*Gender, Race, and Ethnicity
in the Workplace*

Gender, Race, and Ethnicity in the Workplace

*Issues and Challenges
for Today's Organizations*

VOLUME 2

*Legal, Psychological, and Power Issues
Affecting Women and
Minorities in Business*

EDITED BY
Margaret Foegen Karsten

PRAEGER PERSPECTIVES

**Westport, Connecticut
London**

Library of Congress Cataloging-in-Publication Data

Gender, race, and ethnicity in the workplace: issues and challenges for today's organizations / edited by Margaret Foegen Karsten.

    p.   cm.

Includes bibliographical references and index.

ISBN 0-275-98802-3 (set: alk. paper)—ISBN 0-275-98803-1 (v. 1: alk. paper)—
ISBN 0-275-98804-X (v. 2: alk. paper)—ISBN 0-275-98805-8 (v. 3: alk. paper)

    1. Diversity in the workplace—United States.   I. Karsten, Margaret Foegen
HF5549.5.M5G46   2006
658.3008—dc22   2006010950

British Library Cataloguing in Publication Data is available.

This book is included in the African American Experience database from
Greenwood Electronic Media. For more information,
visit www.africanamericanexperience.com.

Library of Congress Catalog Card Number: 2006010950
ISBN: 0-275-98802-3 (set)
       0-275-98803-1 (vol. 1)
       0-275-98804-X (vol. 2)
       0-275-98805-8 (vol. 3)

First published in 2006

Praeger Publishers, 88 Post Road West, Westport, CT 06881
An imprint of Greenwood Publishing Group, Inc.
www.praeger.com

Printed in the United States of America

In gratitude to all the women of strength—colleagues, relatives, and friends both living and deceased—who have influenced my life.

Contents

Acknowledgments

I gratefully acknowledge the University of Wisconsin-Platteville for granting a sabbatical leave that ultimately led to this project and Nicholas Philipson, senior editor, Business and Economics at Praeger, for all his assistance. Furthermore, I thank the contributors for the ideas and insights they shared in their chapters. Dealing with them to complete this set has been a pleasure. Finally, I want to express appreciation to Mary Christoph Foegen for her counsel; J. H. Foegen for instilling in me the desire to write; and my immediate family: children in their birth order, John, Kathryn, and Amy, and my husband, Randy, for their support as I completed two major writing projects in eighteen months.

Margaret Foegen Karsten
March 2006

Introduction

Two generations have grown to adulthood since sweeping federal laws were passed to end employment discrimination based on race, color, religion, sex, and national origin and to ensure that women and men were paid equally for doing the same or substantially similar jobs. Why, then, is it still necessary—even compelling—to have a diverse group of practitioners, academics, and theorists in business, psychology, and related disciplines address issues related to gender, race, and ethnicity in the workplace?

Three reasons, *not* in order of importance, are money, power, and ethics. Women in management and the professions supposedly experience a $2 million lifetime income disparity vis-à-vis their male counterparts.[1] Economists indicate that white women experience a 7 percent wage penalty for *each child* they have.[2] Though no wage penalty is attached to motherhood for black women, they unfortunately tend to be paid significantly less than whites.

Though the sexes have reached numerical parity in management overall, scarcely more than a handful of women lead the powerful Fortune 500 firms in the United States. As of this writing, only one is a woman of color. And 95 percent of top executives in U.S. corporations are white males, though no appreciable difference exists in the percent of women and men who aspire to become chief executives.[3]

If those facts are not persuasive enough, consider that from 2000 through the first half of 2001, twenty-five cases filed with the Equal Employment Opportunity Commission involved egregious racial harassment—the use of nooses reminiscent of lynching.[4] Not in out-of-the way rural areas, the sites of such despicable incidents were cities such as San Francisco and Detroit. Those are only the overt acts; columnist Leonard Pitts commenting on the death of civil rights advocate Rosa Parks in 2005 said, "Racism that was once brazen enough to demand a black woman's bus seat is covert now, a throw-the-rock-and-hide-your-hand charade, its effects as visible as ever, its workings mostly hidden."[5]

How long will it take before repugnant incidents and effects—blatant and subtle—are abolished? When will future U.S. citizens wonder why publications in the early twenty-first century found it necessary to create lists of the top fifty women or blacks in major firms? Those from cultures characterized by extreme time consciousness, a strong streak of individualism, and a desire to pursue promotions into the pinnacles of power have become impatient with the slow pace of change. Incrementalists might urge them to learn from those of other cultural traditions that social change occurs slowly and that forty to fifty years, though a large portion of any person's life, is very little time in the context of social institutions that have existed for centuries. Others are not convinced that change must be slow. They argue that any additional time is too long to wait for those who have been deprived of full participation in and equal benefits of their work in this society.

Corporate downsizing notwithstanding, the United States may again face a shortage of highly skilled professionals. Baby Boomers, born between 1946 and 1964, are starting to retire in record numbers and will be replaced by the much smaller Baby Bust and Generations X and Y. Record numbers of women are in the labor force already, so they will not be a ready supply of additional labor, but women and people of color who are currently marginalized and underutilized may be.[6]

Twenty-five percent of U.S. firms do not have diversity programs.[7] Of those that do, only about one-third succeed; 20 percent fail.[8] This abysmal track record does not promote positive relations among people of various races and ethnicities. The road to a multicultural workplace is uneven and full of potholes; temporary spikes in dysfunctional conflict are to be expected. Miscommunication and misunderstanding even among people of similar backgrounds can result in serious organizational problems. Without honest, open face-to-face dialogue, which presupposes self knowledge such that people can explain who they are, their worldviews, and the factors, including ethnicity and race, that have shaped them, U.S. firms face trying times. Progressing from different starting points on the continuum ranging from monolithic to pluralistic to multicultural organizations will be challenging.

Stereotypes and the debate over the extent to which gender differences in behavior exist and their causes affect the enthusiasm with which workplace diversity is embraced. A 2005 Catalyst study showed that although few managerially relevant behavioral differences exist between the sexes, men are still viewed as more likely to "take charge" and women to "take care" of situations and people.[9] The consequences of such deeply embedded false mindsets are horrendous for women pursuing upward mobility, yet they are as likely to believe the stereotypes as men. A steady stream of contrary information must be presented to root out stereotypes if gender parity is to be a reality by 2019, as the optimistic Committee of 200, an elite group of powerful U.S. women, forecasts.[10] Otherwise, predictions of those who say gender equity will not occur for another 475 years may prove more accurate.[11]

Equity may not be achieved quickly if behavioral variations are primarily attributed to innate sex-based differences. Despite profuse apologies, former Harvard president Lawrence Summers, who resigned from that position on June 30, 2006, unleashed a controversy the previous spring by suggesting that the shortage of female science professors may be due to such distinctions. This rationale alarmed people who believe that nurture or socialization has far more to do with occupational choice than any internal differences, which they maintain are insignificant.

Baron-Cohen, who studies differences in empathizing and systematizing human brains that he believes are hard-wired but that appear in both women and men thinks the situation of those studying biological differences has improved since the 1960s and 1970s. In those days, serious researchers who recognized the role of socialization but wanted to study the impact of biology on sex differences in behaviors were "accused of oppression and of defending an essentialism that perpetuated inequalities between the sexes." Baron-Cohen argues that now the "pendulum has settled sensibly in the middle of the nature-nurture debate."[12]

His assessment is disputed by other researchers, notably Janet Hyde. Her meta-analysis revealed that gender-related behavioral differences long assumed to exist may not or may be highly exaggerated. She found few differences between the sexes and still fewer that were relevant to leadership or management in her studies of gender similarities.[13] False assumptions nonetheless persist and harm both sexes. Women who are not perceived as nice may be penalized in important selection and evaluation decisions; men may be perceived incorrectly and may see themselves as incapable of nurturing.[14]

Implications of many other factors based on which humans experience different workplace opportunity and treatment could have been explored; these volumes address only gender, race, and ethnicity for reasons of relative brevity. The socially constructed term *race* is used reluctantly, recognizing that it is not synonymous with skin color, differs from ethnicity, and may be unrelated to objective reality. The human race truly is the only one that exists.

Over the past two generations, much progress has been made. Things *have* changed, yet some issues in vogue today—such as "on-" and "off-ramps" for those who wish to step out of the fast track to provide care or get more education[15]—are essentially concerns from a quarter century ago that have been repackaged significantly.

A shortage of ideas for creating harmonious diverse workplaces in which all employees flourish is not the problem. We know what to do; now we must figure out how to do it. Ways to implement greater organizational equity must be considered carefully after they have been interiorized and are given high priority. Evaluation, accountability, and follow-up also are crucial to long-term success of equal opportunity efforts.

Consequences of failing in this endeavor could be dire. Some believe corporations are immune from the short-lived social disintegration and racial tension following Hurricane Katrina in 2005, but they may be deluded. Growing gaps between haves and have-nots in the United States, if not remedied, could result in chaos affecting all institutions, including businesses. Though many blacks have increased their incomes, their wealth trails that of the majority group.[16] Native Americans are virtually off the radar in terms of management of major firms, but the underlying leadership principles of some tribal nations are consistent with contemporary management theories, such as stewardship and servant leadership. Continuing to marginalize these and other racial and ethnic minorities is costly and must end.

This comprehensive set examines the status of women and racial/ethnic minorities and discusses challenges they face and the psychological, sociological, and legal contexts in which change must occur. It then suggests actions that organizations and individuals can take to deal with such challenges.

VOLUME 1

Volume 1 sets the stage for in-depth treatment of causes and consequences of workplace and leadership inequity. Perspectives of those who feel disconnected from or outside of the Eurocentric corporate mainstream in the United States, such as Asian Americans, Native American women, and black and white women are explored. Employment statistics pertaining to a spectrum of racial and ethnic minorities and to women are analyzed, as are those focused more narrowly on subgroups of Latinas.

Disaffection is expressed poignantly in the stories of those whose backgrounds would uniquely qualify them to make culturally rich, if thus far unrecognized and unrewarded, contributions to workplace management but for artificial barriers. This illustrates the amount of progress that must be made before those with different but equally valid and valuable perspectives become full partners in societal and business leadership.

Chapters in Volume 1 range from theoretical reflections on leadership to pragmatic analyses of employment statistics. The volume begins with conceptual discussions of leadership that draw on but go beyond experiences of diverse groups, including African American executives and entrepreneurs, skilled tradeswomen who perform managerial functions daily, Asian Americans, and Native American women. Advocated are flexible, holistic, situational leadership approaches that "give voice" to the marginalized, "give back" to the community, add value to society, and distance themselves from either/or dichotomies.

As a group, contributors largely reject hierarchical leadership but reach no consensus about what must replace it. Such agreement may be impossible if leadership depends on the circumstances. Leader effectiveness may demand both meticulous preparation through the study of related disciplines and a simultaneous willingness to "let go" and creatively combine a kaleidoscope of possibilities in new, different ways. The most fitting leadership analogy may be that of the artist whose painting-in-process evolves on an ever-changing canvas, suggested by Adler.

Though technically not managers, skilled craftswomen who eschew the title fulfill leadership roles and engage in traditional management functions of planning, organizing, directing, and controlling. The lack of attractiveness of management as an occupation is not an obstacle that the Glass Ceiling Commission of the 1990s envisioned but is nonetheless problematic. For most skilled tradeswomen, promotions to management would entail less flexible schedules, relative job insecurity associated with nonunionized supervisory positions, and short-term pay cuts due to necessary but unpaid overtime. Thus the short-run lack of incentives for tradeswomen to cross over to management may perpetuate occupational segregation at higher levels.

Such occupational segregation is the topic of later chapters in Volume 1. Contributors differ markedly in their views of this problem and related concepts. For example, Kim decries occupational segregation for its inefficiency in the use of human resources in a meritocracy where rewards are to be based on performance rather than on uncontrollable factors. Rosette, on the other hand, questions the existence of meritocracy due to unearned privilege, which gives advantages to some based on race, ethnicity, or gender.

VOLUME 2

Many legal, judicial, psychological, and sociological forces affect the treatment and advancement prospects of employees and executives based on their gender, race, and ethnicity. This volume discusses selected laws related to equal employment opportunity, affirmative action programs, and the relationship of the relatively neglected topics of racial and ethnic harassment to the more widely researched issue of sexual harassment and of the latter to workplace incivility (rudeness) and violence. The impact of stereotypes, socialization, and power-related concerns on the disenfranchised also are presented.

Twenty-five percent of human resource managers surveyed attribute sexual harassment lawsuits to failed romantic relationships in the workplace.[17] This worries some employers enough to ask the parties to sign so-called love contracts to release their firms from liability for harassment when or if the relationship ends. Unlike harassment, incivility, or violence, however, workplace romances may have a positive side, improving morale and satisfaction of the participants, possible charges of favoritism from co-workers notwithstanding. Romantic workplace relationships are addressed in Volume 2.

Though office romance may have unanticipated favorable effects on those directly involved, many laws and programs designed to rectify employment inequity have unintended harmful effects. For example, affirmative action has been wildly successful at opening previously closed doors for women and minorities — particularly white women — but also has led to consequences that some fear have hampered additional progress.

Furthermore, other equal employment opportunity–related programs focus on superficial problems and fail to discern (let alone address) their root causes. For example, Nydegger and coauthors point out in Volume 2 that workplace incivility and sexual harassment sometimes occur together. Rudeness at work, however, has been virtually ignored. Later, Callahan indicates that sexual harassment training implemented to deal with sexual assault by males in one branch of the military disregards the fact that its higher incidence and an increase in eating disorders among females in the same branch could be caused by perceived loss of personal control due to institutionalized resocialization practices.

In the first chapter of Volume 2, Heilman and Haynes argue that affirmative action may have unintended consequences that should be dealt with. The effects of the Pregnancy Discrimination Act of 1978 (PDA), intended or otherwise, could not be adequately assessed or addressed for many years due to different judicial interpretations. Not until enactment of the Family and Medical Leave Act in 1993 (FMLA) did the debate subside.

At issue was whether the PDA required employers to provide minimum job-protected leave when a woman was physically incapacitated during childbirth and recovery. In some jurisdictions, women could be fired for absenteeism associated with complications of pregnancy or time off for childbirth if their employers lacked temporary disability insurance. Those interpreting the PDA narrowly argued that pregnant women had to be treated only as well or as poorly as "non-pregnant persons" who were disabled for a time, assuming that their employers offered insurance or had other temporary disability policies. Even then, the controversy was resolved only for employees who met eligibility standards and worked for firms covered by the FMLA. Those employed by organizations not required to comply with the FMLA still may have to contend with such interpretations if their state laws provide no additional protection.

The FMLA allows all eligible employees, regardless of sex, unpaid, job-protected leave in an attempt to dispel gender stereotypes about responsibilities for caregiving. Some employees, however, fear their career commitment will be questioned if they take FMLA leave; others cannot afford to do so. Ironically, the FMLA, which was to protect employees' job rights when they needed time off work for caregiving, may deter employees—particularly women wishing to bear children—from job changes needed to advance in their careers because of its restrictive eligibility requirements.

Stereotypes about the career commitment of pregnant women harm all employed women. Such mindsets, though incorrect, readily extend to all in the same general category when they are grouped together based on one uncontrollable factor instead of viewed as individuals.

More than forty years after the *Harvard Business Review* published "Are Women Executives People?"[18] and over twenty-five years after "Women and Men as Managers: A Significant Case of No Significant Difference" appeared in *Organizational Dynamics*,[19] the perception (though not the reality) of a link between management and masculinity persists. Several contributors deal with these stereotypes and the difficulty in eradicating them despite evidence that any true gender differences in leadership are small and situational.[20] Such stereotypes may be all but intractable until women, who now represent half of all managers, professionals, and administrators, are no longer numerical tokens in the executive suite.

Tokenism is another subject examined in this volume. Though much empirical evidence describes the organizational consequences of tokenism for women, the few existing studies on the impact of racial and ethnic minorities are narrow. More should be conducted. Those researching women who are tokens believe the same concepts may apply to minorities and have seen positive results among token women in powerful positions when the organization employing them purposely legitimated their authority.

Any token group has far less power than the dominant class, but power can also be systematically taken from the numerical majority as is done in the military to resocialize recruits. Callahan's previously mentioned chapter illustrates how power and control of one's own life are systematically removed from both male and female air force cadets, resulting in dysfunctional consequences as both strive to regain it. An important distinction is that the women cadets seem to bear the brunt of the negative impact; not only do they experience eating disorders at a higher rate than other female college freshmen as they seek to control their bodies, but they also are targets of sexual assault by men cadets who react to being stripped of power by asserting control over women.

Whether they are military recruits or powerful corporate CEOs, women and men still seem to be evaluated differently. This occurs despite the notion that U.S. institutions including the judiciary are gender-neutral and fair. Those who do not conform to intensified gender-related prescriptions for behavior, which are especially strong stereotypical expectations based on gender, are punished harshly.[21] On the other hand, infractions of those violating relaxed gender-based proscriptions, or behaviors considered inappropriate for any U.S. adult but less so for males, may be dealt with less severely.[22] Though the final verdict is still out at this writing, these findings may be relevant in the respective cases of Martha Stewart and Ken Lay of Enron, discussed in the last chapter of Volume 2.

VOLUME 3

Organizational and individual strategies for dealing with challenges faced by people of color and women based on case studies, personal reflections, and research are presented in Volume 3. Face-to-face interpersonal communication is proposed as the new frontier in which the promised benefits of diversity management will be delivered as individuals begin to know and trust one another. Other chapters dealing with diversity focus on the path Shell Oil U.S. took to become a model firm in terms of not only cultivating a heterogeneous workforce but also using each employee's unique talents fully and best practices in diversity management, which include built-in accountability, top executive support, and aggressive promotion of diversity during recruitment.

Today's diverse workforce consists of about equal percentages of women and men. As the percent of sexual harassment cases filed by men increases, some might think harassment policies should be gender-neutral, but the authors of "Dirty Business," a chapter in Volume 3, disagree. They discuss why sexual objectification of women—even if it occurs off the job—has devastating effects on the workplace, what can be done to change the culture that perpetuates objectification, and who should be involved in effecting such widespread organizational change.

Another change in the workforce with implications for women and minorities involves career planning models. Vestiges from a bygone era that assume uninterrupted vertical movement within one company must be replaced by models with multiple career paths featuring flexible on- and off-ramps, lateral moves, and continuous learning.

Crucial to career advancement of women and racial/ethnic minorities is the cultivation of social capital through developmental opportunities. Those who have lower positions or have been historically underrepresented may need to temporarily gain legitimacy by reflecting that of more powerful organizational members. Role modeling, another avenue for development, deserves more study. Being perceived as and serving as role models also may affect women and minorities positively.

New forms of developmental relationships, such as a network of mentors, may be appropriate for a workplace in which demands for knowledge quickly outpace capabilities of any human, regardless of gender, race, or intellectual endowment. Other alternatives to the master-apprentice model are needed to ease the burden on executive women and minorities who are expected to help others advance but whose ability to sponsor protégés is limited due what has been dubbed a time famine.[23] Some options are virtual-, peer-, and co-mentoring, and mentors-for-hire.

If research supports the importance of developmental relationships for women and people of color, so does the life experience of contributors to this volume. Evans advocates greater use of peer mentoring and coaching and defines networking as "putting people together" for business reasons. Gee lists networking along with self-knowledge and reflection as strategies for dealing with gendered racism.

Though the business literature focuses on developmental relationships and activities occurring at work, one's personal life also can enhance leadership. Too often, personal life is assumed to detract from work, but that occurs only if resources are assumed to be limited. To the extent that multiple roles are energizing,[24] the net result of personal experiences that teach skills transferable to the workplace may be positive, especially for those who have lacked equal access to company-sponsored development programs historically.

Equal access and treatment are necessary but insufficient to create employment equity if certain groups face unequal limitations.[25] All organizations, including those in higher education, must seriously consider personal and professional needs and realities of the employees they seek to attract and retain when formulating work-life policies and programs to minimize disparities in constraints.

Perceived inequities may create stress. Thus, people of color and women are more likely than white male counterparts to encounter gender- and race-related stressors. Glass and concrete ceilings, manifestations of individual and institutional racism, and historical traumas deep enough to wound the soul represent unequal constraints.

The resilience some people of color and women exhibit in coping successfully with profound challenges or stressors is remarkable. It may lead to unparalleled gains in hardiness, self-efficacy, self-esteem, and empathy, qualities that can only help in future personal and professional endeavors. However, not all those in the workplace who have been harmed by "isms" related to gender, race, or ethnicity are gifted with such resilience. They must not be abandoned, nor must their possible future contributions as employees or executives be dismissed. Rather, organizations must fully commit not only to stress-reduction strategies but also to creation of an environment that optimizes the talents of all.

NOTES

1. E. Murphy, *Getting Even: Why Women Don't Get Paid Like Men—And What to Do about It* (New York: Touchstone, 2005).

2. S. A. Hewlett, "Executive Women and the Myth of Having it All," *Harvard Business Review* 80 (2002): 66–74.

3. J. S. Lublin, "Women Aspire to Be Chief as Much as Men Do," *Wall Street Journal* (2004, June 23): D2.

4. A. Bernstein, "Racism in the Workplace: In an Increasingly Multicultural U.S., Harassment of Minorities Is on the Rise," *Business Week* (2001, July 30): 37–43, 64–67.

5. L. Pitts, "Rosa Parks: She Taught Us the Power of One," *Wisconsin State Journal* (2005, Oct. 31): A6.

6. S. A. Hewlett and C. B. Luce, "Off-Ramps and On-Ramps: Keeping Talented Women on the Road to Success," *Harvard Business Review* (March 2005): 43–46, 48, 50–54.

7. T. Joyner, "Ethnicity, Gender Bias Remain Common at Work," *Wisconsin State Journal* (2005, April 15): C9.

8. S. Rynes and B. Rosen, "A Field Survey of Factors Affecting the Adoption and Perceived Success of Diversity Training," *Personnel Psychology* 48 (1995): 247–71.

9. Catalyst, *Women "Take Care," Men "Take Charge": Stereotyping of U.S. Business Leaders Exposed* (New York: Catalyst, 2005).

10. M. Llewellyn-Williams, *The C200 Business Leadership Index 2004: Annual Report on Women's Clout in Business* (Chicago: Committee of 200, 2001–2004).

11. D. L. Corsun and W. M. Costen, "Is the Glass Ceiling Unbreakable? Habitus, Fields, and the Stalling of Women and Minorities in Management," *Journal of Management Inquiry* 10 (March 2001): 16–25.

12. S. Baron-Cohen, "The Essential Difference: The Male and Female Brain," *Phi Kappa Phi Forum* 85(1) (2005): 23.

13. J. S. Hyde, "The Gender Similarities Hypothesis," *American Psychologist* 60 (2005): 581–92.

14. Ibid.

15. Hewlett and Luce, "Off-Ramps and On-Ramps: Keeping Talented Women on the Road to Success," 43–46, 48, 50–54.

16. D. Hajela, "The Color of Money Still Divides Blacks and Whites," *Wisconsin State Journal* (2005, January 18): D1, D9.

17. Society for Human Resource Management, "Workplace Romance Survey (item no. 62.17014)," Alexandria, VA: SHRM Public Affairs Department.

18. G. Bowman, N. Worthy, and S. Greyser, "Are Women Executives People?" *Harvard Business Review* (July–August 1965): 15–28, 164–78.

19. S. M. Donnell and J. Hall, "Men and Women as Managers: A Significant Case of No Significant Difference," *Organizational Dynamics* (Spring 1980): 71.

20. Hyde, "The Gender Similarities Hypothesis."

21. D. A. Prentice and E. Carranza, "What Women and Men Should Be, Shouldn't Be, Are Allowed to Be, and Don't Have to Be: The Contents of Prescriptive Gender Stereotypes," *Psychology of Women Quarterly* 26 (2002): 269–81.

22. Ibid.

23. L. A. Perlow, "The Time Famine: Toward a Sociology of Work Time," *Administrative Science Quarterly* 44 (1999): 57–81.

24. R. Barnett and G. Baruch, "Social Roles, Gender, and Psychological Distress," in R. Barnett, L. Biener, and G. Baruch, eds., *Gender and Stress* (New York: Free Press, 1987), pp. 122–41.

25. L. Bailyn, *Breaking the Mold: Women, Men, and Time in the New Corporate World.* (New York: Free Press, 1993).

1

Affirmative Action:
Unintended Adverse Effects

Madeline E. Heilman and Michelle C. Haynes

Since its inception in the 1960s, affirmative action has provoked intense debate. Originally implemented to rectify past discrimination and prevent it in the future, affirmative action often receives credit for the decided increase in the numbers of women and racial minority members in today's important organizational positions. However, claims have been made that affirmative action and the procedures used to implement it have subtly deleterious consequences. This chapter presents research examining claims of hidden potential costs of affirmative action for organizations and the people who work in them—costs that may work against its intended objectives.

WHAT IS AFFIRMATIVE ACTION?

Affirmative action was instituted as a policy in 1964 when President Lyndon Johnson issued Executive Order 11246. It required organizations with more than fifty employees that wished to enter contracts with federal agencies to take "affirmative action" to ensure that all current and future employees were employed in fair numbers and treated fairly on the job. In addition, regulations set forth by the Secretary of Labor required organizations to develop internal monitoring to identify problem areas and, should underutilization be discovered, required organizations to create goals and timetables to correct these problems. Examples of such affirmative action might entail targeted recruitment, career advancement training, and validation of selection tests.[1]

Although affirmative action originally was designed to overcome discrimination and barriers to equal employment opportunity, more recently it has also been legitimated by the U.S. Supreme Court as a means of realizing diversity goals.[2] Thus, it is used not only to rectify and avert discrimination but also to increase the representation of designated disadvantaged groups, namely, women and ethnic minorities who are underrepresented in the workforce, for example, African Americans and Latinos. Yet affirmative action goes beyond the adoption of equal opportunity practices in which gender and race are to be disregarded when employment decisions are made. Rather, it implies that nondiscrimination is insufficient to combat prejudice; instead, active efforts—explicitly taking group membership into account when making employment decisions—must be made to overcome discrimination.

The Practice of Affirmative Action

Affirmative action has been implemented by a broad range of policies, both mandated and voluntary.[3] Various typologies have been developed as means of classifying the many implementations of affirmative action. For example, Oppenheimer proposed a program model typology.[4] Specifically, Oppenheimer suggested that affirmative action takes form as one of five program models: targeted hiring, in which a position is designated a priori, to be filled by a member of a designated group; quotas, in which specific numerical require-ments are set for hiring members of designated groups; plus factor programs, in which applicants are assigned additional points, based on their group mem-bership, that are used to tally total scores that are compared for selection pur-poses; self-examination programs, which involve monitoring the current status of minorities and women and implementing goals and timetables should un-derrepresentation exist; and outreach programs, in which efforts are made to expand the applicant pool to recruit women and minorities to positions in which they are underrepresented.

Alternatively, following Seligman,[5] a number of researchers have classified the various implementations of affirmative action using a more theoretical ty-pology, conceiving of them as falling along a "hard–soft" continuum. Implemen-tations for which group membership is the primary criterion in decision making are considered to be on the hard end of the continuum, and implementations for which merit is the primary criterion in decision making are on the soft end. Implementations involving a mixture of group membership and merit criteria fall in between.

Despite their repeated inclusion in the various typologies of affirmative action, a review of relevant legislation and case law makes clear that the ex-tremely hard forms of affirmative action—those in which group membership is the exclusive criterion used—are illegal (e.g., federal regulations 41 CFR 60-2(e), 60-2.15, and 60-2.30 explicitly prohibit quotas in employment decisions and the preferential selection of unqualified minority group members over qualified nonminority group members). Nonetheless, the distinction between practices in which merit is central in decision making and those in which group membership plays the major role seems psychologically meaningful both to those targeted by affirmative action efforts and those who are onlookers to these processes.

The Perception of Affirmative Action

Despite the many variations of affirmative action programs, the perception of affirmative action remains largely undifferentiated. Both anecdotal and empirical evidence indicates that people generally assume affirmative action to be little more than preferential selection based on demographic group membership and that they persist in associating affirmative action programs with particularly hard forms of affirmative action based solely on group membership, such as quota systems and set-aside programs,[6] despite the fact that they are illegal. Quotas, in particular, seem to resonate with people's understanding of the implementation of affirmative action. One study conducted by Crosby and colleagues surveying adults in the metropolitan Chicago area found that approximately 40 percent of the respondents understood affirmative action to be a quota system.[7] Moreover, there is evidence that the public believes that with affirmative action, demography trumps merit; results from the General Social Survey report 70 percent of whites think that it is at least somewhat likely that whites lose jobs or promotions to less qualified blacks in today's job market.[8]

The widespread assumption that affirmative action is little more than preferential selection based on demographic group membership has important implications. This assumption about what affirmative action entails, even if it is inconsistent with fact, provides the impetus for reactions to it. The negative effects of affirmative action, when they occur, are not the result of what a particular affirmative action program actually is but the result of what it is perceived to be.

Research indicates that when individuals discount the role of merit criteria in selection, and people are believed to have benefited not because of what they merit but because of the demographic group to which they belong, (1) the selected others can become tainted with a stigma of incompetence, (2) the beneficiaries themselves can suffer in their self-evaluations and work attitudes and behavior, and (3) the nonbeneficiaries can feel cheated and become resentful and demotivated. Each of these potential consequences is discussed in turn in the following sections.

THE STIGMA OF INCOMPETENCE

Several vocal opponents of affirmative action are members of groups targeted to benefit from it.[9] These individuals argue that affirmative action stigmatizes its intended beneficiaries by causing inferences of substandard competence. Thus, Shelby Steele, a prominent black professor, wrote in the *New York Times Magazine*, "the quality that earns us preferential treatment is implied inferiority"—the implication is that special treatment is needed.[10] More recently, Justice Clarence Thomas, in his dissenting opinion to the case upholding the affirmative action policy at the University of Michigan Law School, indicated that students who are associated with affirmative action are "tarred as undeserving."[11]

Some research results are consistent with the claim that affirmative action taints its recipients with a stigma of incompetence, although none test it directly. For example, Garcia and colleagues found that qualifications of minority graduate student applicants were rated less favorably when the university's affirmative action plan was highlighted than when it was not mentioned.[12] Another study reported negative effects on evaluations of female managers when an organization was portrayed as being committed to an affirmative action policy.[13] Northcraft and Martin found that when a black investment banker was reported to be an affirmative action hire, respondents were more likely to pair him, as compared with whites or blacks not associated with affirmative action, with a poor résumé.[14] Finally, Jacobson and Koch found that when selected because of their sex, not merit or chance, female managers were more likely to be seen as the cause of a team's failure and less likely to be given credit for its success.[15]

Why would association with affirmative action result in inferences of incompetence? A consideration of attribution theory and the processes by which we come to understand the cause of events is instructive. Particularly relevant is the discounting principle, which is used to understand the cause for an effect when several causes are possible.[16] Affirmative action, because it is presumed to entail preferential selection based on demographic group membership, provides an alternative, salient, and plausible reason for a person's selection independent of his or her qualifications. Consequently, the importance of the role of the individual's qualifications for the position—his or her skills, abilities, and relevant experience—is likely to be "discounted" and the individual thought to be selected only because of gender or minority status, with qualifications irrelevant in decision making. But because qualifications are typically considered critical to personnel decision making, the assumption that they did not play a role is likely to lead to another assumption—that the person did not "have what it takes" to do the job well and would not have been selected without help from affirmative action. Thus the assumed disregard of ordinary and expected selection criteria, a consequence of perceptions of what affirmative action really entails, provides impetus for the inference of incompetence.

Empirical Evidence of the Stigma of Incompetence

We conducted a series of studies to directly examine the proposition that a stigma of incompetence arises from affirmative action initiatives and to examine the role of the discounting process in bringing this about. In the first study,[17] we sought to determine whether association with affirmative action would affect the perceived competence of its beneficiaries. Specifically we expected that women associated with affirmative action would be evaluated less favorably than men and other women not associated with affirmative action. Moreover, we reasoned that if discounting were truly the underlying process, then perceptions of a woman's lesser competence should not be limited only to jobs for which women typically would be considered poorly qualified. In other words, we expected association with affirmative action to create an unfavorable evaluation of a woman's competence, even in instances when it would not have otherwise occurred.

We used a laboratory experiment to test these ideas. In what was described as research to help understand selection decisions, male and female college students reviewed the application materials of someone said to be recently hired for a job, and then both described what they thought the individual was like and made prognoses about his or her work effectiveness. Research participants received a job description in the form of a recruitment bulletin indicating job requirements and work responsibilities and employment application materials containing information about educational background, work experience, and general demographic information. The job either was strongly male sex-typed (electrician) or more neutral in sex-type (lab technician), with only 8 percent women said to currently populate the former and 41 percent the latter.

In all cases the information provided about the hiree was identical except for his or her sex, which was made evident by the name on the application materials and a photograph (which always depicted a white man or woman). Furthermore, when the person hired was a woman, she either was or was not linked to an affirmative action initiative via handwritten comments written on the application materials. We were interested in ratings of competence.

Results indicated that whatever the degree of sex typing of the job, when there was an association with affirmative action, women were rated not only less competent than men but also less competent than women not associated with affirmative action. In fact, the affirmative action label created problems for women even when their sex by itself did not result in more negative characterizations (neutral sex-typed job), and it clearly worsened problems for women when simply being a woman already was problematic for competence evaluations (male sex-typed job). These data therefore verify the existence of stigma of incompetence for beneficiaries of affirmative action initiatives and indicate the depth of its negative impact. Moreover, consistent with the discounting idea, respondents believed qualifications were far less important when affirmative action was involved in the selection of employees. There were no differences in the responses of male and female respondents.

These results support the idea that affirmative action can give rise to negativity directed at those purported to be its beneficiaries. But they do not make clear how pervasive this effect is. In the workplace, individuals often have more information about others than they did in our study, and this additional information may supersede association with affirmative action as an indicator of an individual's competence. Accordingly, we conducted another study to capture the attitudes of people actually in organizational settings and asked them to draw on their own personal experiences in providing research data.[18] The specific objective was to examine how beliefs about the role that affirmative action played in an individual's career progress relates to competence evaluations of women and minority group members employed in nontraditional positions in actual organizations.

Respondents were white males, ranging in age from twenty-five to forty-seven years (mean age was thirty-four), all of whom were currently employed in a broad range of industries. They were approached in airports, train stations, and outdoor sitting areas near places of employment in Chicago and New York City and asked to complete a brief questionnaire. The questionnaire's cover page described the purpose of the research as the study of working people's impressions of the changing composition of the American workforce. It instructed respondents to think of a specific co-worker, one who had joined their unit in recent years and who is a member of a group that in the past typically did not hold this type of position, and to answer the questionnaire with that individual in mind. No names of respondents were obtained; any respondent who could not think of a co-worker who fit these criteria returned the questionnaire.

The questionnaire was designed to assess both the presumed role of affirmative action in the decision to hire the co-worker (embedded among questions about other possible reasons for the hiring decision) and the perception of the co-worker's competence. The resulting data demonstrated a strong negative correlation; the greater the role affirmative action was believed to have played in a co-worker's hiring, the less competent that co-worker was thought to be. This correlation remained statistically significant regardless of the length of time the respondent had worked with the co-worker; whether the co-worker was the respondent's peer, superior, or subordinate; or whether the co-worker described was a white woman, a black woman, or a black man. Moreover, the greater the presumed role of affirmative action in the hiring decision, the less were qualifications seen as playing a major role in the co-worker's selection and, even more importantly, the less likely the co-worker was viewed as having been qualified to do the job at the time he or she was hired.

The findings of these two studies strongly support the idea that a stigma of incompetence is associated with affirmative action and demonstrate that inferences of incompetence are made whether affirmative action beneficiaries are women or members of racial minorities and whether the evaluators are students, employees, men, or women. But they do not provide evidence of the ultimate impact of these inferences. They do not tell us whether inferences of incompetence persist when information about actual performance, especially that which is inconsistent with the inferences, becomes available. This question led us to another set of studies.[19]

Persistence of the Incompetence Stigma

We expected that information about on-the-job performance effectiveness would only sometimes override the inferences of incompetence arising from association with affirmative action. In particular, we thought this would only occur when the performance information was unambiguous and not amenable to distortion—a not so common occurrence in work organizations in which performance information often lacks precision, is arrived at subjectively, or is unclear with regard to the party responsible for it. Accordingly, we varied the level of ambiguity associated with the performance information provided.

In the first study, the level of ambiguity was varied by the degree of precision of the performance information. Managers from a large insurance company, approximately half male and half female, and ranging in age from twenty-five to fifty-four years old, reviewed materials very much like those in the laboratory experiment described previously. However, in this study, only one job was used, the neutrally sex-typed job of computer programmer. As in the earlier study, participants received packets containing a job description and an employment application containing information about an employee's education and work experience. However, in this study, participants also were given a six-month job activity summary, supposedly written by the employee's supervisor. Following these materials was a questionnaire asking for reactions to the employee, including an assessment of his or her competence.

Using the same procedures as in the earlier study, the employee was depicted as either a man or woman and, when a woman, either associated with affirmative action or not. Performance information was conveyed on the six-month summary by the supervisor's overall rating of the employee's performance, which followed a description of the employee's work activities. The actual response and the response format together were used to vary information ambiguity. In the success conditions, the employee was always rated in the highest category, but the range of categories differed. In the clear success conditions, there were five category ratings: top 5 percent, top 10 percent, top 25 percent, top 50 percent, or bottom 50 percent. In the ambiguous success conditions, there were only two categories: top 50 percent and bottom 50 percent. In addition, there was a condition with no information about success and a condition in which the employee evidently had not been successful and was rated in the bottom 50 percent.

Results indicated, as would be expected based on the earlier studies, that with no information about success, affirmative action women were rated as less competent than both the women not associated with affirmative action and the men. This data pattern persisted when the information provided about success was ambiguous (rated as being in the top 50 percent rather than the bottom 50 percent). Only when the information about success was clear and unequivocal (rated as being in the top 5 percent rather than the other four categories) was there no difference in ratings of the competence of the affirmative action woman and the other employees. Thus, without clear information of success, ratings of the affirmative action woman were as negative as when no information had been provided and, surprisingly, not even any better than when failure information had been provided. The pattern of ratings of proposed salary increases, also obtained in the study, was identical to that of the competence ratings.

A follow-up study was conducted, using managers from the same insurance company as research participants.[20] Similar research materials were used, but in this case, the clarity of success was varied by the source ambiguity of the success information. That is, although all research participants reviewed employees who were depicted as having been highly successful (the supervisor indicated that they had "far exceeded expectations"), additional information provided to them allowed for different interpretations of how the success had been achieved. Specifically, a report that there had been coaching by a senior co-worker who could be used as a consultant whenever needed (in the ambiguous success conditions) was designed to raise questions about the degree to which the target employee was the unique source of his or her success.

Results showed that despite strong indications of success, female affirmative action beneficiaries and male and female nonbeneficiaries were rated equally competent only when information conveyed about those responsible for female beneficiaries' success was unambiguous. When ambiguity existed about responsibility for the success (when there had been a coach involved), competence ratings of affirmative action women differed decidedly from the ratings of the others. Recommendations for a salary increase followed the identical pattern—when the employees were thought to have used coaches, those associated with affirmative action were treated more harshly.

Findings from these two studies suggest that success information does not always dispel the negative competence perceptions that accompany the affirmative action label. Only success that is irrefutable in its implications for an individual's competence—success that cannot be ignored or dismissed either because of its magnitude or because it is absolutely clear who is responsible for it—counteracts the stigma of incompetence. Evidently, lack of clarity can nullify the disconfirming potential of successful performance information. People seem to resist giving up a negative view of those associated with affirmative action; they continue to be viewed as lacking in competence unless they are proved to be otherwise. This point is particularly important because ambiguity about performance is pervasive in organizations where the nature of work products often makes objective evaluation challenging. In addition, work often is performed interdependently in teams and project groups, making individual contribution difficult to determine. Because ambiguity about performance is inherent in so many work settings, this research suggests that the affirmative action stigma is likely to persist despite performance success.

Inferring the Affirmative Action Stigma

Although the role affirmative action has played in a selection decision typically is not explicitly stated, it is nonetheless likely that association with affirmative action often is inferred. Whether association with affirmative action is explicitly stated or inferred should make no difference in its consequences—the stigma of incompetence is likely to predominate in impression formation regardless. But when is affirmative action inferred? When is an individual assumed to have been hired preferentially because of his or her demographic group? The context in which the selection occurs influences inferences about why a person has been chosen for a position. If a hire is out of the ordinary, it is likely to raise attention and provoke efforts to explain its occurrence. Such cues may be the hiring of one black employee into an all-white work group, or the hiring of a woman into a position that up until then was held only by men. Although many possible explanations exist for either occurrence, the recent visibility of affirmative action policies and the widespread belief that affirmative action is a major factor in personnel decision making makes it a salient and highly plausible explanation for the unexpected newcomers.[21]

To demonstrate the proclivity to attribute the selection of those from socially targeted groups when their presence is unusual in the setting, we conducted a study in which student participants reviewed the application materials of a female student who was recently admitted to a doctoral program at their university.[22] This doctoral student was either the only woman among the eight students admitted to the program that year (the other seven were men) or was one of four women (out of eight) accepted for admission. The admissions decision process was said to be one involving preferential selection based on demographic group (affirmative action), individual qualifications as the sole criterion (merit), or no information about the decision process (ambiguous).

Results illustrated that when the admissions process was left ambiguous and only one female was admitted, gender was seen as having played as great a role in selection, and the woman student was seen as having been as poorly qualified, as when an affirmative action policy was explicitly stated. So even without direct information about affirmative action, when selection of a particular student seemed unusual or surprising, respondents (both male and female) behaved as if affirmative action had been taken, in the form of preferential selection, in each case rating the woman far more negatively than when the process had been specified as merit-based. The fact that this result occurred only when the woman chosen was the solo female selected (not when four women were admitted), supports the idea that the out-of-the-ordinary nature of the event triggers the affirmative action inference.

This study's results demonstrate that even in the absence of an explicitly stated selection policy, there is a tendency to assume that an affirmative action policy is being implemented and that demographically based preferential selection has occurred. Thus the problems created by the affirmative action stigma are not confined to those who are officially designated as the program's beneficiaries. Until the concept of affirmative action and its powerful influence in selection processes changes, women and members of minority groups whose success is totally unrelated to affirmative action or preferential selection may be stigmatized by inferred association.

BENEFICIARIES' VIEWS OF SELF-COMPETENCE

Another negative consequence of affirmative action is that it may directly damage those it was designed to benefit by creating feelings of inferiority and by undermining self-esteem. In fact, some have argued that affirmative action feeds the suspicion of those who benefit from it that they are not worthy of the positions they attain or the honors they are awarded. They furthermore contend that these threats to self-esteem can plague those in targeted groups who would have obtained their positions and honors without the help of affirmative action.[23]

In analyzing why affirmative action and the preferential selection processes it is assumed to entail may damage the self-esteem of its intended beneficiaries, considering the differences in the information that a preferential and a merit-based selection procedure provides, in particular the message conveyed about work competence, is instructive. Preferential selection based on one's demographic group implies that a work-irrelevant characteristic had special weight in the decision process, whereas merit-based selection implies that skill and ability were key factors. Consequently, those selected based on merit have received a vote of confidence—they feel they have earned their positions because of their qualifications, and this belief affirms their sense of competence. However, this external verification of competence, which is a natural consequence of merit-based selection, is absent in preferential selection situations. Rather than their competence being affirmed, it is left open to question, and those assumed to have been selected preferentially are therefore vulnerable to feelings of being unqualified for the job in which they are placed. Just as help is sometimes interpreted to indicate that the recipient is not competent enough to help him- or herself,[24] preferential selection may be interpreted to mean that the recipient is not competent enough to be selected on his or her own merits.[25]

But not having verification about one's qualifications for a job does not necessarily have adverse effects on feelings about competence; it is only likely to have this effect if people are unsure of themselves. If an individual feels highly capable of handling a job effectively, then verification of his or her skills and abilities is superfluous; a sense of competence already prevails. If, however, an individual is filled with self-doubt or negative performance expectations, the absence of such verification can feed these insecurities. Thus the ambiguity about competence inherent in preferential selection processes is likely to more detrimentally affect those lacking confidence in their ability to perform the job well.

Performance expectancies are determined not only by individual proclivities but also by group membership. Stereotypes, which are widely shared and often self-defining, exist about characteristics of those who are members of particular ethnic and gender groups. Stereotypes of groups that typically are targets of affirmative action depict their members as having fewer achievement and leadership qualities and skills, deemed essential for high level, prestigious jobs in U.S. culture, than do white men. Consequently, these individuals are more likely than others to approach jobs that are nontraditional for them and thought to require characteristics lacking in members of their groups with a lack of confidence and a low expectation of success.[26] Moreover, because affirmative action focuses on the very reason for beneficiaries' lack of confidence—their group membership—preferential selection based on demographic group should be particularly disturbing for members of targeted groups, adding to their self-doubts. One would therefore expect that whether or not selection was based on merit would have a negligible effect on white men but a strong effect on women and minority group members: Merit-based selection should calm anxieties about their competence; preferential selection procedures should exacerbate them.

Empirical Evidence of Beneficiaries' Negative Self-View of Competence

To directly test these ideas, we conducted a series of studies using the psychology laboratory to create a situation in which preferential selection could occur. Male and female students were chosen for a male sex-typed leadership role either due to their sex (preferentially) or due to merit. Our interest was in the views of self-competence and the consequent self-evaluation of performance and attitudes toward the leadership role that arise from the two different selection procedures. Because of the sex-typed nature of the task, we expected women (but not men) to be insecure about their task-related abilities and therefore negatively affected by the preferential selection procedure.

Research participants were paired with an opposite-sex participant (actually a confederate) and were told that one would be the leader and the other the follower on a spatial communications task in which the leader would teach the follower how to draw geometric figures. Participants then completed a brief test said to reliably assess their task-related spatial communication skills. The test was collected, and in the merit conditions it was scored, but in the preferential treatment conditions it was conspicuously set aside. The task was then described and the leader and follower roles assigned. All participants were told that leaders for the study typically were selected based on their skill and ability as indicated by the test, which they were told provided a highly reliable measure of communication skills. Accordingly, in the merit conditions the participant was informed that he or she was chosen as leader because of his or her score, which was higher than that of the other member of the pair. But in the preferential selection conditions, the participants were told that things had to happen differently today because of a shortage of male (female) participants for the study. The participant was told that regardless of test performance, "because you are a man [woman], you will get to be leader for the task." The twosome then worked on the task and completed a brief questionnaire.

Results of the first study in this series indicated that as we had anticipated, when participants were male, method of selection made no difference.[27] Results for the women, however, indicated that preferential selection can trigger negative self-regard. Compared to those chosen on a merit basis, women who were preferentially selected rated their performance more negatively, viewed themselves as more deficient in leadership ability, and were more eager to relinquish their leadership role. A subsequent study delved further into the differences found in men's and women's reactions to the method of selection, by directly verifying self-confidence level as the factor determining whether preferential selection based on group membership adversely affects self perceptions and evaluations.[28] These studies starkly illustrate how the lack of competence affirmation inherent in preferential selection can, if one has questions about one's task competence, lead to diminished views of self.

Effects on Work Behavior

If the perception of having been selected preferentially based on one's demographic group leads people to view their competence more negatively than when they are selected on a merit basis, then their approach to work also should differ. Self-view of competence influences expectations of performance success, and as a result motivation and actual performance also are likely to be affected. Indeed, in his extensive review of research exploring the relationship between judgments of personal capability, or self-efficacy judgments, and performance-relevant activities, Bandura found repeated evidence that expectations of task competence have a profound effect on work behavior.[29]

A study designed to test the notion that preferential selection rather than merit-based selection of those in targeted groups would have detrimental consequences for their actual work behavior validated these ideas.[30] One of the consequences of negative self-view of competence is reluctance to assume demanding tasks.[31] This consequence is extremely important because seeking and accepting demanding assignments early in one's career affects others' impressions of one's commitment and can therefore affect the nature of subsequent job assignments and the way one's career advances. So if preferentially selected employees tend to avoid taking on the tough jobs, opting instead for those that are safe and easy to accomplish, then their career progress may be hindered.

The study used a similar procedure to the one just described except that the roles assigned were financial services manager and subordinate. All participants were made the manager, and assignment to role was made based either on gender (preferentially) or on diagnostic test results (merit). Participants were subsequently given a choice between two work tasks, both said to be part of the managerial job. One, which involved verifying the subordinate's work, was designed to be far less demanding than the other, which was to make loan decisions.

Results were dramatic. Men overwhelmingly chose the demanding task, regardless of how they were selected for the managerial role. Women selected on the basis of merit also overwhelmingly chose the demanding task—in fact, the frequencies of their choices and those of the men did not differ. But the choices of women who were preferentially selected on the basis of their sex were very different; they chose the undemanding and the demanding task equally often and much more often than women selected on a merit basis. The preferentially selected women also rated their work-related ability and task effectiveness more unfavorably than did women selected on a merit basis; selection method had no effect on men's self-ratings. A second study using the same general procedure verified that it was the negative self-perception of competence that was prompted by preferential selection that was responsible for these timid task choices and negative work-related evaluations.[32] When women were given reason to feel confident about their ability to do the task—and therefore whatever uncertainties they had about their ability were quelled— preferential selection had no adverse effects on task choice or self-evaluations.

The findings of these studies demonstrate that the negative consequences of preferential selection can extend beyond self perceptions and evaluations and affect actual work-related behavior. Apparently, such selection can lead to self-limiting actions by those designated to benefit from it. Because of the extensive literature on the effects of lowered self-efficacy judgments, the findings also suggest other likely consequences of preferential selection for work behavior, including declines in motivation, perseverance, and even performance itself. Recent research in fact documents the negative relationship between preferential selection and performance on a problem-solving task.[33]

REACTIONS OF THOSE WHO FEEL UNFAIRLY BYPASSED

There has long been evidence in the literature,[34] as well as reports in the public press,[35] that many think they have been unfairly bypassed due to affirmative action. In fact, affirmative action has been criticized as constituting reverse discrimination. Complaints by white male managers who feel they have been victimized by preferential selection procedures have become increasingly common; clearly, many believe that affirmative action has thwarted their career advancement. Together with the reduction in high-level managerial jobs due to widespread downsizing and efforts to streamline management levels, affirmative action policies often are viewed as major obstacles to getting ahead.[36]

Underlying the feeling of having been harmed by affirmative action, as with other reactions identified in this chapter, is the belief that it is little more than preferential selection on the basis of demographic group without regard to merit. Preferential selection signals unfair treatment, and, in fact, studies of responses to affirmative action have identified the perception of unfairness as a critical determining factor.[37] The perception of unfairness is likely to affect reactions to affirmative action generally, but it is likely to be particularly salient and to take on special significance for those who see themselves as its victims.

The perception of fairness has two components that are relevant to this issue: fairness in the allocation of organizational outcomes, such as selection and promotion decisions (distributive justice), and the fairness of the process used to allocate these outcomes (procedural justice). Because affirmative action and the preferential selection that it is thought to involve results in the discounting of beneficiaries' qualifications, it is likely they will be seen as less competent.[38] For that reason, those bypassed in these selection decisions may assume beneficiaries have lesser competence and therefore see them as less deserving of the better outcome as compared to themselves; this leads to a feeling of having been cheated out of one's just desserts. Also, because preferential selection processes are thought to advantage individuals based on an ascribed attribute—race, ethnicity, or gender—over which people have no control, they are likely to be seen as unfair procedurally as well.

The consequences of feeling unfairly treated, whether distributively or procedurally, have been repeatedly illustrated.[39] Job satisfaction, organizational commitment, turnover intention, as well as general satisfaction, all have been shown to be affected negatively. Therefore, preferential selection on the basis of demographic group membership is likely to have negative consequences for the work attitudes and behavior of nonbeneficiaries. Furthermore, the intensity of these negative reactions should be related to the perceived degree of unfairness.

Empirical Evidence of Nonbeneficiaries' Negative Reactions

We conducted a study to test the idea that the nonbeneficiaries of affirmative action–based preferential selection have negative reactions to the work setting.[40] The study incorporated both procedural and distributive justice elements. The method of selection and also the perception of deservedness as compared with the other were varied. We used an experimental procedure very similar to that used in earlier studies and described in the last section.[41] In this case, however, participants, all of whom were men paired with female confederates, were assigned to the role of subordinate (as opposed to the more desirable role of leader) for a two-person communication task. They were bypassed for the role of leader either on the basis of their skills and abilities (as measured by a test) or on the basis of their sex. In addition, when bypassed on the basis of sex, they either were left uninformed about their task-related ability compared with their female mate who was assigned the leadership role, or were informed that they were inferior, superior, or equal in ability to her. Last, a justification for the preferential procedure on the basis of compensation for past ills either was or was not included. We measured the male participants' feelings about the task, their ratings of the woman leader, and their intentions to engage in prosocial citizenship behavior.

Results indicated that sex-based preferential selection has negative consequences for nonbeneficiaries. Unless there was clear evidence to the contrary
(the woman beneficiary was reported to be better equipped to handle the position), or very special circumstances (the woman beneficiary was reported to be
equally equipped and justification for the selection procedure was explicitly
provided), male nonbeneficiaries reacted more negatively to the work task than
when merit-based selection had occurred. Importantly, when male nonbeneficiaries were left uninformed about their ability vis-à-vis the woman selected to be leader (the situation most common in organizational settings), they
responded as negatively in terms of motivation, affect, and task attitudes as male
beneficiaries who had been explicitly informed that they were superior in
ability, and they also characterized the female leader as equally incompetent.
This indicates that the prevailing assumption among those bypassed by demographically targeted preferential selection is that they have been denied a de-
served outcome. Furthermore, neither variations in the beliefs about relative
ability nor variations in the presence or absence of justification for the preferential selection procedure affected citizenship intentions; all of those bypassed
because of preferential selection procedures demonstrated a greater reluctance
to engage in helping behavior than those not selected for the position because of
merit. Only judgments about the beneficiary's likeability were spared negativity,
suggesting that hostility may not necessarily be directed at the perceived beneficiaries of affirmative action despite obvious discontent and disaffection on the
part of nonbeneficiaries.

These findings suggest that distributive and procedural justice are both
critical in understanding nonbeneficiaries' negative reactions to preferential selection, but that they each have consequences in different reaction domains.
Specifically, they suggest that distributive justice concerns, and the feeling of
being cheated, influence job-related reactions, whereas procedural justice concerns influence the general orientation toward the work setting. But most important, these findings indicate that the preferential selection process that is
thought to characterize affirmative action can inflame perceptions of unfair
treatment and provoke negative and resentful feelings, attitudes, and behavior in
nonbeneficiaries.

THE EFFECT OF AFFIRMATIVE ACTION POLICY TYPE

Throughout this chapter we have argued that without information to the
contrary, people generally assume that affirmative action is little more than
preferential selection of women and minorities without regard to merit or
qualifications, and this assumption is at the heart of many problems we have
identified. But as pointed out earlier, affirmative action in reality is not one
policy. Affirmative action policies, procedures, and practices have many variations.[42] Indeed, scholars in fields including law, political science, sociology, and

psychology have recognized the distinctions in the practice of affirmative action. Research we have thus far presented tended either to leave the precise nature of the affirmative action policy ambiguous, allowing participants' assumptions about what affirmative action is to have free reign, or to deliberately specify the policy in a way that is consistent with the assumption—as a hard affirmative action policy in which merit criteria for selection were inconsequential. This means that a question can be raised about whether the adverse reactions we identified would ensue when the softer nature of an affirmative action policy is made explicit and preference given for gender or minority group membership is believed to be only a part, not the whole, of the decision process. This question is important for both theoretical and policy reasons.

A series of three studies,[43] each corresponding to the particular set of unintended consequences of affirmative action that have been identified in this chapter, were conducted to shed light on this issue. One focused on others' views of beneficiaries' competence, a second on beneficiaries' self-evaluations and performance assessments, and the third on work-related reactions of non-beneficiaries. In each study, we expected that policies specifying the consideration of merit along with demographic group membership would produce fewer negative reactions than policies in which merit was not believed to be a major factor in selection decision making. The greater the weight reportedly given to merit in decision making, the less negative we expected the reactions to be.

The studies, all of which focused on gender-based preferential selection, closely followed the investigations conducted earlier.[44] However, they each included variations of the specific policy guiding the selection decisions. Five selection policies were presented. One was totally merit-based, indicating that skill level and ability were the main considerations in making the selection decision. The other four policies were variations of affirmative action: group membership used exclusively, minimum qualifications used as a screen before consideration of group membership, equal qualifications required for group membership to be considered in selection, and an ambiguous policy that indicated only that group membership would be taken into account when decisions were made. Research participants were male and female students from undergraduate and MBA programs.

Results indicated that type of policy indeed matters. Although women were found to be regarded as less competent by others whenever they were thought to have been selected on a preferential as opposed to a merit basis, the reported weighting of the merit criterion used made a difference in how they were viewed. When it was made clear that equivalent qualifications were required before their sex was taken into consideration in decision making, the women selectees were rated as more competent than in all other instances in which preferential selection was thought to have occurred.[45]

The effect of an equivalent qualifications policy was even more pronounced in self-evaluations.[46] Although beneficiaries' desire to retain a leadership role was uniformly and negatively affected by preferential selection procedures, when it was clear that equivalent qualifications were required before gender was given preference in decision making, women's assessment of their own performance and leadership ability did not differ from those of women selected on the basis of merit; they also were decidedly more favorable than the self-views reported by preferentially selected women for whom qualifications were only a perfunctory consideration (minimum standards) or no consideration at all.

A similar pattern of results occurred in the reactions of nonbeneficiaries.[47] When the equivalence of qualifications was a prerequisite for preferential selection on the basis of gender, in contrast to the other preferential selection policies, differences from a merit-based selection procedure were not evident in nonbeneficiaries' affective, motivational, and attitudinal reactions to the task or in evaluations of the leader's competence. However, anyone involved in a preferential selection situation, whatever the qualifications criterion, was less prone to be willing to engage in citizenship behavior.

Thus there appear to be very different reactions to affirmative action policies and preferential selection practices depending on the role merit is thought to play in the decision-making process. In others' perceptions of the competence of beneficiaries, in beneficiaries' own self-views and self-assessments, and in work-related reactions of nonbeneficiaries, when merit considerations were said to take priority in selection decisions with equivalent qualifications being necessary for preferential selection to occur, many (but not all) negative reactions abated. However, inclusion of a merit criterion did not always do the trick; in none of the three studies was the minimum requirement policy—in which qualifications were taken into account but were not heavily weighted in decision making—at all successful in mitigating the negativity produced by preferential selection processes.

Finally, it is very important to note the results when the affirmative action policy was left ambiguous and a vague reference was made to "group membership being taken into account" in decision making. In this situation, research participants consistently reacted in the same way as did those who were explicitly informed of a policy in which decision makers had totally disregarded merit criteria. This result, repeated across each of the three studies, lends strong support to the idea that affirmative action is typically assumed to be nothing more than preferential selection based on demographic group membership and that without information to the contrary, people act on this assumption.

On a brighter note, these findings demonstrating the importance of the nature of the affirmative action policy in determining reactions to it suggest that the adverse effects of affirmative action are not inevitable or unavoidable. How it is implemented, and even more crucial, what is believed about how it is implemented, are of paramount importance.

IMPLICATIONS FOR WORK SETTINGS

The research we have presented has important implications for the way affirmative action initiatives are managed in the workplace. First and foremost, care should be taken in formulating policies and implementing procedures concerning affirmative action. The role that merit plays in selection and the weight that it carries are critical factors in determining reactions. Our findings strongly suggest that organizations should embrace policies and procedures allowing traditional merit criteria, such as skill qualifications and past experience, to play a significant role in the selection process.

However, the actual formulation of policies and procedures is not the end of the issue. Because the perception of affirmative action (not the reality of it) provokes the unintended negative reactions that we have identified, conveying the affirmative action policy to members of the organization is very important. Selection procedures and underlying policies usually are invisible to those not directly involved, so the often erroneous assumptions that people hold about affirmative action are not challenged, much less disconfirmed. The nature of affirmative action policy must be publicized to all affected by it to avoid its harmful consequences.

In addition, recognition of the potentially debilitating effects of affirmative action on its beneficiaries can lead to constructive organizational efforts to avert them. The importance of providing competence information to qualified women and minorities is a case in point, because it seems to ward off the negative self-regard and its subsequent effects on work behavior that can ensue from the belief that one has been preferentially selected based on one's gender or minority status. Also, programs and practices that boost confidence in capability, such as social support networks, should help preclude the negative self-regard that can result from an individual's belief that he or she has benefited from demographically based preferential selection.

Recognition of the stigma of incompetence that often burdens those associated with affirmative action efforts also has action implications. Although clear information about the affirmative action policy and its inclusion of merit criteria should help undermine the discounting process that produces the stigma, affirmative action policies probably will remain suspect and assumptions about any one co-worker's competence still will be tinged with negativity. Thus, validating that co-worker's competence by providing information about qualifications that uniquely equip him or her for the position and about his or her performance successes is critical.

Organizations must also recognize the feelings of victimization experienced by nonbeneficiaries who believe that they have been sacrificed in the effort to enhance others' careers. Although such individuals often do not articulate these feelings because of concerns about political correctness, their disillusionment and disenchantment with the organization can have destructive consequences, leading to nonproductive work behaviors and low motivation and commitment.

For these individuals, knowing that the person they believe to be a beneficiary of affirmative action is truly deserving of the position is critical.

Last, our findings indicate that the designation of an individual as an affirmative action beneficiary can be totally arbitrary. Explanations about how people who typically have not held particular roles and positions have attained them often include inferences about affirmative action and preferential selection. These inferences are a product of today's cultural milieu and widespread assumptions about the reach of affirmative action and its general incursion into selection processes. Combating these inferences by being explicit about that organization's selection processes is about the best that can be done; with repeated exposure, such communication can perhaps help reshape the image of affirmative action more generally.

CONCLUSIONS

The research presented throughout this chapter supports the idea that affirmative action can inadvertently have detrimental consequences in work settings. These consequences are at odds with affirmative action's objectives and may undermine its success at reducing discrimination and advancing workplace equality. Being associated with affirmative action can create problems for those it was designed to help, tainting them with a stigma of incompetence, burdening them with negative self-views, and creating an unpleasant work environment in which others around them are disgruntled and resentful.

Although the investigations reported here focus primarily on women as beneficiaries of affirmative action, they are relevant to those in other groups who also are the targets of affirmative action efforts. The psychological processes that lead to affirmative action's unintended consequences operate identically whether gender, race, or ethnicity is the basis of the presumed preferential selection. Also, recent research demonstrates that the findings reported here are not confined to policies labeled as affirmative action. When said to be selected as part of a diversity initiative, women and blacks were viewed as more deficient in competence than when said to be selected on the basis of merit.[48] It appears that whether called affirmative action, managing diversity, or even minority outreach, programs that highlight demographic group membership as a critical feature in decision making risk creating problems for those targeted for benefit.

Although we have focused on the generally accepted assumptions about affirmative action, differences exist in the degree to which people hold negative attitudes toward it as a policy. Thus research has indicated that attitudes toward affirmative action programs are affected not only by the structure of the plan itself,[49] but also by individual differences in race, gender, political ideology, and prejudice, all of which have been found to be related to endorsement of affirmative action policies.[50] Whether these differences in attitudes toward affirmative action affect the perceptions or self-perceptions of purported beneficiaries or attitudes of nonbeneficiaries has yet to be investigated.

In summary, our research suggests that as currently construed, affirmative action policies can have unintended deleterious consequences. Denying individuals the satisfaction of knowing they have attained a position on their own merits can lower their self-efficacy and foster feelings of inadequacy. The stigma associated with affirmative action can feed stereotypic thinking and prejudiced attitudes. The bitterness of feeling victimized and cheated can aggravate workplace alienation and tensions. In fact, as long as affirmative action is associated with an absence of quality standards, it seems as likely to create problems as it is to solve them.

This does not imply that affirmative action is necessarily a bad policy or that we would recommend its abandonment. Its resounding success at increasing the representation of formerly underrepresented groups at all levels of the organizational hierarchy and in society more generally is to be applauded. It does imply, however, that we should work to uncover and address affirmative action's unintended by-products. The research presented throughout this chapter attests to the fact that paradoxically, the aims of affirmative action may be subtly thwarted by the policy itself. Although it provides organizational access to those who may otherwise have been denied entry, affirmative action may produce reactions that ultimately block these same individuals from the opportunity to advance in their careers and reach their full potential.

NOTES

1. K. Green, *Affirmative Action and Principles of Justice* (Westport, CT: Greenwood Press, 1989).

2. *Grutter v. Bollinger*, 539 U.S. 306 (2003), No. 02-241.

3. S. D. Clayton and F. J. Crosby, *Justice, Gender, and Affirmative Action* (Ann Arbor: University of Michigan Press, 1992); F. Crosby, *Affirmative Action Is Dead; Long Live Affirmative Action* (New Haven, CT: Yale University Press, 2004); N. Glazer, "The Future of Preferential Affirmative Action," in P. A. Katz and D. A. Taylor, eds., *Elimination Racism: Profiles in Controversy* (New York: Plenum Press, 1988), p. 329.

4. Cited in R. F. Tomasson, F. J. Crosby, and S. D. Herzberger, *Affirmative Action: The Pros and Cons of Policy and Practice* (Lanham, MD: Rowman and Littlefield, 1996).

5. D. Seligman, "How 'Equal Opportunity' Turned into Employment Quotas," *Fortune* (March 1973): 158–68.

6. Clayton and Crosby, *Justice, Gender, and Affirmative Action*; F. J. Crosby and D. I. Cordova, "Words Worth of Wisdom: Toward an Understanding of Affirmative Action," *Journal of Social Issues* 52 (1996): 33–49; M. C. Haynes and M. E. Heilman, "Perceptions of Affirmative Action Programs: What Are They Anyway?," paper presented at the Academy of Management, New Orleans, LA, August 2004; F. Holloway, "What Is Affirmative Action?" in F. Blanchard and F. Crosby, eds., *Affirmative Action in Perspective* (New York: Springer-Verlag, 1989), pp. 9–19; D. A. Kravitz, "Attitudes toward

Affirmative Action Plans Directed at Blacks: Effects of Plan and Individual Differences," *Journal of Applied Social Psychology* 25 (1995): 2192–220.

7. H. Golden, S. Hinkle, and F. J. Crosby, "Reactions to Affirmative Action: Substance and Semantics," *Journal of Applied Social Psychology* 31 (2001).

8. See M. A. Taylor Carter, D. Doverspike, and K. D. Cook, "The Effects of Affirmative Action on the Female Beneficiary," *Human Resource Development Quarterly* 7 (1996): 31–54.

9. G. Himmelfarb, "Universities Creating Second-Class Faculties: Letter to the Editor," *New York Times*, May 15, 1988; S. Steele, *The Content of Our Character: A New Vision of Race in America* (New York: Morrow, 1990); I. Wilkerson, "Remedy for Racism of Past Has New Kind of Shackles," *New York Times*, September 15, 1991, p. 11; D. Wycliff, "Blacks Debate the Costs of Affirmative Action," *New York Times*, June 10, 1990, p. 3.

10. S. Steele, "A Negative Vote on Affirmative Action," *New York Times Magazine*, May 1990, p. 46.

11. *Grutter v. Bollinger.*

12. L. T. Garcia, N. Erskine, K. Hawn, and S. R. Casmay, "The Effect of Affirmative Action on Attributions about Minority Groups Members," *Journal of Personality* 49 (1981): 427–37.

13. R. J. Summers, "The Influence of Affirmative Action of Perceptions of a Beneficiary's Qualifications," *Journal of Applied Social Psychology* 21 (1991): 1265–76.

14. G. B. Northcraft and J. Martin, "Double Jeopardy: Resistance to Affirmative Action from Potential Beneficiaries," in B. A. Gutek, ed., *Sex Role Stereotyping and Affirmative Action Policy* (Los Angeles: University of California, Institute of Industrial Relations, 1982), pp. 81–130.

15. M. B. Jacobson and W. Koch, "Women as Leaders: Performance Evaluation as a Function of Methods of Leader Selection," *Organizational Behavior and Human Decision Processes* 20 (1977): 149–57.

16. H. H. Kelley, "The Processes of Causal Attribution," *American Psychologist* 28(2) (1973): 107–28; H. H. Kelley, "Attribution in Social Interaction," in E. E. Jones and D. E. Kanouse, eds., *Attribution: Perceiving the Causes of Behavior* (Hillsdale, NJ: Lawrence Erlbaum Associates, 1987), pp. 1–26.

17. M. E. Heilman, C. J. Block, and J. A. Lucas, "Presumed Incompetent? Stigmatization and Affirmative Action Efforts," *Journal of Applied Psychology* 86 (1992): 536–44.

18. Ibid., study 2.

19. M. E. Heilman, C. J. Block, and P. Stathatos, "The Affirmative Action Stigma of Incompetence: Effects of Performance Information Ambiguity," *Academy of Management Journal* 40 (1997): 603–25.

20. Ibid., study 2.

21. M. C. Haynes and M. E. Heilman, "Perceptions of Affirmative Action Programs"; D. A. Kravitz and J. Platania, "Attitudes and Beliefs about Affirmative Action: Effects of Target and of Respondent Sex and Ethnicity," *Journal of Applied Psychology* 78 (1993): 928–38.

22. M. E. Heilman and S. L. Blader, "Assuming Preferential Selection when the Admissions Policy Is Unknown: The Effects of Gender Rarity," *Journal of Applied Psychology* 86 (2001): 188–93.

23. B. Blaine, J. Crocker, and B. Major, "The Unintended Negative Consequences of Sympathy for the Stigmatized," *Journal of Applied Social Psychology* 25 (1995): 889–905; G. Himmelfarb, "Universities Creating Second-Class Faculties: Letter to the Editor," *New York Times*, May 15, 1988; C. Murray, "Affirmative Racism: How Preferential Treatment Works against Blacks," *New Republic*, December 1984, 18–23; Steele, *The Content of Our Character*.

24. A. Nadler and J. D. Fisher, "The Role of Threat to Self-Esteem and Perceived Control in Recipient Reaction to Help: Theory Development and Empirical Validation," in L. Berkowitz, ed., *Advances in Experimental Social Psychology* (Orlando, FL: Academic Press, 1986), pp. 81–112.

25. M. E. Turner, and A. R. Pratkanis, "Affirmative Action as Help: A Review of Recipient Reactions to Preferential Selection and Affirmative Action," *Basic and Applied Social Psychology: Special Social Psychological Perspectives on Affirmative Action* 15 (1994): 43–69.

26. M. E. Heilman, "Sex Bias in Work Settings: The Lack of Fit Model," *Research in Organizational Behavior* 5 (1983): 269–98.

27. M. E. Heilman, M. C. Simon, and D. P. Repper, "Intentionally Favored, Unintentionally Harmed? Impact of Sex-Based Preferential Selection on Self-Perceptions and Self-Evaluations," *Journal of Applied Psychology* 72 (1987): 62–68.

28. M. E. Heilman, J. A. Lucas, and S. R. Kaplow, "Self-Derogating Consequences of Sex-Based Preferential Selection: The Moderating Role of Initial Self-Confidence," *Organizational Behavior and Human Decision Processes* 46 (1990): 202–16.

29. A. Bandura, "The Psychology of Chance Encounters and Life Paths," *American Psychologist* 37 (1982): 747–55; A. Bandura, *Social Foundations of Thought and Action* (Englewood Cliffs, NJ: Prentice Hall, 1986).

30. M. E. Heilman, J. C. Rivero, and J. F. Brett, "Skirting the Competence Issue: Effects of Sex-Based Preferential Selection on Task Choices of Women and Men," *Journal of Applied Psychology* 76 (1991): 99–105.

31. Bandura, *Social Foundations of Thought and Action*; C. S. Dweck, "Motivational Processes Affecting Learning," *American Psychologist: Special Psychological Science and Education* 41(1986): 1040–48.

32. Heilman et al., "Skirting the Competence Issue."

33. R. P. Brown, T. Charnsangavej, K. A. Keough, M. L. Newman, and P. J. Rentfrow, "Putting the 'Affirm' into Affirmative Action: Preferential Selection and Academic Performance," *Journal of Personality and Social Psychology* 79(2000): 736–47.

34. J. R. Kluegel and E. R. Smith, "Affirmative Action Attitudes: Effects of Self-Interest, Racial Affect, and Stratification Beliefs on Whites' Views," *Social Forces* 61 (1983): 797–824; R. W. Nacoste, "But Do They Care about Fairness? The Dynamics of Preferential Treatment and Minority Interest," *Basic and Applied Social Psychology* 8 (1987): 177–91; R. W. Nacoste, "Sources of Stigma: Analyzing the Psychology of Affirmative Action," *Law and Policy* 12 (1990): 175–95.

35. D. Feiden, "Firms Fed up with Affirmative Action," *Crain's New York Business* 1(2) (1992); W. A. I. Henry, "Time," *What Price Preference?* September 1991, 30–31; F. R. Lynch, *Invisible Victims: White Males and the Crisis of Affirmative Action* (New York: Praeger, 1992).

36. M. Scofield, "Off the Ladder," *New York Times Magazine*, June 1993, p. 22.

37. Nacoste, "Sources of Stigma."

38. Heilman et al., "Presumed Incompetent?"

39. T. R. Tyler, R. J. Boeckmann, H. J. Smith, and Y. J. Huo, *Social Justice in a Diverse Society* (Boulder, CO: Westview Press, 1997).

40. M. E. Heilman, W. F. McCullough, and D. Gilbert, "The Other Side of Affirmative Action: Reactions of Nonbeneficiaries to Sex-Based Preferential Selection," *Journal of Applied Psychology* 81 (1996): 346–57.

41. Heilman et al. "Self-Derogating Consequences of Sex-Based Preferential Selection"; M.E. Heilman et al., "Intentionally Favored, Unintentionally Harmed?"

42. D. C. Evans, "A Comparison of the Other-Directed Stigmatization Produced by Legal and Illegal Forms of Affirmative Action," *Journal of Applied Psychology* 88 (2003): 121–30; R. W. Nacoste, "How Affirmative Action Can Pass Constitutional and Social Psychological Muster," *Journal of Social Issues* 52 (1996): 133–44; Taylor Carter et al., "The Effects of Affirmative Action on the Female Beneficiary."

43. M. E. Heilman, W. S. Battle, C. E. Keller, and R. A. Lee, "Type of Affirmative Action Policy: A Determinant of Reaction to Sex-Based Preferential Selection?" *Journal of Applied Psychology* 83 (1998): 190–205.

44. Heilman et al., "Presumed Incompetent?"; Heilman et al., "The Affirmative Action Stigma of Incompetence"; Heilman et al., "Self-Derogating Consequences"; Heilman et al., "Intentionally Favored, Unintentionally Harmed?"

45. Heilman et al., "Type of Affirmative Action Policy."

46. Ibid., study 1.

47. Ibid., study 3.

48. M. E. Heilman and B. Welle, "Disadvantaged by Diversity? The Effects of Diversity Goals on Competence Perceptions," *Journal of Applied Social Psychology* 36 (2006): 1–29.

49. Kravitz, "Attitudes toward Affirmative Action Plans Directed at Blacks"; D. A. Kravitz, and S. L. Klineberg, "Reactions to Two Versions of Affirmative Action among Whites, Blacks, and Hispanics," *Journal of Applied Psychology* 85 (2000): 597–611.

50. D. A. Kravitz, D. A. Harrison, M. E. Turner, E. L. Levine, W. Chaves, M. T. Brannick et al., *Affirmative Action: A Review of Psychological and Behavioral Research* (Bowling Green, OH: Society for Industrial and Organizational Psychology, 1997).

2

Racial and Ethnic Harassment in the Workplace

Tamara A. Bruce

White women continually ask me, "how often do black women wash their hair?" and so I said, "you know this is like the third time you asked me how many times black women wash their hair, you already know the answer."[1]

The incident depicted in the epigraph is a prime example of the unique form that harassing comments may take when directed toward racial and ethnic minorities. Such behaviors, which are often influenced by racial and ethnic stereotypes, characterize an understudied form of workplace discrimination: racial/ethnic harassment. Racial/ethnic harassment in the workplace is a crucial area of research given the current trends in workforce demographic composition. U.S. census data from the past decade (1990–2000) report that every racial minority group has increased its rate of entering the workforce, and the Caucasian group has decreased its rate (Table 2.1).[2] This shift in the composition of the American workforce is best illuminated by estimates that less than 40 percent of it is comprised of Caucasian men.[3] With this backdrop I begin to discuss the history and background of workplace discrimination.

BACKGROUND

Workplace discrimination has received increasing attention both in research and public realms since the late 1970s. Most notably, the introduction of the term *sexual harassment* as a specific form of discrimination has opened the floodgates for researchers and nonresearchers alike to explore the complexities of workplace harassment.

Racial and ethnic harassment, however, has not experienced the proliferation of research and attention that its older sibling sexual harassment has

TABLE 2.1.   U.S. Civilian Employed Workforce 1990–2000

	1990	2000	Change
Black	9.9%	10.1%	2.7%
American Indian, Eskimo, or Aleut	0.6%	0.7%	12.8%
Asian or Pacific Islander	2.9%	3.8%	29.0%
Other race	3.4%	6.7%	98.8%
	16.8%	21.3%	26.9%
White	83.2%	78.7%	−5.4%
Entire workforce change			2.8%

received.[4] Harassment and stress research has often overlooked ethnic minority employees, and that which has been performed has often used convenience samples (e.g., professional society members) unlikely to generalize to the entire worker population.[5] Racial and ethnic harassment has only relatively recently become the primary focus of empirical studies and begun to distinguish itself as a unique form of workplace discrimination.

This chapter explores racial and ethnic harassment in the workplace by detailing primarily empirical research that has been conducted on both racial and ethnic harassment and its related constructs. First, racial and ethnic harassment will be defined to help distinguish it from similar phenomena. Second, the research on racial and ethnic discrimination and the sexual harassment of ethnic and racial minorities will be discussed as a foundation for understanding racial and ethnic harassment. Third, the nature of racial and ethnic harassment and its relationship with other forms of discrimination will be delineated. Finally, I will conclude with a discussion of the challenges faced by racial and ethnic harassment researchers and directions for future study.

Due to the many chapters, articles, and books reviewing the historical and legal background of sexual harassment and well-documented information on racial discrimination, this chapter will only touch on those areas briefly as they apply to racial and ethnic harassment.[6] In addition, this chapter will only focus on U.S.-based experiences, because other countries have different laws and racial/ethnic compositions.[7]

SEMANTIC DISTINCTIONS

To discuss racial and ethnic harassment and its related constructs, a few semantic issues must be addressed initially. Sometimes publications on racial and ethnic harassment and discrimination define race or ethnicity, describe differences between the two constructs, and justify the term chosen for the dialogue. Some key distinctions that are usually mentioned include the difference between a biologically determined framework of race and a socially constructed framework of ethnicity. However, many people today (researchers and nonresearchers alike) use these terms interchangeably and even view the constructs as equivalent.

Nonetheless, race and ethnicity are different by definition, and with the growing Hispanic population in the United States, one of the most common trends is to distinguish between Caucasian Hispanic and Caucasian non-Hispanic ethnicities.[8] Although a person of German descent and one of Latin American descent may both be classified as Caucasian in terms of race, their ethnic classification would be different. Thus, a practical distinction between race and ethnicity is the visibility level of the characteristics. Although an individual's race may not always be easy to determine by observation, it is usually more visible than a person's ethnicity. To establish ethnicity, observers rely more heavily on inferences and other characteristics (e.g., manner of speech).[9]

Given that ethnicity is generally a *less* visible characteristic than race, managing their minority group identity may be easier for ethnic than racial minorities. Stigmatized individuals who have been able to cross group boundaries may enjoy the benefits of majority group membership and feel significantly less stigmatized or not stigmatized at all compared to those who cannot or do not cross such boundaries.[10] Therefore, the nature of ethnic harassment may be qualitatively different from racial harassment because of the increased potential for identity management strategies.

Thus arguments can be made for and against the separation of the ethnic and racial harassment constructs. Some distinguish between the two, whereas others do not; still others simply confuse them.[11] The matter is further complicated by the intimate relationship between the two constructs. Victims of racial or ethnic harassment are likely to be unable to distinguish whether they were targets of harassment because of their race or ethnicity. Finally, these forms of research suffer from a lack of empirical investigations examining the differences between ethnic and racial harassment.

Therefore, for the purposes of this review, the term racial/ethnic harassment (REH) will be adopted in most of the discussion in an attempt to use research on both forms to create on overarching framework for the study of either. Alternatively, the terms racial harassment (RH) and ethnic harassment (EH) will be used only when differences between the two constructs are being directly compared. This approach is not intended to discount the differences between the two constructs but to allow for a more coherent review of the relevant literature. However, I contend that because research about racial and ethnic harassment is still in its infancy, a strategy of integration as opposed to segregation will best serve the advancement of understanding the two phenomena.

Similarly, a variety of terms, such as Caucasian, white, and Anglo American or black, people of color, and African American, are often used to describe like groups of people. Again, to reduce the already present fragmentation in this research resulting from the multiple disciplines and approaches used to study it, certain descriptors will be considered to encompass or be synonymous with other similar ones (e.g., a statement about African Americans should be re-garded as generalizable to blacks and people of color).

DEFINITION OF RACIAL/ETHNIC HARASSMENT

Racial/ethnic harassment has typically been conceptualized as threatening or verbal conduct or exclusionary behavior with a racial/ethnic component and is directed at targets due to their race or ethnicity.[12] Comparatively, racial/ethnic discrimination (RED) involves behaviors or practices that impede career opportunities or earning potential due to race or ethnicity.[13] These definitions are parallel to those of sexual harassment (SH) and sexual discrimination (SD). Like SH and SD, REH and RED are illegal under federal law.

Part of the Civil Rights Act of 1964 made employment discrimination ille-gal. Specifically, Title VII made it unlawful to discriminate against individuals in an employment setting based on their race, sex, color, religion, or national origin.[14] Since 1964, additional federal legislation has expanded the list of pro-tected classes to include age, disability, and familial and veteran status.

In both the empirical and legislative realms, REH, like SH, is considered a specific type of discrimination. Discrimination occurs when a person or group of people is treated differently than another person or group. Although all ha-rassment is considered discrimination, many forms of discrimination would not be defined as harassment.

Two major criteria must be met to label a behavior as a type of harassment as opposed to the more general category of discrimination. First, in harassment, people typically go out of their way to bother others by behaving in a manner that is unrelated to appropriate work conduct (e.g., teasing, fondling, etc.). Harassment therefore consists of behavior outside the scope of necessary job performance presumably engaged in for personal gratification, because of other personal motives, or due to meanness or bigotry. Discrimination claims, by contrast, involve perceptions of unfair outcomes of necessary human resource management processes. The second distinction is that harassment is usually a continual pattern of behaviors, whereas discrimination can be a one-time event (e.g., firing or hiring).

As previously mentioned, although the means by which individuals deter-mine another's race or ethnicity may differ, the forms of behavior that constitute RH and EH appear to be relatively similar. REH behaviors have been categorized into two types, verbal behaviors such as comments, jokes, slurs, and so on related to one's ethnicity or race, and exclusionary behaviors such as being excluded from a social event, not being given necessary information due to one's ethnicity or race, or being pressured to "give up" one's ethnic/racial identity to fit in.[15]

Some have suggested the exclusionary behaviors component of REH as unique to harassment based on ethnicity/race, because previous SH research has not explicitly focused on such behaviors. However, SH inventories may capture some if not all types of exclusionary behaviors based on gender with items asking whether someone has "treated you differently because of your sex (for example, mistreated, slighted, or ignored you)."[16] The focus on exclusionary behaviors in REH but not in SH measures appears to be motivated by their frequency within each harassment type. Thus, research and practice suggest that individuals may encounter exclusionary behaviors based on gender or ethnicity/race, but that those experiencing REH are far more likely to encounter exclusionary behaviors than those facing SH.[17]

In discussions of sexual harassment, many authors have cited the grounding of violence against women in the sociocultural roots of gender and power.[18] Moreover, researchers suggest that any key dimension of social stratification (e.g., race, ethnicity, or gender) is strongly linked to discrimination and harassment and argue that the marginalized status of women and racial/ethnic minorities in our society makes them more susceptible to becoming victims of harassment in general.[19]

RACIAL/ETHNIC DISCRIMINATION

Given that harassment is a specific form of discrimination, much relevant research on REH has actually been performed in the area of RED. Many studies over the years have shown that race, as expected, is an important factor to consider when investigating racial discrimination.[20]

RED has been shown to be related to a host of negative outcomes, including lowered co-worker satisfaction and job satisfaction, poorer mental health and emotional well-being, and poorer physical well-being.[21]

Separation of Harassment and Discrimination

A major problem in investigating REH is that harassment as a form of discrimination is rarely distinguished from its larger parent construct in studies of discrimination, despite evidence showing that the two phenomena result in different workplace outcomes, therefore suggesting that they operate in separate psychological domains within the workplace.[22] Moreover, the ability to distinguish the two constructs is rarely present because many measures of RED (also often called racist events or perceived racism) assess an array of somewhat generic experiences.

For example, Landrine and Klonoff found striking results during their validation of an 18-item measure of racial discrimination on a sample of 153 university-affiliated African American students, faculty, and staff.[23] Nearly all participants reported experiencing some type of racist discrimination in the past year (98.1 percent), and all had encountered it in their lifetime (100 percent). Additionally, 99.4 percent of the sample indicated that such racist events created stress in their lives.

Given these findings, discerning the number of these events that would be classified as REH and RED would be interesting. But further investigation of the measurement items reveals that such distinctions are rather difficult. Some items, such as number fifteen, "How many times have you been called a racist name like _____?" may be relatively easily categorized as racial harassment. However, many others, such as number three, "How many times have you been treated unfairly by your co-workers, fellow students, and colleagues because you are black?" is too broad to determine if respondents are recalling specifically harassing or generally discriminatory events. Such items should not be discounted as potentially reliable and valid measures of racial discrimination, but they impede our ability to measure the unique effects of REH.

Similar difficulties arise with other instruments.[24] Reporting frequencies of individual items that clearly fit into one category or another is possible using such scales. This practice, however, may lead to a distortion and deficiency in measurement of the two constructs. Without racial discrimination surveys that include clear harassment subscales or entire racial harassment instruments themselves, the field will constantly suffer from an inability to determine the true impact of the phenomenon.

ETHNIC/RACIAL MINORITY EXPERIENCES OF SEXUAL HARASSMENT

Interestingly, REH research has been more heavily based on studies dealing with sexual harassment than on those of racial discrimination or racism. In fact, REH research may be seen as the most recent construct development in a progression of research based on SH experiences but departing from the traditional Caucasian female as the victim. To better understand the theoretical and methodological roots of REH, examining the first step in that progression, research on the SH experiences of racial/ethnic minorities, is important. This area of research may be considered as having bridged the gap between studies of SH and REH and, more importantly, introduced the use of SH paradigms when examining harassment experiences affected by racial/ethnic variables.

Since the late 1970s when Catherine MacKinnon published her seminal work on sexual harassment, ethnic or racial minority women have been considered more likely to experience sexual harassment than nonminority women.[25] However, such research is comparatively scarce within the arena of sexual harassment. This is mainly because research on SH has typically relied on samples of Caucasian females.[26] Practically, this has occurred because field studies usually have too few women of color to analyze racial differences, and lab studies rarely specify the race of either the harasser or victim.[27] Additionally, potentially useful data often cannot be utilized by other researchers because information on the racial/ethnic demography of the sample is not included in publications.[28]

Despite these obstacles, usable findings exist. Some claim that experiences of sexual harassment do not differ significantly between racial/ethnic minorities and nonminorities.[29] Others report mixed findings or find that theoretical models of sexual harassment are similar for different ethnic groups.[30]

However, a much larger proportion of studies report that differences between racial/ethnic minorities and nonminorities exist in the severity and amount of the SH, coping strategies, incidence rates, work outcomes, status level and race of perpetrators, and type of harassment.[31] In fact, some researchers have even adapted existing SH measures for use with a specific ethnic population.[32]

In cases comparing multiple racial/ethnic minority groups, some research has found that African American women report the highest incidence of SH (62 percent), followed closely by Latinas (60 percent), European American women (56 percent), and Asian/East Indian American women (46 percent).[33]

INCIDENCE, CORRELATES, AND CURRENT MEASURES OF REH

Contrary to what the empirical literature on sexual harassment suggests, one dominant measure of REH does not seem to exist. Within the past decade, though, researchers have used several approaches to try to assess this elusive construct. Although the relatively recent development of these measures as compared to other workplace discrimination surveys is not surprising given the history of the evolution of REH research, it nonetheless suggests that further empirical exploration and validation of the instruments are important. Moreover, the nuances of the construct of REH and the way each scale captures them can be determined only after each has been used repeatedly in samples with diverse occupational, socioeconomic, and racial/ethnic characteristics.

The purpose of this review of current measures is not to compare or evaluate their validity or utility but to showcase each plan of research to observe the direction current REH research is following. Many other measures not mentioned in this chapter also contain questions and subscales that assess REH (e.g., the Perceived Ethnic Discrimination Questionnaire).[34] However, the focus of these omitted measures is on RED rather than REH specifically, and for that reason they are not discussed.

The first measure is labeled the Ethnic Harassment Experiences scale.[35] It contains seven items ($\alpha = 0.79$) and assesses exposure to threatening behavior in the form of ethnic derogation and social exclusion during the previous twenty-four months. The development of the measure was informed by analysis of employed students' descriptions of ethnic harassment incidents. Sample items include evaluating how often someone in the participant's institution "called [the person] by a racial/ethnic slur," or "excluded [him or her] from social interactions because of . . . race/ethnicity."

Related to this measure, Radhakrishnan and Schneider also developed a Bystander Ethnic Harassment scale,[36] which includes seven items ($\alpha = 0.84$)

assessing bystander harassment that occurs when the person reporting the incident witnesses the harassment of another individual during the previous two years.[37] It was modeled on a measure of bystander sexual harassment. Sample items include determining how often someone in the participant's institution "watched [their] colleagues be the target of racist comments," or "supported a colleague who talked with [them] about being the target of racial harassment."

The Racial Acts, Crimes, and Experiences Survey also evaluates REH.[38] This scale includes 24 items ($\alpha = 0.90$) assessing personal experiences with racism during employment at one's most recent job. Sample items include asking participants if they were ever in a situation in which managers, supervisors, co-workers, or employees "made condescending remarks to [them] about [their] race," or "excluded people of a particular race from organized social activities."

Yet another measure is the Racial Ethnic Harassment Scale, which includes fifteen items evaluating individual exposure to racial/ethnic harassment during the previous twelve months.[39] Respondents are asked to separately indicate their experiences with respect to military and civilian harassers. This scale was modeled on the structure of the Sexual Experiences Questionnaire, Department of Defense (SEQ-DoD) sexual harassment measure.[40] Sample items include asking how often individuals were in circumstances where they thought that someone "made unwelcome attempts to draw [them] into an offensive discussion of racial/ethnic manners" or "made remarks suggesting that people of [their] race/ethnicity are not suited for the kind of work that [they] do."

Finally, the Racialized Sexual Harassment Scale is a seven-item ($\alpha = 0.86$) measure of incidents of racialized sexual harassment during a person's employment at his or her most recent job.[41] Sample items assess participants' experiences with situations in which their managers, supervisors, co-workers, or employees "told jokes or stories that described people of [their] *gender and ethnicity* negatively," or "said they expected [the participants] to behave certain ways because of your *gender and ethnicity.*"

It is interesting that the underlying construct dimensions of REH seem similar across the five measures just described. However, researchers developing these scales have used not only different approaches but also varying semantic choices. Two focus exclusively on ethnicity, one exclusively on race, and the remaining three include both constructs. Four of the five deal with direct harassment, whereas one focuses on bystander harassment. Some incorporate significant sexual harassment content in the measure, and others use sexual harassment models to inform the development of the measure.

An important consideration when reviewing the current REH assessment efforts is that all of these measures were either indirectly or directly influenced by sexual harassment measurement approaches. Although these influences are not only expected and justified, their presence nonetheless has dictated that REH has developed similarly to SH. One wonders what a REH measure would look like if it were developed independently from SH models based on racism frameworks and literature. Have SH influences limited the progress of REH measurement efforts? Answering this question is difficult given the youth of the REH research field and the lack of a parallel workplace harassment construct that has not been heavily based on SH theory. In time, however, any disadvantages of this approach may become evident.

Setting aside potential limitations of the validity of these REH measures, studies using them have reported REH incidence rates of 40–67 percent among employed individuals.[42] These rates have been shown to be affected by the victim's race/ethnicity, religious affiliation, age, country of origin, organizational ethnic/racial composition, and work experience as well as the harasser's employment status.[43] No consistent pattern seems to appear across racial/ethnic groups regarding how most of these variables affect the percentage of individuals who experience REH, most likely due to differing research methodologies of each study. A theme that does emerge is that ethnic/racial minorities experience proportionally more REH than their nonminority counterparts.

Factor analysis suggests that REH consists of two underlying factors, one including nonphysical verbal, symbolic, and exclusionary behaviors, and the other including threatening or harmful behaviors.[44] Additionally, REH experiences have been conceptualized as being more subtle and indirect in form and content.[45] This finding parallels racial and ethnic bias research findings that most such behaviors are subtle, with only a small percentage of the population exhibiting overt behaviors.[46]

REH also appears to lead to lower health satisfaction, lower well-being scores, higher general work stress levels, decreased job satisfaction, negative psychological and physical outcomes, increased substance abuse, and greater negative affectivity.[47] REH is related to worker dissatisfaction, which in turn affects turnover intentions.[48] In the legal realm, a review of 131 civil cases of racial harassment found claimants most likely to be black (63 percent), work in the private sector (76 percent), and be employed in unskilled or semiskilled occupations (59 percent). The employer is also likely to win in court 66 percent of the time.[49] These findings suggest not only that REH is a unique form of workplace discrimination but that its correlates and outcomes are both significant and important to consider when investigating workplace harassment and its impact on individuals.

MULTIPLE FORMS OF HARASSMENT

Given the theoretical similarity of the constructs of racial, ethnic, and sexual harassment, one may wonder if the predictors and outcomes of one form can be explained by that construct's correlation to the others. Fortunately, a few studies have attempted to investigate such relationships. Findings include significant correlations between racial/ethnic and sexual harassment that have ranged from 0.39 to 0.62.[50] Factor analysis also has demonstrated strong associations between racial and sexual harassment variables in the workplace.[51] Though these correlations between constructs are high, they are not perfect, suggesting that the constructs differ on some level. These potential construct distinctions should be established by additional factor analytic work.

Employees subjected to multiple types of harassment have reported worse outcomes than those exposed to fewer forms.[52] When considered simultaneously, SH and REH have been shown to be significantly associated with different outcomes, with SH causally related to self-esteem and depression and REH linked to job and work outcomes, life satisfaction, and posttraumatic stress disorder (PTSD) symptomatology.[53] REH also has been shown to have unique predictive ability beyond the effects of SH in the areas of work withdrawal, somatization, health satisfaction, and PTSD symptomatology.[54] Additionally, bystander REH has been shown to be related to direct ethnic harassment and discrimination.[55] These findings suggest that a climate where harassment of any kind is prevalent and tolerated leads to negative outcomes for employees. Moreover, the unique combined effects of these constructs provide further evidence supporting their differentiation.

As previously suggested, it is likely that many individuals are subjected to multiple forms of workplace harassment as determined by their individual characteristics. Examples of this phenomenon include findings that African American women are more likely to experience multiple forms of harassment and that minority women were significantly more harassed than minority men or majority men or women when looking at an overall combined measure of REH and SH.[56]

Recent research also has posited that various forms of harassment may coexist within individual behavioral incidents. Buchanan and Ormerod propose that the harassment of African American women is likely to be unique both in its perception as well as its form.[57] Specifically, the nature of such sexual harassment is likely to draw on aspects of race, whether subtle or overt, when directed toward women of color. For example, although white women may be referred to as "sluts" or "whores," an African American woman is more likely to be called a "*black* whore," creating an experience that combines aspects of both gender and race. Women in the Buchanan study reported common experiences of racialized sexual harassment (harassment with both racial and sexual overtones) ranging from racial/sexual comments to assumptions about competence, personal hygiene, and typical style of dress.

Similarly, Mansfield and colleagues found that African American tradeswomen had extensive gender-based *and* race-based harassment, suggesting that to some extent the two experiences co-occur among women of color.[58] In their studies of African American women firefighters, Yoder and Aniakudo found that respondents refused to define their experiences as solely racial or sexual, asserting instead that they reflected both forms of harassment simultaneously.[59]

In their study of black college students, Mecca and Rubin found that many African American women described the issue of sexual harassment as inextricably intertwined with racism.[60] In addition, Mecca and Rubin found that a unique category of harassment emerged in which sexual attention was based on racial stereotypes of African American women's sexuality or on physical features thought to vary by race (e.g., that black women have large behinds).

Texeira provided an analysis of the experiences of sixty-five African American women in the law enforcement profession and described their experiences as having components of both sexual harassment and racial overtones, thus labeling such events racialized sexual harassment.[61] Factors such as job tenure, marital status, and race of the harassers also played a role in the experiences.

These studies demonstrate that sexual harassment, when directed toward women of color, often fuses racial and gender domination and may be better defined as racialized sexual harassment (RSH).[62] RSH seems to be a construct that is distinct from either sexual or racial/ethnic harassment.[63] The existence of racialized sexual harassment has begun to be mentioned in the literature and is supported by previous and current research on multiple minority status.[64] Those having this status may experience a situation of multiple advantage or jeopardy.[65] Multiple characteristics can interact to create a unique result that is more than the additive effects of the separate status characteristics.[66]

Harassment combining significant aspects of both SH and REH is an interesting notion. To date, the work on what has been labeled RSH has not thoroughly investigated the proportion of harassment content that may be attributed to sexual overtones, racial influences, or both. Therefore, determining whether such behaviors should be labeled racialized sexual harassment and considered a distinct subtype of SH or sexualized racial harassment and viewed as a specific subtype of REH is difficult. This clouding of constructs has implications for REH research in general. If RSH were to be considered a form of SH, then perhaps any form of harassment with racial content that also has the potential for sexual overtones would be considered a form of SH rather than a separate form of harassment. Because many REH behaviors may incorporate sexual influences simultaneously, REH researchers are left with a difficult situation. If REH continues to distinguish itself through empirical work as a distinct form of workplace discrimination, how should it be conceptualized—as a racially or ethnically based or a sexually based phenomenon? Researchers must seek to answer these questions with future studies.

Climate

Given evidence that multiple forms of harassment (and discrimination) are likely to coexist in the same environment and findings that harassment experiences are related to organizational variables (e.g., work satisfaction), one must question the role of organizational climate in the perpetuation of REH. The organizational model of sexual harassment posits that it is encouraged by organizational structures creating power differentials that harassers can take advantage of. This model also can be applied to REH, as can similar research that has found that harassment is facilitated by the aforementioned power differentials and other organizational characteristics such as male-female ratios, amount of contact between employees, occupational norms, job functions and alternatives, and harassment policies and procedures.[67] These findings suggest that organizational climate variables are likely to be associated with the incidence and outcomes of REH.

Again, borrowing from the sexual harassment literature, we find that the proportion of women experiencing sexual harassment has been correlated with a number of different constructs. These include organizational practices and cultures that do not promote equal treatment for men and women[68] and related factors, such as social norms of the organization, the presence and effectiveness of policies prohibiting harassment, and the general sexual ambience of a workplace and its masculine job gender context.[69] Finally, the percentage of women experiencing harassment has been linked to work groups' perceptions of organizational tolerance for harassment and work climate, acceptance of superior–subordinate dating, and the differences in organizational power and gender between the harasser and victim.[70] Additionally, meta-analytic findings indicate that SH is more prevalent in organizations in which large power differentials are likely to exist between organizational levels.[71]

In sum, these studies on sexual harassment depict the relationship between gender-based harassment and organizational variables that stratify individuals along gender dimensions. Similar relationships are expected to exist for REH, such that variables placing people in the workplace into different tiers according to racial/ethnic dimensions are likely to be associated with REH incidence and outcomes. In fact, recent work has found that an organization's ethnic composition is an antecedent of REH.[72] Therefore, future studies of REH should investigate climate and structural variables as potential antecedents of the phenomenon.

CURRENT ISSUES AND FUTURE DIRECTIONS

So far in this chapter I have outlined the definitions, correlates, and outcomes of REH and its related constructs. At this point, I will discuss ongoing challenges researchers studying these phenomena face, highlight a number of promising plans of research, and finally make suggestions for future endeavors in this arena.

Challenges

Because REH research is similar to SH in its form and structure, many difficulties faced by SH researchers also plague the REH arena. Specifically, one problem that has hindered SH researchers' ability to accurately determine prevalence rates of harassment has been differences in reporting practices. Looking beyond the mere presence of individual personality differences as influences in harassment experiences, SH research has suggested the importance of examining individual variables, such as the nature and frequency of the harassment, organizational status of the harasser, and characteristics of the victim (e.g., age, organizational status, gender, ethnicity, marital status), as important influences on the judgment process victims go through when interpreting potentially harassing events.[73] Perceptions of an organization's climate for sexual harassment have been shown to influence the interpretation of potentially harassing events and to affect perceptions and attitudes toward the organization (e.g., work satisfaction) directly.[74]

How victims interpret an event (i.e., determine it as harassing or not) is directly related to whether they choose to report the harassment and to whom they describe it. Type and severity of experienced harassment seems to affect reporting patterns, and cognitive appraisal of a situation appears to be a significant mediator of the relationship between sexual harassment experiences and reporting behaviors.[75]

In addition to the judgment of whether a particular behavior constitutes harassment, other factors might influence if and to whom a victim's decides to provide details of a harassment experience. When leaders do not support harassment policies and procedures, victims are less likely to report the incident.[76] As a corollary, leaders at multiple organizational levels who make an honest, concerted effort at prevention have been shown to have significant impact on how comfortable subordinates feel coming forward about a sexually harassing encounter.[77] These leadership efforts have an impact that goes beyond implementation of policies and procedures discouraging harassment.[78]

Victims also must consider stigmatization and other negative consequences of reporting the harassment. In many cases, doing so leads to more negative outcomes than not.[79] Thus, fear of being blamed by the harasser and others are deterrents to reporting sexual harassment.[80] Targets' perceptions of whether the organization possesses policies and procedures for effective punishment of harassment are positively correlated to both victim reporting and their likelihood and method of seeking social support.[81] A similar pattern exists for support of such policies and procedures by organizational leaders.[82] Individual differences in witnesses or perpetrators of harassment also may play a role, because sexist attitudes and gender strongly predict the tendency to blame targets of harassment.[83]

Given these findings related to organizational climate and perception differences, the finding that Caucasians are more likely to indicate workplace SH perpetrated by male *superiors* and African American victims have a tendency to describe harassment by *peers or subordinates* is not surprising.[84] In a related vein, the occupational status of harassment victims has been shown to be correlated with likelihood of reporting harassment incidents. Those of higher occupational status report harassment more often than those of lower status. This relationship is explained by beliefs held by higher status persons who are less likely to fear retaliation and possess stronger beliefs about their abilities to create social change.[85] Finally, less sociocultural and organizational power is associated with an increased likelihood of experiencing harassment.[86]

Because the majority of victims of REH are racial/ethnic minorities, incidence rate accuracy problems due to reporting practices are further aggravated. The findings suggest that in general, REH is likely to be underreported, that reported accounts are likely to be heavily influenced by occupational self-preservation concerns, and that REH experiences are likely to be qualitatively different than other forms of harassment. This triple threat translates into a host of difficulties facing current REH researchers.

Cortina and colleagues suggest that sexual harassment incidence rate differences between various ethnic/racial groups could be due to the tendency of some female ethnic/racial groups to underreport incidents involving sexual abuse.[87] This suggestion seems plausible considering that ethnic and racial minority individuals often have relatively low occupational status within an organization either due to their social status or job title. However, it is unclear exactly how such status differences influence harassment incidence rates. Workplace status differentials could either cause minorities' *experiences* to vary or make minorities more likely to *report* incidents differently. Alternatively, such status differences could exert both effects simultaneously. Nonetheless, the disparate impact of reporting practices on incidence rates for REH should be investigated further, with special attention paid to intragroup differences by gender and race/ethnicity.

Another difficulty that sexual harassment researchers encounter involves determining the best method for measuring harassment experiences, particularly when using self-reporting instruments.[88] Meta-analytic findings from sexual harassment research demonstrate that more general, behaviorally anchored items that do not force participants to label behaviors as harassment yield higher incidence rates.[89] However, because REH behaviors tend to be more subtle and indirect in form and content, measures of REH require more descriptive information to determine if the behavior is indeed REH. Put simply, more general abstract items, for instance, "someone said something that bothered you," are more likely to yield higher incidence rates. However the same items are unable to tap into specific REH behaviors and therefore distinguish between REH and other forms of harassment. To fully assess REH, such an item would require additional descriptive information, such as "someone said something *involving racial or ethnic stereotypes* that bothered you." The latter example, though, would be more likely to yield lower, presumably more inaccurate incidence rates. This trade-off is a common concern for REH researchers, who must settle for a relatively narrow set of responses to measure REH precisely. Such limitations on the breadth of responses add to the previously mentioned measurement challenges.

Future Directions

As previously stated, much REH literature has been informed by research on sexual harassment. However, unlike SH, which has historically focused on women's experiences, REH has the potential to affect both minority women and men at relatively similar rates. This fact is important when considering the current shift in racial and ethnic diversity among workers. This demographic change emphasizes that future research must focus on the specific nature of workplace REH using full-time employees rather than school-based REH relying on employed students' experiences. As with any research on workplace phenomena, using student samples is often convenient but frequently fails to provide important information about the nuances of workplace environments.

In addition to increased use of occupational samples, the nature of REH dictates that effects must be examined with respect to both multiple racial/ethnic groups and multiple status dimensions. Such social status stratification characteristics as gender, race, ethnicity, socioeconomic status, and sexual orientation may interact in unique ways such that workplace REH may vary in severity, prevalence, and quality depending on the characteristics one possesses. Furthermore, studying differences between Caucasians and non-Caucasians may dilute the true nature of REH. An example of how complex differences may manifest themselves can be observed in a recent study investigating both REH and SH experiences among different racial/ethnic groups. Results showed that Caucasians reported a higher incidence of SH as compared to REH, whereas all other groups had higher rates of REH as compared to SH. However, a particularly interesting point was that of these other minority groups, the multiracial group had the highest incidence and frequency of both RH and SH.[90] This finding suggests that differences may be found not only between various ethnic/racial groups but also when more than one such race or ethnicity is present in the same person, as in the case of multiracial individuals.

Another aspect of REH that deserves increased attention is impact of the harasser's race on the harassment experience. In a lab study, Shelton and Chavous found that college students rated sexual behavior as more appropriate and humorous depending on the race of the harasser and victim.[91] When the victim was a black woman, the interaction was viewed as less appropriate when the harasser was a white as opposed to a black male. Replication of this finding in a field sample would clarify the mechanism of REH in the workplace. Additionally, if such replication were achieved, the demographic composition of various organizations and occupations may dictate that REH experiences vary as a function of job type or organization. This variation points to another area of much-needed focus with respect to workplace REH, organizational climate.

Organizational climate, as discussed, has been shown to influence the nature of workplace SH and REH in a parallel manner. Variables such as worker composition, embedded organizational status differentials, and formal and informal discrimination and harassment policies may influence REH experiences similarly. Therefore, future studies should fully explore both the effect of work-place climate on REH and the impact of the prevalence and nature of REH in the workplace on the organization's climate.

Another interesting future direction of REH research involves the impact of group and dominant culture identification in the mediation of harassment experiences. Studies have shown that common group identity can be a pro-tective factor against discrimination, although the protective qualities may differ at various levels of discrimination, such that the pride in one's ethnic identity may have little buffer quality at very high levels of discrimination.[92] Similarly, sexual harassment incidence among Hispanic women has been shown to be related to victims' affiliation to the mainstream non-Hispanic white U.S. culture (acculturation), such that Hispanic women with the least affiliation reported the lowest rates of SH experiences, followed by moderately affiliated Hispanic women and non-Hispanic white women.[93] These findings suggest that women with less affiliation with majority cultural norms, though reporting lower rates of SH than those with more affiliation, nonetheless experience worse effects of ha-rassment (in terms of factors such as work and co-worker satisfaction) than peers with greater connection to the mainstream culture. These findings from racial discrimination and sexual harassment suggest that one's acculturation and affili-ation level may cause seemingly similar subjects (e.g., alike in ethnic/racial back-ground and gender) to report qualitatively different experiences or exposure to REH. Investigation of these influences is another topic of study for future researchers.

Finally, one of the most difficult aspects of REH research is that many measurement attempts require participants to make inferences about the mo-tivation underlying the harassment and whether it was driven by racial/ethnic influences. Such inferences are especially central to nonverbal conduct, such as social exclusionary behaviors. The importance of determining the impact of assumptions and inferences in workplace REH is underscored by laws dictating that workers are protected against only forms of harassment related to specific characteristics, such as race, ethnicity, and gender. However if a harasser chooses his or her victim based on an unprotected category, such as sexual orientation, personality, or another arbitrary reason, the behavior is legal. Therefore, exam-ining the possibility of developing measures that do not rely as heavily on in-ferential items to determine the existence of REH in the workplace is important. Respondents could be reporting false positives by viewing harassment based on unprotected categories the same as that based on protected categories, thereby diluting REH measurement efforts. REH researchers are likely to struggle with this dilemma for years to come, particularly because the same issue has not been completely resolved in the SH arena. However, comparisons of different mea-surement approaches, with some using more behaviorally based items and others using more inferential items, would help inform the measurement process.

In sum, workplace REH is a burgeoning area of research that is increasingly important, but it also is plagued by the complicated nature of the construct. As discussed, this chapter has approached REH as a union of research between racial and ethnic harassment investigators. In reality, as research in EH and RH continues, significant distinctions between those two constructs may dictate the need for separation and comparison. Currently, however, the lack of empirical examinations directly comparing RH to EH allows conclusions to be drawn from combined RH and EH research. Among these is the fact that REH is a common occurrence in the workplace that has detrimental effects on its victims. With this thought in mind, occupational researchers and practitioners alike must look toward their future endeavors and consider the impact of this new phenomenon.

NOTES

1. N. T. Buchanan, "The Nexus of Race and Gender Domination: The Racialized Sexual Harassment of African American Women," in P. Morgan and J. Gruber, eds., *In the Company of Men: Re-Discovering the Links between Sexual Harassment and Male Domination* (Boston: Northeastern University Press, 2004), pp. 294–320.

2. S. L. Clark and M. Weismantle, "Employment Status: 2000," Census 2000 Brief (U.S. Department of Commerce, 2003); available online at www.census.gov/prod/2003 pubs/c2kbr-18.pdf.

3. M. Inman, P. Radhackrishnan, and E. Koster, "The Differential Effects of Ethnic Harassment and Discrimination at Work: Support for the Domain-Specific Model," manuscript in preparation.

4. N. T. Buchanan and A. J. Ormerod, "Racialized Sexual Harassment in the Lives of African American Women," *Women and Therapy* 25 (2002): 107–24.

5. K. T. Schneider, R. T. Hitlan, A. X. Estrada, D. Anaya, and M. Delgado, "Bystander Harassment: Attributions Regarding a Climate Tolerant of Harassment," in T. M. Glomb (Chair), *How Detrimental Is Sexual Harassment? Broadening the Boundaries of Research* (Symposium conducted at the 15th Annual Conference of the Society for Industrial and Organizational Psychology, New Orleans, LA, April 2000).

6. For example, see A. Levy and M. Paludi, *Workplace Sexual Harassment*, 2nd ed. (Upper Saddle River, NJ: Prentice Hall, 2002); C. M. Steele, "A Threat Is in the Air: How Stereotypes Shape Intellectual Identity and Performance," *American Psychologist* 52 (1997): 613–29; and J. P. Harrell, S. Hall, and J. Taliaferro, "Physiological Responses to Racism and Discrimination: An Assessment of the Evidence," *American Journal of Public Health* 93(2) (2003): 243–48.

7. For a review of potential cross-cultural differences, especially because researchers and practitioners alike are becoming increasingly interested in the globalization of workforces, see P. Roberts and L. Vickers, "Harassment at Work as Discrimination: The Current Debate in England and Wales," *International Journal of Discrimination and the Law* 3 (1998): 91–114.

8. Clarke and Weismantle, "Employment Status: 2000."

9. K. T. Schneider, R. T. Hitlan, and P. Radhakrishnan, "An Examination of the Nature and Correlates of Ethnic Harassment Experiences in Multiple Contexts," *Journal of Applied Psychology* 85 (2000): 3–12.

10. R. D. Harvey, "Individual Differences in the Phenomenological Impact of Social Stigma," *Journal of Social Psychology* 141(2) (2001): 174–89.

11. For a discussion of the use of race versus ethnicity in ethnic/racial harassment research, see D. S. Blumenthal, "Race versus Ethnicity," *Academic Medicine* 74(12) (1999): 1259.

12. Schneider et al., "An Examination."

13. R. T. Hitlan and P. Radhakrishnan, "The Validity of a Context-Specific Scale of Racial Discrimination," paper presented at the Annual Meeting of the Western Psychological Association, Irvine, CA, April 1999.

14. See E. J. Harrick and G. M. Sullivan, "Racial Harassment: Case Characteristics and Employer Responsibilities," *Employee Responsibilities and Rights Journal* 8 (1995): 81–95, for a review of legal issues and regulations on racial harassment.

15. Schneider et al., "An Examination."

16. L. F. Fitzgerald, S. L. Shullman, N. Bailey, M. Richards, J. Swecker, Y. Gold, A. J. Ormerod, and L. Weitzman, "The Dimensions and Extent of Sexual Harassment in Higher Education and the Workplace," *Journal of Vocational Behavior* 32 (1988): 152–75.

17. Schneider et al., "An Examination."

18. L. M. Cortina, L. F. Fitzgerald, and F. Drasgow, "Contextualizing Latina Experiences of Sexual Harassment: Preliminary Tests of a Structural Model," *Basic and Applied Social Psychology* 24 (2002): 295–311.

19. L. Kalof, K. K. Eby, J. L. Matheson, and R. J. Kroska, "The Influence of Race and Gender on Student Self-Reports of Sexual Harassment by College Professors," *Gender and Society* 15(2) (2001): 282–302; A. J. Murrell, "Sexual Harassment and Women of Color: Issues, Challenges, and Future Directions," in M. S. Stockdale, ed., *Sexual Harassment in the Workplace: Perspectives, Frontiers, and Response Strategies* (Thousand Oaks, CA: Sage, 1996), pp. 51–66.

20. For example, see P. K. Mansfield, P. B. Koch, J. Henderson, J. R. Vicary, M. Cohn, and E. W. Young, "The Job Climate for Women in Traditionally Male Blue-Collar Occupations," *Sex Roles* 25(1–2) (1991): 63–79; S. Valentine, L. Silver, and N. Twigg, "Locus of Control, Job Satisfaction, and Job Complexity: The Role of Perceived Race Discrimination," *Psychological Reports* 84 (1999): 1267–74; Inman et al., "The Differential Effects"; V. M. Mays, L. M. Coleman, and. J. S. Jackson, "Perceived Race-Based Discrimination, Employment Status, and Job Stress in a National Sample of Black Women: Implications for Health Outcomes," *Journal of Occupational Health Psychology* 1(3) (1996): 319–29; J. F. Dovidio, S. L. Gaertner, Y. F. Niemann, and K. Snider, "Racial, Ethnic, and Cultural Differences in Responding to Distinctiveness and Discrimination on Campus: Stigma and Common Group Identity," *Journal of Social Issues* 57(1) (2001): 167–88.

21. P. Radhakrishnan, "Ethnic Harassment and Discrimination," paper presented at the Department of Psychology, Penn State University, University Park, January 1999; E. A. Dietch, A. Barsky, R. M. Butz, S. Chan, A. P. Brief, and J. C. Bradley, "Subtle yet Significant: The Existence and Impact of Everyday Racial Discrimination in the Workplace," *Human Relations* 56(11) (2003): 1299–324; E. Klonoff, H. Landrine, and J. B. Ullman, "Racial Discrimination and Psychiatric Symptoms among Blacks," *Cultural Diversity and Ethnic Minority Psychology* 5(4) (1999): 329–39; see D. R. Williams, H. W. Neighbors, and J. S. Jackson, "Racial/Ethnic Discrimination and Health: Findings from Community Studies," *American Journal of Public Health* 93 (2003): 200–208 for a review of negative mental and physical health outcomes of ethnic/racial discrimination.

22. Schneider et al., "An Examination"; for example, Inman et al., "The Differential Effects."

23. H. Landrine and E. A. Klonoff, "The Schedule of Racist Events: A Measure of Racial Discrimination and a Study of Its Negative Physical and Mental Health Consequences," *Journal of Black Psychology* 22 (1996): 144–68.

24. For example, see Mays et al., "Perceived Race-Based Discrimination"; J. I. Sanchez and P. Brock, "Outcomes of Perceived Discrimination among Hispanic Employees: Is Diversity Management a Luxury or a Necessity?" *Academy of Management Journal* 39 (1996): 704–19; R. J. Contrada, R. D. Ashmore, M. L. Gary, E. Coups, J. D. Egeth, A. Sewell, K. Ewell, and T. M. Goyal, "Measures of Ethnicity-Related Stress: Psychometric Properties, Ethnic Group Differences, and Associations with Well-Being," *Journal of Applied Social Psychology* 31(9) (2001): 1775–820.

25. C. A. MacKinnon, *Sexual Harassment of Working Women: A Case of Sex Discrimination* (New Haven, CT: Yale University Press, 1979); J. E. Gruber and L. Bjorn, "Women's Responses to Sexual Harassment: An Analysis of Sociocultural, Organizational, and Personal Resource Models," *Social Science Quarterly* 67 (1986): 814–26; D. Defour, "The Interface of Racism and Sexism on College Campuses," in Michele Paludi, ed., *The Ivory Tower: Sexual Harassment on Campus* (Albany: University of New York Press, 1990), pp. 45–52; M. F. Karsten, *Management and Gender: Issues and Attitudes* (Westport, CT: Quorum Books, 1994); Murrell, "Sexual Harassment and Women of Color."

26. Cortina et al., "Contextualizing Latina Experiences"; M. E. Bergman and F. Drasgow, "Race as a Moderator in a Model of Sexual Harassment: An Empirical Test," *Journal of Occupational Health Psychology* 8(2) (2003): 131–45; L. M. Cortina, "Assessing Sexual Harassment among Latinas: Development of an Instrument," *Cultural Diversity and Ethnic Minority Psychology* 7(2) (2001): 164–81; S. J. Mecca and L. J. Rubin, "Definitional Research on African American Women and Social/Sexual Interactions in Academia," *Psychology of Women Quarterly* 23 (1999): 813–17; Buchanan, "The Nexus of Race and Gender Domination."

27. J. N. Shelton and T. M. Chavous, "Black and White College Women's Perceptions of Sexual Harassment," *Sex Roles* 40(7/8) (1999): 593–615.

28. Murrell, "Sexual Harassment and Women of Color."

29. For example, Kalof et al., "The Influence of Race and Gender"; C. S. Piotrkowski, "Gender Harassment, Job Satisfaction, and Distress among Employed White and Minority Women," *Journal of Occupational Health Psychology* 3(1) (1998): 33–43; B. A. Gutek, *Sex and the Workplace* (San Francisco: Jossey-Bass, 1985); U.S. Merit Systems Protection Board, "Sexual Harassment in the Federal Government: An Update," Office of Merit Systems Review and Studies/Government Printing Office, Washington, DC, 1988; P. V. DiVasto, A. Kaufman, L. Rosner, R. Jackson, J. Christy, S. Pearson, and T. Burgett, "The Prevalence of Sexually Stressful Events among Females in the General Population," *Archives of Sexual Behavior* 13(1) (1984): 59–67.

30. For example, M. Cortina, E. Shupe, A. Ramos, N. T. Buchanan, and L. F. Fitzgerald, "Effects of Sexual Harassment across Cultures: A Comparison of Hispanic and Non-Hispanic White Women," in L. Fitzgerald (Chair), *Innovations in Sexual Harassment Research and Theory* (Symposium conducted at the 12th Annual Conference of the Society for Industrial and Organizational Psychology, St. Louis, MO, April 1997); E. Shupe, L. M. Cortina, A. Ramos, L. F. Fitzgerald, and J. Salisbury, "The Incidence

and Outcomes of Sexual Harassment among Hispanic and Non-Hispanic White Women: A Comparison across Levels of Cultural Affiliation," *Psychology of Women Quarterly* 26(4) (2002): 298–308; Bergman and Drasgow, "Race as a Moderator."

31. J. E. Gruber and L. Bjorn, "Blue-Collar Blues: The Sexual Harassment of Women Autoworkers," *Work and Occupations* 9 (1982): 271–98; Gruber and Bjorn, "Women's Responses to Sexual Harassment"; Bergman and Drasgow, "Race as a Moderator"; R. R. Cox, P. W. Dorfman, and W. Stephan, "Determinants of Sexual Harassment Coping Strategies in Mexican American and Anglo Women," in K. L. Middleton (Chair), *Sexual Harassment 25 Years After the EEOC Guidelines* (Symposium conducted at the Academy of Management Conference, Honolulu, Hawaii, August 2005); S. A. Wasti and L. M. Cortina, "Coping in Context: Sociocultural Determinants of Responses to Sexual Harassment," *Journal of Personality and Social Psychology* 83 (2002): 394–405; L. M. Cortina and S. A. Wasti, "Profiles in Coping: Responses to Sexual Harassment across Persons, Organizations, and Cultures," *Journal of Applied Psychology* 90(1) (2005): 182–92; Mansfield et al., "The Job Climate for Women"; A. Morris, "Gender and Ethnic Differences in Social Constraints among a Sample of New York City Police Officers," *Journal of Occupational Health Psychology* 1(2) (1996): 224–35; M. A. Paludi, *Sexual Harassment on College Campuses: Abusing the Ivory Power* (Albany: State University of New York Press, 1996); L. D. Bastian, A. R. Lancaster, and H. E. Reyst, "Department of Defense 1995 Sexual Harassment Survey," Report No. 96-014, Defense Manpower Data Center, Arlington, VA, 1996; G. E. Wyatt and M. Riederle, "The Prevalence and Context of Sexual Harassment among African American and White American Women," *Journal of Interpersonal Violence* 10(3) (1995): 309–21; G. E. Wyatt and M. Riederle, "Sexual Harassment and Prior Sexual Trauma among African-American and White American Women," *Violence and Victims* 9(3) (1994): 233–47; Cortina et al., "Effects of Sexual Harassment across Cultures"; A. Culbertson and P. Rosenfeld, "Assessment of Sexual Harassment in the Active-Duty Navy," *Military Psychology* 6 (1994): 69–93.

32. For example, the SEQ-L: Cortina, "Assessing Sexual Harassment among Latinas."

33. L. M. Cortina, S. Swan, L. F. Fitzgerald, and C. Waldo, "Sexual Harassment and Assault: Chilling the Climate for Women in Academia," *Psychology of Women Quarterly* 22 (1998): 419–41.

34. Contrada et al., "Measures of Ethnicity-Related Stress."

35. Schneider et al., "An Examination."

36. K.S.D. Low, P. Radhakrishnan, K. T. Schneider, and J. Rounds, "The Experiences of Bystanders of Ethnic Harassment" (manuscript under review).

37. T. M. Glomb, W. L. Richman, C. L. Hulin, F. Drasgow, K. T. Schneider, and L. F. Fitzgerald, "Ambient Sexual Harassment: An Integrated Model of Antecedents and Consequences," *Organizational Behavior and Human Decision Processes* 71 (1997): 309–28; K. T. Schneider "Bystander Stress: Effects of Sexual Harassment on Victims' Co-Workers," in J. Schmidtke (Chair), *Responses to Sexual Harassment* (Symposium conducted at the annual convention of the American Psychological Association, Toronto, Canada, August 1996).

38. M. E. Bergman and N. T. Buchanan, "Development of the Racial Acts, Crimes, and Experiences Survey" (manuscript in preparation).

39. J. Scarville, S. B. Button, J. E. Edwards, A. R. Lancaster, and T. W. Elig, "Armed Forces Equal Opportunity Survey," Report no. 97-027, Defense Manpower Data Center, Arlington, VA, 1999.

40. L. F. Fitzgerald, V. J. Magley, F. Drasgow, and C. R. Waldo, "Measuring Sexual Harassment in the Military: The SEQ-DoD," *Military Psychology* 11 (1999): 243–63.

41. N. T. Buchanan, "Incorporating Race and Gender in Sexual Harassment Research: The Racialized Sexual Harassment Scale (RSHS)," in N. T. Buchanan (Chair), *Expanding Sexual Harassment Research to Include Diverse Populations and Intersecting Forms of Harassment* (Symposium conducted at the meeting of the International Coalition Against Sexual Harassment, Philadelphia, PA, August 2005).

42. Schneider et al., "An Examination"; Scarville et al., "Armed Forces Equal Opportunity Survey."

43. G. Corbie-Smith, E. Frank, H. W. Nickens, and L. Elon, "Prevalences and Correlates of Ethnic Harassment in the U.S. Women Physicians' Health Study," *Academic Medicine* 74(6) (1999): 695–701; Inman et al., "The Differential Effects"; Scarville et al., "Armed Forces Equal Opportunity Survey."

44. Scarville et al., "Armed Forces Equal Opportunity Survey."

45. Buchanan, "The Nexus of Race and Gender Domination."

46. J. F. Dovidio, "The Subtlety of Racism," *Training and Development* 47 (1993): 51–57; J. F. Dovidio and S. L. Gaertner, "On the Nature of Contemporary Prejudice: The Causes, Consequences, and Challenges of Aversive Racism," in J. L. Eberhardt and S. T. Fiske, eds., *Confronting Racism: The Problem and the Response* (Thousand Oaks, CA: Sage, 1998), pp. 3–32.

47. Radhakrishnan, "Ethnic Harassment"; K. T. Schneider, R. T. Hitlan, M. Delgado, D. Anaya, and A. X. Estrada, "Hostile Climates: The Impact of Multiple Types of Harassment on Targets," in T. M. Glomb (Chair), *How Detrimental Is Sexual Harassment? Broadening the Boundaries of Research* (Symposium conducted at the 15th Annual Conference of the Society for Industrial and Organizational Psychology, New Orleans, LA, April 2000); Corbie-Smith et al., "Prevalences and Correlates"; D. Hughes and M. A. Dodge, "African American Women in the Workplace: Relationships Between Job Conditions, Racial Bias at Work, and Perceived Job Quality," *American Journal of Community Psychology* 25(5) (1997): 581–99; H. J. Erlich and B.E.K. Larcom, "The Effects of Prejudice and Ethnoviolence on Workers' Health," paper presented at the 2nd American Psychological Association and National Institute of Occupational Safety and Health Conference on Work Stress and Health, Washington, DC, November 1992; G. G. Bennett, K. Y. Wolin, E. L. Robinson, S. Fowler, and C. L. Edwards, "Perceived Racial/Ethnic Harassment and Tobacco Use among African American Young Adults," *American Journal of Public Health* 95(2) (2005): 238–40; G. G. Bennett, M. M. Merritt, C. L. Edwards, and J. J. Sollers, "Perceived Racism and Affective Responses to Ambiguous Interpersonal Interactions among African American Men," *American Behavioral Scientist* 47(7) (2004): 963–76.

48. Inman et al., "The Differential Effects."

49. Harrick and Sullivan, "Racial Harassment."

50. Cortina et al., "Contextualizing Latina Experiences"; Buchanan, "The Nexus of Race and Gender Domination"; Schneider et al., "Hostile Climates"; T. A. Bruce and N. T. Buchanan, "Group Differences in the Relationship between Racial and Sexual Harassment and Academic and Health-Related Outcomes," in J. M. Konik and L. M. Cortina (Chairs), *Diversity and Antisocial Behavior in Organizations: New Contributions from Multi-level Research* (Symposium conducted at the Academy of Management Conference, New Orleans, LA, August 2004).

51. Cortina et al., "Contextualizing Latina Experiences."

52. Schneider et al., "Hostile Climates"; Cortina et al., "Contextualizing Latina Experiences."

53. N. T. Buchanan and L. F. Fitzgerald, "The Effects of Racial Harassment, Sexual Harassment, and Appraisals of Harassment Severity on the Psychological Well-Being of African American Women" (manuscript under review); Bruce and Buchanan, "Group Differences."

54. Bruce and Buchanan, "Group Differences."

55. Radhakrishnan, "Ethnic Harassment."

56. Buchanan and Fitzgerald, "The Effects of Racial Harassment"; J. L. Berdahl and C. Moore, "Workplace Harassment: Double Jeopardy for Minority Women," *Journal of Applied Psychology* (in press).

57. Buchanan and Ormerod, "Racialized Sexual Harassment."

58. Mansfield et al., "The Job Climate for Women."

59. J. D. Yoder and P. Aniakudo, "The Response of African-American Women Firefighters to Gender Harassment at Work," *Sex Roles* 32 (1995): 125–37; J. D. Yoder and P. Aniakudo, "When Pranks Become Harassment: The Case of African American Women Firefighters," *Sex Roles* 35 (1996): 253–70; J. D. Yoder and P. Aniakudo, "'Outsider Within' the Firehouse: Subordination and Difference in the Social Interactions of African-American Women," *Gender and Society* 11 (1997): 324–41.

60. Mecca and Rubin, "Definitional Research on African American Women."

61. M. T. Texeira, "'Who Protects and Serves Me?' A Case Study of Sexual Harassment of African American Women in One U.S. Law Enforcement Agency," *Gender and Society* 16 (2002): 524–45.

62. Buchanan and Ormerod, "Racialized Sexual Harassment"; S. E. Martin, "'Outsider Within' the Station House: The Impact of Race and Gender on Black Women Police," *Social Problems* 41 (1994): 383–400; Texeira, "Who Protects and Serves Me?"

63. Buchanan and Ormerod, "Racialized Sexual Harassment."

64. N. T. Buchanan, "Sexual Harassment and the African American Woman: A Historical Analysis of a Contemporary Phenomena," paper presented at the annual meeting of the Association for Women in Psychology, Providence, RI, March 1999; P. H. Collins, *Black Feminist Thought: Knowledge, Consciousness, and the Politics of Empowerment,* 2nd ed. (New York: Routledge, 2000); Defour, "The Interface of Racism and Sexism"; Wyatt and Reiderle, "The Prevalence and Context"; Murrell, "Sexual Harassment and Women of Color."

65. E. Higginbotham, "Moving Up with Kin and Community: Upward Social Mobility for Black and White Women," *Gender and Society* 6 (1992): 416–40; S. Levin, S. Sinclair, R. C. Veniegas, and P. L. Taylor, "Perceived Discrimination in the Context of Multiple Group Memberships," *Psychological Science* 13(6) (2002): 557–60; C. West and S. Fenstermaker, "Doing Difference," *Gender and Society* 9 (1995): 8–37; H. Landrine, E. A. Klonoff, R. Alcaraz, J. Scott, and P. Wikins, "Multiple Variables in Discrimination," in B. Lott and D. Maluso, eds., *The Social Psychology of Interpersonal Discrimination* (New York: Guilford Press, 1995), pp. 183–224; J. Lorber, *Gender Inequality: Feminist Theory and Politics* (Los Angeles: Roxbury, 1998).

66. E. M. Almquist, "Untangling the Effects of Race and Sex: The Disadvantaged Status of Black Women," *Social Science Quarterly* 56 (1975): 129–42; B. Greene,

"Lesbian Women of Color: Triple Jeopardy," in L. Comas-Diaz and B. Greene, eds., *Women of Color: Integrating Ethnic and Gender Identities* (New York: Guilford Press, 1994), pp. 389–427; Landrine et al., "Multiple Variables"; P. T. Reid and L. Comas-Diaz, "Gender and Ethnicity: Perspectives on Dual Status," *Sex Roles* 22 (1990): 397–408; Martin, "Outsider Within"; Murrell, "Sexual Harassment and Women of Color"; Texeira, "Who Protects and Serves Me?"; K. Crenshaw, "Mapping the Margins: Intersectionality, Identity Politics, and Violence against Women of Color," in K. Crenshaw, N. Gotanda, G. Peller, and K. Thomas, eds., *Critical Race Theory* (New York: Free Press, 1995), pp. 357–83.

67. S. S. Tangri, M. R. Burt, and L. B. Johnson, "Sexual Harassment at Work: Three Explanatory Models," *Journal of Social Issues* 38 (1982): 33–54.

68. B. W. Dziech and L. Weiner, *The Lecherous Professor: Sexual Harassment on Campus*, 2nd ed. (Champaign: University of Illinois Press, 1990); S. G. Bingham and L. L. Scherer, "Factors Associated with Responses to Sexual Harassment and Satisfaction with Outcomes," *Sex Roles* 29 (1993): 239–69; E. Lafontaine and L. Tredeau, "The Frequency, Source, and Correlates of Sexual Harassment among Women in Traditional Male Occupations," *Sex Roles* 15 (1986): 433–42; G. Timmerman and C. Bajema, "The Impact of Organizational Culture on Perceptions and Experiences of Sexual Harassment," *Journal of Vocational Behavior* 57 (2000): 188–205.

69. J. B. Pryor, J. L. Giedd, and K. B. Williams, "A Social Psychological Model for Predicting Sexual Harassment," *Journal of Social Issues* 51 (1995): 69–84; J. B. Pryor, C. LaVite, and L. Stoller, "A Social Psychological Analysis of Sexual Harassment: The Person/Situation Interaction," *Journal of Vocational Behavior* 42 (1993): 68–83; M. S. Hesson-McInnis and L. F. Fitzgerald, "Sexual Harassment: A Preliminary Test of an Integrative Model," *Journal of Applied Social Psychology* 27 (1997): 877–901; Gutek, *Sex and the Workplace*; E. Haavio-Mannila, K. Kaupinen-Toropainen, and I. Kandolin, "The Effect of Sex Composition of the Workplace on Friendship, Romance, and Sex at Work," in B. A. Gutek, A. H. Stromberg, and L. Larwood, eds., *Women and Work*, vol. 3 (Beverly Hills, CA: Sage, 1988), pp. 123–38; U.S. Merit Systems Protection Board, "Sexual Harassment of Federal Workers: Is it a Problem?" (Washington, DC: Office of Merit Systems Review and Studies/Government Printing Office, 1981); U.S. Merit Systems Protection Board, "Sexual Harassment in the Federal Government."

70. J. B. Pryor, "The Social Psychology of Sexual Harassment: Person and Situation Factors which Give Rise to Sexual Harassment," paper presented at the 1st National Conference on Sex and Power Issues in the Workplace, Bellevue, WA, March 1992; Pryor et al., "A Social Psychological Analysis"; Fitzgerald et al., "The Dimensions and Extent"; M. J. Zickar, "Antecedents of Sexual Harassment," paper presented at the 9th Annual Conference of the Society for Industrial and Organizational Psychology, Nashville, TN, April 1994; C. L. Hulin, L. F. Fitzgerald, and F. Drasgow, "Organizational Influences on Sexual Harassment," in M. S. Stockdale, ed., *Sexual Harassment in the Workplace: Perspectives, Frontiers, and Response Strategies* (Thousand Oaks, CA: Sage, 1996), pp. 127–50; C. A. Cohorn, C. S. Sims, and F. Drasgow, "Organizational Climate, Sexual Harassment, and Outcomes on United States Military Installations," paper presented at 17th annual conference of the Society for Industrial and Organizational Psychology, Toronto, Canada, April 2001; Lafontaine and Tredeau, "The Frequency, Source, and Correlates"; M. E. Bond, "Division 27 Sexual Harassment Survey: Definitions, Impact, and Environment Context," *Community Psychologist* 21 (1988): 7–10;

J. A. Livingston, "Responses to Sexual Harassment on the Job: Legal, Organizational, and Individual Actions" *Journal of Social Issues* 38 (1982): 5–22; Tangri et al., "Sexual Harassment at Work."

71. R. Ilies, N. Hauserman, S. Schwochau, and J. Stibal, "Reported Incidence Rates of Work-Related Sexual Harassment in the United States: Using Meta-Analysis to Explain Reported Rate Disparities," *Personnel Psychology* 56 (2003): 607–31.

72. Inman et al., "The Differential Effects."

73. Culbertson and Rosenfeld, "Assessment of Sexual Harassment"; T. C. Fain and D. L. Anderton, "Sexual Harassment: Organizational Context and Diffuse Status," *Sex Roles* 17 (1987): 291–311; M. Martindale, "Sexual Harassment in the Military: 1988," *Sociological Practice Review*, 2 (1991): 200–216; Tangri et al., "Sexual Harassment at Work"; U.S. Merit Systems Protection Board, "Sexual Harassment of Federal Workers"; U.S. Merit Systems Protection Board, "Sexual Harassment in the Federal Government."

74. A. Culbertson and W. Rodgers, "Improving Managerial Effectiveness in the Workplace: The Case of Sexual Harassment of Navy Women," *Journal of Applied Social Psychology* 27 (1997): 1953–71.

75. Livingston, "Responses to Sexual Harassment"; D. E. Terpstra and S. E. Cook, "Complainant Characteristics and Reported Behaviors and Consequences Associated with Formal Sexual Harassment Charges," *Personnel Psychology* 38 (1985): 559–74; Gruber and Bjorn, "Women's Responses to Sexual Harassment"; L. Brooks and A. R. Perot, "Reporting Sexual Harassment: Exploring a Predictive Model," *Psychology of Women Quarterly* 15 (1991): 31–57; A. B. Malamut and L. R. Offermann, "Coping with Sexual Harassment: Personal, Environmental, and Cognitive Determinants," *Journal of Applied Psychology* 86 (2001): 1152–66.

76. P. M. Popovich, "Sexual Harassment in Organizations," *Employee Responsibilities and Rights Journal* 1 (1988): 273–82.

77. R. Niebuhr, "Sexual Harassment in the Military," in W. O'Donohue, ed., *Sexual Harassment: Theory, Research, and Treatment* (Needham Heights, MA: Allyn and Bacon, 1997), pp. 250–62; L. R. Offermann and A. B. Malamut, "When Leaders Harass: The Impact of Target Perceptions of Organizational Leadership and Climate on Harassment Reporting and Outcomes," *Journal of Applied Psychology* 87 (2002): 885–93; Pryor et al., "A Social Psychological Analysis."

78. Offermann and Malamut, "When Leaders Harass."

79. M. E. Bergman, R. D. Langhout, P. A. Palmieri, L. M. Cortina, and L. F. Fitzgerald, "The (Un)reasonableness of Reporting: Antecedents and Consequences of Reporting Sexual Harassment," *Journal of Applied Psychology* 87 (2002): 230–42.

80. J. W. Adams, J. L. Kottke, and J. S. Padgitt, "Sexual Harassment of University Students," *Journal of College Student Personnel* 24 (1983): 484–90; Fitzgerald et al., "The Dimensions and Extent"; I. W. Jensen and B. A. Gutek, "Attributions and Assignment of Responsibility in Sexual Harassment," *Journal of Social Issues* 38 (1982): 55–74.

81. Brooks and Perot, "Reporting Sexual Harassment"; Malamut and Offermann, "Coping with Sexual Harassment"; Bingham and Scherer, "Factors Associated with Responses."

82. Popovich, "Sexual Harassment in Organizations."

83. M. De Judicibus and M. P. McCabe, "Blaming the Target of Sexual Harassment: Impact of Gender Role, Sexist Attitudes, and Work Role," *Sex Roles* 44 (2001): 401–17.

84. Wyatt and Riederle, "Sexual Harassment and Prior Sexual Trauma."

85. M. P. Miceli and J. P. Near, "Individual and Situational Correlates of Whistle-Blowing," *Personnel Psychology* 41 (1988): 267–81; J. P. Near and M. P. Miceli, "Effective Whistle-Blowing," *Academy of Management Review* 20 (1995): 679–708; Gruber and Bjorn, "Women's Responses to Sexual Harassment."

86. M. S. Harned, A. J. Ormerod, P. A. Palmieri, L. L. Collinsworth, and M. Reed, "Sexual Assault and Other Types of Sexual Harassment by Workplace Personnel: A Comparison of Antecedents and Consequences," *Journal of Occupational Health Psychology* 7 (2002): 174–88.

87. Cortina et al., "Effects of Sexual Harassment across Cultures."

88. Dietch et al., "Subtle yet Significant."

89. Ilies et al., "Reported Incidence Rates."

90. Bruce and Buchanan, "Group Differences."

91. Shelton and Chavous, "Black and White College Women's Perceptions."

92. Dovidio et al., "Racial, Ethnic, and Cultural Differences"; M. R. Lee, "Resilience against Discrimination: Ethnic Identity and Other-Group Orientation as Protective Factors for Korean Americans," *Journal of Counseling Psychology* 52 (2005): 36–44. See K. James, "Social Identity, Work Stress, and Minority Workers' Health," in G. P. Keita and J. J. Hurrell Jr., eds., *Job Stress in a Changing Workforce: Investigating Gender, Diversity, and Family Issues* (Washington, DC: American Psychological Association, 1994), pp. 127–45 for a review of social identity theory and how it relates to the experiences of racial discrimination at work.

93. Shupe et al., "The Incidence and Outcomes of Sexual Harassment."

3

Incivility, Sexual Harassment, and Violence in the Workplace

Rudy Nydegger, Michele Paludi, Eros R. DeSouza, and Carmen A. Paludi Jr.

> *Domestic and social violence usually starts off with a few angry words and a few hurt feelings that don't get resolved, then escalates into feelings of betrayal, rage and revenge. Inner feelings of rage soon spill over into all aspects of society. Social stress multiplies daily with every new report of political upheaval, child abuse, drug abuse, workplace violence, children bringing guns to school, homelessness, ethnic wars or some other crisis.*
>
> —Doc Childre

In August 1986, Patrick Sherrill, a U.S. postal employee in Edmond, Oklahoma, received a poor performance appraisal from his supervisor. Subsequently, he stole weapons from a National Guard Armory and went to his workplace, where he opened fire, killing fourteen of his co-workers and injuring six more.

In June 2005, David Wilhelm entered the EPAC plastic plant in Savoy, Texas, and killed his estranged wife and her male co-worker Felipe de Leon before shooting himself. The Wilhelms were in the process of divorcing.

In March 1998 at the Connecticut Lottery Corporation, Matthew Beck, age thirty-five, an accountant involved in a pay dispute, fatally shot the president of the organization and three of his supervisors before killing himself.

In Santa Fe Springs, California, in March 1994, Tuan Nguyen was fired from a electronics factory and subsequently used a still valid security code to gain access to the factory where he shot three people to death before killing himself.

In Miami Beach, Florida, in April 2005, Gustavo Velastegui arrived at his wife's workplace, where he shot and killed her before killing himself.

These incidents, like all other human behaviors, need an examination of the social context to be understood. The following are pre-incident indicators that have been identified from research on workplace violence. They focus on symptoms regarding assailants.[1]

- Increased use of alcohol or illegal drugs
- Unexplained increase in absenteeism
- Noticeable decrease in attention to appearance and hygiene
- Depression and withdrawal
- Explosive outbursts of anger or rage without provocation
- Threatened or verbally abused co-workers and supervisors
- Repeated comments that indicate suicidal tendencies
- Frequent, vague physical complaints
- Noticeably unstable emotional responses
- Behavior that is suspect of paranoia
- Preoccupation with previous incidents of violence
- Increased mood swings
- Had a plan to "solve all problems"
- Resistance and overreaction to changes in procedures
- Increase of unsolicited comments about firearms and other dangerous weapons
- Empathy with individuals committing violence
- Repeated violations of company policies
- Fascination with violent or sexually explicit movies or publications
- Escalation of domestic problems, including having restraining orders against them
- Large withdrawals from or closing his or her account in the company's credit union
- Frequent comments about fearing losing their job

Postincident interviews with co-workers of employees who committed a violent act indicated that they observed one of more of these symptoms but considered them insignificant.[2] These employees had not been trained by their employer in symptom recognition of potentially violent behavior, nor were they provided instructions on how to report this behavior. Thus, a common thread among the examples presented at the beginning of the chapter is the extent to which employers could have prevented the assaults and murders.

In previous generations, employees viewed work as a protected environment, one in which they felt safe. This view of workplaces no longer exists. Homicide is the most frequent manner in which women employees are fatally injured at work; it is the number two cause for men.[3] The incidence of workplace violence has increased in the past sixteen years, according to a recent study identified by the Society for Human Resource Management.[4]

Moreover, reported homicides and serious nonfatal assaults are only a small part of workplace violence for women.[5] Approximately 260,000 women are victims of workplace violence annually, according to the U.S. Justice Department. Types of violence against women include 178,400 simple assaults, 55,500 aggravated assaults, 17,400 robberies, and 8,800 rapes.[6]

In this chapter we discuss workplace violence as a continuum with incivility on one end and violence, including homicide, at the other. We note legal issues and psychological dimensions involved in each of these types of violence. In addition, we offer resources for employers, including sample policies on workplace violence, domestic violence in the workplace, and sexual harassment.

Rather than focusing on changing the level of analysis from the systemic to the individual, the goal in dealing with violence in the workplace is to pursue an institutional level of analysis to explain the prevalence of violence and to recognize the contexts within which it is more likely to occur. We note that the broken windows theory can be applied to workplaces trying to prevent and deal with workplace violence.[7] If what is perceived by the organization to be trivial isn't handled immediately, more severe forms of workplace violence may result.

INCIVILITY

Workplace incivility is defined as "low-intensity deviant behavior with *ambiguous* intent to harm the target, in violation of workplace norms for mutual respect. Uncivil behaviors are characteristically rude and discourteous, displaying a lack of regard for others."[8] Ambiguity of the behavior is a key characteristic of incivility, because the perpetrator can easily deny any intent to cause harm, for example, by suggesting that his or her behavior was misinterpreted (e.g., "I was just kidding").

Incivility is an interpersonal process dependent on person–environment factors. It begins with perceptions of interpersonal injustice that causes one to lose face (e.g., the uncivil act is perceived as a threat to one's identity) and feel angry, which fuels a desire for revenge for the perceived organizational or societal norm that has been violated. Note that at any time, one or more parties may choose to act in a civil manner and break the incivility cycle. The following personal factors are related to the escalation of uncivil acts: impulsiveness (e.g., lack of self-control), reactivity (e.g., sensitivity to negative events), and rebelliousness (e.g., independence, self-sufficiency, and resistance to peer pressure).[9] Individuals with one or more of these personality traits tend to handle the daily frustrations at work by engaging in disrespectful or condescending behaviors, which may quickly reach a tipping point that spirals into more severe forms of coercive behaviors (e.g., emotional abuse, bullying, and sexual harassment). Furthermore, to handle occupational stress, individuals with a "hot temperament" may use alcohol or drugs while at work as coping mechanisms, which in turn disinhibit coercive behaviors even more. Last, Anderson and Pearson argue that a climate of informality contributes to incivility at the workplace by adding ambiguity to the boundary of acceptable behavior.[10] Thus, careless bantering may lead to thoughtless remarks that escalate into incivility.[11]

Pearson, Anderson, and Porath conducted 700 interviews and collected questionnaire data from 775 employees throughout the United States.[12] They found that the perpetrator of incivility was typically of higher status than the victim and was male. Interestingly, men were more likely to be uncivil toward subordinates than toward superiors, whereas women were equally likely to behave uncivilly toward their superiors and subordinates. The consequences of incivility included negative effects on victims and organizations, including impaired concentration, reduced organizational commitment and productivity, and increased intentions to quit; in fact, 12 percent of the sample reported having ultimately quit their jobs. Moreover, 75 percent of the victims reported being dissatisfied with how the organization handled uncivil incidents. The authors found scant attention by organizations to address incivility. In fact, some managers even reported that rudeness and disrespect could be beneficial and appropriate in certain organizations.

Cortina, Magley, Williams, and Langhout investigated the incidence and impact of incivility in a sample of 1,662 employees at the U.S. Eighth Circuit federal court system.[13] The authors created the Workplace Incivility Scale (WIS), which has appropriate reliability and validity properties, to measure how often participants experienced incivility (e.g., disrespect, rudeness, and condescension) from superiors or co-workers during the past five years. Participants also completed several job-related as well as psychological and health measures. The authors found that 71 percent of these employees reported some experience with workplace incivility in the previous five years. Women experienced more uncivil acts than men did. However, both men and women experienced similar negative effects. Those who experienced more uncivil acts were less satisfied with their employment (including their jobs, supervisors, co-workers, pay and benefits, and promotional opportunities; they also considered quitting) and suffered greater psychological distress (especially men) than those who experienced less incivility.

The studies indicate that even mild forms of interpersonal mistreatment (i.e., incivility) have negative outcomes and should not be ignored by organizations, as is frequently the case. Now we turn to another type of interpersonal mistreatment that is not only widespread but also illegal.

SEXUAL HARASSMENT

Sexual harassment is a type of sex discrimination that violates Title VII of the Civil Rights Act of 1964.[14] Since 1980, the Equal Employment Opportunity Commission (EEOC) has defined sexual harassment as:

> Unwelcome sexual advances, requests for sexual favors, and other verbal or physical conduct of a sexual nature constitutes sexual harassment when (1) submission to such conduct is made either explicitly or implicitly a term or

condition of an individual's employment, (2) submission to or rejection of such conduct by an individual is used as the basis for employment decisions affecting such individuals, or (3) such conduct has the purpose or effect of unreasonably interfering with an individual's work performance or creating an intimidating, hostile, or offensive work environment.

Parts 1 and 2 are typically referred to as quid pro quo sexual harassment, whereas part 3 is commonly referred to as hostile environment sexual harassment.

Note that victims of sexual harassment also include men; however, only 15.1 percent of the sexual harassment charges were filed by men during 2004.[15] Additionally, the EEOC states the victim does not have to be the target but could be a witness to the harassment. Furthermore, although the victim of sexual harassment does not have to show that she or he suffered psychological harm, the harassment must be unwelcome and must have occurred because of the victim's sex, which is problematic in same-sex harassment cases.[16]

Psychologically, sexual harassment is defined as unwanted sexually offensive behavior that threatens one's psychological health and well-being.[17] The following empirical studies investigated the psychological rather than the legal aspect of sexual harassment by asking respondents if they had experienced a list of unwanted sexual behaviors. Such investigations allow researchers to learn a great deal about gender roles, power dynamics, and coping skills "without focusing on whether particular behavior would rise to the level of actionable conduct in a court of law."[18]

Congress commissioned three large-scale studies to determine the prevalence of sexual harassment across representative national samples of federal workers. The findings showed that 42 to 44 percent of women and 14 to 19 percent of men reported having experienced at least one sexually harassing behavior during the previous twenty-four months.[19]

The findings from these studies conducted on civilian samples parallel those from military samples. The Department of Defense (DoD) conducted a survey in 1988 to assess sexual harassment among active duty military personnel. The DoD survey was modeled after the U.S. Merit Systems protection Board survey. Of the 20,400 participants who completed the survey, 64 percent of the women and 17 percent of the men reported having experienced sexual harassment at least once during the last 12 months.[20]

In 1995, the DoD surveyed the active duty military personnel's experiences of unwanted sexual behavior based on adaptations of Fitzgerald et al.'s Sexual Experiences Questionnaire (SEQ).[21] Of the 28,296 participants who completed the SEQ-DoD survey, 76 percent of the women and 37 percent of the men reported having experienced some form of sexual harassment during the previous twelve months.[22] Overall, these studies show that sexual harassment is much more common among women than men.

Unlike incivility, sexual harassment is illegal behavior that can cost organizations millions of dollars in litigation and monetary awards.[23] Sexual harassment can also cost organizations millions of dollars due to employees' impaired concentration, reduced organizational commitment and productivity, increased intragroup conflict as well as reduced team cohesion and team performance, reduced job satisfaction, and job withdrawal, including turnover intention, actual transference, or termination.[24] In addition, numerous survey studies as well as some experimental and longitudinal studies have shown the ill effects of workplace sexual harassment on the physical and mental health of the victim,[25] including alcohol abuse[26] and eating disorder symptoms among women but not men.[27]

THE ESCALATION: FROM INCIVILITY TO SEXUAL HARASSMENT

Until recently, the literatures on sexual harassment and incivility have not interfaced. In addition, organizations have typically focused on sexual harassment rather than incivility, because the former is illegal but not the latter. As stated earlier, incivility is an interpersonal process that may escalate into more severe forms of interpersonal aggression, such as sexual harassment. One way to bridge the two literatures is to examine the types of sexual harassment to find which one is a link to both incivility and more severe forms of sexual harassment, such as quid pro quo sexual harassment. Thus, we briefly review Fitzgerald and colleagues' typology of sexual harassment.[28]

Fitzgerald et al. developed a behavior-based assessment (the SEQ) based on Till's typology of sexual harassment, which consists of gender harassment (sexist remarks or behavior), seductive behavior (sexual advances or propositions), sexual bribery (sexual favors in exchange for rewards), sexual coercion (sexual advances with a threat of punishment), and sexual imposition (assault).[29] They found that the factor structure of the SEQ failed to validate Till's five-level typology. Instead, a tripartite model (gender harassment, unwanted sexual attention, and sexual coercion) better accounted for the data. Gender harassment consists of sexist behaviors that do not appear to elicit sexual cooperation but rather convey hostile and offensive attitudes toward members of one gender, for example, offensive stories or jokes about women (or men). As the name implies, unwanted sexual attention denotes sexual attention that is unwelcome and unreciprocated, for example, unwanted touching or repeated requests for dates. Sexual coercion includes explicit or implicit bribes or threats to gain sexual favors. The first two types typically parallel the legal definition of hostile work environment, whereas the third parallels the legal definition of quid pro quo. Keep in mind that the SEQ measures behavioral experiences of sexual harassment and not the legal aspects of sexual harassment per se. A legal determination is based on several factors that surveys cannot adequately address.

Research indicates that gender harassment is the most common type of sexual harassment, with sexual coercion being the least frequent and unwanted sexual attention being in between the two.[30] Recently, Lim and Cortina examined the relationships and outcomes of incivility and sexual harassment in two samples of women employed in a large federal judicial circuit.[31] The authors used the WIS and SEQ to measure the frequency of incivility and sexual harassment, respectively. They combined unwanted sexual attention and sexual coercion items into a sexualized harassment composite. The findings showed that incivility and sexual harassment co-occurred. That is, in both samples, gender harassment was strongly related to both incivility and sexualized harassment. There was also a moderate relationship between incivility and sexualized harassment, even after controlling for the correlation between incivility and gender harassment. Almost all women who experienced gender or sexualized harassment also experienced incivility but not vice versa. In addition, confirmatory factor analyses indicated that gender harassment linked incivility to sexualized harassment. These relationships may exist because experiencing one type of interpersonal mistreatment may sensitize victims to notice other types of misconduct.

Moreover, Lim and Cortina used several measures to examine job, psychological, and health outcomes on four groups of women (i.e., those who never experienced incivility, gender harassment, or sexualized harassment; those who experienced only incivility; those who experienced incivility and gender harassment but not sexualized harassment; and those who experienced incivility, gender harassment, and sexualized harassment).[32] The results indicated an incremental worsening of both job outcomes and psychological/health outcomes even after controlling for behavior frequency, with women who experienced incivility, gender harassment, and sexualized harassment having the worst outcomes, followed by women who experienced both incivility and gender harassment. Even women who experienced incivility alone had significantly worse outcomes than those who never experienced incivility, gender harassment, or sexualized harassment. These results suggest that sexual harassment does not happen in a vacuum; rather, it occurs in a climate of disrespect. Thus, multiple forms of interpersonal mistreatment need to be addressed simultaneously rather than in isolation, as is typically the case. As Lim and Cortina put it, "a concerted effort at eliminating all elements of a hostile work environment might be more effective and efficient."[33]

Lapierre et al. conducted a meta-analytic study to compare experiences of sexual nonviolent workplace aggression (i.e., sexual harassment) with nonsexual experiences of nonviolent workplace aggression (including incivility) on employees' overall job satisfaction, which is one of the best indicators of employees' attitude toward the quality of their overall work experience.[34] The authors included in their analyses twenty-five studies on incivility and related constructs, representing a total of twenty-eight independent samples (three of which completed the WIS), and nineteen studies on sexual harassment, representing a total of twenty-two independent samples (twelve of which completed the SEQ). Concerning sexual aggression, because only two samples included women as well as men, the authors compared sexual to nonsexual aggression only among women to hold victims' gender constant. Thus gender comparisons were conducted only on nonsexual aggression. The findings showed that both types of workplace aggression negatively affected victims' overall job satisfaction. When the authors compared the two types of workplace aggression (among women only), they found that nonsexual aggression had a stronger negative relationship with overall job satisfaction than did sexual aggression. Furthermore, nonsexual aggression had a stronger negative relationship with overall job satisfaction among women than among men. Such a finding is inconsistent with earlier research possibly because Lapierre and colleagues used only one outcome of job satisfaction, whereas Cortina et al. used several job-related measures, including other measures to tap psychological and health-related outcomes.[35]

Overall, these findings suggest that because incivility generally happens more frequently than sexual harassment (see previous studies), incivility becomes a systemic organization problem that is often ignored and unpunished. Lapierre et al.'s findings are consistent with prior research on stress. That is, there is a parallel between incivility and daily hassles. Lazarus reported that daily hassles (e.g., workplace incivility) not only negatively affected people's well-being but also had a stronger relationship with well-being than exposure to more severe, but less common incidents (e.g., workplace sexual harassment).[36] We now continue with our continuum of workplace violence by focusing on criminal (not civil) offenses that occur in the workplace.

WORKPLACE VIOLENCE: BACKGROUND

Approximately one out of six crimes committed in the United States occurs in the workplace. According to the Department of Justice, in 1994 1 million employees were assaulted at work in the United States, resulting in 160,000 personal injuries.[37] A more recent study by Bowman and Zigmond found over 2 million workers who reported being attacked at work, which resulted in over $13.5 million in medical costs alone.[38] One very detailed study examined workplace violence from 1987 through 1992 and found about 1 percent of workers reported being victimized by violence at work, and of these, 16 percent reported significant physical injuries. Between 1980 and 1992 the National Institute for Occupational Safety and Health (NIOSH) found that 9,937 homicides in the workplace were reported, which represented about 800 per year, yielding a workplace homicide rate of 0.7/100,000 workers. Workplace homicide is the fastest growing type of homicide in the United States, and other forms of aggression also are increasing. Each year, about 2 million workplace assaults occur, 16 million workers are harassed, and 6 million workers are threatened.[39]

As we endeavor to understand this frightening and expensive problem, we must first be clear as to exactly what we mean by violence. According to Nydegger, violence is "the actual infliction or threat of infliction of physical harm by a person or persons on another person, a group, or the broader organization which includes physical and human components." He goes on to point out the difference between violence and aggression by suggesting that aggression is the intent to harm another or an organization and that this may take several forms: direct aggression, where a person takes action intended to inflict harm on another or an organization; this would also include verbal aggression or bullying.[40] The other form of aggression that he describes is passive-aggression, in which there is intent to harm but in which the act is indirect and often disguised. This type of aggression will be discussed later in this chapter.

Another definition agreed on by the European Commission defines workplace violence as "incidents where persons are abused, threatened or assaulted in circumstances related to their work, involving an explicit or implicit challenge to their safety, well-being, or health."[41] The California Occupational Safety and Health Administration also adds an important way to conceptualize workplace violence. It points out that three distinctly different types of workplace violence exist:

1. Violent acts that occur primarily from robberies with the aim of obtaining cash or other valuables, and which involve situations in which the offender has no legitimate right to be on the work premises.
2. Violent acts from individuals who have a legitimate right to be on the work premises as those who are receiving or providing services that are offered at the workplace—for example, patients, customers, and students.
3. Violent incidents between co-workers, which includes violence committed toward a person or persons in superior, similar, and subordinate positions.[42]

This latter category of events often gets a lot of media attention, but in the United States, being murdered by a fellow employee only accounts for about 4 percent of the homicides, whereas the large majority are committed during robberies.[43] However, Boyd suggests that workplace murders occurring due to "disgruntled" employees is a problem that is most relevant to the United States and probably can be linked to the availability of firearms.[44]

Baron and Neumann reported that of aggressive acts committed in the workplace, 44.5 percent are against co-workers, 31.4 percent are against supervisors, and 26.8 percent are against subordinates.[45] Furthermore, many assert that much workplace violence comes from outside of the organization, and data seem to confirm this. Greenberg and Baron found that 81.82 percent of workplace violence results from robberies and other crimes.[46] Business disputes account for 8.69 percent of the violence, police in the line of duty experience about 5.59 percent of the workplace violence, and personal disputes only account for 3.9 percent of the violent acts in the work environment.

Obviously, the type of workplace violence that is of most concern is homicide. Runyon et al. reported that consistent with some other data, about 1,000 fatalities and over 20,000 nonfatal events occur in the workplace each year.[47] One very concerning statistic is that the rate at which supervisors are murdered doubled between 1985 and 1997. The occupations that are most at risk for homicide are taxi drivers, law enforcement, and retail.[48] According to NIOSH, retail and service industries are high risk for homicide, particularly when the employee handles money or makes deliveries. Although taxi drivers are at the highest risk for workplace homicide, most nonfatal assaults were in the service and retail businesses. In the service business most assaults were in the health care sector, with 27 percent occurring in nursing homes, 13 percent in social service settings, and 11 percent in hospitals. In fact, the assault rates for residential and nursing and personal care workers are more than ten times the rates for employees in private non–health care industries.[49]

More recent research has found similar patterns and reports that workers in retail and service industries are at high risk for workplace violence. Businesses open twenty-four hours/day and those having a history of violent events were at increased risk for employee injury.[50] In studying public employees as a group, Barab found that health care workers, corrections officials, social service workers, teachers, municipal housing inspectors, and public works employees were all in "at-risk" jobs.[51]

Evidence indicates that men are more likely than women to be victims of homicide and physical assault and to be attacked by a stranger. Women, on the other hand, face greater odds of being attacked by someone known to them. This is assumed to be because of women's vulnerable position in the workforce; women are concentrated in the lower paid and lower status positions and are often in occupations with high rates of client violence.[52] Homicide is the second leading cause of workplace death (motor vehicle accidents is first), and although more men are victims of homicides than women, homicide is the leading cause of occupational death for women. Approximately 260,000 women are victims of workplace violence annually, according to the Justice Department. Federal Bureau of Investigation statistics indicate that women who are victims of violence by their mates account for one-quarter of all women who are murdered in a given year.[53] Furthermore, more women in the United States are victimized by their male partners than are harmed because of muggings, automobile accidents, and rapes combined. Thus, although employment may provide an escape from the victimization women experience outside of the workplace by their mates, it also offers a site where the batterer can consistently find his victim.[54]

Although the actual number of workplace homicides has decreased since the mid-1990s, much less is known about the incidence of nonfatal events.[55] Many point out that most workplace aggression is verbal or indirect and passive, which may be very hurtful and harmful, but is harder to recognize. These kinds of behaviors have more recently become the focus of study around the world and have been called various different names. For example, such behavior is referred to as bullying in the United Kingdom and Australia; mobbing in the Scandinavian and German-speaking countries; and workplace harassment, mistreatment, and emotional abuse in the United States.[56]

Einarsen et al. have stated that "bullying emerges when one or several individuals persistently over a period of time perceive themselves to be on the receiving end of negative actions from one or several persons, in a situation where the one at the receiving end has difficulties in defending him/herself against these actions."[57] Keashly defines emotional abuse as verbal and non-verbal behavior that is not explicitly tied to sexual or racial content directed at gaining compliance from others.[58] Yelling, screaming, using derogatory names, giving the silent treatment, withholding important information, making aggressive eye contact, spreading negative rumors, having explosive outbursts of anger, and ridiculing in front of others are examples of emotional abuse. These are very similar to the types of behaviors that are described as bullying.[59]

A similar type of behavior that has been described in the clinical literature for decades but has only recently been addressed in the organizational literature is passive-aggressive. This is very similar in form to some of the other types of behavior that have been described earlier in this chapter. For example, incivility, emotional abuse, mistreatment, and workplace harassment certainly overlap with passive-aggressive behavior. When passive-aggressive is described in the clinical literature it may take the form of the passive-aggressive personality, which is a particular clinical description, or of passive-aggressive behavior, which can occur in any situation and be perpetrated by anyone.

We are primarily concerned here with a type of behavior that has aggressive intent but is also disguised and not always obvious. Thus, passive-aggressive behavior may be found as a subset of some of the other types of workplace mistreatment, but because it has a link to other clinical literature, we chose to set it apart for the present discussion.

Only recently has this become a focus of study in the workplace as well. Passive-aggressive behavior is more common than violence or direct aggression, and it, too, is harmful. Examples of this are such things as intentionally forgetting appointments, not returning calls, being late, spreading rumors, and so on. This type of behavior is hard to recognize as aggression because it usually looks like something else, and when confronted the perpetrator will almost always deny the aggressive intent.

Clearly, violence, aggression, passive-aggression, and all of the other forms of workplace violence and aggression are extremely problematic for employees, managers, and organizations. In the next section, we examine some of the basic explanatory models for workplace violence and aggression in its various forms.

EXPLANATIONS AND SUSPECTED REASONS FOR WORKPLACE VIOLENCE

When we discuss causes of workplace violence it is tempting to try to find simple explanations that seem to fit all situations. Complex problems, however, rarely have simple explanations, and those that exist are usually wrong. Some try to isolate the causal factors within the person, attempting to find out why a particular person committed the violent act. Rarely do we find that a person is uniformly violent in most or all situations, and thus trying to isolate causal factors *only* in the person is rarely adequate. Furthermore, some are tempted to specify social or situational factors as causing violence or aggression. However, if these factors were adequate causes for violence, then everyone who experienced them would be equally violent, and this is never the case.

Thus, it is becoming increasingly obvious that the various causes of workplace violence probably interact in ways that will result in violent or aggressive behavior in some people, in some situations, and with respect to some social factors. The causes of aggression involve personal and workplace factors, and these things typically interact and combine in ways that predict different kinds of aggression against different targets. Keeping this in mind, let us examine some of these factors and the ways in which they might relate to violence or aggression.

Greenberg and Barling found that a history of aggression and the amount of alcohol consumed predicted aggression toward co-workers.[60] Nydegger discussed how a negative affective state (being in a bad mood) often leads to people behaving more aggressively and that these moods also are likely to elicit more aggressive behavior from others.[61]

Another personality variable that has been linked to aggression is self-monitoring. This characteristic indicates how aware people are of their impact on others, and how much they are aware of their own behavior in social situations. People who are low self-monitors tend to be very unaware of their impact on others and are typically not that aware of others' emotional states anyway. Thus, they might be obstructionist or inconsiderate of others and perhaps not even be aware of it. Therefore, they could be making other people very angry and not know it, thereby producing a situation where others might be more likely to be aggressive. Interestingly, low self-monitoring might not necessarily produce aggression in those with the trait, but it could produce it in people around them. However, if the low self-monitoring people consistently elicited hostile or aggressive behaviors from others it might make them more likely to be aggressive themselves. That is, they might develop a hostile-attributional bias, which might cause them to be more aggressive. Thus, if their behavior evoked hostile/aggressive behavior from others, they would not see the cause in their own behavior but would assume that everyone else was hostile or aggressive and that they needed to respond in kind to protect themselves.

Some assume that Type A personalities might also be more prone to violence or aggression because of their own personalities, traits, and behaviors. The Type A person tends to be very achievement-oriented, very busy, time-urgent, and aggressive toward others. Furthermore, they are easily frustrated, and thus may also be predisposed to aggressiveness.[62] However, this variable is a little hard to interpret in this context. Rather than a personality type, this is more accurately a personality dimension that runs from nonproblematic to very problematic. At the problematic extreme, those with Type A personalities may be more disposed to aggression and even violence, but this connection is not clear from the literature.

Interestingly, when people are asked why they committed violent or aggressive acts they typically say that someone did something to them that justified the response.[63] They almost always externalize the responsibility for their behavior (they think that it is usually someone else's fault), and feel that someone "drove" them to do what they did. However, this explanation is rarely satisfying to anyone except the perpetrator.[64]

In addition, some social factors seem to be related to workplace violence. For example, the frustration-aggression hypothesis suggests that aggression is the result of frustration.[65] However, most psychologists would not agree that all aggression is based on frustration, although most would accept the idea that frustration can and does at times lead to aggression. Thus, experiencing frustration in a social situation increases the probability that some people will behave aggressively.

Another social factor that is important has to do with people other than those who are part of the organization. As discussed earlier, most workplace violence is committed by people who come into the organization from outside. For example, Warren et al. showed that workplace violence differs from similar behavior in other settings according to the victim's age, degree of injury, and whether the workplace was a medical setting.[66] They conclude that the differences between workplace and nonworkplace violence is largely explained by the movement of people in and out of the work environment who bring societal violence into the workplace with them. Thus, one social factor we must consider is related to society and people outside the organization. Consequently, the external physical and social environment must also be considered when looking at workplace violence.

This is certainly true with respect to domestic violence that spills over into the workplace. Domestic violence, also referred to as battering, spouse abuse, spousal assault, and intimate partner abuse is defined as violence between adults who are intimates, regardless of their marital status, living arrangements, or sexual orientation.[67] Such violence includes throwing, shoving, and slapping as well as beatings, forced sex, threats with a deadly weapon, and homicide. Abuse in couples' relationships may also include intense criticisms and put-downs, verbal harassment, intimidation, restraint of normal activities and freedoms, and denial of access to resources. Thus violence can be physical, emotional, or sexual and is used by one partner to control another.[68] Domestic violence is about power and control. One partner uses intimidation and control tactics to gain power in the relationship.

Of course, some social factors within the organization are related to workplace violence. For example, when employees feel or perceive that they are treated unfairly, they are at higher risk for violence or aggression. It is not uncommon that employees will even steal from employers or sabotage the workplace to "get even" for real or imagined harm.

One social factor that is becoming more important today is diversity. An increasingly diverse workplace offers many advantages and some problematic circumstances. For example, as organizations become more diverse, violence and aggression will probably escalate.[69] This may happen due to many factors, but it is not usually as simple a situation as to imply that the new and diverse members of the workforce are the problem. Lack of understanding, suspiciousness, lack of trust, stereotypes, communication problems, and so on are apparently the kinds of social factors that are related to the relationship between increasing diversity and higher rates of violence and aggression.

Some organizations may have difficulties with violence and aggression because of their normative system. That is, the social norms and guidelines may actually promote aggression and even violence. In other situations, violating certain norms may result in violence or aggression. Other things that place workers at risk for nonfatal occupational violence include work climate variables (e.g., co-worker support, work group harmony), which were predictive of threats, harassment, and fear of becoming a victim of violence.[70]

Certain factors in many organizations set the stage for heightened violence and aggression. Many firms are making changes that have created conditions directly leading to increased aggression among employees. Even environmental conditions like noise, heat, and humidity can raise workers' stress, producing negative affect, which can contribute to increases in violence and aggression. Cole and colleagues also found that structural aspects of the job like work schedule were also significant in predicting threats and fear of becoming a victim of violence.[71] Another situational factor in organizations is related to management style. Authoritarian management styles and policies are also linked to increases in violence and aggression.[72] Interestingly, in organizations like this, if violence or aggression does not result in loss of work it is typically not reported to supervisors or public authorities and thus may never be recognized or dealt with at all.[73]

Finally, as might be expected, layoffs, downsizing, and wage freezes create hostility in the workforce that can lead to problems involving violence and aggression.[74] Nydegger also pointed out that cost-cutting, budgetary constraints, and other changes might produce problems as well.[75] He suggested that any change— even positive change—produces stress, and we know that any type of stress raises the possibility of violence and aggression.

CONTROLLING VIOLENCE AND AGGRESSION IN THE WORKPLACE

Workplace violence and aggression are significant sources of stress in the work environment and as such impact the personal, health, social, work-related, and management aspects of the whole workforce. Furthermore, employers must address domestic violence in the workplace because it poses a threat not only to the victim but to the safety of co-workers, vendors, and clients. Research indicates that battering annually costs employers more than $200 million in reduced worker productivity, increased turnover, and absenteeism.[76] In addition, approximately 25 percent of women who visit emergency rooms are battered women. They incur more than $70 million in hospital bills annually.[77] Thus, these realities demand that employers take remedial and educational steps to deal with domestic violence and its impact on the workplace.

Certainly, employees and managers are concerned about violence and aggression, and how the work environment can be kept safe without infringing unnecessarily on individual rights and freedoms. It is becoming increasingly clear that employers, administrators, and supervisors share responsibility for controlling workplace violence and aggression, including domestic violence that spills over into the workplace.[78] According to Chappell and DeMartino, dealing with these issues in the workplace requires responses in several different ways:

1. Preventive: employers must look for and deal with the causes.
2. Targeted: all types of violence can't be handled the same way. Determine the type you want to deal with and handle it directly.
3. Multiple: combined responses are needed to deal with complex situations.
4. Immediate: responses to a potentially dangerous situation must be taken without hesitation.
5. Participatory: to be successful, any program must involve relevant employees or at least a representative group of them.
6. Long-term: issues ignored or minimized today are tomorrow's big problems.[79]

Placing this entire problem area in a public health perspective and focusing on prevention seems sensible. Job stress and workplace violence are recognizable, predictable, and even preventable if managed correctly. Prevention means early identification of problems, decreasing risk of disputes, and thoughtful policies on handling stressful situations.[80] Prevention strategies at the organizational level should include an explicit policy statement, investigatory procedures for handling complaints, and training programs for the entire workplace that include the company's policy and procedures so employees know their rights and responsibilities.[81] Sample policies and procedures for workplace and domestic violence as employment concerns are presented in the appendix to this chapter.

In addition, OSHA recommends that a company train a Threat Assessment Team, whose task is to assist with dealing with workplace violence, including domestic violence.[82] Responsibilities of the team include assessing the vulnerability of the company to violence and serving as advocates for victims, including victims of domestic violence that has carried over into the workplace.

The team should include representatives from senior management, employee assistance, security, and human resources staff.

Employers can also assist victims of domestic violence by developing a personalized safety plan for them.[83] This plan can include the following:

- Include the workplace on the restraining order for the victim—copies of the restraining order can be provided to the employee's supervisor, human resource representative, and security;
- Save any threatening email and voicemail messages;
- Identify the parking arrangements and have security escort the employee to his or her car;
- Remove the employee's name and phone number from automated phone directories; and
- Rotate the employee's work site or assignment if such a change would increase the employee's safety at the workplace.

Employees should decide what is needed in their plan because they are more familiar with their abusers. In addition, the company should maintain communication with the employee during that person's absence. The company must maintain confidentiality of the employee's whereabouts.

Recommendations for additional preventative measures include the following:

1. Posting phone numbers at worksites of the following:
   - Employee assistance program
   - Security department
   - National domestic violence hotline number
   - Local domestic violence resources
   - Information on obtaining orders of protection
   - List of certified batterers' intervention programs
2. Developing policies and other educational materials in languages spoken by employees.
3. Modifying any human resource policies that negatively impact victims of domestic violence.
4. Collaborating with domestic violence services available in the community.

In addition to developing and enforcing effective policies and procedures as well as training programs on workplace violence, employers can partner with employee assistance programs in dealing with workplace violence.[84] For example, they may help employees develop a sense of trust and safety in the current environment. Employee assistance programs can also help women employees foster relationships with appropriate nonviolent male models. Furthermore, these programs can help employees counter any sense of guilt about having caused the violence or not being able to prevent the abuse. Trained counselors can offer several treatment modalities for employees, including cognitive and behavioral techniques to deal with specific problem behaviors, such as aggression; play assessment and therapy to encourage preschool children to express feelings about the trauma; individual counseling for children, including specific strategies for creating a better understanding of their reaction to the abuse and their preparation for future violence; information about shelters and employee-children support groups. These services can be integrated with other community agencies.[85]

CONCLUSION

In summary, this review suggests that multiple types of workplace mistreatment need to be researched and confronted simultaneously. It also points to the importance of addressing the organizational climate. Certain climates may be tolerant of incivility and even gender harassment, which may then spiral into more severe forms of coercive behaviors, such as quid pro quo sexual harassment. Conversely, other climates may be intolerant of such behaviors, sending a clear message—through well-disseminated policies and sanctions (see the appendix), and regular training sessions and workshops on the ill effects of such behaviors on the victim—that all employees have the right to work in an environment free of any form of mistreatment. Organizations should also promote organizational and psychological empowerment to increase prosocial behaviors and create a strength-based culture of growth.[86]

APPENDIX: SAMPLE POLICIES

Sample Policy on Domestic Violence as a Workplace Concern

Employees of _____ must be able to work in an atmosphere of mutual respect and trust. As a place of work, _____ should be free of violence and all forms of intimidation and exploitation. _____ is concerned and committed to our employees' safety and health. The Company refuses to tolerate violence in our workplace.

_____ has issued a policy prohibiting violence in the workplace. We have a zero tolerance for workplace violence.

_____ also will make every effort to prevent violent acts in this workplace perpetrated by spouses, mates, or lovers. The Company is committed to dealing with domestic violence as a workplace issue. _____ has a zero tolerance for domestic violence.

Domestic Violence: Definition

Domestic violence—also referred to as battering, spouse abuse, spousal assault, and intimate partner abuse—is a global health problem. This victimization is defined as violence between adults who are intimates, regardless of their marital status, living arrangements, or sexual orientations. Such violence includes throwing, shoving and slapping as well as beatings, forced sex, threats with a deadly weapon, and homicide.

Domestic Violence: Myths and Realities

Myth: Domestic violence affects a small percentage of employees.

Reality: Approximately 5 million employees are battered each year in the United States. Domestic violence is the leading cause of injury and workplace death to women in the United States.

Myth: People must enjoy the battering since they rarely leave the abusive relationship.

Reality: Very often victims of battering do leave the relationship. Women and men remain in a battering relationship not because they are masochistic, but for several well-founded reasons, e.g.,

- Threats to their lives and those of their children, especially after they have tried to leave the batterer
- Fear of not getting custody of their children
- Financial dependence
- Feeling of responsibility for keeping the relationship together
- Lack of support from family and friends

Myth: Individuals who batter or abuse their partners because they are under a great deal of stress, including being unemployed.

Reality: Stress does not cause individuals to batter their partners. Society condones partner abuse. In addition, individuals who batter learn they can achieve their goals through the use of force without facing consequences.

Myth: Children are not affected by watching their parents in a battering relationship.

Reality: Children are often in the middle of domestic violence. They may be abused by the violent parent. Children may also grow up to repeat the same behavior patterns they witnessed in their parents.

Myth: There are no long-term consequences of battering.

Reality: There are significant long-term consequences of battering, including depression, anger, fear, anxiety, irritability, loss of self-esteem, feelings of humiliation and alienation, and a sense of vulnerability.

Myth: Domestic violence only occurs in poor and minority families.

Reality: Domestic violence occurs among all socioeconomic classes and all racial and ethnic groups.

Threat Assessment Team

_____ has established a Threat Assessment Team to assist with dealing with workplace violence. Part of the duties of the Threat Assessment Team is to assess the vulnerability of the Company to domestic violence and serve as advocates for victims of workplace violence, including domestic violence that has carried over into the workplace.

Each of these members of the Threat Assessment Team has received specialized training in workplace violence issues, including domestic violence as a workplace concern.

Services Offered by _____ for Employees Who Are
Victims of Domestic Violence
_____ will offer the following services for our employees who are victims of domestic violence:

- Provide receptionists and building security officer with a photograph of the batterer and a description of the batterer
- Screen employee's calls
- Screen employee's visitors
- Accompany the employee to her/his car
- Permit the employee to park close to the office building
- When there is a restraining order, the Vice President will send a formal notification to the batterer that indicates that his/her presence on the Company premises will result in arrest
- Referrals for individual counseling

Sample Personalized Safety Plan

Name: _____
Date Completed: _____

1. I can inform my immediate supervisor, security, human resources and _____ at work that I am a victim of domestic violence.
2. I can ask _____ to help me screen my telephone calls at work.
3. When leaving work, I can walk with _____ to my car or the bus stop. I can park my car where I will feel safest getting in and out of the car.
4. If I have a problem while driving home I can _____.
5. If I use public transit, I can _____.
6. I will go to different grocery stores and shopping malls to conduct my business and shop at hours that are different from those I kept when residing with my battering partner.
7. I can use a different bank and go at hours that are different from those kept when residing with my battering partner.
8. I can use _____ as my code word with my co-workers when I am in danger so they will call for help.

Important Telephone Numbers:
Police: 911 and _____
Domestic Violence Program: _____
District Attorney's Office: _____
My Supervisor's Home Phone Number: _____
Cell Phone Number: _____

My Clergy's Phone Number: _____

Domestic Violence Shelter: _____

Human Resources Phone Number: _____

Security's Phone Number: _____

Other: _____

Policy on Workplace Violence

Administrators, faculty and employees of _____ must be able to work in an atmosphere of mutual respect and trust. As a place of work, _____should be free of violence and all forms of intimidation and exploitation. _____ is concerned and committed to our employees' safety and health. We refuse to tolerate violence in our workplace and will make every effort to prevent violent incidents in this workplace. All employees at all levels must not engage in violence in the workplace and will be held responsible for insuring that _____ is free from violence. Any employee who engages in such behavior will be subject to disciplinary procedures.

_____ **has a zero tolerance for workplace violence.**

_____ has issued a separate policy dealing with domestic violence as a workplace issue.

What Is Workplace Violence?

Workplace violence includes, but is not limited to, verbal threats, nonverbal threats, pushing, shoving, hitting, assault, stalking, murder, and related actions. These behaviors constitute workplace violence whether they are committed by employees who are in a supervisory position or by co-workers, vendors, clients, or visitors. And, these behaviors constitute workplace violence if they occur between employees of the same sex or between employees of the opposite sex.

Threat Assessment Team

_____has established a Threat Assessment Team to assist with dealing with workplace violence. Part of the duties of the Threat Assessment Team is to assess the vulnerability of _____ workplace violence and serve as advocates for victims of workplace violence, as explained below.

Each of these members of the Threat Assessment Team has received specialized training in workplace violence issues, including prevention.

Reporting Workplace Violence

_____requires prompt and accurate reporting of all violent incidents whether or not physical injury has occurred. Any employee who has a complaint of workplace violence is encouraged to report such conduct to the Threat Assessment Team so that the complaint may be investigated and resolved promptly.

All complaints of workplace violence will be investigated by _____.

Complainants and those against whom complaints have been filed will **not** be expected to meet together to discuss the resolution of the complaint.

Employees who file a complaint of workplace violence may do so orally and/or in writing. A standardized form for filing complaints of workplace violence is included with this policy.

Investigating Complaints of Workplace Violence

_____ will investigate the complaint of workplace violence. The investigation will be limited to what is necessary to resolve the complaint. If it appears necessary for them to speak to any individuals other than those involved in the complaint, they will do so only after informing the complainant and the person against whom the complaint is made.

_____ will endeavor to investigate all complaints of workplace violence expeditiously and professionally. In addition, she will make every attempt to maintain the information provided to her in the complaint and investigation process as confidentially as possible. If warranted, _____ will work with local police officials in resolving the complaint of workplace violence.

Complaints will be investigated in the following manner:

1. Upon receipt of complaints, _____ will ask individuals if they have any witnesses they would like to be interviewed on their behalf. Individuals will complete a form providing names of witnesses as well as the issues to which the witnesses may address. Complainants will provide _____ with a signed statement giving her permission to contact these witnesses.

2. _____ will immediately forward a copy of the complaint, along with a copy of _____ Workplace Violence Policy Statement and Procedures, to the individual complained against and request a meeting with this individual within 3 business days.

3. During the meeting with the respondents, _____ will ask the individuals if they have any witnesses they would like to be interviewed on their behalf. Individuals will complete a form providing names of witnesses as well as the issues the witnesses may address. Complainants will provide _____ with a signed statement giving her permission to contact these witnesses

4. Names or other identifying features of witnesses on behalf of the complainant and respondent will not be made known to the opposing party. This will help ensure participation by witnesses in the investigation.

5. _____ will investigate all complaints of discrimination expeditiously and professionally. To the maximum extent possible, the investigation will be completed within three days from the time the formal investigation is initiated. _____ will also maintain the information provided to her in the complaint and investigation process confidential. Parties to the complaint will be asked to sign a "Confidentiality" form in which they state they will keep the complaint and complaint resolution confidential. They will also be asked to sign a form indicating they will not retaliate against any party to the complaint.

6. A safe environment will be set up for the complainant, respondent, and witnesses to discuss their perspectives without the fear of being ridiculed or judged.

7. No conclusions about the veracity of the complaint will be made until the investigation is completed.

8. All documents presented by the parties to the complaint will be reviewed by _____. Documents include, but are not limited to: letters and notes.
9. Following the completion of an investigation, _____ will make one of the following determinations:
   - Sustain the Complaint: A finding of workplace violence has been made and recommendations for corrective action will be identified, including reprimands, relief from specific duties, transfer, or dismissal.
   - Not Sustain the Complaint: A finding of no workplace violence has been made.
   - Insufficient Information: Insufficient information exists on which to make a determination. _____ will reinvestigate all parties named in the complaint.
10. Following any determination and recommendations for corrective action, _____ will issue a written decision with findings to President_____. President _____ will correspond with the complainant and person complained against of the findings of the investigation and recommendations for corrective action. President _____ will make appropriate statements of apology to individuals involved in the complaint.

There will be no retaliation against employees for reporting workplace violence or assisting the investigators in the investigation of a complaint. Any retaliation against an employee is subject to disciplinary action.

If after investigating any complaint of workplace violence it is discovered that the complaint is not bona fide or that an employee has provided false information regarding the complaint, the employee may be subject to disciplinary action.

Inspection of Company for Workplace Violence

The Threat Assessment Team will review previous incidents of violence at_____. They will review existing records identifying patterns that may indicate causes and severity of assault incidents as well as identify changes necessary to correct these hazards. In addition, the Threat Assessment Team will inspect _____and evaluate the work tasks of all employees to determine the presence of hazards, conditions, operations, and other situations which might place employees at risk of workplace violence. Periodic inspections will be performed every three months, on the first Friday of the month.

The Threat Assessment Team will also survey employees at _____to identify and confirm the need for improved security measures. These surveys will be conducted once a year.

Training

_____will provide training on workplace violence annually to all employees.

Policy Statement on Sexual Harassment

(Name of Company) has an obligation to create a work environment for all employees that is fair, humane, and responsible–an environment that supports, nurtures, and rewards career progress based on relevant factors such as work performance.

All employees of (Name of Company) have a responsibility to cooperate in creating a climate at (Name of Company) where sexual harassment does not occur. We have a zero tolerance for sexual harassment of our employees. All employees at all levels of (Name of Company) must not engage in sexual harassment.

The following policy statement is designed to help employees of (Name of Company) become aware of behavior that is sexual harassment and the procedures (Name of Company) will use to deal with sexual harassment in a way that protects complainants, witnesses, and respondents.

What Is Sexual Harassment?

Sexual harassment is legally defined as "unwelcome sexual advances, requests for sexual favors, and other verbal or physical conduct of a sexual nature" when any one of the following criteria is met:

Submission to such conduct is made either explicitly or implicitly a term or condition of the individual's employment;

Submission to or rejection of such conduct by an individual is used as the basis for employment decisions affecting the individual;

Such conduct has the purpose or effect of unreasonably interfering with an individual's work performance or creating an intimidating, hostile or offensive work environment.

Two types of sexual harassment situations are described by this legal definition: quid pro quo sexual harassment and hostile environment sexual harassment.

Quid pro quo sexual harassment involves an individual with organizational power who either expressly or implicitly ties an employment decision to the response of an employee to unwelcome sexual advances. Thus, a supervisor may promise a reward to an employee for complying with sexual requests (e.g., a better job, promotion, raise) or threaten an employee's job for failing to comply with the sexual requests (e.g., threatening to not promote the employee, threatening to give an unsatisfactory performance appraisal).

Hostile environment sexual harassment involves a situation that creates an atmosphere or climate in the workplace making it difficult, if not impossible, for an employee to work because he or she perceives it as intimidating, offensive, or hostile.

For purposes of this policy, sexual harassment includes, but is not limited to the following:

- Unwelcome sexual advances
- Sexual innuendos, comments and sexual remarks
- Suggestive, obscene or insulting sounds
- Implied or expressed threat of reprisal for refusal to comply with a sexual request
- Patting, pinching, brushing up against another's body
- Sexually suggestive objects, books, magazines, poster, photographs, cartoons, e-mail, or pictures displayed in the work area
- Actual denial of a job-related benefit for refusal to comply with sexual requests

Thus, sexual harassment can be physical, verbal, visual or written. These behaviors constitute sexual harassment if they are committed by individuals who are in supervisory positions or coworkers. They constitute sexual harassment if they occur between individuals of the same sex or of the opposite sex. (Name of Company) prohibits these and other forms of sexual harassment. Any employee who engages in such behavior will be subject to disciplinary procedures.

What Isn't Sexual Harassment?

Sexual harassment does not refer to relationships between responsible, consenting adults. Sexual harassment does not mean flirting. Giving compliments does not mean sexual harassment. Sexual harassment refers to unwanted, unwelcome behavior. Not every joke or touch or comment is sexual harassment. The key is to determine if the behavior is unwanted and unwelcome. Furthermore, sexual harassment interferes with employees' ability to get their work done.

Costs of Sexual Harassment

There are high costs of sexual harassment to individuals. They include depression, feelings of helplessness, headaches, anxiety, sleep disturbances, and disordered eating. The cost of sexual harassment to our company includes decreased productivity, absenteeism, and decreased morale.

What Should Individuals Do If They Believe They Are being Sexually Harassed?

Employees who have complaints of sexual harassment, including any supervisor, co-worker, vendor, client or visitor, are urged to report such conduct to (Name of Investigator) so that (s)he may investigate and resolve the problem. Employees are encouraged to bring their concerns to (Name of Investigator) within 60 days of the alleged incident(s). Employees may ask (Name of Investigator) to postpone an investigation if their performance appraisals will be conducted by the party against whom the complaint is brought.

(Name of Investigator) will investigate all complaints professionally and as expeditiously as possible. The confidentiality of the investigative procedures will be maintained. The complaint will be investigated and resolved typically within a two-week period. Complainants and those against whom complaints have been filed will not be expected to meet together to discuss the resolution of the complaint.

Investigatory procedures have been developed and are fully explained in another memorandum: (Name of Company) **Sexual Harassment Complaint Procedure**.

Any employee who is found to have engaged in sexual harassment will be subject to disciplinary action, as indicated in (Name of Company) complaint procedure.

Discussions about Sexual Harassment: No Complaints

Employees at (Name of Company) have the right to seek advice and information about sexual harassment from (Name of Investigator), who will maintain such consultation in confidence. Such discussions do not constitute filing a complaint of sexual harassment.

Retaliation

There will be no retaliation against employees for reporting sexual harassment or assisting (Name of Investigator) in the investigation of a complaint. Any retaliation against such individuals is subject to disciplinary action, including verbal and written reprimands, transfers, demotions, and dismissal.

False Complaints

If, after investigating any complaint of sexual harassment, it is discovered that the complaint is not bona fide or that an individual has provided false information regarding the complaint, that individual may be subject to disciplinary action, including verbal and written reprimands, transfers, demotions, and dismissal.

Recommended Corrective Action

The purpose of any recommended corrective action to resolve a complaint will be to correct or remedy the injury, if any, to the complainant and to prevent further harassment. Recommended action may include: a private or public apology, written or oral reprimand of the individual who engaged in sexual harassment, relief from specific duties, suspension, transfer, or dismissal of the individual who engaged in sexual harassment.

If complainants are not satisfied with the attempts to resolve the sexual harassment, they may seek resolution through other sources, for example, the (Name of State) Division of Human Rights or the Equal Employment Opportunity Commission.

Policy Review

This policy will be reviewed periodically by (Name of Investigator) and by (Name of President), who welcome comments on the policy, its interpretation or implementation.

For additional information regarding sexual harassment, contact (Name of Investigator) or (Name of President). They have been trained in complaint resolution and receive additional education about sexual harassment law and its management and psychological applications. Both (Name of Investigator) and (Name of President) will be responsible for a program of information and education concerning this policy and procedures relating to sexual harassment.

Office Numbers and Phone Numbers:(Of Investigator)(Of President)

Sexual Harassment Complaint Procedure

Employees of (Name of Company) who have complaints of sexual harassment by anyone at this Company, including any supervisors, are encouraged to report such conduct to (Name of Investigator) so that (s)he may investigate and resolve the problem. Individuals who feel subjected to sexual harassment should report the circumstances orally and/or in writing within 60 days to (Name of Investigator).

(Name of Investigator) will maintain confidentiality in her/his investigation of complaints of sexual harassment.

Any employee pursuing a complaint may do so without fear of reprisal.

Informal Advice and Consultation

Employees may seek informal assistance or advice from (Name of Investigator). All such consultations will be confidential and no action involving any individual beyond (Name of Investigator) and the employee will be taken until a formal complaint has been made.

(Name of Investigator) may, however, take action, within the context of its existing policy and procedures, that (s)he deems appropriate on the basis of information received to protect all employees of (Name of Company).

Resolutions of Informal Complaints

Any employee may discuss an informal complaint with (Name of Investigator). If the employee who discusses an informal complaint is not willing to be identified to the person against whom the informal complaint is made, (Name of Investigator) will make a confidential record of the circumstances and will provide guidance about various ways to resolve the problem.

If the employee bringing the complaint is willing to be identified to the person against whom the complaint is made and wishes to attempt an informal resolution of the problem, (Name of Investigator) will make a confidential record of the circumstances (signed by the complainant) and undertake appropriate discussions with the person complained about.

When a number of people report incidents of sexual harassment that have occurred in a public context (for example, offensive sexual remarks in an office setting) or when (Name of Investigator) received repeated complaints from different employees that an individual has engaged in sexual harassment, the person complained against will be informed without revealing the identity of the complainants.

Resolutions of Formal Complaints

If an employee wishes to pursue the matter through a formal resolution, a written complaint must be submitted to (Name of Investigator), giving details of the alleged harassment, including dates, times, places, name(s) of individual(s) involved and names of any witnesses.

The complaint must be addressed to (Name of Investigator).

Formal complaints will be investigated in the following manner:

Upon receipt of a written complaint, (Name of Investigator) will immediately forward a copy of the complaint, along with a copy of (Name of Company) Sexual Harassment Policy Statement and Procedures, to the individual complained against and request a meeting within 3 days.

The investigation will be limited to what is necessary to resolve the complaint or make a recommendation. If it appears necessary for (Name of Investigator) to speak to any individuals other than those involved in the complaint, (s)he will do so only after informing the complainant and person complained against.

(Name of Investigator) will investigate all complaints of sexual harassment expeditiously and professionally. To the extent possible, the investigation will completed within two weeks from the time the formal investigation is initiated.

(Name of Investigator) also will maintain the information provided to her/him in the complaint and investigation process confidential. The only other employee of (Name of Company) who will be informed about the investigation is (Name of President), President of (Name of Company). (Name of Company)'s first priority will be to attempt to resolve the complaint through a mutual agreement of the complainant and the person complained against.

If an employee making a formal complaint asks not to be identified until a later date (e.g., until the completion of a performance appraisal), (Name of Investigator) will decide whether or not to hold the complaint without further action until the date requested.

If a formal complaint has been preceded by an informal investigation, (Name of Investigator) shall decide whether sufficient grounds exist to warrant a formal investigation.

The names or other identifying information regarding witnesses for either party involved in the complaint will not be made known to the opposing party. Referrals for therapists and medical personnel for all individuals involved in an investigation will be made available upon request.

Following the completion of an investigation, (Name of Investigator) will make one of the following determinations:

Sustain the Complaint: A finding of sexual harassment has been made and recommendations for corrective action will be identified. Recommended corrective action may include an apology, written or oral reprimand, relief from specific duties, suspension, dismissal, or transfer of the employee found to have engaged in sexual harassment.

Not Sustain the Complaint: A finding of no sexual harassment has been made.

Insufficient Information: Insufficient information exists on which to make a determination. (Name of Investigator) will reinvestigate all parties named in the complaint.

Following any determination and recommendations for corrective action, (Name of Investigator) will issue a written decision with findings of fact and reason to (Name of President). (Name of President) will correspond with the complainant and person complained against of the findings of the investigation and recommendations for corrective action. Appropriate statements of apology will be made to employees involved in the complaint by (Name of President).

If complainants are not satisfied with the attempts to resolve their complaint of sexual harassment, they may seek resolution through other sources, for example, the (Name of State) Division of Human Rights or the Equal Employment Opportunity Commission.

For additional information regarding (Name of Company) zero tolerance of sexual harassment, contact

Name of Investigator
    Office Number
    Phone Number
Name of President
    Office Number
    Phone Number

Both (Name of Investigator) and (Name of President) are trained in complaint resolution and receive additional education about sexual harassment law and its management and psychological applications.

In addition, (Name of President) and (Name of Investigator) will be responsible for a program of information and education concerning sexual harassment in general and (Name of Company) policy and procedures.

NOTES

1. G. K. Moffatt, "Subjective Fear: Preventing Workplace Homicide," *American Management Association Human Resource Focus* 75 (1998): 11.

2. S. Einarsen et al., eds., *Bullying and Emotional Abuse in the Workplace: International Perspectives in Research and Practice* (London: Taylor and Francis, 2003).

3. G. VandenBos and E. Bulatao, eds., *Violence on the Job* (Washington, DC: American Psychological Association, 1996).

4. E. Esen, SHRM *Workplace Violence Survey* (Alexandria, VA: Society for Human Resource Management, 2004).

5. R. Dobash and R. Dobash, *Rethinking Violence against Women* (New York: Sage, 1998).

6. K. Bjorkqvist et al., "Aggression in the Workplace: Sex Differences in Covert Aggression among Adults," *Aggressive Behavior* 20 (1994): 27–30.

7. G. Kelling and C. Coles, eds., *Fixing Broken Windows: Restoring Order and Reducing Crime in our Communities* (New York: Free Press, 1996).

8. L. Anderson and C. Pearson, "Tit for Tat? The Spiraling Effect of Incivility in the Workplace," *Academy of Management Review* 24 (1999): 452–71; emphasis added.

9. Ibid.

10. Ibid.

11. C. Pearson and C. Porath, *Rude Awakening: Detecting and Curtailing Workplace Incivility* (London, Ontario: Richard Ivey School of Business, University of Western Ontario, 2002).

12. C. Pearson et al., "Assessing and Attacking Workplace Incivility," *Organizational Dynamics* 29 (2000): 123–37.

13. C. Cortina et al., "Incivility in the Workplace: Incidence and Impact," *Journal of Occupational Health Psychology* 6 (2001): 64–80.

14. E. DeSouza and J. Solberg, "Incidence and Dimensions of Sexual Harassment across Cultures," in Michele Paludi and Carmen Paludi Jr., eds., *Academic and Workplace Sexual Harassment: A Handbook of Cultural, Social Science, Management, and Legal Perspectives* (Westport, CT: Praeger, 2003).

15. EEOC, "Sexual Harassment Charges EEOC & FEPAs Combined: FY1992-FY 2004," available online at www.eeoc.gov/stats/harass.html.

16. J. Solberg and E. DeSouza, "An Update on Same-Sex Harassment Since Oncale: Employees Still Face Hurdles" (paper presented at the Academy of Legal Studies in Business, Ottawa, Canada, August 19, 2004).

17. L. Fitzgerald et al., "But Was it Really Sexual Harassment? Legal, Behavioral, and Psychological Definitions of the Workplace Victimization of Women," in W. O'Donohue, ed., *Sexual Harassment: Theory, Research, and Treatment* (Boston: Allyn and Bacon, 1997).

18. B. Gutek and R. Done, "Sexual Harassment," in R. Unger, ed., *Handbook of the Psychology of Women and Gender* (New York: Wiley, 2001).

19. U.S. Merit Systems Protection Board, *Sexual Harassment in the Federal Government: Trends, Progress, Continuing Challenges* (Washington, DC: Government Printing Office, 1995).

20. M. Martindale, "Sexual Harassment in the Military: 1988," *Sociological Practice Review* 2 (1991): 200–216.

21. L. Fitzgerald et al., "The Incidence and Dimensions of Sexual Harassment in Academia and the Workplace," *Journal of Vocational Behavior* 32 (1988): 152–75.

22. L. Bastian et al., *Department of Defense 1995 Sexual Harassment Survey* (Arlington, VA: Defense Manpower Data Center, 1996).

23. M. Paludi and C. Paludi Jr., eds., *Academic and Workplace Sexual Harassment: A Handbook of Cultural, Social Science, Management, and Legal Perspectives* (Westport, CT: Praeger, 2003).

24. L. Fitzgerald et al., "The Antecedents and Consequences of Sexual Harassment in Organizations: A Test of an Integrated Model," *Journal of Applied Psychology* 82 (1997): 578–89.

25. C. Avina and W. O'Donohue, "Sexual Harassment and PTSD: Is Sexual Harassment Diagnosable Trauma?" *Journal of Traumatic Stress* 15 (2002): 69–75.

26. S. Freels et al., "Gender Differences in the Causal Direction between Workplace Harassment and Drinking," *Addictive Behaviors* 30 (2005): 1454–58.

27. M. Harned and L. Fitzgerald, "Understanding a Link between Sexual Harassment and Eating Disorder Symptoms: A Mediational Analysis," *Journal of Consulting and Clinical Psychology* 70 (2002): 1170–81.

28. L. Fitzgerald et al., "Measuring Sexual Harassment: Theoretical and Psychometric Advances," *Basic and Applied Social Psychology* 17(1995): 425–45.

29. F. Till, *Sexual Harassment: A Report on the Sexual Harassment of Students* (Washington, DC: National Advisory Council on Women's Educational Programs, 1980).

30. J. Pryor and L. Fitzgerald, "Sexual Harassment Research in the United States," in S. Einarsen, ed., *Bullying and Emotional Abuse in the Workplace: International Perspectives in Research and Practice* (London: Taylor and Francis, 2003).

31. S. Lim and L. Cortina, "Interpersonal Mistreatment in the Workplace: The Interface and Impact of General Incivility and Sexual Harassment," *Journal of Applied Psychology* 90 (2005): 483–96.

32. Ibid.

33. Ibid.

34. L. Lapierre et al., "Sexual versus Nonsexual Workplace Aggression and Victims' Overall Job Satisfaction: A Meta-Analysis," *Journal of Occupational Health Psychology* 10 (2005): 155–69.

35. L. Cortina et al., "Incivility in the Workplace: Incidence and Impact," *Journal of Occupational Health Psychology* 6 (2001): 64–80.

36. R. Lazarus, "Puzzles in the Study of Daily Hassles," *Journal of Behavioral Medicine* 7 (1984): 375–89.

37. U.S. Department of Justice, *Violence and Theft in the Workplace* (NJC-148199) (Annapolis Junction, MD: Bureau of Justice Statistics, 1994).

38. J. Bowman and C. Zigmond, "State Government Responses to Workplace Violence," *Public Personnel Management* 26 (1997): 289.

39. Ibid.

40. R. Nydegger, "Violence, Aggression and Passive-Aggression in the Workplace," *Management Development Forum* 3 (2000): 121–41.

41. R. Wynne et al., *Guidance on the Prevention of Violence at Work* (Brussels: European Commission, DG-V, Ref. CE/V1-4/97, 1997).

42. California Occupational Safety and Health Administration, *Cal/OSHA Guidelines for Workplace Security* (San Francisco: State of California, Department of Industrial Relations, Division of Occupational Safety and Health, 1995).

43. G. Toscano and W. Weber, "Violence in the Workplace," Bureau of Labor Statistics, available online at www.bls.gov/osh/cfar0005.pdf.

44. N. Boyd, "Violence in the Workplace in British Columbia: A Preliminary Investigation," *Canadian Journal of Criminology* October (1995): 491–519.

45. R. Baron and J. Neumann, "Workplace Violence and Workplace Aggression: Evidence on their Relative Frequency and Potential Causes," *Aggressive Behavior* 22 (1996): 161–73.

46. J. Greenberg and R. Baron, *Behavior in Organizations*, 6th ed. (Upper Saddle River, NJ: Prentice Hall, 1997).

47. C. Runyon et al., "Administrative and Behavioral Interventions for Work-place Violence Prevention," *American Journal of Preventive Medicine* 18 (2000): 116–27.

48. Ibid.

49. K. Varner and J. Varner, "Workplace Violence," *Journal of Health Education* 29 (1998): 140–43.

50. K. Schaffer et al., "A Case-Site/Control-Site Study of Workplace Violent In-jury," *Journal of Occupational and Environmental Medicine* 44 (2002): 1018–26.

51. J. Barab, "Public Employees as a Group at Risk for Violence," *Occupational Medicine* 11 (1996): 257–67.

52. A. Meleis, ed., *Women's Work, Health, and Quality of Life* (New York: Haworth Medical Press, 2001).

53. A. Roberts, *Handbook of Domestic Violence Intervention Strategies: Policies, Programs, and Legal Remedies* (New York: Oxford University Press, 2002).

54. L. Johnny, *Addressing Domestic Violence in the Workplace* (New York: HRD Press, 2004).

55. C. Peek-Asa et al., "The Role of Surveillance and Evaluation Research in the Reduction of Violence against Workers," *American Journal of Preventive Medicine* 20 (2001): 141–48.

56. L. Price Spratlen, "Interpersonal Conflict which Includes Mistreatment in a University Workplace," *Violence and Victims* 10 (1995): 285–97.

57. S. Einarsen et al., *Mobbing og Harde Person Konflikter. Helsefartig samspill på arbeidsplassen* (London: Sigma Forlag, 1994).

58. L. Keashly, "Emotional Abuse in the Workplace: Conceptual and Empirical Issues," *Journal of Emotional Abuse* 1 (1998): 85–117.

59. L. Greenberg and J. Barling, "Predicting Employee Aggression against Co-workers, Subordinates and Supervisors: The Role of Person Behaviors and Perceived Workplace Factors," *Journal of Organizational Behavior* 20 (1999): 897–913.

60. Ibid.

61. Nydegger, "Violence, Aggression and Passive-Aggression in the Workplace."

62. D. Holmes and M. Will, "Expression of Interpersonal Aggression by Angered and Non-Angered Persons with Type A and Type B Behavior Patterns," *Journal of Personality and Social Psychology* 40 (1985): 723–27.

63. T. Harris, *Applied Organizational Communication: Perspectives, Principles and Pragmatics* (Hillsdale, NJ: Lawrence Erlbaum Associates, 1993).

64. B. Torestadt, "What Is Anger-Provoking: A Psychophysiological Study of Per-ceived Causes of Anger," *Aggressive Behavior* 16 (1990): 9–16.

65. J. Dollard et al., *Frustration and Aggression* (New Haven, CT: Yale University Press, 1939).

66. J. Warren et al., "The Organizational Context of Non-Lethal Workplace Vio-lence: Its Interpersonal, Temporal, and Spatial Correlates," *Journal of Occupational and Environmental Medicine* 41 (1999): 567–81.

67. L. Walker, *The Battered Woman Syndrome* (New York: Springer, 2000).

68. L. Walker, *Battered Woman* (New York: Harper, 1980).

69. A. Tsui et al., "Being Different: Relational Demography and Organizational Attachment," *Administrative Science Quarterly* 37 (1992): 549–79.

70. L. Cole et al., "Psychosocial Correlates of Harassment, Threats, and Fear of Violence in the Workplace," *Scandinavian Journal of Work and Environmental Health* 23 (1997): 450–57.

71. Ibid.

72. B. Sharif, "Understanding and Managing Job Stress: A Vital Dimension of Workplace Violence Prevention," *International Electronic Journal of Health Education* 3 (2000): 107–16.

73. R. Johnson and J. Indvik, "Workplace Violence: An Issue in the 90's," *Public Personnel Management* 23 (1994): 515–22.

74. J. Brockner et al., "Layoffs, Job Insecurity, and Survivor's Work Effort: Evidence of an Inverted U Relationship," *Academy of Management Journal* 35 (1992): 413–25.

75. R. Nydegger, "Stress and Job Satisfaction in White- and Blue-Collar Workers," *International Business and Research Journal* 1 (2002): 35–44.

76. V. Bowie et al., *Workplace Violence: Issues, Trends, Strategies* (New York: Willan, 2005).

77. S. Baron, *Violence in the Workplace: A Prevention and Management Guide for Businesses* (New York: Pathfinder, 2001).

78. W. Umiker, "Workplace Violence: The Responsibility of Employers and Supervisors," *Health Care Supervisor* 16 (1997): 29–41.

79. D. Chappell and V. DeMartino, *Violence at Work* (Geneva: International Labor Office, 1998).

80. M. Stewart and B. Kleiner, "How to Curb Workplace Violence," *Facilities* 15 (1997): 5–11.

81. C. Paludi and M. Paludi, "Developing and Enforcing Effective Policies, Procedures, and Training Programs for Educational Institutions and Businesses," in M. Paludi and C. Paludi, eds., *Academic and Workplace Sexual Harassment: A Handbook of Cultural, Social Science, Management, and Legal Perspectives* (Westport, CT: Praeger, 2003).

82. J. Turner and M. Gelles, *Threat Assessment: A Risk Management Approach* (New York: Haworth Press, 2003).

83. See U.S. Department of Labor, Occupational Safety and Health Administration, www.osha.gov.

84. J. Swanberg and T. Logan, "Domestic Violence and Employment: A Qualitative Study," *Journal of Occupational Health Psychology* 10 (2005): 3–17.

85. C. Paludi and M. Paludi, "Developing and Enforcing an Effective Workplace Policy Statement, Procedures, and Training Programs on Domestic Violence," paper presented at the Conference on Domestic Violence as a Workplace Concern: Legal, Psychological, Management, and Law Enforcement Perspectives, Nashua, NH, October 2000.

86. N. Peterson and M. Zimmerman, "Beyond the Individual: Toward a Nomological Network of Organizational Empowerment," *American Journal of Community Psychology* 34 (2004): 129–45.

4

Romantic Relationships in the Workplace

Donna Castañeda

Movies, magazines, and novels are replete with depictions of romantic relationships in the workplace. This stands in contrast to the research literature, where studies of workplace romance, although increasing, are relatively few. Furthermore, although popular culture depictions of workplace romance may be positive—that is, the participants fall in love, marry, and live happily ever after—organizations show ambivalence toward such relationships or view them negatively. The existing literature on workplace romance tends to emphasize the legal, emotional, and work performance pitfalls, rather than the benefits to individuals or organizations, although the empirical research that may illuminate the true consequences of workplace romance for all involved is still to be done.[1]

The purpose of this chapter is to review pertinent research and theory on the prevalence, antecedents, and consequences of romantic relationships in organizational settings and discuss the implications they may have for women in particular. In this effort, the possible link between sexual harassment and workplace romantic relationships will also be discussed.

DEFINITION OF WORKPLACE ROMANTIC RELATIONSHIPS

A workplace romance refers to a relationship between two individuals in the same organization that includes mutual sexual attraction that is acknowledged, and consensually and autonomously acted on, by both participants in some form of intimate behavior, such as dating.[2] The fact that the relationship may or may not be known to co-workers or supervisors is an important aspect of workplace romances that distinguishes them from romantic relationships that occur outside a work setting.[3] A workplace romance, whether known about or merely suspected by others, can impact their work behavior and thus its effects occur not only at the couple level but also at the organizational level.

A definition of workplace romantic relationships does not include married couples.[4] Married couples can work together either in a family-owned business or as co-workers in an organization, but compared to those in a dating relationship that originates and is played out in the workplace, married couples are not viewed in entirely the same way either by co-workers or the organization.[5] Formal regulations may more explicitly apply to married than to dating couples. For example, company policy may prohibit married couples from working together on evaluation or performance teams, projects, or dual receipt of travel or other company funds. Greater research is needed on the experience of married couples in the workplace, particularly how being married to a co-worker affects women's professional performance evaluation and upward mobility in organizations,[6] but this experience will not be dealt with here.

The setting for workplace romances is often perceived to be a white-collar one. In fact, the phrase "office romance" is sometimes colloquially used to refer to these relationships. However, the organizational setting of these relationships varies and can include factories, hospitals, retail businesses, construction sites, restaurants, and shop floors. The individuals' connection to the workplace can be varied as well and can include co-workers, vendors, team members, clients, and contractors. They may work side by side or in different offices, divisions, or geographical locations, such as different neighborhoods, cities, states, or countries.

For the most part, researchers assume a workplace romantic relationship to be heterosexual and the participants to be European American, although clearly this need not be the case. Nevertheless, researchers are only beginning to recognize the importance of studying same-sex workplace romances and the role of culture, social class, and race/ethnicity in them. Indeed, same-sex workplace romances may be subject to greater implications for participants because they tend to receive more negative responses from society.[7] Furthermore, at least in some workplaces, those from already marginalized groups (the working class, certain ethnic or cultural groups) who engage in workplace romantic behavior may be more likely to be targeted for enforcement of existing workplace sexual harassment policies than those from socially dominant groups.[8]

PREVALENCE OF WORKPLACE ROMANTIC RELATIONSHIPS

The traditional conceptualization of the workplace is one that is, ideally constructed, is free of intense emotionality, sexual attraction, and sexual behavior. In this work context, job positions are concrete but depersonalized, and they can hypothetically be filled by any qualified worker regardless of gender, race/ethnicity, or social class. Workers are seen as interchangeable, bodiless abstractions.[9] In this conception of the workplace, sexual and emotional passion, which are very much embodied experiences, are seen as a threat to an organization's effectiveness.[10]

On the other hand, although the definitive prevalence study of workplace romance has yet to be done, available research suggests the workplace is an arena in which intimate romantic and sexual relationships are frequently formed. According to an American Management Association survey conducted among its members and customers,[11] 26 percent of men and 36 percent of women report having dated a workplace colleague. The proportion was higher among workers under forty-nine years old, 37 percent, compared to workers fifty years old and above, 22 percent. More men had dated a subordinate, 20 percent, compared to 2 percent for women, whereas more women had dated a superior, 18 percent, compared to 5 percent for men. In another survey of 610 employees representing a variety of industries across the United States, 58 percent reported engaging in an office romance, up from 46 percent in the same survey two years prior.[12] The results in this survey were not broken down by gender, but 14 percent reported dating a superior and 19 percent said they dated a subordinate.

Not only is the prevalence high for those who report engaging in a workplace romance, but many workers indicate they have been exposed to their co-workers' workplace romances. In one of the first studies of the extent of workplace romance, Quinn found that 62 percent of respondents said they knew of at least one such relationship.[13] Later, Anderson and Hunsaker found that 86 percent of respondents had been exposed to one or more workplace romantic relationships.[14] Most recently, the Vault survey found that 43 percent of respondents knew of a currently occurring workplace romance in their organization.[15]

Often overlooked is that the workplace is an important source of partners for serious relationships, including marriage. For example, 22 percent of respondents in one survey reported meeting their spouse or long-term significant other in the workplace;[16] in another survey, 45 percent of women and 43 percent of men who engaged in a workplace romance reported that the relationship had resulted in marriage.[17]

These results mirror those from social network research demonstrating that the workplace is one of the leading locations in which marriage partners are found. Furthermore, although organized settings such as family and neighborhood networks continue to influence choice of marriage partner, since 1945 the workplace (along with school) has increased in its importance as a site from which marriage partners are selected.[18] Internet relationships notwithstanding, a close relationship can develop only between people with whom we actually meet and interact, and the workplace provides a pool of persons to choose from and an organized setting for social interaction. Of course, personal preferences influence the particular individual who is ultimately chosen as a romantic partner, but the opportunities to meet someone are often influenced by the organized settings traversed daily, such as schools, neighborhoods, family networks, and the workplace.[19]

The workplace is not only a site where romantic relationships can develop and ultimately culminate in marriage, it is also a location where various types of sexual behavior may take place.[20] Such behavior can include sexual banter, touching, even fondling.[21] As further evidence of sexual behavior in the workplace, the Vault survey found that 23 percent of respondents reported they had had a "tryst" there.[22] These sexual encounters took place primarily in offices, but other locations were reported as well, such as restrooms, conference rooms, stairwells, elevators, and even the boss's office. To the extent that the data in these studies on sexual behavior are not constrained by lack of clarity in terminology or social desirability bias, they indicate a fair amount of sexual behavior literally taking place in the workplace.

ANTECEDENTS OF WORKPLACE ROMANTIC RELATIONSHIPS

As organizations confront the issue of romantic relationships among employees, the question arises: What factors facilitate initiation of a workplace romance? An important contribution to answering this question comes from the conceptual model of workplace romance developed by Pierce, Byrne, and Aguinis.[23] They demonstrate that workplace romances are essentially similar to nonworkplace romances, and their development can be understood from the perspective of classic interpersonal attraction theory in social psychology. Important elements in this perspective include attitude similarity,[24] proximity,[25] repeated exposure,[26] physical attractiveness,[27] reciprocity of liking,[28] and physiological arousal.[29]

In many ways, the workplace is an ideal location for these interpersonal attraction processes to occur. Employees in the same organization who are likely to have shared work goals and interests (attitude similarity) come together regularly, sometimes for long hours (proximity, repeated exposure). If a worker is physically attractive, this will lead to positive interpersonal perceptions of her or him, that is, that she or he is good, intelligent, kind, and so on. Employees have the opportunity to get to know one another and provide positive responses to what each says and does (reciprocity of liking), and they may have joint experiences that create physiological arousal, such as overcoming work-related challenges, meeting deadlines, or competitive behavior. This arousal from one source may then be mislabeled and interpreted as sexual attraction for the co-worker. Taken together, these processes could contribute to initiation of a romantic relationship.

In addition to the interpersonal attraction processes, other elements that can contribute to development of a workplace romance are positive attitudes toward workplace romance and to flirting in the workplace,[30] and the extent that an individual perceives her or his job as autonomous,[31] although one study found that job autonomy was positively related to workplace romance only for men.[32] Other variables that have been identified as influencing the incidence of workplace romance are self-rated sociability for both women and men, and among men only, having a disharmonious atmosphere in the workplace.[33]

Another influence on workplace romance is an individual's motive for engaging in the relationship. Early on, Quinn developed a typology of motives for participation in a workplace romance that continues to influence current thinking on this topic.[34] The motives he outlined were (1) job-related, such as advancement, increased power, job security; (2) ego, such as excitement, ego satisfaction; and (3) love, such as true love or desire for a spouse. Given the complexity of close relationships, one can assume that more than three motives, or even mixed motives, exist for engaging in a workplace romance.[35] However, the three motives that Quinn identified are those most often examined in the research literature.

The most frequent motive overall for engaging in a workplace romance is not clear, but counter to what is often believed, job-related reasons are *not* the top motives associated with workplace romance participation. For example, one study of co-worker perceptions of motivation for workplace romance found that ego motives were most often attributed to men and love motives to women.[36] In another study of hierarchical workplace romance, ego motives were most often attributed to both the senior- and lower-level participants in the relationship.[37]

Gender seems to play an important role in perception of reasons for engaging in a workplace romance. With regard to co-worker reactions to those involved in a workplace romance, love motives are perceived more positively than job-related or ego motives.[38] This may be because those in a workplace romance who are believed to be motivated by love are viewed as more sincere and less likely to be a threat to their own work-related rewards or status in the organization. But Dillard found that men who were perceived as having a love motive for workplace romance were evaluated more favorably than women.[39] Although love motives in general are considered positive, men seem to accrue points for them, possibly because many are socialized to consider love and intimacy as women's domain.[40] We may expect men to be less interested in love and intimacy, and when they do show interest, we may be pleased and surprised.

Hierarchical workplace romances are considered most disruptive and viewed most negatively by co-workers and organizations, but again, gender plays a role in evaluations of motives for engaging in them.[41] For example, an investigation of perceptions of hierarchical workplace romances found that male married (as compared to female single) team leaders were more frequently assigned an ego motive.[42] Even in nonhierarchical workplace romances, men, compared to women, were significantly more likely to be assigned ego motives.[43]

Interestingly, at least one study found that women in hierarchical romances were no more likely, either as senior- or lower-level relationship participants, to be assigned job-related motives,[44] although a later study found the opposite—job-related motives were more likely to be attributed to a female than to a male lower-level employee.[45] Furthermore, in this later study hierarchical workplace romances were regarded as a more serious problem for the organization when the lower-level employee was perceived to be motivated by job-related concerns.[46] Another study of nonhierarchical workplace romances found that although job-related reasons accounted for less than 10 percent of the attributed motivations for engaging in a workplace romance, the woman in the relationship was ten times more likely than the male to be perceived as exploiting sexuality for gain.[47] Furthermore, co-workers respond more negatively to women than to men who are perceived as engaging in a workplace romance for job-related motives.[48]

Love relationships are used to meet a variety of psychological, emotional, and practical needs, and a workplace romance is no different in this respect. Greater investigation with samples of those actually involved in workplace romances is needed to uncover the full dimensionality of participant motives. The studies outlined here suggest, however, third-party perceptions of the cause of workplace romance, rather than what members of a couple in this situation truly feel, have the most serious implications for the couple. According to attribution theory, people have a need for a coherent and predictable environment, and because of this propose explanations for the behavior of other people.[49] These explanations then guide their actions with those other individuals in subsequent situations.[50] Available studies tell us that women's and men's motives for engaging in a workplace romance are perceived differently, and these perceived motives tend to be consistent with gender stereotypes depicting men as uncaring and seeking self-gratification in relationships and women as using sexuality to gain resources from men. Neither stereotype is positive or even particularly accurate, but due to their overall lesser power and influence in society and the workplace, women may be the most harmed when co-workers, managers, and organizations develop policies regarding these relationships.[51]

Organizational culture refers to the common values, beliefs, norms, and customs of an organization's employees. It is the system of meanings produced and reproduced when people interact and includes a group's basic assumptions that are taken for granted as the most correct way to behave in the environment.[52] Thus, organizational culture is another element that can influence workplace romance by letting employees know what is considered appropriate or inappropriate behavior.[53] Mainiero suggests that workplace romances are more likely to develop in organizations with a more liberal culture,[54] where creativity and innovation are valued. Such organizations are more likely to tolerate workplace romances. Conversely, organizations with a conservative culture, where traditional values and practices are highly regarded, are less accepting of workplace romances, and they may occur in such organizations less frequently. Although some organizations may accurately be described as having a liberal or conservative culture, most probably fall somewhere in between these two extremes. Therefore, the organizational culture that characterizes a particular workplace likely has both facilitative and prohibitive effects on workplace romance.

Beside whether it can be characterized as liberal or conservative, other aspects of organizational culture, such as the type of gender meanings that pervade the organization, may influence workplace romance. Parkin and Maddock identify a gender typology of organizational cultures that they contend is influential in perpetuating women's inequality in the workplace.[55] Although not the focus of their work, the gendered organizational cultures Parkin and Maddock identify may have significant effects on women's and men's initiation of and experience within workplace romances. Among others, these gendered organizational cultures include "the gentlemen's club," "the locker room," and "the smart macho," all of which tend be hostile to women and distinctly hierarchical, with sexualized work atmospheres.

CONSEQUENCES OF WORKPLACE ROMANCE

Workplace romances are often difficult to keep hidden, and if they become known, they can influence work environments and co-workers.[56] Of most interest are the potential effects of workplace romances on job performance, but studies of this topic provide mixed messages. Some show that involvement in a workplace romance does not result in decrements in work performance, and in some cases, it is related to improvement.[57] In fact, involvement in a romantic relationship, in or out of the workplace, has been positively linked to one's own work motivation, job involvement, and satisfaction with type of work.[58] In at least one study, motives for engaging in a workplace romance affected work performance. In this case, women (and to a lesser extent men) who engaged in workplace romance due to love were more likely to increase their work performance and job involvement than those who engaged in it due to job-related or ego motives.[59]

Research on the effects of workplace romance on co-workers tends to show more negative consequences. If the workplace romance is seen as hierarchical, exploitive, or due to job-related motives, it can reduce the morale and productivity of co-workers who may fear resulting unfairness in task and career rewards.[60] It can also lead to increased gossip among co-workers. Gossip is communication *about* someone, rather than communication directly with that individual. Though gossip can be benign, it also can be an expression of co-worker anxieties surrounding a workplace romance and an effort to build alliances against the couple.[61] Furthermore, gossip about those involved in a workplace romance is not gender-neutral.[62] It is most negative toward females in a workplace romance who are perceived to have job-related motives.

Other aspects of co-worker response to workplace romance relate to preferences for and responses to managerial interventions. According to a model developed by Foley and Powell,[63] when co-workers perceive that a workplace romance will lead to a conflict of interest or work disruption, this, along with several other factors they specify, will result in a preference for management intervention. To the extent that co-workers perceive this intervention process to be fair and the outcomes just, co-worker productivity and morale will not be negatively affected. Critical to co-worker perceptions of fairness and justness are congruence between (1) the severity of actions co-workers prefer and managers take in response to the workplace romance and (2) co-worker beliefs about a just process for managerial decision making and the actual process. This model implies that the most effective interventions in workplace romances occur when managers understand what employees consider to be a fair and just response in a specific case.

Another study of the perception of fairness of organizational workplace romance policies found that co-workers perceived a managerial policy of counseling the couple on the risks of workplace romances as the most fair approach, as opposed to no policy, or more strict approaches such as verbal reprimand, written warning, transfer, or termination.[64] Stricter policies were perceived as fair if the couple's work performance declined. If it improved, however, taking no action was perceived as more just than any other managerial intervention.

Research on perceptions of fairness in managerial interventions in workplace romance is helpful and goes beyond simple advice on managerial action. It does not suggest prohibition of workplace romances but provides insight into how co-workers may perceive and react to various managerial interventions. Currently, the most common managerial approach to workplace romance is to either ignore the relationship or take no action. Few organizations have written or informal unwritten policies about how to approach workplace romances, despite repeated exhortations in the literature that such policies are needed to protect organizations against potential legal risks.[65]

The underlying tension for organizations in their attempt to manage workplace romances is the understanding that they are difficult if not impossible to prevent, but that they must be regulated due to concerns about their assumed negative effects on the organization. Part of the difficulty is that although advice about how to manage workplace romance is abundant, very little is based on adequate empirical research. The little research available shows that nonhierarchical workplace romances have either no effects or somewhat positive effects on job performance, but this is not the impression one gains from articles on workplace romance. Terms such as *pitfalls*, *landmine*, and *threat* are not uncommon in descriptions of the topic.

Another challenge associated with advice on organizational response to workplace romance is lack of understanding of the variable, emergent, and uncharted nature of these relationships for participants themselves. For example, companies may require employees to report their involvement in a workplace romance to their supervisors, especially if it involves a hierarchical relationship. With this disclosure they may even be asked to sign a love contract ensuring that the relationship is consensual and unrelated to the company to eliminate any employer liability.[66] However, at what point in the relationship is this done? After the first date, first sexual relations, after the partners mutually acknowledge that they have fallen in love? Do they tell their family, friends, or company officials first? How do couples even discuss something as logical as when to inform a supervisor of their relationship when they may still be trying to understand their own feelings for each other?

At this point, management intervention in a workplace romance on a case-by-case basis appears to be the approach that is most often recommended.[67] Much depends on how the participants in the relationship behave in the work setting. Only when work performance of the couple or co-workers declines do managers feel compelled to intervene.[68] This approach is more flexible and realistic, particularly considering the many interests that must be balanced, including employee privacy rights, respect for employees' personal lives, organizational interests, and co-worker needs and concerns.[69]

THE LINK BETWEEN SEXUAL HARASSMENT
AND WORKPLACE ROMANCE

A major organizational concern surrounding workplace romance is the potential for sexual harassment claims that may result when the relationship fails. Some data indicate a link between the two. A quarter of the respondents to a survey conducted by the Society for Human Resource Management indicated that sexual harassment claims in their organizations were due to workplace romances.[70] These data are third-party observations, but they are still disquieting. Of particular concern are dissolved hierarchical relationships, especially direct reporting ones, as they are thought to contain greater potential for sexual harassment claims for several reasons. First, although one or both partners may have negative feelings, they must continue to work with one another after the relationship is over. In addition, the lower-level partner in such relationships may have had job-related motives for entering them, which have now been thwarted. This could lead to resentment by the lower-level employee. Finally, a power differential between the two exists that could lead to sexual coercion or discriminatory managerial decision making.[71]

With respect to a dissolved workplace romance, judgments of responsibility for the sexual harassment and decisions about subsequent managerial intervention do not stem solely from the objective behaviors of the former relationship partners. The characteristics of observers and aspects of the former workplace romance play a role in perceptions of responsibility and intervention decisions. For example, Pierce and colleagues found that assessment of the immorality of the sexually harassing behavior mediated decisions about whether the accused or complainant had greater responsibility for it.[72] Assessment of responsibility in turn influenced disciplinary action decisions that ranged from no response to punitive consequences. However, the assessment of immorality was influenced by factors completely unrelated to the specific harassing behavior. If the prior workplace romance had been hierarchical, the company had a workplace romance policy in place, and the sexually harassing behavior was quid pro quo rather than hostile environment, the behavior was considered immoral.

Motives for engaging in a workplace romance, as well as gender of the relationship partner, also play a key role in perceptions of judgments of responsibility for sexual harassment. In a study where a woman was the complainant and a man was the accused, perceptions of their job motives affected judgments of responsibility. In this case, the accused was considered most responsible when he had an ego motive and the complainant had a love motive and least responsible when he had a love motive and the complainant had a job-related motive for participation in the relationship. Conversely, the complainant was judged as most responsible for the harassment when she had a job-related or ego motive compared to a love motive and the accused had a love compared to ego motive for participation in the relationship. This study also found that observers considered disciplining the accused as an appropriate action when the romance had been a hierarchical one, but if the complainant in a hierarchical workplace romance was perceived to be motivated by job-related factors, male (but not female) observers did not consider company-funded counseling as an appropriate intervention.[73]

The growing research on the potential link between workplace romance and sexual harassment provides insight into the complex social and cognitive processes involved in coworker responses to sexual harassment claims by former workplace romance participants. Again, the importance of motives observers perceive for the romance is demonstrated, and even if erroneous, they must be taken seriously. However, a more fundamental and crucial issue surrounding workplace romances and sexual harassment remains unexamined. Although women are acknowledged to more likely be victims of sexual harassment, the reasons for this are not questioned. Therefore, the deeper causes of sexual harassment in the workplace are not addressed. Sexual harassment claims are a legitimate organizational concern, however, the rationale for organizational attempts to prevent them is usually based on their negative organizational consequences, such as low staff morale, high turnover, and reduced productivity, and less on their harmful impact on women.[74] The view implicit in advice to organizations is that sexual harassment is due to individual aberrant behavior and is containable and readily resolved by following a checklist of managerial actions. This traditional approach to sexual harassment obscures the highly gendered power relations in organizations that structure and perpetuate women's inequality in the workplace. One expression of this workplace inequality is sexual harassment.

Much research demonstrates the structures and processes in organizations such as hiring, evaluation, salary, maternity leave, traditional work schedules, and so on, are linked, both overtly and subtly, to gender inequality. These gendered structures and processes make up the context in which workplace romances occur.[75] The experience of sexuality and being in love can make people feel the most authentic, but this experience is influenced by social and cultural context more than generally realized.[76] The workplace does not operate in isolation from the world, and all cultures contain attitudes and practices that impede women's social, political, and economic equality.[77] These operate in the work world as in any other social context.

This may be a reason why women tend to have more negative attitudes toward workplace romantic relationships, especially hierarchical ones, than do men.[78] They may correctly understand that women in these associations will be evaluated more negatively and therefore have more to lose.[79] Furthermore, they may better understand and possibly fear that their claims of sexual harassment after a workplace romance has ended will be taken less seriously due to their involvement in the relationship.[80]

We often think of biology as immutable, but humans routinely transcend biology—some examples are in vitro fertilization, vaccines against disease, and organ transplants. Far more difficult to change are social and cultural norms, attitudes, and behaviors. Because of this, modifications in gender relations that would lead to true solutions to sexual harassment are difficult for organizations to make. But organizations are human creations and as such "can be re-structured, reordered, and re-created in any form that people deem feasible."[81] They need only make sincere attempts.

CONCLUSIONS

Workplace romances cannot be eliminated from organizations; romance, sexuality, intimacy, and love are part of life, both in and out of the workplace. Indeed, organizations can benefit from fostering truly caring and effective relationships between women and men in the workplace.[82] In that effort, we must continue to investigate the risks for involvement in workplace romance, particularly for women, because many questions are yet unanswered. For example, the integration of race/ethnicity, social class, and sexual orientation in research on workplace romance is minimal or nonexistent; in fact, an invisibility and silence surrounding the organizational lives of women of color is only recently being lifted.[83] How do sexuality and race/ethnicity intersect in the workplace? Differential history and social relationships may affect the association between these elements for women of color. For example, Aida Hurtado explains that women of color and European American women have a different relationship to European American men.[84] European American women experience oppression, but through sexuality, they also have access to the privileges that European American men can offer. This option is not open to women of color. How might this reality be reflected in the experience of workplace romance for women of color? Studies of married couples who share the same workplace show that the wife's work may be perceived as lesser in quality than the husband's.[85] Does this happen when women are involved in a workplace romance? What are the short- and long-term effects of workplace romance on women's career choices, on-the-job performance, salary, turnover, and progression in their fields? As mentioned previously, much of the current research on workplace romance assumes a couple is heterosexual, and very little is known about how lesbians and gay men navigate romantic relationships in the workplace. Companies can be very positive or very negative toward openly lesbian and gay workers, but how does an organization's attitudes toward them influence its policies toward same-gender workplace romance?[86] In addition, despite some evidence of a link between dissolved workplace romances and sexual harassment, very little clarity exists concerning the true affective, cognitive, and behavioral mechanisms that may connect these two elements.

Finally, these questions and others would benefit from investigation with actual workplace romance participants. Recruitment of adequate sample sizes of individuals currently involved in a workplace romance is difficult but certainly not impossible. Greater integration of theory and methodologies from the burgeoning field of close relationship research could enhance the research strategies used in the study of workplace romance.[87] Until more studies of actual participants are done, understanding of such relationships will remain incomplete.

NOTES

1. Gary N. Powell and Sharon Foley, "Something to Talk About: Romantic Relationships in Organizational Settings," *Journal of Management* 24 (1998): 421–48; Christine L. Williams, Patti A. Giuffre, and Kirsten Dellinger, "Sexuality in the Workplace: Organizational Control, Sexual Harassment, and the Pursuit of Pleasure," *Annual Review of Sociology* 25 (1999): 73–93.

2. Lisa A. Mainiero, "Dangerous Liaisons? A Review of Current Issues Concerning Male and Female Romantic Relationships in the Workplace," in Ellen A. Fagenson, ed., *Women in Management: Trends, Issues, and Challenges in Managerial Diversity*, vol. 4 (Newbury Park, CA: Sage Publications, 1993), pp. 162–85; Charles A. Pierce, Donn Byrne, and Herman Aguinis, "Attraction in Organizations: A Model of Workplace Romance," *Journal of Organizational Behavior* 17 (1996): 5–32; Powell and Foley, "Something to Talk About."

3. Mainiero, "Dangerous Liaisons"; Powell and Foley, "Something to Talk About."

4. Powell and Foley, "Something to Talk About."

5. Elizabeth M. Street and Warren R. Street, "Marriage to a Co-Worker in an Academic Setting," *Behavior Analysis and Social Action* 6 (1988): 34–39.

6. Rebecca B. Bryson, Jeffrey B. Bryson, Mark H. Licht, and Barbara G. Licht, "The Professional Pair: Husband and Wife Psychologists," *American Psychologist* 31 (1976): 10–16.

7. Powell and Foley, "Something to Talk About"; Cindy M. Schaefer and Thomas R. Tudor, "Managing Workplace Romances," *S.A.M. Advanced Management Journal* 66 (2001): 4–10.

8. Williams et al., "Sexuality in the Workplace."

9. Joan Acker, "Hierarchies, Jobs, Bodies: A Theory of Gendered Organizations," *Gender and Society* 4 (1990): 139–58.

10. Gibson Burrell, "Sex and Organizational Analysis," *Organization Studies* 5 (1984): 97–118; Margaret Mead, "A Proposal: We Need a Taboo on Sex at Work," in Dail A. Neugarten and Jay. M Shafritz, eds., *Sexuality in Organizations* (Oak Park, IL: Moore, 1980), pp. 53–56.

11. American Management Association, "AMA's 2003 Survey on Workplace Dating," available online at www.amanet.org/research/archives.html (accessed September 14, 2005).

12. Vault, "Cupid in the Cubicle, Says New Vault Survey," available online at www.thevault.com/nr/printable.jsp?ch_id=420&article_id=235 (accessed September 14, 2005).

13. Robert E. Quinn, "Coping with Cupid: The Formation, Impact, and Management of Romantic Relationships in Organizations," *Administrative Science* 22 (1977): 30–45.

14. Carolyn I. Anderson and Phillip L. Hunsaker, "Why There's Romancing at the Office and Why it's Everybody's Problem," *Personnel* 62 (1985): 57–63.

15. Vault, "Cupid in the Cubicle."

16. Ibid.

17. American Management Association, "AMA's 2003 Survey."

18. Matthijn Kalmijn and Henk Flap, "Assortative Meeting and Mating: Unintended Consequences of Organized Settings for Partner Choices," *Social Forces* 79 (2001): 1289–312.

19. Ibid.

20. Kirsten Dellinger and Christine L. Williams, "The Locker Room and the Dorm Room: Workplace Norms and the Boundaries of Sexual Harassment in Magazine Editing," *Social Problems* 49 (2002): 242–57; Patti A. Giuffre and Christine L. Williams, "Boundary Lines: Labeling Sexual Harassment in Restaurants," *Gender and Society* 8 (1994): 378–401; Williams et al., "Sexuality in the Workplace."

21. Dellinger and Williams, "The Locker Room and the Dorm Room"; Giuffre and Williams, "Boundary Lines."

22. Vault, "Cupid in the Cubicle."

23. Pierce et al., "Attraction in Organizations."

24. Donn Byrne and Don Nelson, "Attraction as a Linear Function of Proportion of Positive Reinforcements," *Journal of Personality and Social Psychology* 1 (1965): 659–63.

25. Jill Gilbertson, Kathryn Dindia, and Mike Allen, "Relational Continuity Construction Units and the Maintenance of Relationships," *Journal of Social and Personal Relationships* 15 (1998): 774–90.

26. Robert B. Zajonc, "Attitudinal Effects of Mere Exposure," *Journal of Personality and Social Psychology Monograph Supplement* 9 (1968): 1–27.

27. Karen K. Dion, Ellen Berscheid, and Elaine Walster, "What Is Beautiful Is Good," *Journal of Personality and Social Psychology* 24 (1972): 285–90.

28. Rebecca C. Curtis and Kim Miller, "Believing Another Likes or Dislikes You: Behaviors Making Beliefs Come True," *Journal of Personality and Social Psychology* 51 (1986): 284–90.

29. Donald G. Dutton and Arthur P. Aron, "Some Evidence for Heightened Sexual Attraction under Conditions of High Anxiety," *Journal of Personality and Social*

Psychology 30 (1974): 510–17; for additional discussions of these concepts as applied to workplace romance, see Jeanette N. Cleveland, Margaret Stockdale, and Kevin R. Murphy, "Physical Attractiveness, Interpersonal Relationships, and Romance at Work," in *Women and Men in Organizations: Sex and Gender Issues at Work* (Mahwah, NJ: Lawrence Erlbaum Associates, 2000), pp. 67–92; Powell and Foley, "Something to Talk About."

30. Theresa J. Brown and Elizabeth Rice Allgeier, "The Impact of Participant Characteristics, Perceived Motives, and Job Behaviors on Co-Workers' Evaluations of Workplace Romances," *Journal of Applied Social Psychology* 26 (1996): 577–95; Elina Haavio-Mannila, Kaisa Kauppinen-Torpainen, and Irja Kandolin, "The Effect of Sex Composition of the Workplace on Friendship, Romance, and Sex at Work," in Barbara Gutek, Ann H. Stromberg, and Laurie Larwood, eds., *Women and Work: An Annual Review*, vol. 3 (Newbury Park, CA: Sage, 1988), pp. 123–38; Gwen E. Jones, "Hierarchical Workplace Romance: An Experimental Examination of Team Member Perceptions," *Journal of Organizational Behavior* 20 (1999): 1057–52; Charles A. Pierce, "Factors Associated with Participating in a Romantic Relationship in a Work Environment," *Journal of Applied Social Psychology* 28 (1998): 1712–30.

31. Pierce, "Factors Associated."

32. Haavio-Mannila et al., "The Effect of Sex Composition of the Workplace."

33. Ibid.

34. Quinn, "Coping with Cupid."

35. Claire J. Anderson and Caroline Fisher, "Male-Female Relationships in the Workplace: Perceived Motivations in Office Romance," *Sex Roles* 25 (1991): 163–80; James P. Dillard, "Close Relationships at Work: Perceptions of the Motives and Performance of Relational Participants," *Journal of Social and Personal Relationships* 4 (1987): 179–93.

36. Anderson and Fisher, "Male-Female Relationships in the Workplace."

37. Jones, "Hierarchical Workplace Romance."

38. Brown and Allgeier, "The Impact of Participant Characteristics"; Dillard, "Close Relationships at Work."

39. Dillard, "Close Relationships at Work."

40. Francesca M. Cancian, "Feminine and Masculine Love," in *Love in America: Gender and Self-Development* (Cambridge: Cambridge University Press, 1987), pp. 69–80.

41. Mainiero, "Dangerous Liaisons"; Gary N. Powell, "Workplace Romances between Senior-Level Executives and Lower-Level Employees: An Issue of Work Disruption and Gender," *Human Relations* 54 (2001): 1519–44.

42. Jones, "Hierarchical Workplace Romance."

43. Anderson and Fisher, "Male-Female Relationships in the Workplace."

44. Jones, "Hierarchical Workplace Romance."

45. Powell, "Workplace Romances between Senior-Level Executives."

46. Ibid.

47. Anderson and Fisher, "Male-Female Relationships in the Workplace."

48. Dillard, "Close Relationships at Work."

49. Fritz Heider, *The Psychology of Interpersonal Relations* (New York: Wiley, 1958).

50. Edward. E. Jones and Keith E. Davis, "A Theory of Correspondent Inferences: From Acts to Dispositions," in Leonard Berkowitz, ed., *Advances in Experimental Social Psychology*, vol. 2 (New York: McGraw-Hill, 1965), pp. 219–66.

51. Anderson and Hunsaker, "Why There's Romancing at the Office"; Lisa A. Mainiero, "A Review and Analysis of Power Dynamics in Organizational Romance," *Academy of Management Review* 11 (1986): 750–62.

52. Sylvia Gherardi, "Organizational Symbolism, Culture, and Gender," in *Gender, Symbolism, and Organizational Cultures* (Thousand Oaks, CA: Sage, 1995), pp. 7–37.

53. Cleveland et al., "Women and Men in Organizations."

54. Lisa A. Mainiero, *Office Romance: Love, Sex, and Power in the Workplace* (New York: Rawson Associates/Macmillan, 1989).

55. Su Maddock and Di Parkin, "Gender Cultures: How They Affect Men and Women at Work," in Marilyn J. Davidson and Ronald J. Burke, eds., *Women in Management: Current Research Issues* (London: Paul Chapman, 1994), pp. 29–40.

56. Anderson and Hunsaker, "Why There's Romancing at the Office."

57. Dillard, "Close Relationships at Work"; James P. Dillard and Scott M. Broetzman, "Romantic Relationships at Work: Perceived Changes in Job-Related Behaviors as a Function of Participant's Motive, Partner's Motive, and Gender," *Journal of Applied Social Psychology* 19 (1989): 93–110; Pierce, "Factors Associated."

58. Pierce, "Factors Associated."

59. Dillard, "Close Relationships at Work"; Dillard and Broetzman, "Romantic Relationships at Work."

60. Anderson and Hunsaker, "Why There's Romancing at the Office"; Mainiero, "Dangerous Liaisons"; Mainiero, "Office Romance"; Pierce et al., "Attraction in Organizations."

61. Harriet Lerner, "Your Anxious Workplace," in *Fear and Other Invited Guests* (New York: HarperCollins, 2004), pp. 92–116.

62. Dillard, "Close Relationships at Work"; Quinn, "Coping with Cupid."

63. Sharon Foley and Gary N. Powell, "Not All Is Fair in Love and Work: Coworkers' Preferences for and Responses to Managerial Interventions Regarding Workplace Romances," *Journal of Organizational Behavior* 20 (1999): 1043–56.

64. Katherine A. Karl and Cynthia L. Sutton, "An Examination of the Fairness of Workplace Policies," *Journal of Business and Psychology* 14 (2000): 429–42.

65. Theresa J. Brown and Elizabeth Rice Allgeier, "Managers' Perceptions of Workplace Romances: An Interview Study," *Journal of Business and Psychology* 10 (1995): 169–76; Charlotte Denaud and Ghita Fizazi, "The Pitfalls of Workplace Romance," *Washington Times* (February 14, 2005), available online at washingtontimes.com/upi-breaking/20050211-053555-5686r.htm (accessed September 14, 2005); Sue Shellenbarger, "Employers Often Ignore Workplace Romances," *Wall Street Journal*, available online at www.careerjournal.com/columnists/workfamily/20050311-wor (accessed September 14, 2005).

66. Braun Consulting News, "Workplace Romance: How about a Love Contract?" Winter 1999, available online at www.braunconsulting.com/bcg/newsletters/winter99.html (accessed September 14, 2005).

67. Foley and Powell, "Not All Is Fair in Love and Work"; Sharon A. Lobel, "Sexuality at Work: Where Do We Go from Here?" *Journal of Vocational Behavior* 42 (1993): 136–52; Mainiero, "Office Romance"; Gary N. Powell and Laura M. Graves, "Dealing with Sexuality in the Workplace," in *Women and Men in Management*, 3rd ed. (Thousand Oaks, CA: Sage, 2003), pp. 157–82.

68. Brown and Allgeier, "Managers' Perceptions of Workplace Romances"; Kathy Gurchiek, "Be Ready for Slings, Arrows of Cupid in the Cubicles," *HR Magazine* 50 (2005): 27, 36–37.

69. Margaret F. Karsten, "Sexual and Racial Harassment and Corporate Romance," in *Management and Gender: Issues and Attitudes* (Westport, CT: Quorum Books, 1994), pp. 57–72; Rebecca J. Wilson, Christine Filosa, and Alex Fennel, "Romantic Relationships at Work: Does Privacy Trump the Dating Police?" *Defense Council Journal* 70 (2003): 78–88.

70. Society for Human Resource Management, "Workplace Romance Survey (item no. 62.17014)," Alexandria, VA: SHRM Public Affairs Department.

71. Charles A. Pierce and Herman Aguinis, "Bridging the Gap between Romantic Relationships and Sexual Harassment in Organizations," *Journal of Organizational Behavior* 18 (1997): 197–200.

72. Charles A. Pierce, Brandee J. Broberg, Jamie R. McClure, and Herman R. Aguinis, "Responding to Sexual Harassment Complaints: Effects of a Dissolved Workplace Romance on Decision-Making Standards," *Organizational Behavior and Human Decision Processes* 95 (2004): 66–82.

73. Charles A. Pierce, Herman Aguinis, and Susan K. R. Adams, "Effects of a Dissolved Workplace Romance and Rater Characteristics on Responses to a Sexual Harassment Accusation," *Academy of Management Journal* 43 (2000): 869–80.

74. Harriet Samuels, "Sexual Harassment in the Workplace: A Feminist Analysis of Recent Developments in the UK," *Women's Studies International Forum* 26 (2003): 467–82.

75. Rosabeth Moss Kanter, *Men and Women of the Corporation* (New York: Basic Books, 1977); Leslie Salzinger, "Trope Chasing: Making a Local Labor Market," in *Genders in Production: Making Workers in Mexico's Global Factories* (Berkeley: University of California Press, 2003), pp. 35–50; Christine L. Williams, "Femininity in the Marine Corp," in *Gender Differences at Work: Women and Men in Nontraditional Work* (Berkeley: University of California Press, 1989), pp. 45–87.

76. Donna Castañeda and Alyson Burns-Glover, "Gender, Sexuality, and Intimate Relationships," in Michele A. Paludi, ed., *The Praeger Guide to the Psychology of Gender* (Westport, CT: Praeger, 2004), pp. 69–91.

77. Maddock and Parkin, "Gender Cultures"; Virginia E. Schein, "Managerial Sex Typing: A Persistent and Pervasive Barrier to Women's Opportunities," in Marilyn J. Davidson and Ronald J. Burke, eds., *Women in Management: Current Research Issues,* (London: Paul Chapman, 1994), pp. 41–54.

78. Pierce, "Factors Associated"; Pierce et al., "Attraction in Organizations."

79. Anderson and Fisher, "Male-Female Relationships in the Workplace"; Gary Powell, "Workplace Romance in the Public Sector: Sex Differences in Reactions to the Clinton-Lewinsky Affair," *Psychological Reports* 87 (2000): 1043–49; Powell, "Workplace Romances between Senior-Level Executives."

80. Pierce et al., "Responding to Sexual Harassment Complaints."

81. Ellen A. Fagenson and Janice J. Jackson, "Final Commentary," in Ellen A. Fagenson, ed., *Women in Management: Trends, Issues, and Challenges in Managerial Diversity* (Newbury Park, CA: Sage), p. 305.

82. Lobel, "Sexuality at Work."

83. For discussion of this issue see Patricia S. Parker, "Visions of Leadership in Traditional (White Masculine) and (White) Feminine Leadership Approaches: A Review and Critique," in *Race, Gender, and Leadership* (Mahwah, NJ: Lawrence Erlbaum Associates, 2005), pp. 3–19; Lynn Weber and Elizabeth Higginbotham, "Black and White Professional-Managerial Women's Perception of Racism and Sexism in the Workplace," in Elizabeth Higginbotham and Mary Romero, eds., *Women and Work: Exploring Race, Ethnicity, and Class* (Thousand Oaks, CA: Sage, 1997), pp. 153–75.

84. Aida Hurtado, "Relating to Privilege and Political Mobilization: Toward a Multicultural Feminism," in *The Color of Privilege: Three Blasphemies on Race and Feminism* (Ann Arbor: University of Michigan Press, 1996), pp. 1–44.

85. Bryson et al., "The Professional Pair."

86. Micah E. Lubensky, Sarah L. Holland, Carolyn Wiethoff, and Faye J. Crosby, "Diversity and Sexual Orientation: Including and Valuing Sexual Minorities in the Workplace," in Margaret S. Stockdale and Faye J. Crosby, eds., *The Psychology and Management of Workplace Diversity* (Malden, MA: Blackwell, 2004), pp. 206–23.

87. Benjamin R. Karney and Thomas N. Bradbury, "The Longitudinal Course of Marital Quality and Stability: A Review of Theory, Method, and Research," *Psychological Bulletin* 118 (1995): 3–34; Benjamin R. Karney, Joanne Davila, Catherine C. Cohan, Kieran T. Sullivan, Matthew D. Johnson, and Thomas N. Bradbury, "An Empirical Investigation of Sampling Strategies in Marital Research," *Journal of Marriage and the Family* 57 (1995): 909–20.

5

Pregnancy Discrimination: Laboring under Assumptions in the Workplace

Julie Manning Magid

Assumptions are made about pregnant women who work. For example, it is assumed that they will require extended leaves to give birth and care for their infants, change work patterns after giving birth, or have more than one child, thereby affecting their employer not once but possibly several times. Statistics can be found to support each of these assumptions. Working women in the United States who became first-time mothers from 1991 to 1994 averaged nearly three months leave after the birth of their child.[1] Mothers with infants under age one are more likely to work part-time than other women, and 45 percent do not participate in the workforce.[2] Many women bear more than one child; in the 1990s, U.S. fertility rates averaged two births per woman, an increase from the 1970s.[3]

These assumptions culminate in an idea that is devastating for pregnant working women—the assumption that their level of commitment to work is forever changed. This notion affects not just pregnant women but all women. An overwhelming majority of women will give birth at some point in their lives.[4] Thus from the moment women enter the workforce, they bear the weight of all these (statistically accurate) assumptions, which remain with them throughout most of their work lives.

Assumptions are often the source of pregnancy discrimination in the workforce. Statistics about women in the workplace help document trends and calculate averages but do not determine or predict how a given woman will organize her work life in relation to her family life. Each woman should make individual decisions about work and family based on her particular circumstances. If a woman is pregnant, the law should respect the dignity of her decisions concerning work and family by allowing her to work free from the burden of assumptions about parenting responsibilities and future pregnancies.

Employers run afoul of the law if the workplace environment is based on predetermined notions and expectations about how women should organize their work and families. Despite laws prohibiting pregnancy discrimination in the workplace, women believe preset notions about pregnancy and family life underlie employers' actions all too often. The number of pregnancy discrimination complaints filed with the Equal Employment Opportunity Commission (EEOC) increased nationwide by 10 percent between 2001 and 2002.[5] Although the number decreased slightly the following year, a long-term trend indicates complaints concerning discrimination based on pregnancy have risen 39 percent since 1992.[6] During the same time period, the nation's birth rate dropped by 9 percent. Pregnancy discrimination claims filed with the EEOC now climb each year at a rate exceeding the increase in filings for either sex discrimination or sexual harassment claims.

Why is pregnancy discrimination a growing concern? Employment trends suggest some reasons why the number of claims is increasing. More women now remain in their jobs while pregnant. In this era of leaner workforces, the time away from work often associated with pregnancy may create resentment. Managing parental leaves creates challenges for employers, particularly smaller ones. Finally, employers are less aware of prohibitions concerning pregnancy discrimination than of other federal discrimination laws.

Women represent about 47 percent of the labor force, and estimates are that the percentage will continue to grow.[7] While they are pregnant, women often remain in the workforce; in the 1990s, only 27 percent of pregnant women quit their jobs.[8] During the same decade, however, employers fired pregnant women at a higher rate than in the 1980s.[9] As more working women remain in their jobs while pregnant, incidents of discriminatory conduct rise. Women often resent the assumptions made about their work and family life and decide to file complaints when they determine the work environment is intolerable.[10]

Economic trends are related to the increase in pregnancy discrimination complaints. Productivity demands of lean workforces mean that employees work longer hours. If a woman takes maternity leave or other time off during pregnancy, overworked co-workers usually must share her job responsibilities. This is a particularly acute problem for smaller employers with fewer employees among whom additional work responsibilities can be divided.

In addition to the cost of lost productivity and efficiency during pregnancy or maternity leave, pregnancy raises employers' health insurance costs. However, pregnancy discrimination is expensive for employers too. In fiscal year 2005, the EEOC and state and local agencies collected $11.3 million from employers for violations of pregnancy discrimination laws.[11] This amount does not include the cost of litigation and damages paid when employees filed a lawsuit in federal or state courts.

The increase in complaints filed with the EEOC indicates that federal legislation has failed to end pregnancy discrimination. Although Congress attempted to include pregnancy discrimination as part of sex discrimination legislation generally, many courts interpret pregnancy discrimination law dissociated from gender stereotypes. Thus employers and employees alike are confused by varying interpretations of the legal parameters. More recent legislation used a gender-neutral approach to prohibiting discrimination based on family-related commitments. However, this approach did not account for the biological reality of childbirth and resulted in the unintended consequence of making it more difficult for women to maintain legislative protection than men.

An overview of pregnancy discrimination law's laborious development is described in this chapter. Uncertainties remain concerning the legality of crucial employer policies and procedures. Organizations' efforts to comply with anti-discrimination legislation are compromised by the lack of clarity of the underlying statutes and the differing interpretations. This chapter highlights the areas of greatest ambiguity concerning pregnancy discrimination law. In addition, the overlap between federal family leave legislation is analyzed. Two of the most important issues emerging in the context of pregnant employees—benefits policies and defining which aspects of motherhood are included in pregnancy discrimination legislation—are assessed.

Before turning to the legislative landscape, however, a recent court decision provides an example of the assumptions that prevent women from contributing to an organization. Eliminating these assumptions, as demanded by the court in this case, offers the best opportunity to promote organizational excellence and workplace equity.

Compared to other types of discrimination, that based on pregnancy is less well known. Although the Civil Rights Act of 1964 prohibited sex discrimination in employment, the U.S. Supreme Court did not interpret sex discrimination as including differential treatment based on pregnancy. In 1978, fourteen years after Congress passed this major federal antidiscrimination law, it was amended to include pregnancy.

Unfortunately, courts interpreting pregnancy discrimination law have reached vastly different conclusions concerning the parameters of this protection.[12] Some interpret pregnancy discrimination bans narrowly so that many pregnant women have no opportunity to redress this type of workplace discrimination. Although other courts take a broader view concerning the types of employment actions that are prohibited legally, these different interpretations leave employers and employees alike confused about the law and the nature of pregnancy discrimination. The increasing number of pregnancy discrimination complaints filed with the EEOC and federal courts indicates a wide range of conduct result in women seeking to redress discrimination through the law.

Elana Back, an elementary school psychologist who filed a discrimination claim against her employer for assumptions about her commitment to work following her pregnancy, had received several positive performance reviews. Following the birth of her first child and three months of maternity leave, however, Back's career path derailed due to her employer's concern that she could not be a good mother and remain devoted to her job. Back believed that her supervisor relied on predetermined notions about women and their family responsibilities to inquire repeatedly about her plans for additional pregnancies. In particular, the supervisor asked about how Back would "space" her pregnancies, requested that she not become pregnant again until the supervisor retired, and suggested that Back should wait until her first child was in kindergarten before conceiving again.

As Back approached job tenure, her supervisor expressed growing concern about her work and family priorities. The supervisor told Back that it was impossible to be a good mother and have her job. In addition, the supervisor was concerned that after the school awarded Back tenure, her level of job commitment would drop because she had "little ones at home." The supervisor believed another year before recommending tenure would give her time to assess Back's child care situation.[13]

Back asked a federal court, the Court of Appeals for the Second Circuit, to determine whether her employer's stereotypical statements and actions about motherhood and the qualities of a good mother were a form of gender discrimination. The Second Circuit concluded that questioning a woman's abilities and workplace commitment based on her status as a mother strikes at the heart of gender stereotyping. The court referenced a recent U.S. Supreme Court decision that characterized persistent generalizations based on gender, such as those Back described, as the fault line between work and family life that is an enduring obstacle in employment opportunity.[14] The court held that "the notions that mothers are insufficiently devoted to work, and that work and motherhood are incompatible, are properly considered to be, themselves, gender-based."[15]

Although the ruling in the *Back* decision is limited to the states within the Second Circuit, nonetheless, the court's recognition of the link between gender and pregnancy—including postpregnancy assumptions about family planning and responsibilities—is an important step toward reuniting pregnancy discrimination law with gender discrimination. All too often, assumptions about women in the workplace correspond with those about their role as mothers. The history of gender discrimination law, however, shows a concerted effort to dissociate gender discrimination from pregnancy and parenting. Such dissociation ignores the reality of women's experience in the workplace.

When Congress enacted Title VII of the Civil Rights Act of 1964 to address employment discrimination based on race, color, religion, sex, and national origin,[16] pregnancy discrimination received no specific consideration. In fact, the legislative history of Title VII suggests that some members of Congress did not intend to include sex as a protected class. Congressman Howard Smith of Virginia, a representative with little commitment to the civil rights bill, amended the pending legislation to include sex as a protected class in what some speculate was a maneuver to defeat the law's passage.[17] Following Smith's amendment, debate concerning the amendment was lighthearted and humorous.[18] Although Title VII survived with the amendment intact, the less-than-serious discussion concerning protection from gender discrimination left only a brief and often unhelpful legislative history.[19]

The EEOC, the agency responsible for administering Title VII, issued inconsistent interpretations concerning the role pregnancy played in gender discrimination. Initial EEOC opinions permitted maternity, pregnancy, and childbirth exclusions from employers' benefit plans under Title VII. By 1972, however, the EEOC reversed its earlier opinions and promulgated guidelines indicating that pregnancy, childbirth and recovery, and related medical conditions had to be treated the same as other temporary disabilities for insurance purposes in employee benefit plans. Thus, if an employer's plan provided time off for other temporary disabilities, it also had to allow women the same amount of time for temporary disability for pregnancy-related reasons.

The Supreme Court addressed pregnancy discrimination within the meaning of Title VII in a 1976 case, *General Electric v. Gilbert* (referred to as *Gilbert*). In that case, a group of female employees filed a lawsuit against their employer based on its insurance plan. It covered employees who became disabled due to illness or injury. It also covered procedures specific to male reproduction, such as vasectomies, but excluded disabilities resulting from pregnancy. The female employees claimed this exclusion violated Title VII.

In the *Gilbert* decision, the Supreme Court determined that discrimination because of sex, as prohibited by Title VII legislation, did not include pregnancy discrimination. The Court reasoned that the employer's insurance policy excluding pregnancy disability did not distinguish between males and females but between "pregnant persons and non-pregnant persons." This was not understood to represent a gender-based classification because the group of nonpregnant persons included both men and women. The Court found pregnancy was not "a disease or disability comparable in all other respects to covered diseases or disabilities and yet confined to the members of one sex or race."[20] This ruling denied disability coverage to pregnant women under the private employer's insurance plans. In an earlier case, the Court upheld an exclusion of pregnant women from disability coverage under a state insurance plan.[21]

Not all members of the Court agreed with the *Gilbert* decision. Justice William Brennan authored a dissenting opinion that asserted the Court had lost sight of Title VII's intent when it held that pregnancy discrimination was not gender discrimination. Brennan appealed for the Court to approach the issue with a broader understanding of gender. In the dissenting opinion he wrote, "surely it offends common sense to suggest that a classification revolving around pregnancy is not, at a minimum, strongly 'sex related.'"[22] Similarly, Justice John Paul Stevens's dissenting opinion rejected dividing the pool of employees into pregnant women and nonpregnant persons. Instead, he argued for an implicit recognition that biological females cannot be dissociated from the reality of pregnancy. Stevens stated: "The classification is between persons who face a risk of pregnancy and those who do not."[23]

The dissents by Brennan and Stevens received full vindication when Congress responded to the *Gilbert* decision by amending Title VII "to prohibit sex discrimination on the basis of pregnancy." The House and Senate Reports specifically acknowledged that Brennan's and Stevens's dissents reflected congressional intent in enacting Title VII. The Pregnancy Discrimination Act (PDA) amended Title VII by providing that

> the terms "because of sex" or "on the basis of sex" include, but are not limited to, because of or on the basis of pregnancy, childbirth, or related medical conditions; *and* women affected by pregnancy, childbirth, or related medical conditions shall be treated the same for all employment-related purposes, including receipt of benefits under fringe benefit programs, as other persons not so affected but similar in their ability or inability to work.[24]

The PDA's dual purpose of addressing the definition of sex discrimination and overruling the controversial *Gilbert* decision is evident in the congressional committee reports as well as the language of the amendment. The bill "was introduced to change the definition of sex discrimination in Title VII to the commonsense view and to ensure that working women are protected."[25] The Supreme Court recognized Congress's expression of its intent to prohibit discrimination based on pregnancy by enacting the PDA.[26] The Court noted the act's proponents "repeatedly emphasized that the Supreme Court had erroneously interpreted congressional intent and that amending legislation was necessary to reestablish the principles of Title VII law as they had been understood prior to the *Gilbert* decision."[27]

In a later case, the Court debated whether the PDA preempted a California statute requiring employers to provide four months of unpaid maternity leave and guaranteed reinstatement to pregnant employees.[28] If the PDA had preempted the statute, states could not mandate broader pregnancy discrimination laws than the PDA. With a fractured majority, the Court concluded Congress did not mean to prohibit employers from giving preferential treatment to pregnant employee in enacting the PDA. Instead, the Court emphasized the broad goals of the PDA by noting, "rather than limiting existing Title VII principles and objectives, the PDA extends them to cover pregnancy."[29] As a result of this decision, some states require private employers to provide rights to its pregnant employees beyond those identified in the PDA.

Defining the prohibitions under the PDA has proved challenging. For instance, does it apply to women who are not pregnant? Mary Craig was one such woman. She had a decision to make in 1982. She could lose her job or be sterilized and present evidence of her sterility to her employer. Her co-worker, Elsie Nason, was not willing to be sterilized to keep her job and because of that, she received less pay in a job to which she was involuntarily transferred. Another co-worker, Donald Penney, however, did not receive a requested leave from his job. He was required to remain in a position that threatened his future children through high lead exposure. These are the representatives of the class who challenged their employer's fetal protection policy by filing a federal lawsuit.[30]

The employer, a battery manufacturer, had a valid concern about its legal liability. During the manufacturing process, employees were exposed to lead.

The Occupational Safety and Health Administration had determined that such exposure sometimes resulted in blood lead levels exceeding the critical level for an employee who planned to have biological children. Parents' high levels of exposure to lead increased the risk that their children would suffer serious birth defects. After eight of its employees became pregnant with blood lead levels regularly exceeding the critical level, the employer instituted a new policy affecting all women employees (although male exposure could result in birth defects of biological children as well): "It is policy that women who are pregnant or who are capable of bearing children will not be placed into jobs involving lead exposure or which could expose them to lead through the exercise of job bidding, bumping, transfer or promotion rights."[31]

One federal appeals court judge characterized this case as "likely the most important sex-discrimination case in any court since 1964, when Congress enacted Title VII."[32] None of the three employees who filed the lawsuit was pregnant or planned on becoming pregnant. Mary Craig chose sterilization to comply with the company policy and therefore was medically incapable of becoming pregnant. Nonetheless, their status as nonpregnant persons did not exclude them from the discrimination prohibitions under Title VII as amended by the PDA. The Supreme Court noted the employer's policy explicitly categorized employees based on the "potential for pregnancy," "[The company] has chosen to treat all of its female employees as potentially pregnant; that choice evinces discrimination on the basis of sex."[33] The Court found this stereotype of women goes to the very heart of what is prohibited by the PDA: "Congress in the PDA prohibited discrimination on the basis of a woman's ability to become pregnant. We do no more than hold that the PDA means what it says."[34]

The law is clear, then, that employers cannot institute employment policies that single out female employees based on the assumption that these employees may become pregnant. They cannot bar women, but not men, from jobs involving exposure to substances known to harm the human reproductive system. Less clear and far more problematic are the decisions made about employees who are pregnant and require leave. The wording of the PDA is convoluted and subject to differing interpretations. Specifically, courts have long discussed whether Congress intended the amendment broadly to incorporate pregnancy with gender discrimination or if the PDA addresses more specifically the medical leave associated with pregnancy and childbirth.

The debate arises from the specific language of the PDA, which was quoted earlier. Two clauses are joined by the conjunction *and*. Often these clauses are read together to limit the PDA to outlawing discrimination only as it relates to the disability associated with pregnancy. In this interpretation, the conjunction is defined as meaning "therefore." That interpretation unnecessarily narrows the discrimination that women encounter in the workplace. The reading of the clauses of the PDA most supported by the legislative history and the Supreme Court's rulings is to consider them independently. The meaning of the first clause is not limited by the specific language in the second. This interpretation means the conjunction is defined as "in addition," a more common definition of *and* than "therefore." The second clause directly overturns the *Gilbert* case by explaining the application of the general principle to women employees disabled by pregnancy, childbirth, and related conditions.[35]

Perhaps the most notable decision limiting the language of the PDA to disability leave concerns a department store employee. The following federal Court of Appeals decision is notable due to its narrow interpretation of pregnancy discrimination and its impact on decisions concerning pregnancy discrimination claims filed in many federal courts. A department store fired its pregnant employee, Kimberly Hern Troupe, one day before her scheduled maternity leave. Her employer stated the termination was not due to pregnancy but due to repeated absences and tardiness caused by her severe morning sickness. The employee countered that the employer's explanation for termination was nonsensical given that she was one day away from the maternity leave that would resolve the issue of morning sickness. The court drew a now often cited comparison to resolve this issue:

> Suppose that Lord & Taylor had an employee named Jones, a black employee scheduled to take a three-month paid sick leave for a kidney transplant; and whether thinking that he would not return to work when his leave was up or not wanting to incur the expense of paying him while he was on sick leave, the company fired him. In doing so . . . the company could not be found guilty of racial discrimination unless . . . there was evidence that it failed to exhibit comparable rapacity toward similarly situated employees of the white race.[36]

This example of a black employee in need of a kidney transplant is irrelevant to the situation of an employee who no longer will need leave following giving birth. As a commentator has described the difference, "the black kidney patient does not undergo transplant surgery because he is black. Rather, he happens to be a man of color who also needs a kidney transplant. A working woman like Troupe, on the other hand, must take a maternity leave precisely for the reason that the law protects her from discrimination: her pregnancy."[37] Nonetheless, other courts adopted this rationale in pregnancy discrimination cases. In doing so, several courts support the rationale first voiced by the court deciding Troupe's claim of pregnancy discrimination: "Employers can treat pregnant women as badly as they treat similarly affected but non-pregnant employees."[38]

However, pregnancy is not the same as other employees' disabilities. As one judge noted, "if Congress intended to equate pregnancy with a temporary disability . . . it afforded pregnant women precious little protection when it enacted the PDA."[39] Characterizing pregnancy as a disability further dissociates pregnancy from the reality of women in the workplace. Assumptions concerning loyalty to the job, future time off, and parenting are not made when an employee needs a kidney transplant. Pregnancy is unique in these assumptions and in the gender it affects. Furthermore, most individuals do not intend to become disabled or expect it as a logical result of their actions. Pregnancy often is an intended and expected result.

Therefore, although no one would suggest Jones should consider the impact medical leave will have on his job in deciding whether to have a kidney transplant, employers often expect women to consider timing of pregnancies to minimize the impact on their job. As one court noted about a comparison between men on sick leave and women on maternity leave, "the men were incapacitated while the women were not. . . . One can draw no valid comparison between people, male or female, suffering extended incapacity from illness or injury and young mothers wishing to nurse little babies."[40] As this opinion indicates, disability is considered a more acceptable reason to take time away from work than leave associated with pregnancy. Unfortunately, women's pregnancy-related leaves too often are viewed as an admission of women's disinterest in their work or career.

A comparison between pregnancy and disability is inappropriate because the former is plagued by unique stereotypes and assumptions that include not only pregnancy itself but also motherhood and childrearing. By its nature, however, pregnancy carried to term will result in a short-term medical disability. Nonetheless, some courts hold this disability is not covered by the PDA and that the PDA does not include protection of pregnant employees' jobs if the employees take time away from work. The recovery from pregnancy, although medically recognized, is not consistently interpreted as protected by the PDA's discrimination prohibitions. One court rejected the claim that more than one week of incapacitation was required after giving birth.[41] However, other courts hold this narrow interpretation of the PDA is a violation of the letter as well as the spirit of Title VII and the PDA.[42] "A short-term inability to work is bound up with the very nature of pregnancy and childbirth" and it is therefore a violation of the PDA to dismiss an employee for taking leave under the PDA.[43]

The PDA, according to a federal Court of Appeals, "was not designed to handcuff employers by forcing them to wait until an employee's pregnancy causes a special economic disadvantage."[44] Instead, the court noted that the bank employing Jessica Maldonado as a part-time teller would not violate the PDA by terminating her if her pregnancy leave would affect the bank's functioning. The court held that "an employer cannot take anticipatory adverse action[45] against a pregnant employee," however, "an employer may . . . project the normal inconveniences of pregnancy and their secondary effects in the future and take actions in accordance with and in proportion to those predictions."[46] The "normal inconveniences" that may result in adverse action, including termination of a pregnant employee, include "the need to take more frequent snack and restroom breaks and the need to take some time off, at the very least, to give birth."[47]

This conclusion is perhaps understandable given the fundamental misunderstanding of the PDA's purpose. The court deciding Maldonado's discrimination claim posited that "the PDA was designed to allow individual women to make independent choices about whether to continue to work while pregnant."[48] This statement is not a true reflection of the congressional record when Congress amended Title VII to explicitly include pregnancy as gender discrimination. Rather, a sponsor of the PDA, Senator Williams, explained that the "entire thrust" of the PDA "is to guarantee women the basic right to participate fully and equally in the workforce, without denying them the fundamental right to full participation in family life."[49] Representative Tsongas stated, "Title VII and the PDA are designed to 'put an end to an unrealistic and unfair system that forces women to choose between family and career.'"[50] An employer who terminates an employee because she needs time off to give birth is forcing the employee and her family to choose between work and family.

A division exists between those federal appellate courts that hold pregnancy requires employers to grant some leave for the disability associated with giving birth and those that hold the PDA does not require any leave for pregnant employees if the employer does not offer leave to other employees with similar temporary disabilities. Therefore, a pregnant employee's job may depend on where she lives, not federal law.

In 1993, Congress implicitly acknowledged that Title VII—and the PDA specifically—failed to eliminate pregnancy discrimination. Therefore, it enacted new federal legislation to address the issue of pregnancy as well as other disabilities and family care–related leaves. As a whole, the legislation promoted work and family life balance but failed to address some of the most pressing pregnancy discrimination concerns.

The Family and Medical Leave Act of 1993 (FMLA) offered far more comprehensive protection concerning employment policies affecting pregnancy and maternity leave than the PDA.[51] By specifying leave provisions related to pregnancy and childbirth, it clarified for affected employers their obligations concerning pregnant employees. After holding hearings concerning parental leave, Congress determined that "historically, denial or curtailment of women's employment opportunities has been traceable directly to the pervasive presumption that women are mothers first and workers second. This prevailing ideology about women's roles has in turn justified discrimination against women when they are mothers or mothers-to-be."[52] The FMLA was enacted to minimize the potential for discrimination against women by making leave for family related commitments available to everyone, regardless of gender.

The FMLA requires employers to allow employees to return to work following a leave for the birth of a child, adoption of a child, or the serious health condition of employees or members of the employees' immediate family. It eliminates the difficulty in taking leave for prenatal care or childbirth and the confusion about whether such leave is required by the PDA by specifically addressing these aspects of pregnancy. Typically, employers may require employees to have their health care providers certify that their requests for leave meet the parameters of the FMLA. Employees must notify employers of the need for leave in advance. However, Congress recognized the unique needs of pregnant employees by providing some latitude from these documentation requirements.[53]

Under the FMLA, pregnant employees can miss work for morning sickness without obtaining a doctor's note. Absences related to pregnancy and prenatal care are permitted in short time increments. Therefore, an employee who is protected by the FMLA may arrive to work one hour late every day if she is ill as a result of her pregnancy, and her employer may not take any disciplinary action against her. Similarly, that employee may be late to work one day, leave at noon the following day, and continue that pattern for weeks, all without discipline or other adverse employment action.

Although the FMLA is important legislation, it has several important drawbacks. First, it only applies to employers who have fifty or more full-time employees for twenty or more calendar weeks. This includes the largest employers but excludes most employees. Second, and importantly for working women, the FMLA only covers employees who have been employed full-time for at least one year. The firing of Troupe one day before her maternity leave and Maldonado if she would have asked for a day off to give birth would not have violated the FMLA. Neither Troupe nor Maldonado was employed full-time for one year when terminated.

One way Congress tried to consider employers' needs was by requiring employees to work full-time for one year before receiving the benefits of the FMLA. Congress also attempted to end the stigma associated with family leave by making it available to both sexes. However, the FMLA has the unintended consequence of perpetuating women's career stagnation based on pregnancy. It prevents many women from changing jobs to advance their careers and increase their earning power because of its limited coverage. Although men who take family leave when a child is born most likely do not need it before that time, women may need leave throughout the pregnancy. Therefore, to be protected by the FMLA they must work twelve months before conceiving. The inexact nature of conception makes many women leery of changing jobs if they believe they might conceive prior to their first twelve months of employment. Retaining parental leave protection is more difficult for women than for men, but the FMLA coverage provisions do not recognize this gap in coverage. A gender-neutral approach to family leave protection ignores the reality that working women may become pregnant throughout the majority of their working lives.

In addition to limitations concerning the employees covered by the FMLA, the leave it guarantees is limited to twelve weeks in a twelve-month period and is unpaid. Each increment of absence, whether fifteen minutes or several hours, is counted toward the total of twelve weeks. This is both an administrative problem for many employers and a disadvantage of the FMLA for employees who have difficult pregnancies. Absences during pregnancy count against the time employees have to recover from childbirth and care for their infants. Women suffering complications of pregnancy may deplete their entire leaves before their infants are born. Because FMLA leaves are unpaid, financial concerns may prevent women from taking additional leave even if their employers permit an extension. Women's short-term medical disability following childbirth does not entitle them to additional leave time. After the twelve-week total, they must return to work or risk termination.

The Supreme Court described the FMLA as a positive advance to eliminate the stereotypes confronting working women.

> By creating an across-the-board, routine employment benefit for all employees, Congress sought to ensure that family-care leave would no longer be stigmatized as an inordinate drain on the workplace caused by female employees, and that employers could not evade leave obligations simply by hiring men. By setting a minimum standard of family leave for all eligible employees, irrespective of gender, the FMLA attacks the formerly state-sanctioned stereotype that only women are responsible for family care-giving, thereby reducing employers' incentive to engage in discrimination by basing hiring and promotion decisions on stereotypes.[54]

The Court extended FMLA coverage to state employees and large private employers after agreeing that Congress, in legislative hearings prior to passage of the FMLA, recorded a pattern of state constitutional violations based on gender discrimination. The Court found the FMLA was an appropriate remedy for these violations because statutes such as Title VII that merely demanded gender equality without requiring any actions to achieve that result had proved ineffective.[55]

Despite congressional efforts to make pregnancy a more gender-neutral event by passing the FMLA, the biological reality is that pregnancy affects women, and gender distinctions remain barriers to their employment opportunities. An issue receiving much attention in this regard is the exclusion of contraception from employers' benefit plans. Courts have revisited the PDA and Title VII to test the intersection of employer's insurance plans and sex discrimination based on pregnancy-related issues. In *Erickson v. Bartell Drug Co.*, the employer no longer requires employees to avoid childbearing to qualify for the best jobs, as did the employer in *Gilbert*, but an employee is seeking employer support of her decision not to have children.[56] The resulting issue is whether the PDA and Title VII address pregnancy prevention rather than pregnancy or the capacity to become pregnant.

Bartell Drug, an employer in Washington state, included a comprehensive prescription plan in its employee benefits package. The plan was self-insured and covered all prescription drugs, including several preventive drugs and devices, such as blood pressure- and cholesterol-lowering drugs, hormone replacement therapies, prenatal vitamins, and drugs to prevent allergic reactions, breast cancer, and blood clotting. It specifically excluded a handful of products, including contraceptive devices such as birth control pills, Norplant, Depo-Provera, intrauterine devices, and diaphragms. Prescribed weight reduction, infertility, smoking cessation, and experimental drugs also were excluded, as were derma-tological treatments for cosmetic purposes and growth hormones.

The employer maintained that its prescription plan was unrelated to the gender equality provisions of Title VII and the PDA. The district court disagreed, stating:

> The legislative history of Title VII does not forecast how the law was to be interpreted by future courts faced with specific examples of allegedly dis-criminatory conduct. The truth of the matter is, Congress' intent regarding the evolution of a law is rarely apparent from fragments of legislative history. Long before this particular dispute arose, the protections of Title VII had no doubt been applied in ways that were never anticipated by the Representatives and Senators who voted for it or the President who signed it into law. Nevertheless, Congress has generally chosen to interfere with the judiciary's interpretation of Title VII only where the courts attempted to restrict its application.[57]

Although the control of fertility, enabled by the excluded contraceptives, does not correlate with the terms of "pregnancy, childbirth or related medical conditions" in the language of the PDA, the district court interpreted this pro-vision broadly based on the PDA's history. It found that Congress "clearly had in mind the obvious and then-commonplace practice of discriminating against women in all aspects of employment, from hiring to the provisions of fringe benefits, based on an assumption that women would get pregnant and leave the workforce."[58] Sex-based categorization violates Title VII as amended by the PDA. The court ruled that exclusion of a woman-only benefit, such as female con-traception, from a comprehensive prescription benefit plan is sex discrimination in violation of federal law.

This case represented the first time a federal court ruled on the issue of contraception exclusion from a prescription plan. As a district court decision, the ruling is limited to western Washington state. However, the EEOC reached the same decision in a similar case. Although EEOC decisions are not binding on courts interpreting the law, they carry some weight with the courts, as the fol-lowing EEOC decision did with the *Erickson* court.

The EEOC heard a case brought by nurses whose employer did not cover contraception in its health insurance plan. In finding this exclusion discrimi-natory, the EEOC reasoned that only women can become pregnant. This gender distinction cannot, under employment discrimination laws, affect women's terms and conditions of employment in any way. "Contraception is a means by which a woman controls her ability to become pregnant. The PDA's prohibition on discrimination against women based on their ability to become pregnant thus necessarily includes a prohibition on discrimination related to a woman's use of contraceptives."[59]

The EEOC found additional support for this contention from language in the PDA exempting employers from any obligation to pay for abortions. If Congress explicitly made this exception, Congress also could have exempted employers from an obligation to include contraception in their benefit plans but did not. Therefore, employers providing benefits must do so without discriminating under the PDA.

Increasingly, state law prohibits many employers from excluding prescription contraceptives from comprehensive insurance coverage of prescriptions. The state laws generally require insurance plans to provide equal coverage for FDA-approved prescription contraceptives and related outpatient care as other preventive prescription drugs and outpatient care.[60] Many employees do not benefit from these state laws, however, because federal law governs employers who are self-insured.[61] Therefore, future court decisions will determine how broadly the PDA is interpreted in instances of contraceptive exclusion from an employer's benefit plan.

Another emerging issue concerning pregnancy discrimination focuses on defining when it starts and ends. One view is that pregnancy is an easily definable biological condition. While the biological condition exists, adverse employment action based on the pregnancy itself is prohibited. Related implications of pregnancy, such as absence not covered by the FMLA, are not based on the pregnancy but on the employer's expectations of job performance. As one court has described it, firing a pregnant employee because of excessive absences due to pregnancy-related illness is harsh but is not discrimination.[62] This rationale is based on the assumption the employer would terminate any employee with excessive absences. This of course ignores the stereotypes and preset notions that Congress recognized were associated with pregnancy when it enacted both the PDA and the FMLA.

If pregnancy is not purely a biological condition but a gender distinction that includes conception, as some courts recognize, what other elements of a working woman's life are associated with pregnancy? Assumptions about working mothers with infants increasingly are the source of complaints filed with the EEOC and the courts.

The typical scenario is that experienced by Celena Venturelli when she was pregnant and working as a temporary employee in a not-for-profit corporation. Her supervisors were impressed by her work and decided to offer her a permanent position. When a supervisor met with her to discuss the permanent job offer, the discussion was not about employment but about her impending status as a new mother. The supervisor maintained he wanted to be sensitive to Venturelli's pregnancy and not make her feel that the employer was rushing her into larger responsibilities. If this was the intent, it was not what was communicated in the conversation. Instead, the supervisor discussed in detail Venturelli's pregnancy and how she would deal with it in a permanent job with the employer. He made comments about women changing their minds about working after they hold their babies in their arms. The supervisor suggested she take the time necessary to stay at home with her child.

Venturelli was stunned into silence. Rather than viewing the discussion as sensitivity to her situation, she was offended by the stereotypes of mothers that were irrelevant to offering her a permanent job. After this conversation, Venturelli no longer wanted the job she once hoped for because she did not want to work for a discriminatory employer. The employer lost the individual it determined was the best candidate for the job because of the supervisor's conduct.[63]

Many courts view pervasive assumptions about a new mother's work life as "callous" but not discriminatory.[64] Supervisors' expressions that a woman will not return to work full-time after having a baby are insufficient evidence of pregnancy discrimination.[65] Instead, some discriminatory action during pregnancy often is required. For instance, a district manager's instructions to others to reduce efforts to train a pregnant employee due to the manager's doubts about whether she would return from maternity leave could constitute evidence of discrimination. The employee did not receive training because of her pregnancy.[66]

Requiring such a close connection to action during pregnancy directly contradicts the congressional record concerning passage of the PDA. Congress intended the PDA to address "the assumption that women will become [pregnant] and leave the labor force [which] leads to the view of women as marginal workers, and is at the root of the discriminatory practices which keep women in low-paying and dead-end jobs."[67] These interpretations of pregnancy discrimination allow assumptions to eliminate women's decisions about organizing work and family. Such assumptions negatively impact the family generally, making this an issue affecting both men and women.

For women to participate fully in the workforce, pregnancy discrimination must confront the assumptions and stereotypes surrounding roles of mother or caregiver. Even the most conscientious and concerned employer, as Venturelli's supervisor professed to be, may create a difficult work environment because pervasive stereotypes are accepted as the norm in the workplace. Employers must understand these stereotypes and accept each woman's individual decision about whether to have children and how to be a parent.

The major challenge for working women today is to make decisions about their family relationships free from the weight of expectations and assumptions. Not all working women will have children during their work lives. Each pregnancy represents a unique and unpredictable experience for each working woman who has a biological child, and each family adjusts differently. Accepting the uniqueness of the parenting situation rather than relying on personal past experience or statistical averages is the key to treating working women with dignity. Allowing women the dignity of defining their parenting role within their employers' organizational requirements eliminates the many facets of pregnancy discrimination before, during, and after pregnancy.

NOTES

1. Kristen Smith, Barbara Downs, and Martin O'Connell, *Maternity Leave and Employment Patterns: 1961–1995*, Current Population Reports, U.S. Census Bureau.

2. Barbara Downs, *Fertility of American Women: June 2002*, Current Population Reports, U.S. Census Bureau.

3. Ibid.

4. Ibid.

5. The Civil Rights Act of 1964 (known as Title VII) established the EEOC. This federal administrative agency enforces the federal statutes prohibiting employment discrimination.

6. Pregnancy Discrimination Charges EEOC and FEPAs Combined: FY 1992–FY 2004, U.S. Equal Employment Opportunity Commission.

7. *Women at Work: Looking behind the Numbers 40 Years after the Civil Rights Act of 1964*, National Partnership for Women and Families (July 2004).

8. Smith et al., *Maternity Leave and Employment Patterns*.

9. Ibid.

10. See, for example, *Venturelli v. ARC Comm. Servs., Inc.*, 350 F.3d 592 (7th Cir. 2003).

11. EEOC, available online at www.eeoc.gov/types/pregnancy.

12. See Julie Manning Magid, "Contraception and Contractions: A Divergent Decade Following Johnson Controls," *American Business Law Journal* 41 (2003): 115.

13. *Back v. Hastings on Hudson Union Free Sch. Dist.*, 365 F.3d 107, 115 (2004).

14. *Nev. Dep't of Human Res. v. Hibbs*, 538 U.S. 721, 738 (2003).

15. *Back v. Hastings on Hudson*, 121.

16. 42 U.S.C. § 2000e. Title VII regulates the conduct of employers with fifteen or more employees. However, smaller employees typically are covered under similar state legislation prohibiting employment discrimination.

17. "The Civil Rights Act of 1964 was the culmination of decades of debate and political maneuvering over various civil rights proposals. In the end, it took three momentous events to finally propel the bill to the top of the agenda of Congress and the Administration. The first was the August 1963 march on Washington during which Dr. Martin Luther King, Jr., gave his famous 'I have a dream' speech. The second was the September 1963 bombing of a black church in Birmingham, Alabama, in which four little girls were killed. The third was the assassination of President Kennedy, whose support for the bill carried even more weight in Congress and with the public after his untimely death. It was in this time that Bob Dylan warned, 'Come Senators, Congressmen, please heed the call. Don't stand in the doorway, don't block up the hall,' Bob Dylan, The Times They Are A-Changin', on The Times They Are A-Changin' (Sony Music Entertainment/Columbia Records 1964). After months of debate and a seventy-five day filibuster in the Senate, the bill finally passed and was signed into law by President Johnson on July 2, 1964." *Erickson v. Bartell Drug Co.*, 141 F.Supp. 2d 1266, 1269 n. 4 (W.D. Wash. 2001).

18. Francis J. Vass, *Title VII: Legislative History*, Boston College Industrial and Commercial Law Review 7 (1966): 431.

19. *Gen. Elec. v. Gilbert*, 429 U.S. 125, 143 (1976).

20. Ibid., 136.

21. *Geduldig v. Aiello*, 417 U.S. 484 (1974).

22. *Gen. Elec. v. Gilbert*, 149.

23. Ibid., 161 n. 5.

24. 42 U.S.C. § 2000e(k).

25. H.R. Rep. No. 948, 95th Cong., 2d Sess. at 3 (1978), 1978 U.S. Code Cong. & Ad. News at 4751.

26. See Julie Manning Magid, "Pregnant with Possibility: Reexamining the Pregnancy Discrimination Act," *American Business Law Journal* 38 (2001): 819.

27. *Newport News Shipbuilding & Dry Dock Co. v. EEOC*, 462 U.S. 669, 679 (1983).

28. *Cal. Fed. Sav. & Loan Ass'n. v. Guerra*, 479 U.S. 272 (1987).

29. Ibid., 272, 288–89.

30. *UAW v. Johnson Controls*, 499 U.S. 187 (1991).

31. Ibid., 187, 191–92.

32. *UAW v. Johnson Controls*, 886 F.2d 871, 920 (7th Cir. 1989).

33. *UAW v. Johnson Controls*, 499 U.S. 187, 199 (1991).

34. Ibid., 187, 211.

35. *Erickson v. Bartell Drug Co.*, 141 F.Supp. 2d 1266, 1270 (W.D. Wash. 2001).

36. *Troupe v. May Dep't. Store*, 20 F.3d 734, 738 (7th Cir. 1994).

37. Ann C. McGinley and Jeffrey W. Stempel, "Condescending Contradictions: Richard Posner's Pragmatism and Pregnancy Discrimination," *Florida Law Review* 46 (1994): 193, 210 n. 166.

38. *Troupe v. May Dep't. Store*, 734, 738.

39. *In re Carnegie Ctr. Assocs.*, 129 F.3d 290, 304 (3rd Cir. 1997).

40. *Barrash v. Bowen*, 846 F.2d 927 931-32 (4th Cir. 1988).

41. *EEOC v. Elgin Teachers Assoc.*, 27 F.3d 292, 295 (7th Cir. 1994).

42. *Abraham v. Graphic Arts Int'l Union*, 660 F.2d 811, 819 (D.C. Cir. 1981).

43. *Smith v. F.W. Morse & Co., Inc.*, 76 F.3d 413,424 (1st Cir. 1996).

44. *Maldonado v. U.S. Bank*, 186 F.3d 759, 767 (7th Cir. 1999).

45. "Adverse action" in employment law is any change in employment status that negatively impacts the employee. Such actions include demotion, discipline, termination, changes in job responsibilities, and negative evaluations.

46. *Maldonado v. U.S. Bank*, 759, 767.

47. Ibid.

48. Ibid.

49. 123 Cong. Rec. 29658 (daily ed. Sept. 16, 1977).

50. 124 Cong. Rec. 21442 (1978).

51. 29 U.S.C. § 2601.

52. The Parental and Medical Leave Act of 1986: Joint Hearing before the Subcommittee on Labor-Management Relations and the Subcommittee on Labor Standards of the House Committee on Education and Labor, 99th Cong., 2nd Sess., 100 (1986).

53. 29 CFR § 825.114 (e). "Absences attributable to incapacity [due to pregnancy or for prenatal care] qualify for FMLA leave even though the employee...does not receive treatment from the health care provider during the absence.... [For example, an] employee who is pregnant may be unable to report to work because of severe morning sickness."

54. *Nev. Dep't of Human Res. v. Hibbs*, 721, 737.

55. Ibid., 721.

56. *Erickson v. Bartell Drug Co.*, 1266.

57. Ibid., 1266, 1269.

58. Ibid., 1266, 1274.

59. *Decision on Coverage of Contraception*, EEOC Report, available online at www
.eeoc.gov/docs/decision-contraception.

60. Susan A. Cohen, "Federal Law Urged as Culmination of Contraceptive Insurance Coverage Campaign," *Guttmacher Report* 4(5) (October 2001).

61. ERISA, 29 U.S.C. 1144(b)(2)(B).

62. *Dormeyer v. Comerica Bank*, No. 96 C 4805, 1998 U.S. Dist. LEXIS 16585, at
*28–29 (N.D. Ill. 1998).

63. *Venturelli v. ARC Comm. Servs., Inc.*, 592.

64. Ibid., 592, 604.

65. *Ilhardt v. Sara Lee Corp.*, 118 F.3d 1151, 1156 (7th Cir.1997).

66. *Briody v. Am. Gen. Fin. Co.*, No. 98-2728, 1999 U.S. Dist. LEXIS 8405, at *9
(E.D. Pa. May 27, 1999).

67. H.R. Rep. No. 948, 95th Cong., 2d Sess. 3 (1978).

6

The Family and Medical Leave Act: Lost in Translation

Joan E. Gale

The Family and Medical Leave Act of 1993 (FMLA) provides up to twelve weeks of unpaid, job-protected leave in a twelve-month period to eligible employees necessitated by their own serious health condition or to care for employees' parent, child, or spouse with a serious health condition or a child born or placed for adoption or foster care with employees.[1] During an FMLA leave, employees' health benefits must be maintained on the same basis as if they were working their regular schedule. To be eligible, employees must have worked for the employer for at least twelve months, have worked at least 1,250 hours in the twelve-month period prior to the commencement of the leave, and must be employed at a facility with fifty or more employees within a seventy-five-mile radius. The core concept of the FMLA is job-protected leave.

Most would agree that the basic premise of the FMLA is good; it has sometimes run aground due to the way the U.S. Department of Labor (DOL), the agency charged with enforcing the provisions of the act, has exercised its interpretive authority. In some areas, the act's original purpose has been obscured by the DOL's sometimes surprising interpretations and pronouncements. As a result, some employees have used the FMLA to circumvent their employers' attendance and sick leave policies, which was never the intent or purpose of the act.

Under the auspices of a business-friendly administration, those advocating on behalf of employers would like to see the DOL overhaul some of its FMLA regulations. Conversely, employee advocates want to see the current regulatory scheme remain as is but also would like Congress to expand the act's coverage to include smaller employers and require mandatory paid leave. Currently, the act only covers public and private employers with fifty or more workers and provides only unpaid leave.

So far, the DOL has been slow to respond to the calls for change. Although one of its regulations was invalidated by the U.S. Supreme Court in *Ragsdale v.*

Wolverine World Wide, Inc.,[2] the DOL did not seek comments on proposed new language to replace the defunct regulation until June 2006, even though updating the rule has been on the DOL's agenda since 2003. At this juncture, the DOL has given no indication on how it intends to proceed, aside from indicating that it will revise the regulation invalidated by *Ragsdale*. In the absence of a DOL pronouncement at this writing, this chapter examines some areas in which compliance with the act has frustrated employers and will suggest ways to ease their dissatisfaction.

WHAT THE LAW WAS INTENDED TO ACCOMPLISH

On February 5, 1993, President Bill Clinton signed the FMLA into law. The law went into effect in August of that year. In his remarks on the occasion of the signing, Clinton observed that the United States was "virtually the only advanced industrialized country without a national family and medical leave policy."[3] A Senate Report issued prior to the law's signing surveyed maternity or parental leave available in other industrialized countries.[4] The report found that Japan provided twelve weeks of partially paid pregnancy leave, Canada allowed women to take up to forty-one weeks of maternity leave (of which they received 60 percent of their salary during the first fifteen weeks of their leave), Sweden provided eighteen months of family leave (at approximately 90 percent of an employee's gross pay) to both men and women, and Norway provided paid leave equal to the employee's income covered by pensions for up to one month a year to care for a terminally ill close relative.[5] The Senate Report further found that partially paid maternity leave was the norm among other industrialized countries; 127 of the 135 countries surveyed offered maternity leave and some wages.[6]

While acknowledging that some employers already offered leave benefits such as those provided for in the new law, Clinton noted that many other employees still had no such coverage in the early 1990s.[7] Citing U.S. Bureau of Labor Statistics data for 1991, the president observed that only 37 percent of full-time employees in private businesses with 100 or more workers received unpaid maternity leave. Only 14 percent of employees of private employers with fewer than 100 workers received unpaid maternity leave.[8] In summary, the president stated: "This legislation balances the demands of the workplace with the needs of families. In supporting families, it promotes job stability and efficiency in the American workplace."[9]

When enacted in 1993, the FMLA was not without its detractors. Some senators believed that Congress had no business mandating family and medical leave benefits for employers.[10] Rather, they argued that employers should be "encouraged through a policy of providing incentives and lifting legal restrictions" to offer family and medical leave benefits to "preserve the elements of choice and flexibility inherent to the successful employer–employee relationship and necessary for us to remain competitive in a global economy."[11]

Although the FMLA marked the first federal foray into mandating family leave benefits, when it was enacted, twenty-nine states plus the District of Columbia and Puerto Rico had already adopted some form of protected family or medical leave.[12] Today, all but five states have passed some type of family or medical leave legislation covering workers in the private and/or public sector(s).[13] States currently without any protected family or medical leave legislation include Arkansas, Michigan, Mississippi, Nevada, and Wyoming.

FMLA ENFORCEMENT STATISTICS (2001–2004)

According to recent FMLA enforcement statistics issued by the DOL, the number of complaints filed with the DOL declined in fiscal year 2004, after reaching a high of 3,565 in fiscal year 2003.[14] A total of 3,350 new complaints were filed in 2004, the first year since 2001 that the number of new complaints did not exceed the previous year's filings.[15] As had been the case in previous years, the most common reason for filing was because the complainant was wrongfully terminated for exercising rights under the FMLA (1,473); the second and third most frequently cited reasons involved discrimination claims (763) and the refusal to grant FMLA leave (697), respectively.[16] The least common reason for filing a complaint was the employer's failure to maintain the employee's health benefits while on leave.[17] In fiscal year 2004, the DOL found no FMLA violation in 1,848 cases and discovered such violations in 1,502 cases.[18] The DOL did not explain why fewer complaints were filed in fiscal year 2004.

SURVEY FINDINGS

In 1995 and 2000, the federal government had studies conducted to measure the impact of the FMLA on private sector employers and employees.[19] In 1995, the Commission on Family and Medical Leave, a bipartisan group established by the act, authorized the first study, and five years later, the DOL commissioned two additional surveys to update the 1995 findings.[20]

The 1995 findings, based on a survey conducted so soon after the act's effective date, probably do not provide as accurate a picture of the law's impact on business operations as do later studies. In 1995, many employees were not yet familiar with the new law, and utilization rates were low. Although the 2000 survey showed a moderate increase in the act's utilization compared to the 1995 findings, a noticeable shift occurred in employers' attitudes toward the act. They became more negative, a trend that continues to this day.

The DOL did not commission a new survey on the law's tenth anniversary. The few sources that provide insight into employers' views of the act today include the Society for Human Resource Management (SHRM), an association that represents human resources professionals, which conducted a survey in 2003, and the Employment Policy Foundation, a public policy research group, which in 2005 released questionnaire results based on data collected in 2004.

Survey Findings: 1995 and 2000

In 1995 and 2000, similar percentages of private sector employees worked for firms covered by the act and were familiar with their rights under the FMLA.[21] In addition, the percent of employees who took a leave only once in the eighteen months prior to the survey remained fairly stable, as did the leave's median length and the percent of workers who wanted to take a leave but did not.[22] Sixty percent of employees worked for covered employers in 1995, as did 58 percent in 2000, and about 59 percent were familiar with their rights under the law in both years.[23] Approximately three-quarters of private sector workers taking a leave did so only once in 1995 and 2000; the median length in both years was ten days.[24] In 1995, 3.1 percent of private sector workers wanted to take a leave but did not; this figure dropped to 2.4 percent in 2000.[25] The three main reasons why employees who desired a leave did not take it were identical in both years: they could not afford an unpaid leave; work was too important; or they feared losing their job.[26]

Table 6.1 presents selected characteristics of leave takers and shows that in both 1995 and 2000, a majority were female.[27] Nearly three-quarters of those using FMLA leave were married in 2000, up from about 71 percent in 1995.[28] Regardless of marital status, nearly 60 percent of employees using FMLA leave in 2000 had children, compared to about 55 percent in 1995.[29]

The age of the FMLA leave takers most and least likely to take FMLA leave barely budged from 1995 to 2000.[30] An equal percent of those most likely to use leaves had average earning levels of between $30,000 and $50,000 and between $50,000 and $75,000 in 2000; in 1995, slightly more of those most likely to use leave had average earnings of between $30,000 and $50,000.[31] In both years, less than 3 percent of employees aged sixty-five and over used leave, and only 11 percent of the eighteen- to twenty-four-year old workers took leave in 1995.[32] The comparable figure for that latter age group in 2000 was 10 percent.[33] Though not indicated in Table 6.1, an identical percentage of employees (54.5) using leave earned an hourly wage rather than a salary in 1995 and 2000, and leave taking was greatest among those working for manufacturing firms with 250 or more employees.[34]

The percent of survey respondents who perceived that administrative and benefits costs rose due to the act were similar, though slightly higher, in 2000 than in 1995, whereas the percent who thought the law led to higher training and hiring costs jumped. Forty-seven percent said administrative costs had increased due to the act in response to the earlier questionnaire; 51.5 percent said so in 2000.[35] Percentages who believed the FMLA led to higher benefits costs moved from 34.3 to 36.2, respectively, in 1995 and 2000; 23.7 percent thought

TABLE 6.1. Selected Characteristics of FMLA Leave Takers: 1995 and 2000 (Percent)

Year	Sex		Marital Status		Children		Age Group Least Likely to Take Leave		Age Group Most Likely to Take Leave	Annual Avg. Earnings of Those Most Likely to Take Leave	
	F	M	Married	Not	Yes	No	18–24	>65	30–39	$30–$50k	$50–$75k
1995	56.2	43.8	70.9	29.1	54.5	45.5	11.1	2.9	40.8	30.6	NA
2000	58.1	41.9	75	25	59.6	40.4	10	2.1	39.7	25.5	25.7

TABLE 6.2.   Reasons for Longest FMLA Leave in 1995 and 2000 (Percent)

Reason	1995	2000
Care for own serious health condition	61.4	47.2
Care for newborn/adopted infant or child	14.3	17.9
Care for sick child	8.5	11.4
Care for sick parent	7.6	7.8
Maternity/disability	4.6	5.9
Care for sick spouse	3.6	5.9

Note: Disability due to pregnancy is actually considered a serious health condition leave; however, the data broke out leave due to pregnancy disability separately.

the law increased hiring and training costs in 1995 compared to 34.1 percent who believed similarly in 2000.[36]

Larger employers seemed to experience higher costs of compliance with the act than smaller employers in 2000. Among those with 250 or more employees, over 75 percent had increased administrative costs, and over half said they had greater benefit and hiring/training costs due to the FMLA.[37]

Table 6.2 indicates the reason for taking the longest FMLA leave in the two years studied.[38] The only appreciable decline from 1995 to 2000 was seen among employees taking leave for their own serious health conditions. Several other reasons for taking leave, such as the care of a sick child or spouse, increased in the latter survey and may explain why fewer employees took leave for their own health concerns.

Several distinctions between answers of survey respondents in 1995 and 2000 seem noteworthy and may warrant further analysis. For example, the FMLA-covered employees who were eligible to take leave rose from 46.5 to 61.7 percent from 1995 to 2000;[39] the percent covered and eligible using any kind of FMLA leave increased from 11.6 to 18.3;[40] and the percent of employees denied leaves they had requested went from 9.9 to 20.8 percent over the same five-year span.[41]

As Table 6.3 shows, the vast majority of respondents noticed no effect of the act on various business and employee outcomes in either 1995 or 2000. The percent who said the law had no noticeable impact on employee productivity, however, dropped during that time frame.[42]

TABLE 6.3.   Percentage of Employers Finding No Noticeable Effect of the FMLA on Business and Employee Outcomes in 1995 and 2000

Year	Business Productivity	Business Profitability	Business Growth	Employee Productivity	Employee Absences
1995	86.4	92.5	95.8	82.7	89.5
2000	76.5	87.6	87.7	67.0	76.3

TABLE 6.4.   Percentage of Employers Finding Compliance with the FMLA Very or Somewhat Difficult

	1995	2000
Administer the FMLA's notification, description, certification requirements	Not asked	54.4
Coordinate the FMLA with other federal laws	25.7	52.8
Maintain additional recordkeeping	24.0	38.0
Coordinate state and federal leave policies	18.9	42.9
Coordinate the FMLA with other leave policies	21.1	40.1
Coordinate the FMLA with company attendance policies	Not asked	34.5
Determining whether medical condition is a serious health condition	Not asked	42.3

Seven years after its enactment, employers still held a relatively favorable view of the act, but those finding compliance somewhat or very difficult rose from 14.9 percent to 36.4 percent from 1995 to 2000.[43] Specific areas of compliance found to be challenging are listed in Table 6.4.[44]

Intermittent leave use was analyzed closely in 2000 but not in 1995. Though relatively few employees took such leave in 1995, 39.2 percent of employers indicating experience with intermittent leave said they had difficulty managing it.[45] In 2000, 53.9 percent of intermittent leave users said that less than half of their FMLA leave was taken intermittently, and 86.6 percent said they took this type of leave on an "as-needed basis."[46] Reasons for use were more likely to involve care for a child, parent, or spouse than self-care.[47] Overall, most employers said intermittent leave had no impact on their productivity or profitability, but slightly less than one-third of larger employers (with 250 or more employees) said it negatively affected productivity, and 17.4 percent of this latter group said it adversely affected profitability.[48]

2003 Survey Results

In 2003, in conjunction with the law's tenth anniversary, the SHRM queried its membership on its perceptions of the FMLA. This survey was in follow-up to the association's initial FMLA survey, conducted in 2000.[49]

The 2003 survey found that on average, less than half (48 percent) the employees who took FMLA leave scheduled it in advance but also noted a wide degree of variation among the responses. In the earlier survey (2000), participants reported that on average, 40 percent of the employees who took FMLA leave scheduled it in advance. The 2003 survey found that employees were twice as likely to take FMLA leave for a medical as for a family reason. Thirty-four percent of employees took leave for a medical reason, whereas 17 percent took leave for a family reason. However, responses varied widely based on employer size. For instance, small employers (50–99 employees) reported that 7 percent of their employees took FMLA leave for family reasons, and large employers (500+ employees) indicated that 21 percent of their employees took leave for family reasons.[50]

Asked about the ease of determining whether an employee was entitled to leave under the act, 52 percent of the respondents to the 2003 survey had granted FMLA requests they did not believe were legitimate due to the DOL's regulations and interpretations. Large employers were even more likely to approve dubious leave requests than smaller employers (63 percent versus 24 percent) according to the 2003 questionnaire. In 2000, the same percentage of employers reported approving leave requests of questionable legitimacy.

Asked about the ease of administering intermittent leave, 62 percent of employers responding to the 2003 survey reported that it was extremely difficult or difficult to track their employees' use of intermittent leave. This was down slightly from the 2000 findings in which 77 percent of employers indicated that tracking such leave was extremely difficult or difficult. The percentage of employers reporting no difficulty tracking intermittent leave remained the same between 2000 and 2003, at 6 percent.

Very few employers stated that they had calculated the cost of complying with the FMLA. Only 3 percent provided an approximate cost, and 69 percent said that they had not bothered to compute the cost of administering the FMLA. Although most employers had not placed a dollar figure on the cost of administering the act, they were aware of the act's impact on employee morale. Slightly more than one-third of the employers (35 percent) polled stated that they were aware of employee complaints from co-workers because of another worker's questionable use of FMLA leave. The 2000 survey findings were similar.

2005 Survey Results

The Employment Policy Foundation (EPF) conducted a survey of FMLA use in 2004; its results were released in 2005.[51] The survey, which looked at FMLA utilization in both the public and private sectors, found that on average, 14.5 percent of employees took FMLA leave in 2004. However, the survey found wide variation in FMLA use among industries. For instance, FMLA use was greatest among telecommunication workers (>20 percent) and least among education workers (5 percent).

Consistent with the 1995 and 2000 survey findings, the EPF survey found that the average FMLA leave lasted 10.1 days in 2004, but the leave's duration varied widely depending on the industry. In the telecommunications industry, more than 40 percent of the FMLA leave taken was for one day or less. Among all employers, 50 percent of FMLA leave was taken for fewer than five days.

The EPF survey found that 35 percent of FMLA users took leave under the act more than once in 2004. Chronic health conditions accounted for 27 percent of the FMLA leave taken in that year. In some industries, at least 50 percent of the leave taken was for a chronic health condition. Fifty-eight percent of FMLA leave taken was for that reason in the transportation industry; in the telecommunications industry, which had the second highest percent of leave taken to cope with a chronic health condition, the rate was 42 percent.

The EPF survey noted that most leave takers did not give their employer advance notice of their leave. Only 35 percent provided at least a week's notice or more before they took FMLA leave. Fifty percent gave no notice before taking leave, and 11 percent provided notice at the time their leave began or shortly thereafter.

The EPF survey estimated that employers incurred *direct* costs totaling $21 billion in connection with FMLA compliance. Direct costs consider lost productivity, cost of continuation benefits, and labor replacement costs. This amount, according to the EPF, still underestimated the "true cost" of complying with the FMLA because it excluded the administrative costs employers incur in having to track employees' leave usage and did not reflect the "secondary economic impacts of declining profitability on economic activity."

Among the three factors used to compute the FMLA's direct cost to employers, the EPF survey found that labor replacement costs were the most expensive. Overall, employers spent $10.3 billion to replace workers on leave. Not surprisingly, the transportation and telecommunications industries incurred the largest replacement costs—each paying the equivalent of nearly 1.7 percent of its compensation costs to cover replacement. The next most costly expense was for continuation of benefits. Employers paid an additional $5.9 billion, or nearly 2 percent of their total health care expenses, to continue health benefits. Finally, the survey estimated that in 2004, employers lost $4.8 billion in profits due to FMLA leave.

SUGGESTED REVISIONS TO THE DOL REGULATIONS

In 2002, the U.S. Office of Management and Budget asked the public to nominate federal regulations it believed should be revised. Among those nominated, the FMLA regulations received over 1,000 comments, the most "votes" tabulated by any federal regulation.[52] Many objections to the FMLA's current regulatory scheme were first raised by employer groups during the public comment phrase, prior to the release of the final regulations in January 1995.[53] Employers' objections have largely turned on their belief that the DOL, in preparing the regulations, failed to draw their essence from Congress' stated intentions. One of the most frequently cited examples of this is the definition of a "serious health condition." This represents a fundamental difficulty employers experience in trying to comply with the FMLA, but employees and their advocates regard it as a sacred cow. As employees and employers await the DOL's next move, the rest of this article will explore how the DOL might revise some of the regulations to respond to the concerns employers have raised since the act's inception.

Remove Minor, Short-Term Illnesses from the Definition of a Serious Health Condition

The expansive definition of "serious health condition" has been an early and constant source of frustration for employers who must determine whether an employee is entitled to protection under the FMLA. Not surprisingly, the question of whether an employee is suffering from a serious health condition is one of the act's most litigated provisions.[54] Under the act, an employee has two ways to satisfy the definition of a serious health condition. An employee suffers from a serious health condition if he or she is receiving:

   a. care as a patient in a hospital, hospice, or residential medical care facility; or
   b. continuing treatment by a health care provider.[55]

The first listed item is relatively self-explanatory, but the second needs further clarification, which the DOL chose to provide via regulation. Although the DOL stated in its comments in response to the FMLA regulations that it was mindful of the act's legislative history, the regulations ignore the very guidance that the DOL indicated helped shape them.

From the record, Congress clearly did not intend a serious health condition to include short-term conditions that would typically fall within the "most modest sick leave policies," such as minor illnesses lasting only a few days and surgical procedures entailing no hospitalization and only a brief recovery period.[56] The DOL's interpretive guidance on what Congress meant by "continuing treatment" has greatly expanded the definition of a serious health condition. Title 29 C.F.R. § 825.114 states that those undergoing continuing medical treatment satisfy the definition of a serious health condition when they are:

   1. unable to work for more than three consecutive calendar days, and
   2. are undergoing treatment by a health care provider involving:
       a. treatment two or more times by a health care provider, or
       b. treatment by a health care provider at least once which results in a regimen of continuing treatment under a health care provider's supervision.[57]

On April 7, 1995, the day after the FMLA Final Rule was effective, the DOL appeared to retreat from its expansive stance and issued an advisory opinion letter to respond to a writer's concerns that the DOL's definition of a serious health condition did not "reflect the intent of the Act's authors and [was] being applied inconsistently."[58] The DOL explained that even if employees had been sick for more than three days, had been seen by a health care provider at least once, and were on a regimen of continuing treatment, they would not qualify for FMLA protection if they were merely suffering from a common cold without complications.[59] The DOL's response was encouraging. It suggested that the analysis explained in § 825.114 would not ignore basic common sense notions about what medical conditions are *serious* in nature.

Reliance on the DOL's common sense approach proved to be short-lived. Eighteen months later, the DOL withdrew its opinion letter of April 7 in a new advisory opinion letter dated December 12, 1996.[60] The DOL indicated that it was withdrawing the earlier letter because it contained an "incorrect construction" of the definition of a serious health condition.[61] The new opinion letter stated that employees who were ill with a common cold or flu would be entitled to FMLA protection if they met the test set forth in § 825.114. In addition, according to the new DOL opinion letter, employees did not have to demonstrate that complications occurred to satisfy the definition of a serious health condition.[62] Although hinting that these conditions (common cold or flu) might not routinely meet the regulatory threshold for a serious health condition, the DOL concluded there was no basis to exclude such conditions from protection if they in fact met the stated criterion.[63]

Not only did the DOL's remarks soundly reject its earlier ruminations on what constitutes a serious health condition, the DOL effectively struck the portion of the regulation stating that conditions such as the common cold, flu, earaches, upset stomach, minor ulcers, headaches (other than migraines), routine dental or orthodontic problems, and periodontal disease would not qualify as serious health conditions *unless there were accompanying complications.*[64]

One need only look at the case law to see that the DOL's construction of serious health condition has turned the FMLA into the national sick leave policy Congress expressly did not envision.[65] Courts have found that employees suffering from the flu, upper respiratory inflections, and stomach problems were entitled to protection under the FMLA.[66] Although many courts have refused to find that the act applies to such minor conditions, the haphazard interpretation of the term *serious health condition* has led many employers to err on the side of inclusion to avoid a potential lawsuit.[67]

In comments on the FMLA submitted to the U.S. House of Representatives Congressional Committee on Education and the Workplace Subcommittee on Oversight and Investigations in 1997, one company described its difficulties trying to comply with the act's requirements.[68] Kansas City, Missouri–based Hallmark Cards viewed the agency's definition of serious health condition as going well beyond the scope of what Congress intended. It thus enabled employees to potentially receive protected leave for such conditions as a bladder infection, stress caused by divorce, a "personal family crisis," and a gum infection—none of which the company believed were entitled to FMLA protection based on the act's legislative history.[69] The lack of predictability or useful guidance has left employers feeling that they have the burden to prove that an employee's health condition is not covered by the FMLA, rather than the other way around.

Various suggestions have been made for reworking the definition of *serious health condition*. Foremost, the definition must only address medical conditions that are genuinely serious in nature. To do so, the analysis should not require employers (or judges) to suspend disbelief in favor of a rigid test that discourages people from using their common sense in answering the question—as is currently the case.

At minimum, § 825.114 should be revised to require that an employee be totally incapacitated (unable to perform most or all of his or her job duties or the normal activities of daily living) for at least seven to ten consecutive calendar days. The current threshold of more than three days enables too many minor medical conditions to satisfy the definition. Additionally, the "continuing treatment" requirement should not be satisfied by a mere showing that an individual has been prescribed a course of prescription drug therapy, without considering the specific medical condition being treated, the type of drug therapy prescribed, and the drug's side effects. A prescription drug regimen alone is a poor gauge for assessing whether someone suffers from a serious health condition. Perhaps twenty years ago, when doctors were more circumspect about prescribing medication, such treatment might have indicated a serious health condition, but not today.

The regulation's analysis should be treated as a minimum threshold from which employers should be permitted to take into account all relevant information that turns on the question of whether the employee is suffering from a serious health condition.

Allow Employers to Obtain More Information from the Employee's Health Care Provider

As the EPF survey observed, few employers are receiving advance notice of an employee's need for FMLA leave. Even when the employee gives notice and provides supporting medical certification, the information justifying the leave request is often incomplete or raises more questions than it answers about the employee's need for leave. Although an employer is permitted to send an employee for a second (or third) opinion at its own expense if it questions the validity of certification, the current scheme has proved to be both protracted and costly.[70]

Among the obstacles imposed on employers is that they generally not permitted to contact an employee's doctor about a medical certification.[71] An employer, through its health care provider representative, may contact an employee's physicians for purposes of "clarification and authenticity of the medical certification" only if the employee agrees.[72] The lack of unfettered and direct access to an employee's doctors to quickly and efficiently resolve questions pertaining to the medical certification is an immense handicap. Asking an employee to resubmit a certification form several times before determining entitlement to FMLA leave is not unusual for employers. The process could be greatly streamlined if the employer did not have to obtain an employee's permission before contacting his or her doctors.

The right to send employees for a second opinion, in principle, sounds like a good idea. In practice, however, the option fails to consider the real costs employers incur by doing so. Hallmark Cards told a House Committee in 1997 that the cost of obtaining a second opinion was "extremely expensive." Citing two instances in which it sent employees for a second opinion—one for a back injury and the other for a mental health condition—Hallmark Cards paid $700 and $600, respectively, for each examination. Considering that over 1,900 of its employees took FMLA leave in 1996, Hallmark Cards stated that the cost of obtaining a second—let alone a third—opinion was "a real deterrent" to its ability to manage FMLA leaves. Very few employers—large or small—are likely to have the financial resources to assume this expense.[73]

An additional obstacle to the use of second and third opinions is that employees are not required to provide copies of their medical records to doctors hired to conduct an exam and provide second/third opinions.[74] The absence of this information can be particularly problematic when employees no longer suffer from the condition that prompted the original need for FMLA leave. This places the doctors, through no fault of their own, at a significant disadvantage. Practically speaking, without this information, referring physicians may lack the necessary background information to form a reasonable opinion.

Second and third opinions also are of limited usefulness to determine if relatively minor acute conditions (i.e., those falling within the category of more than three consecutive calendar days plus treatment) are in fact serious health conditions. Often, by the time employees finally see the second or third opinion physician, determining whether they were incapacitated at the time of the absences is impossible.

Finally, if the third opinion finds that employees do not have a serious health condition, the employer may be faced with difficult decisions. If employees have been taking intermittent leave and the third opinion concludes that they do not have a serious health condition, the decision to take action, such as termination, should be relatively defensible because the absences would not be protected. This presumes that the employer has a reasonably well-defined attendance policy that has been consistently applied. On the other hand, if employees have missed a block of time while the issues were being sorted out, that time cannot be counted against their FMLA entitlement, but it may not be equitable or in accordance with policy to terminate them. In this circumstance, the employer is sometimes better off assuming the time was FMLA qualifying so that it could be counted.

Fortunately, current limits placed on the free exchange of relevant employee medical information can be addressed. Unquestionably, employers must have greater access to employees' health care providers to resolve any questions arising in conjunction with the employees' medical certification. Employers should not be forced to incur unnecessary medical expenses simply because employees will not permit them to speak to employees' doctors. If employers were allowed to communicate with employees' providers directly, employers could ensure that providers had an accurate understanding of the physical requirements of their patients' jobs and had been fully apprised of other relevant information, such as the pattern and frequency of employees' absences.

At the same time, employers must limit their inquiry to employees' reason for requesting FMLA leave. They should not be able to request medical documentation beyond the information required on the medical certification form. If, however, employers still find it necessary to send an employee for a second/third opinion, employees should be required to produce all relevant medical records to the second/third opinion doctors. These records must be returned to the employees or their health care providers after the doctors have completed their reports and must be kept confidential in accordance with applicable law, unless specifically released to the employers.

Revise the Notice Requirements Raised by *Ragsdale* to Make Them Less Onerous for Employers

In 2002 the U.S. Supreme Court invalidated the following portion of the regulation, 29 C.F.R. § 825.700(a): "If an employee takes paid or unpaid leave and the employer does not designate the leave as FMLA leave, the leave taken does not count against an employee's FMLA entitlement." Another portion of the regulations, §825.301(b)(2), requires employers to notify employees of their rights and obligations under the FMLA within one to two business days of learning of the need for FMLA leave.[75] The Supreme Court's reason for striking down the first provision as contrary to the act and beyond the DOL's authority was twofold. First, the regulation relieved employees of the burden of providing any proof that their rights had been impaired or that they were prejudiced by the employer's failure to properly designate their leave. Second, it amended the act's most fundamental right—the guaranteed twelve work weeks of leave during any twelve-month period.[76] The employer in *Ragsdale* had provided much more leave than the twelve weeks the FMLA requires but had not specifically designated the leave as FMLA-qualifying.

Following the decision in *Ragsdale*, federal courts have held that employees have no claim against employers for failing to designate leave on a timely basis unless the employees can show that they were prejudiced by the employers' actions or would have exercised their rights under the FMLA differently had proper notice been given. In the dozen or so cases that have been decided since *Ragsdale*, most employees have been unable to satisfy this burden—usually because they were medically unable to return to work after exhausting their leave rights.[77]

The quoted section of §825.700(a) should be removed from the regulations. Additionally, §825.301(b)(2) should be revised to allow a longer time period for notice to be sent, for example, ten business days instead of the current one to two. Furthermore, the regulations should be revised so that employers are not penalized for failing to timely or properly designate employees' leave as long as employees receive the substantive benefits of the act (i.e., job-protected leave and continuation of benefits). Thus, the regulations should not arbitrarily impose any penalty on employers who fail to provide proper notice. This construction is consistent with the Supreme Court's analysis in *Ragsdale*.

Curb the Abuse of Intermittent Leave

Intermittent and reduced-schedule leave are often used interchangeably because they both connote leave taken on a less than full-time basis. As the FMLA has evolved, intermittent leave generally refers to unplanned sporadic leave, most often for a chronic serious health condition. Reduced work schedule leave, on the other hand, generally is a regular part-time arrangement needed to accommodate planned medical treatment(s) or employees' inability to work a full-time schedule. Of the two forms of part-time leave, unplanned intermittent leave is the more difficult for employers to administer. Both types are available to employees if they are experiencing—or their covered family members are dealing with—a serious health condition, provided that intermittent or reduced leave is medically necessary. Conversely, employees who wish to take intermittent or reduced leave due to the birth of a child, adoption, or foster care placement must obtain their employers' permission before taking such leave.[78]

Currently, employers cannot compel employees to take more time off than is necessary.[79] The only limitation the regulations allow is an employer "may limit leave increments to the shortest period of time that the employer's payroll system uses to account for absences or use of leave, provided it is one hour or less."[80] For some employers, this increment of time can be as small as fifteen minutes.[81]

Unplanned intermittent leave presents a serious problem for many employers, who often struggle to keep track of employees' intermittent leave usage and who, with little or no advance warning, must scramble to meet their staffing needs. Unlike the Americans with Disabilities Act, the FMLA has no hardship component. So if a high percentage of employees in a department or on a work shift have certifications for intermittent leave, employers have few choices. As employees become more sophisticated in their understanding of the FMLA, an increasing problem is that a small percentage use intermittent leave to make an end run around their employers' policies. Some request intermittent leave to avoid written warnings or other disciplinary measures for tardiness.[82] Others claim they cannot work overtime due to an FMLA-qualifying reason or use intermittent leave on weekends, before holidays, or on other undesirable shifts at the last minute. Because such leave can be taken with little or no warning, employers exercise minimal control over the time when employees take it. Although the legislative history suggests that intermittent leave was expected to be used for such scheduled activities as radiation therapy, chemotherapy, and dialysis, in practice it has been used primarily for unscheduled leaves associated with chronic serious health conditions, such as migraine headaches, backaches, depression, and allergies.[83]

Furthermore, even though the regulations require employees and employers to cooperate to devise intermittent leave schedules that are not "unduly disruptive" to employers' operations, this presumes that employees know ahead of time when they need to take intermittent leave, which is generally not the case.[84] The only other tool employers have to minimize the disruption caused by employees certified to take intermittent leave is to reassign them to other positions that may better accommodate their unplanned and reoccurring absences.[85] But here again, the regulations speak in terms of transfer for planned medical treatment and do not expressly permit transfer for unplanned intermittent leave takers whom employers probably want to transfer. The regulation should be changed to allow transfer in this situation.

If employers question the legitimacy of employees' needs for intermittent leave, the regulations enumerate circumstances in which employees can be asked to recertify their continued need for intermittent leave for a pregnancy or a chronic or permanent/long-term serious health condition.[86] In 2004, the DOL issued an advisory opinion letter in which it provided further clarification on when employers can request recertification.[87]

Generally, employers may not seek a recertification before the conclusion of the stated duration of the medical condition as set forth in the original certification supporting an employee's request for intermittent leave.[88] If the original request stated that the duration was unknown or unspecified, with some exceptions, employers may ask for recertification no more than every thirty days and only in connection with an employee's absence.[89] Exceptions are provided by regulation 29 C.F.R. § 825.308, which states that employers are allowed to request recertification at "any reasonable interval" (less than thirty days) in any of the following circumstances: (1) the employee seeks to extend the period of time during which intermittent leave is needed, (2) the medical condition or circumstances related to it have changed significantly since the original request was made, or (3) employers receive information casting doubt on the employee's reason for leave.[90] The DOL's advisory opinion letter further provides that employers may ask for recertification for intermittent leave more often than every thirty days if their request is made in conjunction with an employee's absence, the basis for which is questionable due to a suspicious pattern of occurring immediately before or after a weekend or holiday.[91]

The current regulatory scheme has placed few restraints on intermittent leave usage, according to the EPF's survey. Overall, in 2004, the EPF survey found that 20 percent of all FMLA leave taken was for periods of one day or less. Nearly half of those taking FMLA leave in 2004 did so more than once, with nearly 15 percent taking six or more leaves within the year.[92] Chronic serious health conditions account for a vast majority of the intermittent leave used, according to the EPF's survey.[93] As mentioned earlier, a staggering 58 percent of the workers taking FMLA leave in the transportation industry, followed by 42 percent of telecommunication workers, did so for a chronic health condition.[94]

Another way to control intermittent leave abuse is to insist that employees take leave in blocks of time no less than a half day. This would dissuade employees who use their intermittent leave to sidestep their employer's attendance policies (to avoid disciplinary action for arriving late to work) and encourage them to be more selective about when they take their leave. Requiring employees to take their intermittent leave in larger time blocks also should facilitate employer tracking of employee FMLA leave usage.

Abuse of intermittent leave also can be reduced by requiring employees (and their health care providers) to give more specific guidance about how much leave is anticipated. Currently, many intermittent leave takers provide certifications that simply say the need for leave is "unknown" or "lifelong" with no estimate of the number of days off to be taken or the frequency of the absences. This sort of certification provides carte blanche for employees who have no desire to work full-time but want to maintain full-time health benefits.

Employee advocates do not favor policy changes discussed in the previous paragraphs. They believe that the incidence of abuse is negligible and that employees with a legitimate basis for taking intermittent leave will be the only ones to suffer if such modifications are made. Furthermore, employee advocates argue that employees could exhaust their intermittent leave allotment before their need for such leave lapses if they are required to use more than they actually need.[95] Currently, many employees never exhaust their intermittent leave because they may take it in such small time increments.[96] Although some employees may be penalized if forced to take intermittent leave in fixed units of time or provide more detail about the scope of their leaves, the current regulatory scheme is neither practical nor workable.

Allow Employers to Require Light Duty as an Alternative to FMLA Leave

The regulations now provide that employers cannot mandate that employees who have asked for FMLA leave remain at work in a light-duty capacity, even if the position is within the employees' work restrictions.[97] The DOL unnecessarily focuses on the fact that employees would have to transfer to jobs that do not contain the same essential functions as their permanent position to explain why they should not be compelled to remain at work on light duty due to their reassignment rights. This reading ignores the reality of today's workplace.[98]

Regulations should be amended to permit employers to require employees to accept light-duty job assignments when employees' physicians agree that workers can perform duties of the alternative job assignment safely. Though this change in policy might seem to run counter to the act's purpose, which is to provide protected leave to employees, it enables the parties to consider reasonable and legitimate ways to keep employees on the job or allow them to return from leave at an earlier date without jeopardizing their health. By offering light duty as a legitimate alternative to taking leave, employers regain some of the control to address staffing needs that they have lost.

Allow Employers to Obtain Second/Third Opinions after a Recertification

The regulations prohibit employers from obtaining a second/third opinion after employees have provided a recertification of their serious health condition.[99] Unfortunately, in some situations, employers may have accepted the original certification without challenge only to have issues regarding the duration, frequency, and legitimacy of the absences arise after recertification. The regulation arbitrarily prohibits a second/third opinion in such cases, which severely limits employers' rights to challenge the legitimacy of employees' continued rights to FMLA leave. This section of the regulations should be amended to allow a second/third opinion after a recertification is received on the same basis that second/third opinions are permitted for the initial certification.[100]

CONCLUSION

The FMLA has been in effect for thirteen years. In many ways, it works very well, and most employees who take advantage of its provisions do so legitimately and as Congress intended. To address instances where employees have used (and abused) the FMLA in ways never intended, additional safeguards should be built into the regulations so employers can make sure that leave being taken is in accordance with the law. Only then will the FMLA truly accomplish its stated purpose of providing a balance for employees "in a manner that accommodates the legitimate interests of employers."[101]

NOTES

The author extends her deep gratitude to Ina R. Silvergleid, whose assistance in the preparation of this chapter was invaluable.

1. 29 U.S.C.A. §§ 2601–2654 (1999).
2. 535 U.S. 81 (2002)
3. Statement by President Bill Clinton upon Signing H.R. 1 [FMLA] (Feb. 5, 1993), reprinted in 1993 U.S.C.C.A.N. (United States Codes Congressional Record and Administrative News) 54, 55 (hereafter "President's Statement").

4. S. Rep. No. 103-3, at 19 (1993), reprinted in 1993 U.S.C.C.A.N. 21 (hereafter "Senate Report").

5. Ibid.

6. Ibid.

7. President's Statement, 55.

8. Ibid.

9. Ibid.

10. Senate Report, 51–53.

11. Ibid.

12. Ibid. The Senate Report did not specify whether these laws covered employees in the private or public sector.

13. Currently, the following states have laws mandating some form of family or medical leave for workers in the private sector: California, Colorado, Connecticut, Hawaii, Iowa, Kansas, Kentucky, Louisiana, Maine, Maryland, Massachusetts, Minnesota, Montana, New Hampshire (law does not mandate a fixed amount of leave, requires that employer allow employee leave for a temporary disability related to pregnancy or childbirth), New Jersey, New York, Ohio (regulation does not mandate a fixed amount of leave, provides that women are entitled to a reasonable period of leave for childbearing), Oklahoma, Oregon, Pennsylvania, Rhode Island, South Carolina (similar to Ohio, regulation provides that an employer cannot deny an employee maternity leave), Tennessee, Vermont, Washington, and Wisconsin. Some of these laws only provide leave for women in conjunction with the birth of a child. This list does not include those states that have passed laws covering leave for organ/bone marrow donors, crime or domestic violence victims, school visitation.

14. FMLA enforcement data is available online at www.dol.gov/esa/whd/statistics/200411.htm.

15. Ibid.

16. Ibid.

17. Ibid.

18. Ibid.

19. "Balancing the Needs of Families and Employers: Family and Medical Leave Surveys," U.S. Dept. of Labor (2000) (hereafter "2000 Survey Update"); "A Workable Balance: Report to Congress on Family and Medical Leave Policies," U.S. Dept. of Labor (1996) (hereafter "Workable Balance Report"). Because the 2000 Survey Update summarizes much of the findings contained in the earlier report, this chapter will cite primarily the later report because it presents the 1995 and 2000 findings in tables that allow the reader to compare the data for the two years.

20. 2000 Survey Update.

21. Ibid., 3-3, 11; A-2-21.

22. Ibid. A-2-1, 2-3; 2-14, 16.

23. Ibid., 3-3, 11; A-2-21.

24. Ibid., A-2-1; 2-3.

25. Ibid., 2-14.

26. Ibid., 2-16.

27. Ibid., A-2-4.

28. Ibid.

29. Ibid.

30. Ibid.
31. Ibid.
32. Ibid.
33. Ibid.
34. Ibid.
35. Ibid., A-2-62.
36. Ibid.
37. Ibid., A-2-61.
38. Ibid., 2-4, 6.
39. Ibid., 1-9, 3-3; A-2-21.
40. Ibid., 3-14.
41. Ibid., 2-16.
42. Ibid., 6-11.
43. Ibid., 6-9.
44. Ibid.
45. Workable Balance Report, App. E, table 6.A.
46. 2000 Survey Update, 2-11, 12.
47. Ibid., 2-13.
48. Ibid., A-2-59.
49. SHRM 2003 FMLA Survey. This survey can be obtained from the SHRM Web site, www.shrm.org.
50. Similar findings were made by Commerce Clearing House (CCH) in its annual *Unscheduled Absence Survey for 2003*. The CCH survey found that 38 percent of unscheduled absences were taken for a personal illness, and 23 percent of unscheduled absences were taken for family reasons.
51. EPF, Issue Backgrounder, *The Cost and Characteristics of Family and Medical Leave* (April 19, 2005) (hereafter "EPF Survey"). The Issue Backgrounder is available online at www.epf.org.
52. Testimony by Nancy McKeague on behalf of the SHRM and the FMLA Technical Corrections Coalition, before the Government Reform Committee Subcommittee on Energy Policy, Natural Resources and Regulatory Affairs, U.S. House of Representatives (Nov. 17, 2004), 3 (hereafter "McKeague Testimony").
53. The Family and Medical Leave Act of 1993, Summary of Major Comments, Subparts A-F, 60 *Fed. Reg.* 2180, 6658, 16,382 (1995).
54. Nucleus Solutions, *The State of FMLA: How to Get a Handle on the Family Medical Leave Act* (Dec. 2001), reprinted June 2003.
55. 29 U.S.C.A. § 2611(11).
56. Senate Report, 30.
57. 29 C.F.R. § 825.114(a)(2)(i)(A)–(B) (2004). To date, the U.S. Supreme Court has declined to address the reasonableness of the DOL's construction of serious health condition. The two federal courts of appeal to consider this question upheld the department's rule-making authority. See *Miller v. AT&T Corp.*, 250 F.3d 820 (4th Cir. 2001) (found that department's definition of "treatment" was not overly broad and that § 825.114 did not contravene the underlying purpose of the statute); *Thorson v. Gemini, Inc.*, 205 F.3d 370 (8th Cir.), cert. denied, 531 U.S. 871 (2000).
58. Opinion FMLA-57 (April 7, 1995).
59. Ibid.

60. Opinion FMLA-86 (Dec. 12, 1996).

61. Ibid.

62. Ibid.

63. Ibid.

64. 29 C.F.R. § 825.114(c).

65. McKeague Testimony, 5.

66. See, e.g., *Miller* (flu); *Thorson v. Gemini, Inc.*, 205 F.3d 370 (8th Cir.), cert. denied, 531 U.S. 871 (2000) (diarrhea and stomach cramps); *Wheeler v. Pioneer Developmental Servs.*, 2004 U.S. Dist. LEXIS 24960 (D. Mass. Dec. 8, 2004) (upper respiratory infection); *Corcino v. Banco Popular De P.R.*, 200 F. Supp. 2d 507 (D.V.I. 2002) (pharyngitis); *Summerville v. Esco Co.*, 52 F. Supp. 2d 804 (W.D. Mich. 1999) (heel spurs).

67. SHRM 2003 FMLA Survey, found that more than half (52 percent) of the human resources professionals questioned had granted FMLA requests that they did not believe were legitimate, in response to the DOL's shifting interpretations of the regulations.

68. Comments of Hallmark Cards, Inc. on the Implementation of the Family and Medical Leave Act Submitted to the Committee of Education and the Workforce Subcommittee on Oversight and Investigations, U.S. House of Representatives (June 10, 1997), 6–8 (hereafter "Hallmark Cards Comments").

69. Ibid.

70. 29 C.F.R. § 825.307(a)(2); Hallmark Cards Comments, 10–11.

71. The one exception to this rule arises where the employee's FMLA leave runs concurrently with his or her worker's compensation leave, and the state worker's compensation statute permits the employer to have direct contact with the employee's physician, the employer may follow the state statute. 29 C.F.R. § 825.307(a)(1).

72. 29 C.F.R. § 825.307(a).

73. There is a split in the case law as to whether an employer's failure to go through the second/third opinion process is a waiver of the employer's right to challenge whether an employee has a serious health condition at the litigation stage. See, e.g., *Rhoads v. FDIC*, 257 F.3d 373 (4th Cir. 2001), cert. denied, 535 U.S. 933 (2002) (no waiver found; ruling at odds with court's earlier decision in *Thorson*); *Stekloff v. St. John's Mercy Health Sys.*, 218 F.3d 858 (8th Cir. 2000) (no waiver found); *Thorson v. Gemini, Inc.*, 205 F.3d 370 (8th Cir. 2000) (waiver found); *Wheeler v. Pioneer Developmental Servs.*, 2004 U.S. Dist. LEXIS 24960 (D. Mass. Dec. 8, 2004) (waiver found); *Dillaway v. Ferrante*, 2003 U.S. Dist. LEXIS 23468 (D. Minn. Dec. 9, 2003) (no waiver found); *Smith v. Univ. of Chi. Hosps.*, 2003 U.S. Dist. LEXIS 20965 (N.D. Ill. Nov. 20, 2003) (waiver found); *Porter v. N.Y. Univ. Sch. of Law*, 2003 U.S. Dist. LEXIS 14674 (S.D.N.Y. Aug. 22, 2003) (no waiver found).

74. Hallmark Cards Comments, 11.

75. 29 C.F.R.§825.301(b)(2).

76. *Ragsdale*, 89, 93–95.

77. See, e.g., *Conoshenti v. Public Serv. Elec. & Gas Co.*, 364 F.3d 135 (3d Cir. 2004) (found that plaintiff may have exercised his FMLA rights differently if properly notified); *Fogleman v. Greater Hazleton Health Alliance*, 2004 U.S. App. LEXIS 26861 (3d Cir. Dec. 23, 2004) (no prejudice found); *Duty v. Norton-Alcoa Proppants*, 293 F.3d 481 (8th Cir. 2002) (affirmed jury award for employee who detrimentally relied on employer's erroneous statement regarding his FMLA rights); *Miller v. Personal-Touch of*

Va., Inc., 342 F. Supp. 2d 499 (E.D. Va. 2004) (no interference with plaintiff's FMLA rights found); *Wright v. Owens-Illinois, Inc.*, 2004 U.S. Dist. LEXIS 8535 (S.D. Ind. May 14, 2004) (no harm to plaintiff found); *Roberts v. Owens-Illinois, Inc.*, 2004 U.S. Dist. LEXIS 8534 (S.D. Ind. May 14, 2004) (no prejudice found); *Donahoo v. Master Data Ctr.*, 282 F. Supp. 2d 540 (E.D. Mich. 2003) (no prejudice found); *Farina v. Compuware Corp.*, 256 F. Supp. 2d 1033 (D. Ariz. 2003) (no prejudice or detrimental reliance found); *Phillips v. Leroy-Somer N. Am.*, 2003 U.S. Dist. LEXIS 5349 (W.D. Tenn. Mar. 28, 2003) (no prejudice found); *Kelso v. Corning Cable Sys. Int'l Corp.*, 224 F. Supp. 2d 1052 (W.D.N.C. 2002) (no prejudice found); *Summers v. Middleton & Reutlinger, P.S.C.*, 214 F. Supp. 2d 751 (W.D. Ky. 2002) (no prejudice found).

78. 29 C.F.R. § 825.203.

79. 29 C.F.R. § 825.203(d).

80. Ibid.

81. Eric Lekus, "Two Hundred Organizations Sign Letter Urging DOL to Keep Leave FMLA Intact," *Daily Labor Report* 72 (April 15, 2005): A-10.

82. Fawn H. Johnson, "'Roundtable' Panel Debates Usefulness of 'Intermittent Leave' in Family Leave Law," *Daily Labor Report* 121 (June 24, 2005): A-10; Stephanie Armour, "Family, Medical Leave Act at Center of Hot Debate," *USA Today* (May 25, 2005), available online at www.usatoday.com/money/employment/2005-05-05-medical-leave-usat_x.htm.

83. McKeague Testimony, 8; Senate Report, 28.

84. 29 C.F.R. § 825.302(f).

85. 29 C.F.R. § 825.204.

86. 29 C.F.R. § 825.308.

87. Opinion FMLA 2004-2-A (May 25, 2004).

88. 29 C.F.R. § 825.308(b)(2).

89. 29 C.F.R. § 825.308(a).

90. 29 C.F.R. § 825.308(c).

91. In addition to these scenarios, a DOL pronouncement by Michael Ginley, Office of Enforcement Policy, confirmed that effective May 25, 2004, the DOL would "not cite an employer's request for a new medical certification in conjunction with the employee's first absence in a new 12-month period as a violation of section 103 of the FMLA." This allows an employer to seek a second/third opinion, even though there may have been a recertification in the prior leave year. See also Opinion FMLA-112 (Sept. 11, 2000) (if an employer calculates an employee's entitlement to FMLA leave as of the date the employee takes leave, an employer can seek recertification twelve months from the date the employee's intermittent leave commenced).

92. EPF Survey, 2.

93. Ibid., 2-3.

94. Ibid.

95. Lekus, "Two Hundred Organizations."

96. Hallmark Cards Comments, 13; Eric Lekus, "Business Groups Urge DOL to Reopen Regulations, Reform Medical Leave Rules," *Daily Labor Report* 71 (April 14, 2005): A-9.

97. 29 C.F.R. §§ 825.207(d)(2), 825.702(d)(1).

98. See, e.g., *Artis v. Palos Community Hosp.*, 2004 U.S. Dist. LEXIS 20150 (N.D. Ill. Sept. 22, 2004). In that case, the court granted summary judgment to the employer

despite a last-minute argument by the plaintiff that she was coerced into remaining at work in a light-duty position after a work-related injury resulted in restrictions in the performance of her duties as a certified nursing assistant. The court reasoned that the employee was not released to return to her former position until more than twenty weeks had elapsed from when she suffered her injury, and therefore the employee was afforded greater job protection than she was entitled to under the act.

   99. 29 C.F.R. § 825.308(e).

   100. 29 C.F.R. § 825.307 allows for a second/third opinion where the employer has reason to doubt the validity of the certification. As noted (EPF Survey, 2), it is permissible to require a "new" certification once twelve months have elapsed from the date of the original certification.

   101. 29 U.S.C. § 2601(b).

7

Gender and Managerial Stereotypes: Have the Times Changed?

Gary N. Powell, D. Anthony Butterfield, and Jane D. Parent

Stereotyping of group members may occur on the basis of gender, race, and ethnicity as well as many other dimensions of diversity. In this chapter, we examine stereotypes of the managerial role in relation to gender stereotypes. How well do gender stereotypes, which represent stereotypical views of male–female differences in general, apply to the managerial ranks in particular? We know that the face of management has changed considerably over the last quarter-century. That face is now female at least 40 percent of the time in at least twenty countries from A (Argentina, Australia) to U (United Kingdom, United States) (Powell & Graves, 2003). As an example of the magnitude of change, the proportion of women managers in the United States increased from 26 percent in 1980 to 45 percent in 2000. No matter what the starting point, the trend in almost all countries has been in the same direction, toward the increased representation of women in the managerial ranks. Have these changes in the face of management led to changes in views of what constitutes a good manager to incorporate a greater emphasis on "feminine" traits associated with women or a lesser emphasis on "masculine" traits associated with men? The study reported in this chapter, which is the third in a series of studies conducted since the mid-1970s, addresses this question.

There has been a considerable increase in the proportion of women managers in recent years, from 21 percent in 1976 to 46 percent in 1999, and a call for "feminine leadership" to capitalize on this increase. The present study examines whether there has been a corresponding change in men's and women's stereotypes of managers such that less emphasis is placed on managers' possessing masculine characteristics. Data from 348 undergraduate and part-time graduate business students indicate that although managerial stereotypes place less emphasis on masculine characteristics than in earlier studies (Powell & Butterfield, 1979, 1989), a good manager is still perceived as predominantly masculine.

Stereotypes are "beliefs about the characteristics, attributes, and behaviors of members of certain groups" (Hilton & von Hippel, 1996, p. 240). Stereotyping is an enduring human phenomenon (Fiske, 1998), partly because stereotypes are so convenient to use. For example, stereotypes may be used to simplify the demands on the perceiver. They make information processing easier by allowing people to substitute previously acquired information for incoming information. When people are identifiable as members of a larger group (e.g., the male or female sex), stereotyping makes it easier for others to remember and categorize them (Klatzky & Anderson, 1988). Stereotypes may also be used to justify the current assignment of social roles. However, stereotypes often operate to the disadvantage of women in work settings (Carli & Eagly, 1999; Deaux & La-France, 1998). Consider the case of managerial stereotypes.

In prior studies (Powell & Butterfield, 1979, 1989), women and men have described a good manager as possessing predominantly masculine characteristics that are traditionally associated with males (e.g., assertiveness, independence, and willingness to take risks). Thus, women who aspire to management positions have to contend with common stereotypes of being unfit for the role. These stereotypes disadvantage women at all levels of management (Powell, 1999). When decision makers believe that masculine characteristics are best suited for managerial roles and that men possess these characteristics in greater abundance than women, they are more likely to select men for open management positions than equally qualified women (Heilman, 1995); they are also likely to evaluate male managers more favorably than female managers who have exhibited equivalent performance (Bartol, 1999; Heilman, 1983; Nieva & Gutek, 1980). Further, women who hold these beliefs may hold back in seeking management positions (Powell & Butterfield, 1979). However, since the mid-1970s, there has been a considerable increase in the proportion of women in management (U.S. Department of Labor, Bureau of Labor Statistics, 1983, 1999) and a call for "feminine leadership," that is, a greater emphasis in management on feminine characteristics that are traditionally associated with females (e.g., compassion, sensitivity to the needs of others, and understanding), to take advantage of this increase (e.g., Helgesen, 1990; Loden, 1985; Rosener, 1995). The purpose of this study was to examine whether there has been a corresponding change in men's and women's stereotypes of managers such that less emphasis is placed on managers' possessing masculine characteristics.

STEREOTYPES

Stereotypes tend to be durable over time (Hamilton & Sherman, 1994). This is because stereotypes are reinforced by both cognitive and social mechanisms. According to a cognitive perspective of stereotyping, individuals categorize people into groups and then develop self-enhancing beliefs about the attributes held in common by members of different groups, including their own (Ashforth & Humphrey, 1995; Tajfel & Turner, 1986); these beliefs in turn act as self-fulfilling prophecies through processes of expectancy confirmation (Darley & Fazio, 1980; Merton, 1948). According to a sociocultural perspective of stereotyping, individuals learn stereotypes of different groups in their formative years from their parents, teachers, and other significant adults in their lives as well as from the public media (Hamilton & Sherman, 1994).

Both of these perspectives have been supported in research on gender stereotypes. Stereotypes of males and females have remained essentially stable over time in different cultures, even as attitudes about women's rights and roles have changed (Deaux & Kite, 1993; Deaux & LaFrance, 1998; Williams & Best, 1990). In general, research on gender stereotypes reveals that people consider women to have more communal qualities (e.g., are more gentle, kind, supportive, expressive, affectionate, and tactful) and men more agentic qualities (e.g., are more assertive, competitive, daring, and courageous) (Broverman et al., 1972; Carli & Eagly, 1999; Deaux & Kite, 1993; Williams & Best, 1990).

However, stereotypes may change over time in the presence of disconfirming information. Rothbart (1981) distinguished between two models of stereotype change—the bookkeeping model and the conversion model. According to the bookkeeping model, stereotypes are continually open to revision as new pieces of information, either confirming or disconfirming, are received; stereotypes change gradually if there is a steady stream of disconfirming information. According to the conversion model, stereotypes change suddenly in response to highly salient and critical pieces of disconfirming information. Thus, if new information about the accuracy of a particular stereotype has been moderately disconfirming, the bookkeeping model would predict modest change in the stereotype, and the conversion model would predict no change. If new information has overwhelmingly discredited the stereotype, both models would predict substantial change in it.

A third model of stereotype change focuses on the typing of group members. When a few members of a group do not conform to the group stereotype, the observer may break down the larger group into subgroups and categorize the small group exhibiting the unexpected behavior as "deviants." This cognitive response enables preservation of the general stereotype for the group through the establishment of subgroup stereotypes (Weber & Crocker, 1983). Further, an exemplar-based model assumes that stereotypes consist of representations of specific individuals; thus, stereotypes may change as new exemplars replace and differ in personal characteristics from earlier exemplars (Smith & Zárate, 1992).

However, the literature on stereotypes has placed far greater emphasis on cognitive processes that reinforce the durability of stereotypes than their changeability (e.g., Darley & Fazio, 1980; Fiske, 1998; Hamilton & Sherman, 1994; Merton, 1948). In general, it is assumed that it is easier for an individual to maintain a stereotype than to change it (Hilton & von Hippel, 1996).

GENDER STEREOTYPES AND MANAGERIAL STEREOTYPES

In this section, we review prior research on the relationship between gender stereotypes and managerial stereotypes. Note that our concern is with gender stereotypes, not with fundamental conceptualizations of sex, gender, or androgyny, about which there has been much controversy. See Korabik (1999) for a recent review of this controversy.

There have been two streams of research on the relationship between gender stereotypes and managerial stereotypes (see Butterfield & Grinnell, 1999). Schein (1973, 1975) initiated one stream when she hypothesized that gender stereotyping impeded the progress of women in management through the creation of occupational sex typing: since the vast majority of managers were men, the managerial job could be classified as a masculine occupation calling for personal attributes thought to be more characteristic of men than women. In support of her hypothesis, she found that both male and female middle managers believed that a successful middle manager possessed personal characteristics that more closely matched beliefs about the characteristics of men in general than beliefs about the characteristics of women in general. In later studies, the managerial job was no longer sex-typed by female middle managers (Brenner et al., 1989) or female management students (Schein et al., 1989). In addition, sex typing of the managerial job was reduced when contextual information such as level of success was available. However, when women were depicted as managers, they were still seen as more different from successful managers than men (Heilman et al., 1989). The belief of "think manager— think male" seems to be a global phenomenon, especially among males (Schein & Mueller, 1992; Schein et al., 1996).

The other stream of research on the relationship between gender stereotypes and managerial stereotypes is the focus of this study. Bem (1974, 1975) directly challenged the traditional assumptions and beliefs that males were supposed to be masculine, females were supposed to be feminine, and anyone who fell in the middle or at the "wrong" end of the scale was maladjusted and in need of help (Broverman et al., 1972). She argued that masculinity and femininity should be regarded as independent dimensions rather than as opposite ends of the same dimension and that the concept of androgyny, defined as a high propensity toward both feminine and masculine characteristics, offered a more appropriate standard for both sexes than did the traditional standard for each sex. An association between androgyny and more effective behavior was soon observed in a variety of nonorganizational settings (e.g., Bem, 1975; Bem & Lenney, 1976; Spence et al., 1975). Powell and Butterfield (1979) applied Bem's concept of androgyny to individuals' concept of management. They asked part-time graduate business students (evening MBAs), nearly all of whom worked full-time, and undergraduate business students during 1976–77 to describe both themselves and a "good manager" using the Bem Sex Role Inventory (BSRI), the instrument Bem (1974) developed. In 1976, when they began their data collection, the proportion of women in management positions in the United States was 21 percent, an increase from 16 percent in 1970 (U.S. Department of Labor, Bureau of Labor Statistics, 1983). Based on Bem (1974, 1975) and the recent increase in the proportion of women in management, Powell and Butterfield (1979) hypothesized that a good manager would be seen as androgynous (i.e., high in both masculine and feminine characteristics). However, contrary to their hypothesis, a good manager was seen as possessing predominantly masculine characteristics by all groups of respondents, including undergraduate and part-time graduate males and females. Thus, a belief of "think manager—think masculine" prevailed in that study.

Powell and Butterfield (1989) conducted a replication of their original study during 1984–85 using a refined and abbreviated version of the original BSRI instrument called the Short BSRI (Bem, 1981); they also rescored their original results using only the items that belonged to the Short BSRI. In 1984, when this data collection effort began, the proportion of women in management in the United States was 35 percent (U.S. Department of Labor, Bureau of Labor Statistics, 1985), a considerable increase from 21 percent in 1976. Powell and Butterfield (1989) hypothesized that the further increase in the proportion of women in management since their earlier study would now lead to a good manager being viewed as androgynous. However, their new results were consistent in direction with their earlier results, even when the earlier results were rescored.

A good manager was still seen as possessing predominantly masculine characteristics by all groups of respondents. In fact, contrary to the bookkeeping, conversion, and exemplar-based models of stereotype change (Rothbart, 1981; Smith & Zárate,1992), some groups exhibited strengthened support since the earlier study for the belief that a good manager is masculine.

By 1999, the proportion of women managers in the United States was 46 percent (U.S. Department of Labor, Bureau of Labor Statistics, 1999), a further substantial increase from 35 percent in 1984. Having a woman manager has become a more routine and less novel experience for male and female subordinates. Thus, management as a whole should no longer be viewed as a sex-typed occupation; the managerial role is not as associated statistically with men as it once was. However, is the managerial role still associated with the possession of predominantly masculine characteristics?

If women truly bring a different set of personal characteristics to the managerial role than men, there may be a sufficient amount of new information disconfirming the belief in a good manager as masculine since the mid-1970s to cause a rethinking of managerial stereotypes. In this event, given that the proportion of women managers has more than doubled since 1976 and is now almost half of all managers, a change in managerial stereotypes should be predicted by the bookkeeping, conversion, and exemplar-based models of stereotype change (Rothbart, 1981; Smith & Zárate, 1992). Managerial stereotypes may place less emphasis on the masculine characteristics traditionally associated with men than in the past and greater emphasis on the feminine characteristics traditionally associated with women or an androgynous combination of characteristics (i.e., high in both masculine and feminine characteristics). Although there has been mixed evidence over three decades of research as to whether men and women differ as leaders (Butterfield & Grinnell, 1999), some recent evidence has supported the existence of such differences (e.g., Bass et al., 1996). Moreover, several writers (e.g., Grant, 1988; Helgesen, 1990; Loden, 1985; Rosener, 1990, 1995) have argued that organizations need to place greater emphasis on feminine characteristics associated with women managers (e.g., caring, compassionate, understanding, collaborative) to be successful in an increasingly diverse and competitive economic environment.

However, the top ranks of management are still male-dominated, and a glass ceiling that is keeping women as a group from reaching these ranks still seems to prevail (Catalyst, 2000b; Davidson & Cooper, 1992; Morrison & Von Glinow, 1990; Powell, 1999). For example, the proportion of women in corporate officer positions in Fortune 500 corporations, although much higher than in the 1970s (Epstein, 1975), is only 13 percent (Catalyst, 2000a).

If top managers still believe in and adhere to the traditional stereotype of managers as masculine, women as well as men may feel compelled to display personal characteristics that are consistent with this stereotype to be selected for and successful in managerial roles. If this were the case, there would be little reason to expect managerial stereotypes to have changed with the increased proportion of women managers or the increased call for an emphasis on feminine characteristics in management.

The present study was designed to explore these speculations further. It replicated Powell and Butterfield (1979, 1989) using the Short BSRI as an instrument. Consistent with the bookkeeping and conversion models of stereotype change (Rothbart, 1981), it was hypothesized that a good manager would be seen as possessing less masculine characteristics in 1999 than in 1984–85 (Powell & Butterfield, 1989) or 1976–77 (Powell & Butterfield, 1979).

METHOD

Data were collected in 1999 at two American universities from two groups of subjects who differed considerably in age, education, and work experience. One group consisted of 206 undergraduate business students; their mean age was 21.2 years, and 43 percent were female. The second group consisted of 142 part-time graduate business students (i.e., evening MBAs), nearly all of whom held full-time jobs. Their mean age was 31.7 years, and 44 percent were female.

The present study used these data in addition to data collected from the same two groups in 1984–85 (Powell & Butterfield, 1989) and 1976–77 (Powell & Butterfield, 1979).

The 1984–85 sample consisted of 201 undergraduate business students with a mean age of 20.9 years (57 percent were female) and 127 part-time MBA students with a mean age of 29.0 years (42 percent were female). The 1976–77 sample consisted of 574 undergraduate business students with a mean age of 20.7 years (30 percent were female) and 110 part-time MBA students with a mean age of 28.0 (18 percent were female).

Each respondent in the 1999 and 1984–85 samples completed the Short BSRI (Bem, 1981) both for him- or herself and for a good manager. The Short BSRI contains ten items characteristic of the masculine sex role stereotype, ten items characteristic of the feminine sex role stereotype, and ten filler items not associated exclusively with either stereotype.

The masculine items are: defend my own beliefs, independent, assertive, strong personality, forceful, have leadership abilities, willing to take risks, dominant, willing to take a stand, and aggressive. The feminine items are: affectionate, sympathetic, love children, eager to soothe hurt feelings, compassionate, understanding, warm, tender, sensitive to the needs of others, and gentle. The filler items are: moody, conceited, conscientious, reliable, jealous, tactful, truthful, secretive, adaptable, and conventional. Items were rated on a seven-point scale, ranging from "never or almost never true" (1) to "always or almost always true" (7).

Each respondent in the 1976–77 sample completed the Original BSRI (Bem, 1974) both for him- or herself and for a good manager. The Original BSRI included twenty items designated as masculine that were independently judged by both females and males to be more desirable in American society for a man than a woman and twenty items designated as feminine that were similarly judged to be more desirable for a woman than a man. It contained all of the items in the Short BSRI but contained twice as many items in each category. Only those items appearing in the Short BSRI were used in the present study. Masculinity and femininity items in the Original BSRI were selected for the Short BSRI to maximize both the internal consistency of the masculinity and femininity scales and the orthogonality between them (Bem, 1981). Also, some of the femininity items in the Original BSRI with relatively low social desirability ratings were excluded from the Short BSRI to make the overall social desirability of the masculine and feminine items more similar. For further discussion of the development of the Original BSRI and Short BSRI, see Bem (1974, 1981) and Powell and Butterfield (1989).

Masculinity and femininity "self-scores" were calculated for each respondent as the average of scores on the masculine and feminine items in his or her self-description. Coefficient alpha was 0.85 for the masculinity self-score and 0.87 for the femininity self-score. Median masculinity and femininity scores on the Short BSRI were calculated for the combined 1999, 1984–85, and 1976–77 samples. Undergraduate males, undergraduate females, graduate males, and graduate females were weighted equally for the purposes of calculating these median scores (Bem, 1981). Each respondent was then classified into an androgynous, masculine, feminine, or undifferentiated "self-group" according to his or her self-description as shown below.

Masculinity and femininity "good manager scores" were calculated from each respondent's description of a good manager using the same procedure as for the self-description. Coefficient alpha was 0.74 for the masculinity good manager score and 0.86 for the femininity good manager score. The good manager description was classified as androgynous, masculine, feminine, or undifferentiated according to the median masculinity and femininity self-scores, that is, relative to the same medians used to classify respondents into self-groups, to allow direct comparisons of how respondents described a good manager and themselves.

Thus, each respondent was classified into a "good manager group" as follows:

Femininity "self-score" or "good manager score"	Masculinity "self-score" or "good manager score"	
	Below median	*Above median*
Above median	Feminine	Androgynous
Below median	Undifferentiated	Masculine

It was possible that the results of the study would be at least in part a function of the differing percentages of women at each time period. To address this possibility, we used a random sample of respondents at each time period and level (undergraduate and part-time graduate) to equalize the percentage of women across time periods within each level. The sampling procedure is summarized first for undergraduates and then for graduates.

The average percentage of undergraduate women across the three time periods was 43 percent. However, the percentage of undergraduate women was lower than 43 percent in 1976–77 (30 percent), higher than 43 percent in 1984–85 (57 percent), and equal to 43 percent in 1999. Thus, for 1976–77, we used all of the undergraduate women and a random sample of the undergraduate men. For 1984–85, we used all of the undergraduate men and a random sample of the undergraduate women. For 1999, we used all of the undergraduate women and men in the sample.

The average percentage of graduate women across the three time periods was 35 percent. However, the percentage of graduate women was lower than 35 percent in 1976–77 (18 percent) and higher than 35 percent in 1984–85 (42 percent) and 1999 (44 percent). Thus, for 1976–77, we used all of the graduate women and a random sample of the graduate men. For 1984–85 and 1999, we used all of the graduate men and a random sample of the graduate women. Further analyses were conducted on these samples.

RESULTS

Table 7.1 presents good manager group and self-group distributions for undergraduate business students and part-time graduate business students sampled in each of the three periods of data collection. Table 7.2 presents mean masculinity and femininity good manager scores and self-scores for the same groups of students. Although the emphasis of this study was on changes in descriptions of a good manager over time, self-descriptions are reported for purposes of comparison. These two tables comprehensively display the newly obtained results of the present study as well as the results of the two earlier studies (Powell & Butterfield, 1979, 1989). Because (1) the median self-scores used to determine good manager group and self-group distributions were calculated for the combined samples across all time periods and (2) the sampling procedure resulted in the loss of some subjects at various time periods, the good manager group and self-group distributions for 1984–85 and 1976–77 differ from those reported previously by Powell and Butterfield (1979, 1989).

Further, because many comparisons were made across time (six comparisons for each type of distribution in Table 7.1, twelve comparisons for each type of score in Table 7.2), the possibility existed for a study-wise Type 1 error. To minimize this possibility, a Bonferroni-type adjustment was implemented, whereas a more stringent test of significance was used for each comparison to keep the level of significance across all comparisons at a reasonable level (Tabachnick & Fidell, 1989, p. 52). Specifically, each Chi-square test in Table 7.1 used a significance level of 0.01. In addition, one-way ANOVAs reported in Table 7.2 used the Bonferroni multiple comparison test at a significance level of 0.01. Since four comparisons were made at a time for each group of subjects (masculinity and femininity good manager scores and self-scores), the significance level for each comparison was equivalent to approximately 0.01/4, or 0.0025. A significance level of 0.01 was used for comparisons within the 1999 sample that are not reported in the tables.

We shall review the results for the 1999 sample first and then compare these results with those from earlier samples.

Results for the 1999 Sample

Both undergraduate business students and part-time graduate business students viewed a good manager as possessing predominantly masculine characteristics. Considering good manager group distributions as seen in Table 7.1, a good manager was described as masculine by 44.1 percent of undergraduate males, 52.3 percent of undergraduate females, 57.5 percent of graduate males, and 55.8 percent of graduate females; additional analyses indicated that all of these proportions were above random ($p < 0.01$). In contrast, a good manager was described as feminine by only 8.5 percent of undergraduate males,

TABLE 7.1. Good Manager Group and Self-Group Distributions

	Good Manager Group Distribution						Self-Group Distribution					
	1976–77		1984–85		1999		1976–77		1984–85		1999	
Sample	N	%	N	%	N	%	N	%	N	%	N	%
Undergraduate business students												
Total												
Androgynous	103	26.1	38	24.8	61	29.6	101	25.6	48	31.4	75	36.4
Masculine	212	53.7	100	65.4	98	47.6	65	16.5	44	28.8	44	21.4
Feminine	18	4.6	4	2.6	14	6.8	115	29.1	36	23.5	46	22.3
Undifferentiated	62	15.7	11	7.2	33	16.0	114	28.9	25	16.3	41	19.9
	395		153		206		395		153		206	
	$\chi^2_6 = 15.84^*$						$\chi^2_6 = 25.91^*$					
Males												
Androgynous	58	25.8	22	25.3	34	28.8	63	28.0	24	27.6	41	34.7
Masculine	121	53.8	54	62.1	52	44.1	46	50.4	34	39.1	26	22.0
Feminine	10	4.4	2	2.3	10	8.5	43	19.1	11	12.6	16	13.6
Undifferentiated	36	16.0	9	10.3	22	18.6	73	32.4	18	20.7	35	29.7
	225		87		118		225		87		118	
	$\chi^2_6 = 9.91$						$\chi^2_6 = 15.96^*$					
Females												
Androgynous	45	26.5	16	24.2	27	30.7	38	22.4	24	36.4	34	38.6
Masculine	91	53.5	46	69.7	46	52.3	19	11.2	10	15.2	18	20.5
Feminine	8	4.7	2	3.0	4	4.5	72	42.4	25	37.9	30	34.1
Undifferentiated	26	15.3	2	3.0	11	12.5	41	24.1	7	10.6	6	6.8
	170		66		88		170		66		88	
	$\chi^2_6 = 9.50$						$\chi^2_6 = 23.21^*$					

Part-time graduate business students

	N	%	N	%	N	%	N	%	N	%	N	%
Total												
Androgynous	15	26.3	22	19.3	21	17.1	13	22.8	25	21.9	25	20.3
Masculine	38	66.7	71	62.3	70	56.9	16	28.1	33	28.9	48	39.0
Feminine	0	0	2	1.8	3	2.4	15	26.3	28	24.6	29	23.6
Undifferentiated	4	7.0	19	16.7	29	23.6	13	22.8	28	24.6	21	17.1
	57		114		123		57		114		123	
	$\chi^2_6 = 9.89$						$\chi^2_6 = 4.27$					
Males												
Androgynous	11	29.7	12	16.2	13	16.3	7	18.9	14	18.9	16	20.0
Masculine	23	62.2	47	63.5	46	57.5	12	32.4	26	35.1	34	42.5
Feminine	0	0	2	2.7	3	3.8	11	29.7	12	16.2	14	17.5
Undifferentiated	3	8.1	13	17.6	18	22.5	7	18.9	22	29.7	16	20.0
	37		74		80		37		74		80	
	$\chi^2_6 = 7.44$						$\chi^2_6 = 5.46$					
Females												
Androgynous	4	20.0	10	25.0	8	18.6	6	30.0	11	27.5	9	20.9
Masculine	15	75.0	24	60.0	24	55.8	4	20.0	7	17.5	14	32.6
Feminine	0	0	0	0	0	0	4	20.0	16	40.0	15	34.9
Undifferentiated	1	5.0	6	15.0	11	25.6	6	30.0	6	15.0	5	11.6
	20		40		43		20		40		43	
	$\chi^2_4 = 4.79$						$\chi^2_6 = 7.17$					

Note: Chi-square values apply to the comparison of the distributions for the 1976–77, 1984–85, and 1999 samples.
* $p < 0.01$.

153

TABLE 7.2. Mean Good Manager Scores and Self-Scores

Sample	Good Manager Scores					Self-Scores				
	1 (1976–77)	2 (1984–85)	3 (1999)	F^a	Significant Contrasts[a]	4 (1976–77)	5 (1984–85)	6 (1999)	F^a	Significant Contrasts[b]
Undergraduate business students										
Total										
Masculinity	5.55	5.82	5.60	9.18*	1 < 2, 2 > 3	4.86	5.15	5.17	13.83*	4 < 5, 4 < 6
Femininity	4.87	4.73	4.96	3.48		5.29	5.26	5.42	2.20	
Males										
Masculinity	5.54	5.78	5.49	5.32*	1 < 2, 2 > 3	4.98	5.33	5.19	7.21*	4 < 5
Femininity	4.85	4.71	4.98	2.72		5.15	5.01	5.21	1.60	
Females										
Masculinity	5.57	5.87	5.74	5.90*	1 < 2	4.71	4.92	5.15	9.67*	4 < 6
Femininity	4.89	4.76	4.93	.97		5.48	5.58	5.70	2.62	
Part-time graduate business students										
Total										
Masculinity	5.69	5.55	5.41	4.93*	1 > 3	5.14	5.07	5.15	0.30	
Femininity	4.87	4.71	4.62	2.22		5.17	5.09	5.04	0.54	
Males										
Masculinity	5.67	5.48	5.41	2.24		5.13	5.08	5.17	0.28	
Femininity	4.88	4.67	4.66	1.12		5.16	4.86	4.93	2.04	
Females										
Masculinity	5.74	5.68	5.39	4.02		5.15	5.07	5.11	0.08	
Femininity	4.86	4.79	4.54	1.86		5.19	5.53	5.23	1.75	

[a] F-values apply to the comparison of the mean scores for the 1976–77, 1984–85, and 1999 samples.
[b] Pairwise mean scores were compared using the Bonferroni multiple comparison test ($p < 0.01$). Column numbers are used to designate the type of score and sample.
* $p < 0.01$.

4.5 percent of undergraduate females, 3.8 percent of graduate males, and no graduate females; all of these proportions were below random ($p < 0.01$).

Considering good manager scores as seen in Table 7.2 and consistent with these results, masculinity good manager scores were higher than femininity good manager scores for all groups ($p < 0.01$, results not reported).

Good manager group distributions (Table 7.1) did not differ according to gender for either undergraduates ($\chi_3^2 = 3.11$, $p > 0.01$) or graduates ($\chi_3^2 = 1.83$, $p > 0.01$). Also, self-group distributions did not differ according to gender for graduates ($\chi_3^2 = 5.45$, $p > 0.01$).

However, self-group distributions differed according to gender for under-graduates ($\chi_3^2 = 23.00$, $p < 0.01$); undergraduate females were more likely to classify themselves into the feminine self-group (34.1 percent) than under-graduate males (13.6 percent). The gender difference in self-group distributions for undergraduates was due to femininity self-scores (Table 7.2) being higher for females ($M = 5.70$) than males ($M = 5.21$, $t_{204} = -4.40$, $p < 0.01$); masculinity self-scores did not differ for undergraduate females ($M = 5.15$) and males ($M = 5.19$, $t_{204} = 0.38$, $p > 0.01$). As a result, undergraduate females tended to describe a good manager as less like themselves than undergraduate males did, specifically in feminine characteristics.

Comparison of Results for the Three Samples

Good manager group distributions (Table 7.1) differed between the 1999, 1984–85, and 1976–77 samples for undergraduate business students ($\chi_6^2 = 15.84$, $p < 0.01$). The proportion of undergraduates who described a good manager as masculine increased from 53.7 percent in 1976–77 to 65.4 percent in 1984–85 and then decreased to 47.6 percent in 1999.

Consistent with these differences, undergraduates' masculinity good manager scores (Table 7.2) were higher in 1984–85 ($M = 5.82$) than in 1976–77 ($M = 5.55$) or 1999 ($M = 5.60$); undergraduates' femininity good manager scores did not differ over time. Thus, in support of the hypothesis, undergraduates viewed a good manager as possessing less masculine characteristics in 1999 than in 1984–85. Contrary to the hypothesis, undergraduates tended to view a good manager as possessing similar amounts of masculine characteristics in 1976–77 and 1999.

Good manager group distributions (Table 7.1) did not differ over time for part-time graduate business students ($\chi_6^2 = 9.89$, $p > 0.01$), although the pro-portion of graduates who described a good manager as masculine decreased from 66.7 percent in 1976–77 to 62.3 percent in 1984–85 and 56.9 percent in 1999, and the proportion of graduates who described a good manager as undifferentiated increased from 7.0 percent in 1976–77 to 16.7 percent in 1984–85 and 23.6 percent in 1999. However, graduates' masculinity good manager scores (Table 7.2) declined over time ($M = 5.69$ in 1976–77 to $M = 5.41$ in 1999); graduates' femininity good manager scores did not vary over time. Thus, in support of the hypothesis, graduates viewed a good manager as possessing less masculine characteristics over time.

DISCUSSION

Have the times changed regarding the relationship between gender stereotypes and managerial stereotypes? Results for the 1999 sample, when compared with results for the 1984–85 sample (Powell & Butterfield, 1989) and the 1976–77 sample (Powell & Butterfield, 1979), suggest that the answer to this question is both yes and no. Despite the considerable increase in the proportion of women managers over this period of time (from 21 percent in 1976 to 46 percent in 1999) and the emergent call for a greater emphasis on feminine characteristics in management, men and women of varying age, education, and work experience still described a good manager as possessing predominantly masculine characteristics.

However, the preference for masculine characteristics decreased between 1984–85 and 1999 for undergraduate business students. Further, the preference for masculine characteristics decreased between 1976–77 and 1999 for part-time graduate business students. Thus, the hypothesis that a good manager would be seen in 1999 as possessing less masculine characteristics than in earlier years was generally supported; perhaps the increased proportion of women managers is beginning to have an effect. In summary, a comparison of results from all three samples suggests both persistence and change in the nature of managerial stereotypes over time.

Why have managerial stereotypes persisted in placing primary emphasis on masculine characteristics? Powerful forces serve to perpetuate existing stereotypes, whatever group of people is being stereotyped and whatever the content of its stereotype may be (Hamilton & Sherman, 1994; Hilton & von Hippel, 1996; Fiske, 1998). In the case of managerial stereotypes, men and women who are choosing a career track may not seek to be managers if they do not see themselves as fitting the prevailing stereotype of managers. In addition, organizations may only select applicants for entry-level managerial positions whom they see as adhering to managerial stereotypes. Further, organizations tend to exert strong pressures on their members to conform to ways acceptable to other members, particularly those in power. Despite the remarkable progress of women in attaining managerial positions over the last three decades, the proportion of women who have made it to the very top positions in organizations, that is, broken through the glass ceiling, remains small. Recall that the proportion of women in corporate officer positions in Fortune 500 companies, although minuscule in the 1970s (Epstein, 1975), is still only 13 percent (Catalyst, 2000a). Women's impact on managerial stereotypes may not be felt until more of them are in the top ranks of management. As long as predominantly masculine characteristics are highly valued in the top management ranks, all individuals who enter the management ranks at any level will be expected to act accordingly. Thus, forces of self-selection, organizational selection, and organizational socialization all contribute to managerial stereotypes acting as self-fulfilling prophecies (Darley & Fazio, 1980; Merton, 1948) and reinforce a belief in the good manager as masculine.

Why have managerial stereotypes changed in the direction of placing less emphasis on masculine characteristics? According to both the bookkeeping and conversion models of stereotype change, stereotypes are likely to change in the presence of massive amounts of disconfirming information (Rothbart, 1981). Some evidence (Butterfield & Grinnell, 1999) suggests that women bring a different set of personal characteristics to the managerial role than men. Since the proportion of women in management positions has approached that of men, female managers may feel that their increased strength in numbers gives them more license to be themselves without having to conform to traditional managerial stereotypes.

If female managers do not exhibit predominantly masculine characteristics when they are being themselves, they may be contributing as exemplars (Smith & Zárate, 1992) to a long-term change in managerial stereotypes.

In addition, the increased call for feminine leadership (Grant, 1988; Helgesen, 1990; Loden, 1985; Rosener, 1990, 1995) suggests that organizations benefit when their managers display a high amount of feminine characteristics. Today's workplace is characterized by an increased emphasis on self-management, empowerment, continuous improvement, and organizational learning (Cooper & Lewis, 1999). It has been suggested that organizations that are continually able to transform themselves will have the best chance of survival in the new millennium. Being a good manager has become less about competitiveness, aggression, and task orientation and more about good communication, coaching and people skills, and being intuitive and flexible, all stereotypically feminine characteristics (Cooper & Lewis, 1999). Some managers, whatever their gender and other personal characteristics may be, may have responded to these changing demands, thereby further disconfirming the belief in a good manager as masculine.

However, the decreased emphasis on masculine characteristics in managerial stereotypes over time did not necessarily imply an increased emphasis on feminine characteristics. Indeed, the endorsement of feminine characteristics by the two groups of respondents varied little over time. Instead, the more experienced, part-time graduate business students, most of whom were working full-time and likely to focus on their own jobs and work context, described a good manager as possessing significantly less masculine characteristics over time. As a result, although such respondents still tended to prefer a masculine manager overall, they were tending to display an increasing preference for an undifferentiated manager, or one low in both feminine and masculine characteristics. In addition, undergraduate business students in the 1999 sample, most of whom had little full-time work experience and may have been relying more on expectations than reality, described a good manager as possessing less masculine characteristics than those in the 1984–85 sample.

These results suggest that different groups of respondents may have been receiving similar messages but from different sources about what a good manager looks like. Undergraduate business students may have become particularly aware of the increase in the proportion of women in management between 1984–85 and 1999 from observing their parents and elders as well as from the public media.

Since there was a gender difference in self-descriptions, with women more inclined to assign themselves to the feminine self-group than men, female undergraduates may have thought that having more women in management would mean that a good manager is less masculine, if not more feminine. In contrast, part-time graduate business students were closer to business realities and did not differ according to gender in self-descriptions. They were more in a position to observe the influence of the continued male domination of the top ranks of management, which may have suppressed any inclinations that female managers at lower levels might have had to exhibit a greater amount of feminine characteristics than when their numbers were fewer. Extension of this research to include respondents at different managerial levels is recommended to provide insight into whether a good manager is seen in more masculine terms by managers at higher levels.

LIMITATIONS AND CONCLUSIONS

The limitations of this replication study should be noted. Butterfield and Grinnell (1999) concluded from a review of research on managerial stereotypes over three decades that context is extremely important in mitigating the effects of gender stereotypes. For example, factors such as the duration of managers' interactions with their subordinates, the level of success they have experienced in their jobs, and the nature of their managerial assignments affect the extent to which managers are viewed in gender-stereotypical terms. One drawback of the present study was that it lacked context. Extension of this line of research into specific organizational settings in which the influence of contextual effects can be examined is recommended. However, although context is an issue, graduate business students have experience and knowledge about the work setting that their undergraduate counterparts lack. This could explain why views of a good manager differed between the two types of respondents.

A further limitation of this study is that it relied on responses of student samples. However, this was not as serious a drawback. Similar data were collected in the past from actual managers in three insurance companies (Powell, 1993), with results indicating an overall preference for masculine characteristics as in the present and previous studies of business students (Powell & Butterfield, 1979,

1989). Although it is important to examine the views of practicing managers, their views of a good manager were likely to be consistent with those of part-time graduate business students, most of whom either already held or expected to hold managerial positions. Also, the views of undergraduate business students are of interest because of their implications for career choice. As in earlier samples, undergraduate females in the 1999 sample see a good manager as less like themselves than undergraduate males.

Given this perception, these women may be less inclined to pursue managerial careers than men with the same educational background, leading to a restricted supply of female applicants from which organizations may select entry-level managers compared with the supply of male applicants.

Finally, this study did not examine the cognitive and social mechanisms by which stereotypes develop and change. It suggested that consistent with the bookkeeping, conversion, and exemplar-based models of stereotype change (Rothbart, 1981; Smith & Zárate, 1992), the increased proportion of women in management and the increased call for feminine leadership in the workplace may have led to the decreased emphasis on masculine characteristics in managerial stereotypes. However, we did not collect the full data that would be necessary to demonstrate such a causal connection. Additional research on the mechanisms by which managerial stereotypes are developed and modified that directly tests prevailing theories of stereotype formation and change (e.g., Fiske, 1998; Hamilton & Sherman, 1994; Hilton & von Hippel, 1996; Rothbart, 1981; Smith & Zárate, 1992; Weber & Crocker, 1983) is recommended.

In conclusion, the question of what constitutes a good manager continues to be of interest both to organizational scholars and the general public. If the proportion of women in top management positions becomes more similar to the proportion of men in such positions or further evidence is accumulated about the advantages of feminine leadership to organizations, managerial stereotypes may continue to change in the direction of placing less emphasis on masculine characteristics. However, for the time being, managerial stereotypes continue to emphasize a belief of "think manager—think masculine."

NOTE

Adapted from Gary N. Powell et al., "Gender and Managerial Stereotypes," *Journal of Management* 28(2) (2002): 177–93, by permission of the publisher. Copyright © Elsevier Inc.

REFERENCES

Ashforth, B. E., & Humphrey, R. H. (1995). Labeling processes in the organization: Constructing the individual. In L. L. Cummings & B. M. Staw (Eds.), *Research in organizational behavior* (Vol. 17, pp. 413–461). Greenwich, CT: JAI Press.

Bartol, K. M. (1999). Gender influences on performance evaluations. In G. N. Powell (Ed.), *Handbook of gender and work* (pp. 165–178). Thousand Oaks, CA: Sage.

Bass, B. M., Avolio, B. J., & Atwater, L. (1996). The transformational and transactional leadership of men and women. *Applied Psychology: An International Review, 45,* 5–34.

Bem, S. L. (1974). The measurement of psychological androgyny. *Journal of Consulting and Clinical Psychology, 42,* 155–162.

Bem, S. L. (1975). Sex role adaptability: One consequence of psychological androgyny. *Journal of Personality and Social Psychology, 31,* 634–643.

Bem, S. L. (1981). *Bem sex role inventory: Professional manual.* Palo Alto, CA: Consulting Psychologists Press.

Bem, S. L., & Lenney, E. (1976). Sex typing and the avoidance of cross-sex behavior. *Journal of Personality and Social Psychology, 33,* 48–54.

Brenner, O. C., Tomkiewicz, J., & Schein, V. E. (1989). The relationship between sex role stereotypes and requisite management characteristics revisited. *Academy of Management Journal, 32,* 662–669.

Broverman, I. K., Vogel, S. R., Broverman, D. M., Clarkson, F. E., & Rosenkrantz, P. S. (1972). Sex role stereotypes: A current appraisal. *Journal of Social Issues, 28*(2), 59–78.

Butterfield, D. A., & Grinnell, J. P. (1999). "Re-viewing" gender, leadership, and managerial behavior: Do three decades of research tell us anything? In G. N. Powell (Ed.), *Handbook of gender and work* (pp. 223–238). Thousand Oaks, CA: Sage.

Carli, L. L., & Eagly, A. H. (1999). Gender effects on social influence and emergent leadership. In G. N. Powell (Ed.), *Handbook of gender and work* (pp. 203–222). Thousand Oaks, CA: Sage.

Catalyst. (2000a). *Census of women corporate officers and top earners.* New York: Catalyst.

Catalyst. (2000b). *Cracking the glass ceiling: Catalyst's research on women in corporate management 1995–2000.* New York: Catalyst.

Cooper, C. L., & Lewis, S. (1999). Gender and the changing nature of work. In G. N. Powell (Ed.), *Handbook of gender and work* (pp. 37–46). Thousand Oaks, CA: Sage.

Darley, J. M., & Fazio, R. H. (1980). Expectancy confirmation processes arising in the social interaction sequence. *American Psychologist, 35,* 867–881.

Davidson, M. J., & Cooper, C. L. (1992). *Shattering the glass ceiling: The woman manager.* London: Paul Chapman.

Deaux, K., & Kite, M. (1993). Gender stereotypes. In F. L. Denmark & M. A. Paludi (Eds.), *Psychology of women: A handbook of issues* (pp. 107–139). Westport, CT: Greenwood.

Deaux, K., & LaFrance, M. (1998). Gender. In D. T. Gilbert, S. T. Fiske, & G. Lindzey (Eds.), *The handbook of social psychology* (4th ed., Vol. 1, pp. 788–827). Boston: McGraw-Hill.

Epstein, C. F. (1975). Institutional barriers: What keeps women out of the executive suite? In F. E. Gordon & M. H. Strober (Eds.), *Bringing women into management* (pp. 7–21). New York: McGraw-Hill.

Fiske, S. T. (1998). Stereotyping, prejudice, and discrimination. In D. T. Gilbert, S. T. Fiske, & G. Lindzey (Eds.), *The handbook of social psychology* (4th ed., Vol. 2, pp. 357–411). Boston: McGraw-Hill.

Grant, J. (1988). Women as managers: What they can offer to organizations. *Organizational Dynamics, 16*(3), 56–63.

Hamilton, D. L., & Sherman, J. W. (1994). Stereotypes. In R. S. Wyer Jr., & T. K. Srull (Eds.), *Handbook of social cognition* (2nd ed., Vol. 2) *Applications* (pp. 1–68). Hillsdale, NJ: Lawrence Erlbaum Associates.

Heilman, M. E. (1983). Sex bias in work settings: The lack of fit model. In L. L. Cummings, & B. M. Staw (Eds.), *Research in organizational behavior* (Vol. 5, pp. 269–298). Greenwich, CT: JAI Press.

Heilman, M. E. (1995). Sex stereotypes and their effects in the workplace: What we know and what we don't know. *Journal of Social Behavior and Personality, 10*(6), 3–26.

Heilman, M. E., Block, C. J., Martell, R. F., & Simon, M. C. (1989). Has anything changed? Current characterizations of men, women, and managers. *Journal of Applied Psychology, 74*, 935–942.

Helgesen, S. (1990). *The female advantage: Women's ways of leadership.* New York: Currency Doubleday.

Hilton, J. L., & von Hippel, W. (1996). Stereotypes. In J. T. Spence, J. M. Darley, & D. J. Foss (Eds.), *Annual review of psychology* (Vol. 47, pp. 237–271). Palo Alto, CA: Annual Reviews.

Klatzky, R. L., & Anderson, S. M. (1988). Category-specific effects in social typing and personalization. In T. K. Srull, & R. S. Wyer Jr. (Eds.), *Advances in social cognition* (pp. 91–101). Hillsdale, NJ: Lawrence Erlbaum Associates.

Korabik, K. (1999). Sex and gender in the new millennium. In G. N. Powell (Ed.), *Handbook of gender and work* (pp. 3–16). Thousand Oaks, CA: Sage.

Loden, M. (1985). *Feminine leadership, or how to succeed in business without being one of the boys.* New York: Times Books.

Merton, R. K. (1948). The self-fulfilling prophecy. *Antioch Review, 8*, 193–210.

Morrison, A. M., & Von Glinow, M. A. (1990). Women and minorities in management. *American Psychologist, 45*, 200–208.

Nieva, V. F., & Gutek, B. A. (1980). Sex effects on evaluation. *Academy of Management Review, 5*, 267–376.

Powell, G. N. (1993). *Women and men in management* (2nd ed.). Newbury Park, CA: Sage.

Powell, G. N. (1999). Reflections on the glass ceiling: Recent trends and future prospects. In G. N. Powell (Ed.), *Handbook of gender and work* (pp. 325–345). Thousand Oaks, CA: Sage.

Powell, G. N., & Butterfield, D. A. (1979). The "good manager": Masculine or androgynous? *Academy of Management Journal, 22*, 395–403.

Powell, G. N., & Butterfield, D. A. (1989). The "good manager": Did androgyny fare better in the 1980s? *Group and Organization Studies, 14*(2), 216–233.

Powell, G. N., & Graves, L. M. (2003). *Women and men in management* (3rd ed.). Thousand Oaks, CA: Sage.

Rosener, J. B. (1990). Ways women lead. *Harvard Business Review, 68*(6), 119–225.

Rosener, J. B. (1995). *America's competitive secret: Utilizing women as a management strategy.* New York: Oxford University Press.

Rothbart, M. (1981). Memory processes and social beliefs. In D. L. Hamilton (Ed.), *Cognitive processes in stereotyping and intergroup behavior* (pp. 145–181). Hillsdale, NJ: Lawrence Erlbaum Associates.

Schein, V. E. (1973). The relationship between sex role stereotypes and requisite management characteristics. *Journal of Applied Psychology, 57*, 95–100.

Schein, V. E. (1975). Relationships between sex role stereotypes and requisite management characteristics among female managers. *Journal of Applied Psychology, 60,* 340–344.

Schein, V. E., & Mueller, R. (1992). Sex role stereotyping and requisite management characteristics: A cross cultural look. *Journal of Organizational Behavior, 13,* 439–447.

Schein, V. E., Mueller, R., & Jacobson, C. (1989). The relationship between sex role stereotypes and requisite management characteristics among college students. *Sex Roles, 20,* 103–110.

Schein, V. E., Mueller, R., Lituchy, T., & Liu, J. (1996). Think manager—think male: A global phenomenon? *Journal of Organizational Behavior, 17,* 33–41.

Smith, E. R., & Zárate, M. A. (1992). Exemplar-based model of social judgment. *Psychological Review, 99,* 3–21.

Spence, J. T., Helmreich, R., & Stapp, J. (1975). Rating of self and peers on sex role attributes and their relation to self-esteem and conceptions of masculinity and femininity. *Journal of Personality and Social Psychology, 32,* 29–39.

Tabachnick, B. G., & Fidell, L. S. (1989). *Using multivariate statistics* (2nd ed.). New York: HarperCollins.

Tajfel, H., & Turner, J. C. (1986). The social identity theory of intergroup behavior. In S. Worchel, & W. G. Austin (Eds.), *Psychology of intergroup relations* (2nd ed., pp. 7–24). Chicago: Nelson-Hall.

U.S. Department of Labor, Bureau of Labor Statistics. (1983). *Handbook of labor statistics: 1983.* Washington, DC: Government Printing Office.

U.S. Department of Labor, Bureau of Labor Statistics. (1985). *Employment and earnings,* 32(1), 36, Table A-22.

U.S. Department of Labor, Bureau of Labor Statistics. (1999). *Employment and earnings,* 46(12), 33, Table A-19.

Weber, R., & Crocker, J. (1983). Cognitive processes in the revision of stereotypic beliefs. *Journal of Personality and Social Psychology, 45,* 961–977.

Williams, J. E., & Best, D. L. (1990). *Measuring sex stereotypes: A multination study* (rev. ed.). Newbury Park, CA: Sage.

8

Gender and Race-Related Stereotypes
in Management

Joan E. Riedle

Some suggest that the "traditional" gender stereotypes and roles did not develop until the Victorian age. Whether an accurate supposition or not, the Victorian age was certainly the time when Sigmund Freud first explicitly expressed stereotypes about masculinity and femininity.[1] Freud described women as vane, envious, narcissistic, masochistic; preferring to be passive, overly emotional, dependent; and having a weak sense of right from wrong.[2] His ideas were further codified in the writings of Helene Deutsch, who defined masculine as active and feminine as passive.[3] Without question, the Freudians offered a strongly negative view of normal women and gave such beliefs the appearance of scientific credibility.

Empirical attempts to clarify the masculine and feminine stereotypes followed, with the 1970 project by Inge Broverman, Donald Broverman, Frank Clarkson, Paul Rosenkrantz, and Susan Vogel being a highly influential example.[4] Broverman et al. asked mental health professionals to describe either a normal adult woman, a normal adult man, or a normal adult person. Their survey instrument presented a series of 122 bipolar adjectives (e.g., aggressive — not aggressive), and respondents selected the pole which they felt better fit the category of person. Because the authors were examining gender stereotypes, their discussion focused on the thirty-eight traits on which men and women were placed on opposite poles. Of those traits, they found that normal men and persons shared twenty-nine desirable characteristics that women lacked (e.g., aggressive, independent, not emotional, objective). Normal women and persons shared only eleven desirable characteristics that men lacked (e.g., talkative, tactful, gentle, aware of the feelings of others). Thus twenty-nine of a normal woman's thirty-eight feminine characteristics were socially undesirable when observed in an adult person. It is noteworthy that Broverman et al.'s male and female respondents described normal women similarly.

Shortly after the Broverman et al. project, Virginia Schein applied a similar survey method to a study of managers, with 300 male insurance executives describing either men in general, women in general, or a successful middle manager.[5] Schein's participants rated how characteristic each of ninety-two traits was of the person being described. Schein's numerical response scale allowed her to correlate the ratings for the various categories of person. The ratings for men and managers showed impressive similarity ($r = 0.81$), with men and managers sharing sixty characteristics that women lacked (e.g., emotionally stable, aggressive, leadership ability, self-reliant). The ratings for women and managers did not correlate significantly ($r = 0.10$), with women and managers but not men sharing only eight characteristics. The complete list of traits shared by women and managers included understanding, helpful, sophisticated, aware of feelings of others, intuitive, neat, not vulgar, and having humanitarian values. Schein's results imply that men would be at a marked advantage when applying for a management position. In being male, men would be assumed to have sixty of the sixty-eight requisite characteristics and would only have to prove they possessed the missing eight. Women, obviously, would have to overcome a much greater perceived deficit. Thus, the early empirical work on gender stereotypes presented a bleak picture for women in general and women managers in particular.

Schein's 1973 sample had included only male respondents.[6] In 1975 she replicated her project with a sample of women managers from a variety of insurance companies.[7] A significant correlation was found in the perceptions of men in general and managers ($r = 0.54$) and in the perceptions of women in general and managers ($r = 0.30$), though the second correlation was significantly lower. Respondents with fewer than five years of tenure perceived little to no similarity between the characteristics of women and those of managers ($r = 0.17$). Men and managers but not women were reported to share thirty-nine traits, whereas women and managers but not men shared only fourteen. Overall, these results from female respondents are a bit more positive about women in general, particularly with regard to characteristics related to emotionality (emotionally stable and steady) and rational thinking (logical, analytical thinking, and consistent), but the pattern is still discouraging. Schein concludes that sex role stereotypes foster the view that women are less qualified than men for management positions and that both male and female managers are likely to make employment decisions in favor of men. Masculine is the model for success in management, especially in the minds of men.

THINK MANAGER—THINK MALE

Work on gender stereotypes in management has continued since the 1970s, and although the picture has moderated somewhat, women have not come to be viewed as having qualifications comparable to those of men. Some of the work on gender stereotypes has explored the perceived masculinity and femininity of managers; that work is addressed in the chapter by Gary Powell,

Anthony Butterfield, and Jane Parent (reprinted in this volume).[8] The focus of the present chapter will be the thirty years of replications and extensions of the Schein methodology.

O. C. Brenner, Joseph Tomkiewicz, and Schein conducted a fifteen-year follow-up of Schein's original project.[9] The number of women managers had increased greatly during that time span; perhaps attitudes about women in management had improved. In their 1989 study, the responses of 173 women were contrasted to those of 420 men from a variety of manufacturing and service firms. Responses from male participants indicated a strong correlation between the characteristics of men in general and successful middle managers ($r = 0.72$), but no relationship between the traits of women in general and successful middle managers ($r = -0.01$), replicating the findings from fifteen years prior. Responses from women participants, however, indicated an encouraging change of views. For the women respondents, the correlations between men and successful middle managers ($r = 0.59$) and between women and successful middle managers ($r = 0.52$) were both strong and equally significant. Interestingly, women and men were found to agree on the characteristics that make a good manager ($r = 0.95$). If women and men agree on what it takes to be a successful middle manager and men do not believe that women in general have those characteristics, then it appears that the source of any changes rests in women's perceptions of women in general; by 1989 women saw women in general as possessing many of the traits necessary for success in middle management. Brenner et al. conclude that given the views of men have changed so little, a strong case can be made for continuing affirmative action efforts for initial entry-level positions and for extending those efforts to upper levels. The persistence of men's stereotyped attitudes could severely limit women's abilities to advance into positions of power and influence. (It is noteworthy that Brenner and colleagues did not find a pattern related to age or tenure of the respondent, nor do most of the studies that follow.)

A question that readily comes to mind when reading the Schein and the Brenner et al. studies concerns the choice of the terms women "in general" and men "in general." Are women (and men) generally interested in management positions? Might a respondent who feels women "in general" do not possess the characteristics needed to become a manager still recognize that many women do? Jennifer Deal and Maura Stevenson asked introductory psychology students to indicate whether ninety-one of Schein's traits were characteristic or not characteristic of either a successful manager, a successful male manager, or a successful female manager.[10] Male and female participants agreed more on the characteristics of managers (forty-two of sixty) and male managers (forty-eight of sixty) than on the characteristics of female managers (thirteen of sixty). For example, male participants were likely to describe female managers as bitter, nervous, passive, quarrelsome, and uncertain, whereas female participants were likely to describe female managers as assertive, competent, emotionally stable, and industrious. Given perceptions of managers and male managers were similar across the sexes, and only the perceptions of male respondents were highly negative of female managers, the authors concluded that negative perceptions of female managers are largely a function of the sex of the perceiver. With this study, the pattern of male respondents showing greater bias regarding women in management is strengthened and the relevance of the prior findings to women managers is clarified.

Does it matter if we know about the effectiveness of the job holders? Madeline Heilman, Caryn Block, and Richard Martell addressed this issue by having respondents describe the attributes of six categories of persons: women in general, men in general, women managers, men managers, successful women managers, and successful men managers.[11] They had 224 male managers each rate one of those persons on forty-two of Schein's original traits. The traits had been previously grouped into seven work-relevant categories (work competence, activity/potency, emotional stability, independence, rationality, concern for others, and hostility toward others). Five of those categories were considered to be stereotypically masculine: competent, active, emotionally stable, independent, and rational. Of those masculine trait categories, women managers were rated more positively than women in general on all five, women managers were rated less positively than men managers on all but independence, and successful women and men managers differed only on rationality. Thus, participants recognized that women managers are distinct from women in general and the word *successful* did much to improve the respondents' assumptions about women managers.

Sadly, all was not positive, even for the successful women managers. Successful women managers and women managers were thought to display less concern for others than women in general, and successful women managers and women managers were thought to show more hostility than women in general. It appears that the characterization that resulted for successful women managers included "strongly negative qualities indicative of a hostile-toward-others, 'bitch' caricature of the high-powered career woman."[12] This evaluative ambivalence was not replicated in perceptions of men managers, particularly men managers attributed with success. On the six masculine traits, men managers did not differ significantly from men in general, consistent with the prior findings that men as a group are perceived to have the skills requisite for management positions, and those same traits were rated as more characteristic of successful men managers than of men in general. Successful men managers were also more concerned with others than men managers or men in general, and successful men managers and men managers both showed less hostility toward others than men in general. Thus, successful men managers were given a consistent and desirable description. The authors conclude that job-relevant information can serve to lessen the stereotype process, given that the term *successful* resulted in more positive impressions of both women and men. Information that legitimates a leader has previously been shown to be beneficial to women[13] and provides a promising lead for addressing potential bias.

The preceding studies have explored the traits needed for success in middle management. Women have made significant progress in securing middle-management positions in recent decades but remain severely underrepresented at the executive level. It seems feasible that women aspiring to executive positions are perceived as even more in violation of sex role expectations than those looking at middle management and consequently, the path to the upper echelon remains blocked.

The attributes needed for success in upper management positions were explored by Richard Martell, Christopher Parker, Cynthia Emrich, and Marnie Swerdlin Crawford.[14] Participants included 132 male middle- or senior-level managers, who described either men middle managers, women middle managers, successful men middle managers, or successful women middle managers on four attributes deemed essential for success in executive positions. Those attributes included being a change agent, having managerial courage, having leadership ability, and being results-oriented. Successful managers were judged to be stronger on all four executive attributes than those not designated as successful. Men managers were judged to be stronger than women managers on being agents for change and on managerial courage. Successful men managers and successful women managers did not differ on leadership ability, but when success was not specified men managers were thought to have more leadership ability than women managers.

Thus, in Martell et al.'s study, the specification *successful* attenuated perceived gender differences only on the executive characteristic of leadership and explicit verification of managerial success did less to eliminate stereotyping than had been expected. The authors acknowledged that the gender stereotyping effects in the study were small to moderate but argued that "small amounts of sex bias are sufficient to seriously stunt the upward mobility of women managers,"[15] and that "it is with good reason that women believe that the prevalence of sex stereotypes continue to impede their upward mobility."[16]

Richard Martell and Aaron DeSmet criticized the works described for having focused on trait-like measures of leadership and not on actual leadership behaviors.[17] They employed a set of fourteen behavioral categories (delegating, inspiring, intellectual stimulation, mentoring, modeling, monitoring, networking, problem solving, rewarding, supporting, upward influence, consulting, planning, and team building) which were presented with fixed behavioral anchors. Participants included 151 managers who described either male middle managers and female middle managers or male successful middle managers and female successful middle managers, by indicating the percentage likely to effectively demonstrate each leadership behavior. Male respondents indicated that male managers (regardless of success designation) were more likely than female managers to display behaviors related to delegating, inspiring, intellectual stimulation, and problem solving. They also expected male managers to network more than female managers, but this difference disappeared if the female managers were designated as successful. Furthermore, they expected female managers to consult more than male managers, but this difference disappeared when successful was specified. Interestingly, male and female managers were not thought to differ in team building, but successful male managers were thought to engage in that activity more than successful female managers. Female respondents indicated that female managers were more likely to display behaviors related to inspiring, mentoring, problem solving, rewarding, and supporting, whereas male managers were more likely to delegate. Furthermore, though both female managers and successful female managers were perceived as consulting more than male managers, the difference was more stark for those designated as successful.

Overall, male and female respondents did not stereotype on the behaviors of modeling, monitoring, planning, and upward influence, male respondents favored male managers on five behaviors and female managers on one, female respondents favored female managers on six behaviors and male managers on one. Martell and DeSmet suggest that theirs is one of the first studies to demonstrate female bias against males.[18] An alternative and somewhat more positive wording might be to describe their findings as an example of same-sex or in-group favoritism.[19]

Gender stereotypes in management and leadership positions have received extensive study, but Lisa Boyce and Ann Herd extended the work into the very specific, male-dominated domain of the military.[20] These authors suggest that cadets are "strongly steeped in the attitudes, norms, and traditions within the academy walls."[21] Students at a military service college, including 635 men and 140 women, participated. Doing so involved rating how characteristic each of Schein's ninety-two traits was of either women in general, men in general, or successful officers. For male cadets, the descriptions of officers and of men in general correlated significantly ($r = 0.41$), whereas those for officers and women in general did not ($r = -0.11$). For female cadets, the correlation between officers and men in general approached significance ($r = 0.25$), and that for officers and women in general was significant ($r = 0.30$). Overall, male and female respondents agreed that successful officers and men in general but not women shared five characteristics (authoritative, self-reliant, feelings not easily hurt, frank, and not submissive), and successful officers and women in general but not men shared four (cheerful, kind, neat, and sympathetic).

An additional analysis considered the perceived effectiveness of the cadets on a scale of military performance. Boyce and Herd had expected but did not find that the successful female cadets would gender-type the officer job as requiring feminine characteristics (consistent with the same-sex favoritism found in Martell and DeSmet).[22] Responses from female cadets judged above average in their military performance showed a slightly stronger correlation between the characteristics of officers and men in general ($r = 0.37$) than between officers and women in general ($r = 0.29$), but both were significant. Contrary to expectations, responses from female cadets judged below average in military performance showed no correlation between ratings for officers and men in general ($r = -0.01$), but a significant correlation for officers and women in general ($r = 0.34$). The finding that the less successful female cadets were the ones to feminize the leadership role may explain their lack of success, as they would strive to display a feminine leadership style but be judged by others employing a masculine standard. It is also apparent that the correlations in this study were generally lower than in previous studies; apparently even men "in general" are somewhat lacking in the traits needed for success as a military officer.

Overall, it appears that *think manager—think male* is still strongly evidenced in the perceptions of men but more weakly evidenced in the perceptions of women. Furthermore, when leadership is defined behaviorally, female respondents may actually judge women to be better leaders. Additional studies have addressed whether similar patterns of bias exist outside of the United States and within the United States but across racial groupings.

THINK MANAGER—THINK MALE AS A GLOBAL PHENOMENON

Research on stereotypes of managers has been extended through a variety of cross-nationality comparisons. Virginia Schein and colleague Ruediger Mueller had management students in Germany, Great Britain, and the United States respond to Schein's original set of ninety-two adjectives, each describing either women in general, men in general, or successful middle managers.[23] Male respondents in all three countries showed the typical pattern of bias, with the characteristics of men in general and managers correlating significantly and those for women in general and managers having virtually no similarity. Women from Germany showed almost as much bias as the men, women from Great Britain also sex-typed but saw women in general as having a few more relevant characteristics, and women from the United States did not sex-type the position of manager. Similarly, Virginia Schein, Ruediger Mueller, Teri Lituchy, and Jiang Liu extended the work to China and Japan.[24] Males from both countries demonstrated sex typing similar to that in the United States. Unlike recent findings from the United States but similar to those from Germany, women from China and Japan saw little resemblance between women and managers. These findings led Schein to conclude in 2001 that *think manager—think male* is a global phenomenon, particularly among males and despite the many historical, political, and cultural differences that exist among countries.[25] She suggests that with women's greater participation in management in the United States, improved attitudes of women toward women in management have emerged, and the same may follow in the views of American men and citizens of other countries. Unfortunately, given that men in most countries continue to be the decision makers who control advancement into upper management, the rate of increase in women's participation may be slow.

THINK MANAGER—THINK WHITE

To determine if the managerial stereotype was actually a white managerial stereotype, comparisons of the traits characteristic of whites in general, African Americans in general, and successful middle managers were explored by Joseph Tomkiewicz, O. C. Brenner, and Tope Adeyemi-Bello.[26] A sample including 305 white male managers and 120 white female managers from manufacturing and service firms completed their survey. The characteristics of whites in general and successful middle managers were found to correlate significantly $(r=0.54)$, whereas those for African Americans in general and successful middle managers did not $(r=0.17)$. (The response patterns for male and female participants were similar.) Thus, it appears that we may not only *think manager—think male* but also *think manager—think white*.

Joseph Tomkiewicz and O. C. Brenner note that Hispanics are the fastest-growing segment of the American population and are projected to surpass the number of African Americans by 2010.[27] Management students (110 males and 122 females, race unspecified) described either Hispanics in general, whites in general, successful Hispanic managers, or middle managers in general. The descriptions for whites and middle managers $(r=0.80)$ and Hispanics and middle managers $(r=0.35)$ both showed significant relationships, though the correspondence for Hispanics and managers was significantly lower. Furthermore, male respondents indicated more similarity of Hispanics and middle managers $(r=0.47)$ than did female respondents $(r=0.21)$. Given that the characteristics of Hispanics in general were perceived to have rather marginal overlap with those of middle managers, it is somewhat surprising that the ratings for successful Hispanic managers and middle managers were markedly similar $(r=0.86)$. The designation *successful* had a pronounced positive effect, particularly on the perceptions of female respondents. It again appears that information that legitimates a manager (such as the designation successful) has the power to overcome otherwise powerful stereotypes.

DESCRIPTIVE VERSUS PRESCRIPTIVE NORMS

Gender stereotypes generate expectations for behavior; expected behaviors are referred to as *norms*. Norms can be descriptive—what we feel men and women actually or typically do; norms can be prescriptive—what we believe men and women should do. The preceding studies used wordings that fit with descriptive norms, most frequently asking what men and women are like, sometimes what percent was likely to demonstrate a characteristic, other times asking if a trait was characteristic or not. The distinction between descriptive and prescriptive norms, and the level of gender stereotyping associated with each, were explored by Sabine Sczesny in the context of leadership.[28] Deborah Prentice and Erica Carranza further develop the concept of prescriptive norms in both the broad context of American society and the specific context of Princeton University.[29]

Sczesny asked 215 German management students to describe one of five categories of persons (leaders in general, women, men, female leaders, or male leaders) on twenty person-oriented and twenty task-oriented leadership characteristics.[30] (An additional group of respondents generated a self-description.) The descriptive norm was assessed by having respondents indicate what percent of the group they were describing possessed a characteristic and the prescriptive norm by asking how important they thought the characteristic was for a member of that group. Comparisons of women, men, and leaders in general were thought to be global in nature, whereas those of female leaders, male leaders, and leaders in general were considered more specific. Descriptively, Sczesny found that leaders in general were thought to be more likely to possess task-oriented skills (65.9 percent) than person-oriented skills (45.9 percent) but prescriptively, the two sets of skills were rated as equally important. Furthermore, when asked if they had thought of a man, a man and a woman, or a woman when describing a leader, 55.6 percent had thought of a man and 44.5 percent had pictured men and women; no respondent thought exclusively of a female leader.

Descriptively, Sczesny's male and female respondents reproduced what could here be termed a *think leader—think male* pattern.[31] With regard to the more global women and leader in general comparisons, both men and women described women as having stronger person-oriented skills and weaker task-oriented skills than leaders; the same was true for the more specific woman leader and leader in general comparisons. Person and task skills were thought to be equally important to men and leaders in general and to men leaders and leaders in general. Thus, the traditional gender stereotypes were strongly evidenced in the descriptive norms. That both male and female respondents expressed equal support for traditional stereotypes is not surprising, when one remembers that German women and men have both been shown to endorse traditional biases.[32]

Sczesny described the prescriptive responses as more androgynous.[33] A variety of gender differences emerged (e.g., male respondents thought task-related skills were markedly less important for women in general than for men or leaders in general), but the differences were small and the overall patterns were not consistent with the gender stereotypes. In this way, the prescriptive norms were less gender stereotyped than those expressed descriptively. Sczesny concludes that gender stereotypes may have a greater influence on descriptive norms (what a person is actually like) than on prescriptive norms (what a person should be like).

A different and perhaps more thorough understanding of gender-related prescriptions comes from the work of Prentice and Carranza, who also introduce the idea of gender-related proscriptions.[34] The projects discussed to this point have focused primarily on the positive traits people are supposed to have by virtue of their gender; this study also considered sex-typed negative traits. Prentice and Carranza suggest that many characteristics are prescribed by our culture; they are desirable and expected characteristics. Other characteristics are proscribed by our culture; they are undesirable and prohibited characteristics. Furthermore, the level of prescription and proscription can vary depending on the sex of the person. As depicted in box 1 of Table 8.1, gender intensified prescriptions are desirable characteristics that are more desirable in one of the sexes than for the typical person, whereas gender-intensified proscriptions are viewed as more undesirable in either men or women than for persons in general. Gender-relaxed prescriptions are good traits that are less expected from one sex than from the typical person, and gender-relaxed proscriptions are undesirable characteristics that are more tolerated from one sex.

In Prentice and Carranza's first data set, respondents described persons in American society.[35] Participants rated how desirable each of 100 traits was for

TABLE 8.1. Gender Prescriptions and Proscriptions as Defined and Identified by Prentice and Carranza (2002)

	More Desirable for the Specified Sex	Less Desirable for the Specified Sex
Socially Desirable	Gender-intensified prescription	Gender-relaxed prescription
Socially Undesirable	Gender-relaxed proscription	Gender-intensified proscription
	More Desirable for the Female Sex	Less Desirable for the Female Sex
Socially Desirable	Warm & kind ($n = 16$) Friendly ($n = 11$)	Intelligent ($n = 27$) Active ($n = 23$)
Socially Undesirable	Yielding ($n = 10$) Emotional ($n = 8$)	Rebellious ($n = 6$) Intimidating ($n = 8$)
	More Desirable for the Male Sex	Less Desirable for the Male Sex
Socially Desirable	Business sense ($n = 18$) ($n = 0$)	Happy ($n = 18$) Enthusiastic ($n = 7$)
Socially Undesirable	Rebellious ($n = 8$) Domineering ($n = 1$)	Emotional ($n = 12$) Shy ($n = 6$)

Note: The examples in the second and third boxes are of traits more strongly prescribed or proscribed for the specified sex than for the person in general. The first trait in each box was offered for comparisons "in America" and the second trait for comparisons "at Princeton." The number of traits in each category (n) is indicated.

male, female, and gender-unspecified persons (generating prescriptions and proscriptions) and how typical each trait was of males and females (generating descriptions). The set of traits included seventy-five positive and twenty-five negative gender-correlated attributes. In their second data set, respondents described a male undergraduate at Princeton (which the authors maintain is a very male-dominated environment), a female undergraduate at Princeton, and a person at Princeton. Participants again rated desirability and typicality of 100 traits, but the set of traits was modified to fit a college scenario.

Prentice and Carranza found that the prescriptions and proscriptions for men and for persons in American society were more similar than those for women and persons.[36] Their respondents indicated that it was

> less desirable for a woman but not more desirable for a man to be intelligent and mature, to have common sense and a good sense of humor, to be concerned for the future, principled, efficient, clever, worldly, and persuasive, and to defend beliefs than it was for a person to have these qualities. Similarly, they indicated that it was less desirable for a man but not more desirable for a woman to be happy, helpful, enthusiastic, optimistic, creative, and devoted to a religion than it was for a person to have these qualities.[37]

Prescriptions and proscriptions for male undergraduates and persons at Princeton were even more similar than in the first data set (they did not differ on any intensified prescription and differed on only one relaxed proscription) and more similar than those for female undergraduates and persons. (Sample items from both data sets are available in boxes 2 and 3 of Table 8.1.) Apparently *think person—think male* is still the norm in America and *think person—think male* is the rule at Princeton.

Descriptive norms were also assessed by Prentice and Carranza through their ratings of the typicality of each trait.[38] Although most traits that differed in socially desirable for the sexes (prescriptive norms) also differed in perceived typicality (descriptive norms), there were exceptions. In particular, ten of the twenty-seven relaxed prescriptions for women in America (intelligent, mature, common sense, concern for future, principled, efficient, rational, disciplined, clever, and worldly) were thought to be equally typical of women and men. Five of the twenty-three relaxed prescriptions for women at Princeton (intelligent, active, competent, articulate, and overachieving) did not differ in typicality. Apparently many nonstereotypical characteristics needed by women to function in what are increasingly common nontraditional roles are now perceived to be typical of women in general. Women were described as having the qualities prescribed by traditional gender roles and many of those required by nontraditional roles, so their prescribed characteristics and descriptive traits did not match, and their descriptive norms were less stereotypical. Men have less disjunction between their stereotypical and actual roles, so their prescriptive and descriptive norms were more consistent. In addition, many positive traits did not differ in desirability for the sexes but were perceived as more typical of women, with the end result being an overall more positive description of women. It is noteworthy that sex of participant did not enter into any significant results.

Violations of stereotypes can take multiple form, according to Prentice and Carranza, and those violations elicit different responses.[39] Violations of gender-intensified prescriptions are punished, as happens to women who are not interested in having children and men who are not decisive. Violating a gender-intensified proscription involves failure to comply with both a gender norm and a social desirability norm and receives a more extremely negative response, as occurs for men who display feminine qualities and women who behave arrogantly. Violations of the relaxed prescriptions and proscriptions may elicit rewards, provided one does not simultaneously violate other aspects of the gender stereotype. Thus, women may be goal-oriented if also well-groomed; men may be warm and kind if also goal-oriented. Prentice and Carranza conclude that the descriptive aspects of the gender stereotype may lead to the perception that women are unqualified for stereotypically masculine positions, thus agreeing with Sczesny that descriptive norms can be quite traditional.[40] They also conclude that prescriptive norms may result in disparate treatment, as when women who violate prescriptions are responded to with hostility.

Prentice and Carranza's participants appear to have painted a markedly more positive picture of women and for women than did Sczesny's.[41] Although men and the generic person shared more characteristics than women and the generic person in both studies, Prentice and Carranza's participants gave an overall more socially desirable description of the women. The two studies differ in many ways. Prentice and Carranza employed American college students with various majors as respondents and couched their studies in the context of American society and Princeton University; Sczesny employed German management students who evaluated the traits relative to leaders. Prentice and Carranza also made a point to bring in the desirability and typicality of negative traits, which Sczesny did not. Although it is not clear which factors led to the differences in their findings and conclusions, the following research studies make the case that aspects of the persons being researched, aspects of the context in which they are making their decisions, and the interaction of personal and contextual factors could all moderate level of gender bias.

CONTEXTUAL FACTORS AND POSSIBLE SOLUTIONS

Through what mechanisms does gender actually affect selection decisions? Elissa Perry, Alison Davis-Blake, and Carol Kulik explore both contextual and cognitive explanations for gender segregation, and conclude in favor of the interaction of the two.[42]

Contextual factors may include the demographic composition of the applicant pool and the workforce. For example, applicants often learn about jobs from similar (same-sex) others who are already in those jobs, leading the gender composition of the applicant pool to stay stable; individuals tend to hire and promote others similar to themselves, leading the gender composition of incumbents to stay stable. Contextual factors also involve the structure and size of the organization. For example, large firms tend to have more formal structures and ladders, and formal job ladders are often separated by gender with women's job ladders offering less mobility. Contextual factors may relate to the power of key interest groups, both within and outside of the organization. For example, when affirmative action officers have little power (within the company) gender segregation tends to persist, and when an organization's hiring practices are not exposed to external scrutiny (little power from outside the company) there is often less gender integration. Perry et al. surmise that these contextual factors likely inhibit the career progress of women.[43]

Gender stereotypes are central to the cognitive perspective. According to Perry et al., the cognitive perspective argues that organizational decision makers are imperfect evaluators whose judgments about applicants and position holders can be biased by societal factors. Evaluators employ a jobholder stereotype (or schema) that should include attributes essential for effective performance. Jobholder stereotypes may be developed from repeated observations of similar events, and if the holders of those jobs are of one sex, gender may become part of the stereotype. Furthermore, the content of the jobholder stereotype may be explicitly taught or socialized, leading to an expectation that the jobholder will be of a specific sex or will have specific gender-related attributes (e.g., warm and caring). A job applicant who displays many of the attributes requisite to the jobholder stereotype will be perceived as highly qualified. If the jobholder stereotype includes that the candidate should be female, females will be advantaged in the hiring process; if the jobholder stereotype includes that the person should be warm and caring, females will again be advantaged because we consider those attributes to be more typical of women.[44]

Perry et al. contend that the best explanations for gender segregation involve the interaction of cognitive and contextual factors, stating that "decision makers' propensity to use gender as a basis for selection and promotion decisions varies across organizational contexts."[45] They offer a variety of predictions as to when gender stereotypes are likely to be activated.

- Gender is more likely to be included in a decision maker's jobholder stereotype (cognitive) when the applicant pool is of primarily one gender (contextual), and gender-associated jobholder stereotypes are more likely to be activated (cognitive) if the job applicants are primarily of one sex (contextual).
- Gender is more likely to be part of the stereotype for a leader (cognitive) when most occupants of leadership positions are of one sex (contextual), and gender-associated jobholder stereotypes are more likely to be activated (cognitive) if the job incumbents are primarily of one sex (contextual).

- The number of job titles within an organization (contextual) may relate to the level of stereotyping (cognitive). Stereotypes tend to develop with repeated observation. Perry et al. surmise that if each job has a different title, then observers are encouraged to think of those positions as unique. If the holders of these very specific job titles tend to be of one sex, or if a position only has one occupant, then the observer is encouraged to gender-type the position.
- The jobholder stereotype is more likely to include gender (cognitive) when a formal job ladder is in place (contextual). Thus, in hierarchical organizations with many job titles and formal structures, gender stereotyping is more likely.
- The jobholder stereotype is less likely to include gender (cognitive) if leaders formally express a desire to hire and promote persons of both sexes (contextual).

Perry and colleagues recommend the standardization of personnel functions as a method of reducing the use of gender-associated stereotypes.[46] Organizations may change decision makers' stereotypes through education and incentives. Gender-neutral terms may be used in job descriptions (e.g., *supervisor* is more gender neutral than *manager*). Accountability of the decision maker may reduce reliance on gender stereotypes, so monitoring of the decision-making process may reduce gender stereotyping. Furthermore, reliance on gender stereotypes tends to be greater in situations with time pressure and work overload (e.g., Martell).[47] More detailed and specific examples of the interaction of contextual and cognitive factors are provided by Sabine Sczesny and Ulrich Kühnen;[48] by Alice Eagly, Steven Karau, and Mona Makhijani;[49] and by Robin Ely.[50]

Sczesny and Kühnen provide evidence that a decision maker's intentional efforts to control for the effects of gender stereotyping may result in over-correction (contrast effects), such that women are inappropriately favored.[51] In effect, participants who are aware of the nondesirable effects of stereotyping sometimes overcompensate. Participants in Sczesny and Kühnen's study evaluated a candidate for a leadership position. The candidate was either male or female and was dressed in either a masculine or feminine manner. Respondents evaluated their candidate on leadership competence and indicated whether they would recommend hiring the person. Some respondents were required to memorize a nine-digit number while processing the information about the candidate (high cognitive work load), and others were not (low cognitive work load). When working under a light load, such that personal concerns about stereotyping could be attended to, women were favored. However, when working under a heavy load such that participants were cognitively stressed, men were favored. It is an unfortunate reality that today's corporate decision makers, managers, and supervisors seldom have light work loads, which means that stereotyping disadvantaging women is likely.

Clearly, work load becomes another important contextual factor. An additional aspect of Sczesny and Kühnen's project added greater detail on the interaction of work load and personal factors. Many different classes of stereotypes can affect impressions, and concerns with limiting their impact may vary. As noted earlier, Sczesny and Kühnen also manipulated the gender-stereotypical physical appearance of the job candidates.[52] Most people do not have personal concerns with regard to managing stereotypes in this area and cognitive load was not found to moderate its effects; generally the masculine appearing candidates were attributed with more leadership competence. (The one exception was that female participants also attributed the femininely dressed female candidate with this characteristic.) Thus, Sczesny and Kühnen provide evidence that cognitive factors (awareness of which stereotypes are socially undesirable) interact with contextual variables (work load).

Eagly, Karua, and Makhijani conducted a meta-analysis on leadership studies to determine if one sex was actually more effective in leadership roles and if there were conditions (contextual factors) that tended to produce differences in effectiveness.[53] In the process, they compared theories that focus on cognitive factors as predictors of perceived effectiveness, such as stereotypes regarding the sex of the appropriate jobholder, with those that emphasize contextual factors, such as whether leadership in the particular position has been defined in masculine, feminine, or androgynous terms. Leadership effectiveness may depend on the match of these various factors, such that in androgynous positions women and men may be equally effective but in sex-typed positions (which would activate gender stereotyping) the incumbent of the expected sex would be advantaged. Thus, Eagly et al. appear to argue for the interaction of cognitive and contextual factors as posed by Perry and colleagues.[54]

Considering the aggregate of studies reviewed, Eagly et al. conclude that male and female leaders do not differ in effectiveness.[55] However, that general conclusion obscured a more complex pattern involving the above-mentioned contextual factor. In leadership roles that were male-dominated and involved working with male subordinates, specifically the military, male leaders were judged to be markedly more effective. Several other types of organizations were found to slightly favor female leaders, those being government and social service agencies, educational institutions, and to a lesser extent, business settings. Furthermore, men fared better in entry-level leadership positions and women in middle-level positions. Eagly et al. interpret this latter finding as consistent with prior reports that lower-level management often relies heavily on technical skills, whereas middle management relies more on relationship skills. Clearly gender was not unimportant in the organizations and groups studied, as gender when combined with leadership context moderated effectiveness. The importance of male-dominated roles as a contextual factor is similarly illustrated in the findings of Ely.[56]

Ely explored gender as a social construction.[57] Specifically, she examined how women's proportional representation in the upper management levels of an organization affects the stereotypical nature of their professional roles. Thus, her study provides an additional example of contextual factors (proportional representation) interacting with cognitive factors (gender stereotyping of roles). Ely explored level of sex typing in the perceptions of women lawyers, who were employed as associates in either male-dominated (5 percent or fewer female partners) or sex-integrated (15 percent or more female partners) law firms. Although much of Ely's project focused on qualitative interview responses, participants also rated themselves, professional women, professional men, and what it takes to be successful in their firm on thirty-six behavioral and psychological attributes. The ratings for professional men and women correlated more strongly in the sex-integrated firms than in the male-dominated, as did the ratings for professional women and what it takes to be successful. Furthermore, women in sex-integrated firms were more able to integrate masculinity and femininity, seeing their femininity as a source of strength and competence. It appears that a more androgynous stereotype was evidenced in the sex-integrated firms. Ely acknowledged that her study did not clarify whether the combination of masculine and feminine traits that was accepted in sex-integrated firms for female attorneys would be equally embraced for males, but she clearly documented the interaction of cognitive factors (gender stereotypes) and context (sex integration of the firm).

Evidently, if we are to lessen the impact of gender stereotypes in management and other leadership positions, a variety of factors must be considered as must their possible interactions. Gender is more likely to be included in the jobholder stereotype if the applicant pool is of only one sex and if the job incumbents are of one sex, and those conditions are more likely to exist when job titles are very narrow. Organizations can take steps to change jobholder stereotypes, to make jobholder stereotypes more gender-neutral, and to discourage the use of gender stereotypes in hiring. Organizations can lessen the effects of gender stereotypes by including information that legitimates the jobholder (e.g., recognize the individual's successes) and by allowing decision makers to consider applicants under circumstances of low work load. Organizations that do not involve the military and are not heavily male-dominated will be more successful at making such changes. A multitude of findings suggest that having females involved in decision making greatly improves the chances of women being perceived as eligible candidates; certainly organizations can take steps to maintain and increase the involvement of females on selection committees.

The early work on gender stereotyping in the United States painted a bleak picture for women in management, and the same is true for more recent studies about women in some specific contexts and from a variety of countries. Furthermore, even in the United States, racial stereotypes may hinder the advancement of Hispanics and African Americans. The picture is not all negative, however, when one considers the options for lessening the impact of these stereotypes by altering the many contextual factors with which they are known to interact.

NOTES

1. Miriam Lewin, "The Victorians, the Psychologists, and Psychic Birth Control," in Miriam Lewin, ed., *In the Shadow of the Past: Psychology Portrays the Sexes* (New York: Columbia University Press, 1984), pp. 39–76.

2. Miriam Greenspan, *How Psychotherapy Fails Women and What They Can Do about It: A New Approach to Women and Therapy* (New York: McGraw-Hill, 1985), p. 92.

3. Helene Deutsch, *The Psychology of Women: A Psychoanalytic Interpretation* (New York: Grune and Stratton, 1944).

4. Inge K. Broverman, Donald M. Broverman, Frank E. Clarkson, Paul S. Rosenkrantz, and Susan R. Vogel, "Sex-Role Stereotypes and Clinical Judgments of Mental Health," *Journal of Consulting and Clinical Psychology* 34 (1970): 1–7.

5. Virginia E. Schein, "The Relationship between Sex Role Stereotypes and Requisite Management Characteristics," *Journal of Applied Psychology* 57 (1973): 95–100.

6. Ibid.

7. Virginia E. Schein, "Relationships between Sex Role Stereotypes and Requisite Management Characteristics among Female Managers," *Journal of Applied Psychology* 60 (1975): 340–44.

8. Gary N. Powell, D. Anthony Butterfield, and Jane D. Parent, "Gender and Managerial Stereotypes: Have the Times Changed?" *Journal of Management* 28 (2002): 177–93.

9. O. C. Brenner, Joseph Tomkiewicz, and Virginia E. Schein, "The Relationship between Sex Role Stereotypes and Requisite Management Characteristics Revisited," *Academy of Management Journal* 32 (1989): 662–69.

10. Jennifer J. Deal and Maura A. Stevenson, "Perceptions of Female and Male Managers in the 1990s: Plus Ça Change . . . ," *Sex Roles* 38 (1998): 287–300.

11. Madeline E. Heilman, Caryn J. Block, and Richard F. Martell, "Sex Stereotypes: Do They Influence Perceptions of Managers?" in Nancy J. Struthers, ed., Gender in the Workplace [special issue], *Journal of Social Behavior and Personality* 10 (1995): 237–52.

12. Ibid., p. 249.

13. Janice D. Yoder, Thomas L. Schleicher, and Theodore W. McDonald, "Empowering Token Women Leaders: The Importance of Organizationally Legitimated Credibility," *Psychology of Women Quarterly* 22 (1998): 209–22.

14. Richard F. Martell, Christopher Parker, Cynthia G. Emrich, and Marnie Swerdlin Crawford, "Sex Stereotyping in the Executive Suite: Much Ado about Something," *Journal of Social Behavior and Personality* 13 (1998): 127–38.

15. Ibid., p. 136.

16. Ibid., p. 137.

17. Richard F. Martell and Aaron L. DeSmet, "A Diagnostic-Ratio Approach to Measuring Beliefs about the Leadership Abilities of Male and Female Managers," *Journal of Applied Psychology* 86 (2001): 1223–31.

18. Ibid.

19. Henri Tajfel, *Human Groups and Social Categories: Studies in Social Psychology* (London: Cambridge University Press, 1981).

20. Lisa A. Boyce and Ann M. Herd, "The Relationship between Gender Role Stereotypes and Requisite Military Leadership Characteristics," *Sex Roles* 49 (2003): 365–78.

21. Ibid., 367.

22. Ibid.

23. Virginia E. Schein and Ruediger Mueller, "Sex Role Stereotyping and Requisite Management Characteristics: A Cross Cultural Look," *Journal of Organizational Behavior* 13 (1992): 439–47.

24. Virginia E. Schein, Ruediger Mueller, Terri Lituchy, and Jiang Liu, "Think Manager—Think Male: A Global Phenomenon?" *Journal of Organizational Behavior* 17 (1996): 33–41.

25. Virginia E. Schein, "A Global Look at Psychological Barriers to Women's Progress in Management," *Journal of Social Issues* 57 (2001): 675–88.

26. Joseph Tomkiewicz, O. C. Brenner, and Tope Adeyemi-Bello, "The Impact of Perceptions and Stereotypes on the Managerial Mobility of African Americans," *The Journal of Social Psychology* 138 (1998): 88–92.

27. Joseph Tomkiewicz and O. C. Brenner, "The Relationship between Race (Hispanic) Stereotypes and Requisite Management Characteristics," *Journal of Social Behavior and Personality* 11 (1996): 511–20.

28. Sabine Sczesny, "A Closer Look beneath the Surface: Various Facets of the Think-Manager—Think-Male Stereotype," *Sex Roles* 49 (2003): 353–63.

29. Deborah A. Prentice and Erica Carranza, "What Women and Men Should Be, Shouldn't Be, Are Allowed to Be, and Don't Have to Be: The Contents of Prescriptive Gender Stereotypes," *Psychology of Women Quarterly* 26 (2002): 269–81.

30. Sczesny, "A Closer Look."

31. Ibid.

32. Schein and Mueller, "Sex Role Stereotyping and Requisite Management Characteristics."

33. Sczesny, "A Closer Look."

34. Prentice and Carranza, "What Women and Men Should Be."

35. Ibid.

36. Ibid.

37. Ibid., p. 272.

38. Ibid.

39. Ibid.

40. Sczesny, "A Closer Look."

41. Prentice and Carranza, "What Women and Men Should Be"; Sczesny, "A Closer Look."

42. Elissa L. Perry, Alison Davis-Blake, and Carol T. Kulik, "Explaining Gender-based Selection Decisions: A Synthesis of Contextual and Cognitive Approaches," *Academy of Management Review* 19 (1994): 786–820.

43. Ibid.

44. Ibid.

45. Ibid., p. 787.

46. Ibid.

47. Richard F. Martell, "What Mediates Gender Bias in Work Behavior Ratings?" *Sex Roles* 35 (1996): 153–69.

48. Sabine Sczesny and Ulrich Kühnen, "Meta-Cognition about Biological Sex and Gender-stereotypic Physical Appearance: Consequences for the Assessment of Leadership Competence," *Personality and Social Psychology Bulletin* 30 (2004): 13–21.

49. Alice H. Eagly, Steven J. Karau, and Mona G. Makhijani, "Gender and the Effectiveness of Leaders: A Meta-Analysis," *Psychological Bulletin* 117 (1995): 125–45.

50. Robin J. Ely, "The Power of Demography: Women's Social Constructions of Gender Identity at Work," *Academy of Management Journal* 38 (1995): 589–634.

51. Sczesny and Kühnen, "Meta-Cognition about Biological Sex."

52. Ibid.

53. Eagly et al., "Gender and the Effectiveness of Leaders."

54. Perry et al., "Explaining Gender-Based Selection Decisions."

55. Eagly et al., "Gender and the Effectiveness of Leaders."

56. Ely, "The Power of Demography."

57. Ibid.

9

Impact of Gender on Leadership

Shelly Grabe and Janet Shibley Hyde

As is reviewed elsewhere in this volume (e.g., Chapter 7), women made tremendous gains in leadership within organizations from the 1970s to the 1990s. According to the U.S. Bureau of Labor Statistics, women held half of all management, professional, and related occupations in 2004.[1] Despite these gains, women continue to be sparsely represented at higher levels of organizations and are extraordinarily rare in top managerial positions of businesses and corporations.[2] In this chapter we discuss the role of gender in leadership positions in the context of gender role socialization. We begin by briefly reviewing traditional theories and styles of leadership to provide a framework for an extensive review of gender similarities and differences in leadership. We follow that with a discussion of how social role theory may help one understand gender differences in leadership roles. Finally, we propose an alternative model of leadership characterized by a nonhierarchical and cooperative framework.

TRADITIONAL THEORIES AND STYLES OF LEADERSHIP

Traditional models of leadership that have been given the most attention by researchers are hierarchical in nature and therefore tend to focus on the role and achievements of the leader, with little attention paid to group processes.[3] For example, *trait* theories of leadership tend to emphasize attributes of leaders such as intelligence and action-oriented judgment,[4] whereas *behavior* theories focus on measurable definitions of leadership (e.g., goal attainment).[5] *Transformational* leadership theories reflect a more collaborative view of group process in that leadership is enacted to inspire members of the group being led.[6] The review in this chapter will focus on research that has been conducted within the framework of these traditional theories because almost all empirical research has been based in them.

Researchers in the area of leadership focus on specific *styles* of leadership within the theories just laid out. The bulk of research on leadership styles that was conducted prior to 1990 distinguished between two approaches to leadership: *task-oriented style*, defined as a concern with accomplishing assigned tasks by organizing task-relevant activities, and *interpersonally-oriented style*, defined as a concern with maintaining interpersonal relationships by tending to others' morale and welfare.[7] A smaller number of studies distinguished between leaders who behaved *democratically* as opposed to *autocratically*. Democratically oriented leaders allow subordinates to participate in decision making, whereas autocratically oriented leaders tend to discourage such participation from subordinates.[8] These styles of leadership can be loosely mapped onto gender stereotypes to the extent that women are traditionally viewed as more interpersonal and cooperative than men and men as more authoritative and directive than women.

A shift in focus by several leadership researchers in the 1980s and 1990s led to the study of new types of styles.[9] In particular, there has been recent focus on transformational versus transactional leadership. *Transformational* leadership is defined by an interest in serving as a role model and empowering followers. Transformational leaders tend to innovate to develop followers' full potential and thereby contribute more to their organization.[10] Researchers have contrasted transformational leaders with *transactional* leaders, who appeal to subordinates' self-interest by establishing exchange relationships with them.[11] This type of leadership involves managing in the more conventional sense of clarifying subordinate responsibilities, rewarding them for meeting objectives, and correcting them for failing to meet objectives. In addition to these two styles, researchers distinguish a laissez-faire style as that marked by a general failure to take responsibility for managing.

THE ROLE OF META-ANALYSIS IN RESEARCH ON LEADERSHIP AND GENDER

The work of Alice Eagly and colleagues has provided the most comprehensive source of scholarship on gender differences in leadership. In particular, Eagly and colleagues have conducted synthesized reviews and meta-analyses in the areas of leadership style, effectiveness, emergence of leaders, evaluation, and motivation.

Meta-analysis is a method used to review or survey research literature, and it applies statistical methodology to the task of integrating relevant research. Meta-analysis is a technique designed to permit researchers to evaluate the empirical evidence on a particular question by systematically cumulating data from numerous studies. In meta-analytic work, an effect size, d, is calculated to reflect the difference between the two groups of interest—in this case, women and men.[12] The use of meta-analytic techniques in the area of leadership research has allowed researchers to estimate the overall magnitude of gender differences and compare them to other known gender differences. Given the depth and scientific rigor of the meta-analytic investigations that Eagly and colleagues have conducted on gender differences in leadership, this chapter will focus on the results reported in these quantitative reviews as opposed to the review of individual studies within the area. Therefore, the review of gender differences and similarities that follows is based on systematic and quantitative integrations of relevant research on several aspects of female and male leadership. The comprehensive use of quantitative methods permitted us to examine the extent to which there were notable gender differences in several aspects of leadership and compare the gender differences in one area of leadership (e.g., effectiveness) to another (e.g., evaluation). The effect sizes reported in this review are summarized in Table 9.1.

The use of quantitative review methods also has allowed researchers to examine the extent to which gender differences were consistent across studies within each review. In other words, inconsistencies between studies could be examined to identify potential variables that moderated the gender difference in leadership roles. Thus, when relevant, the following review will discuss variables that differentially predict gender differences in leadership.

ARE THERE GENDER DIFFERENCES IN LEADERSHIP? REVIEW OF META-ANALYTIC RESULTS

Before gender became a focus of study within the leadership literature, most research was conducted on task-oriented versus interpersonally oriented styles; however, as increasing numbers of women enter leadership roles, researchers have begun to question whether differences exist between women and men in various aspects of leadership. The following review will take a comprehensive look at a number of ways women's and men's leadership may be similar or different and conclude with suggestions regarding leadership that moves away from a traditional focus on aspects of masculinity.

Leadership Style

Many studies have explored the leadership styles of women and men to determine whether they carry out leadership roles differently. To investigate whether the styles that have been the traditional focus of research (task-oriented style versus interpersonally-oriented style; democratic versus autocratic) differed by gender, Eagly and Johnson conducted a meta-analysis of the 162 available studies that had compared women and men on these styles.[13] Their comprehensive review of the literature between the years of 1961 and 1987 found that styles were somewhat gender stereotypic in laboratory experiments that used student participants and in assessment studies that investigated the leadership styles of people not selected for occupancy of leadership roles (e.g., samples of

TABLE 9.1. Summary of Mean Effect Sizes for Reviewed Meta-Analyses

Leadership Dimension Assessed	d	Interpretation of d
Traditional leadership style (Eagly and Johnson, 1990)		Positive scores indicate stereotypic differences.
All types of leadership	0.03	
Interpersonally oriented style (assessment setting)	0.25	
Interpersonally oriented style (laboratory setting)	0.37	
Democratic versus autocratic style (assessment setting)	0.08	
Democratic versus autocratic style (laboratory setting)	0.19	
Democratic versus autocratic style (organizational setting)	0.21	
Contemporary leadership style (Eagly et al., 1991)		Positive scores indicate males scored higher than females.
Transformational style	−0.10	
Individualized consideration	−0.23	
Management by exception	0.27	
Contingent reward	−0.13	
Laissez-faire	0.16	
Effectiveness in leadership (Eagly et al., 1995)		Positive scores indicate males scored higher than females.
Overall effectiveness	−0.02	
Effectiveness excluding military	−0.12	
Effectiveness rated by judges	−0.12	
Effectiveness rated by subordinates	−0.19	
Effectiveness rated by other leaders	0.07	
Effectiveness when assessed by ability	0.28	
Effectiveness when assessed by satisfaction	−0.16	
Effectiveness when assessed by motivation	0.01	
Effectiveness when assessed by performance	0.05	
Emergence of leaders (Eagly and Karua, 1991)		Positive scores indicate males scored higher than females.
Overall emergence	0.32	
Task leadership	0.41	
Unspecified leadership	0.29	
Social leadership	−0.18	
<20-minute interaction	0.58	

(continued)

TABLE 9.1. (Continued)

Leadership Dimension Assessed	d	Interpretation of d
More than one meeting held	0.09	
Tasks with high social complexity	0.55	
Tasks with low social complexity	0.23	
Evaluation of leaders (Eagly et al., 1992)		Positive scores indicate males scored higher than females.
Overall evaluation	0.05	
Autocratic leadership style	0.30	
Roles occupied mainly by men	0.09	
Roles occupied equally by men and women	−0.06	
Motivation to lead (Eagly et al., 1994)		Positive scores indicate males scored higher than females.
Overall motivation	0.22	
Competitive games	0.31	
Competitive situations	0.15	
Assertive role	0.27	
Imposing wishes	0.19	
Standing out from the group	0.12	
Authority figures	−0.17	
Routine administrative functions	−0.09	

employees). In general, the authors found that the average weighted effect size across all types of leadership style was slightly but significantly stereotypic ($d = 0.03$, representing a very small effect by Cohen's criteria;[14] a positive sign was given to stereotypic differences (e.g., women more interpersonally oriented), and a negative sign to counterstereotypic differences). Thus, the overall findings suggest similarities in leadership style.

To test whether gender differences in leadership style varied based on the setting, the authors divided the studies into organizational, laboratory, or assessment settings. Interestingly, they found that in the assessment and laboratory settings women tended to manifest relatively interpersonally oriented ($d = 0.25$ and $d = 0.37$, respectively) and democratic styles ($d = 0.08$ and $d = 0.19$, respectively) in comparison to men, who tended to exhibit task-oriented and autocratic styles. In contrast, gender differences were more limited in organizational studies assessing managers' styles: The only demonstrated difference between female and male managers was that women adopted a somewhat more democratic or participative style and a less autocratic or directive style than did men ($d = 0.21$). Male and female managers in organizational contexts did not differ in their tendencies to use interpersonally oriented and task-oriented styles.

Thus, although overall gender-related difference in leadership styles across all contexts were close to zero, more notable gender differences in leadership style only emerged in certain situational contexts, but those differences are still relatively small. Finally, it appears the most consistent finding from this review was that on average, female leaders adopted a relatively democratic and participative style consistent with the female gender role.

In a more recent study examining contemporary leadership styles, Eagly, Johannesen-Schmidt, and van Engen examined research that compared women and men on transformational, transactional, and laissez-faire leadership styles.[15] The meta-analysis of forty-five studies examining gender-related differences in these leadership styles found that on average, female leaders were slightly more transformational than male leaders in their leadership ($d = -0.10$). In this review, the authors selected studies using the most widely employed measure of transformational and transactional leadership—the Multifactor Leadership Questionnaire (MLQ).[16] Predicted gender-related differences were also found when the transformational and transactional scales of the MLQ were broken down into their respective subscales. For example, women scored higher than men on the transformational subscale of individualized consideration ($d = -0.23$). Men scored higher than women on one of the transactional subscales: management by exception-passive ($d = 0.27$), whereas women scored slightly higher on the contingent reward subscale ($d = -0.13$). Men also scored higher on laissez-faire leadership ($d = 0.16$). The overall comparisons on transformational leadership, as well as its subscales, show significantly higher scores among women than men, whereas men obtained significantly higher scores on management by exception and laissez-faire styles. However, it should be noted that using Cohen's categories for classifying average effect sizes ($0.20 =$ small, $0.50 =$ moderate, $0.80 =$ large), these are all considered "small" effects that suggest that although there are differences in leadership styles between women and men, they are not great.

Transformational leadership may be favored by women because it allows them to avoid a traditionally masculine approach characterized by exercising hierarchical control and agentic leadership behavior.[17] The transformational style may therefore allow women to address the conflict that may be introduced when conforming to their leader role is inconsistent with their gender role. Similarly, Eagly and colleagues suggested that transformational leadership may be congenial to women because the relatively communal behaviors characteristic of this style help female leaders deal with the special problems of lesser authority and legitimacy that they face to a greater extent than their male counterparts. Furthermore, women may employ contingent reward behaviors, which include noticing and praising subordinates' good performance, more than men because they foster positive, supportive work relationships.

Interestingly, the authors found that the reported gender differences in leadership style were moderated by setting and publication year. In particular, the authors found the smallest differences in business settings ($d = -0.07$), as opposed to governmental $(d = -0.11)$ or educational settings $(d = -0.21)$. Furthermore, when publication year was taken into account, findings revealed that the gender difference reported in transformational style went more strongly in the female direction in recent years. Over time, perhaps women have perceived less pressure to conform to a traditionally masculine style of leadership and have experienced more freedom to lead in a manner with which they are comfortable.

In summary, transformational leadership, as well as the contingent reward aspects of transactional leadership, may provide a particularly comfortable context for women's enactment of competent leadership. Although this approach to leadership may be effective in men as well, it may be more critical for women than men to display their competence in a manner that is explicitly supportive of subordinates and the organization as a whole.

Effectiveness of Leaders

Another rich area of research that examines gender-related differences in leadership is the investigation of the relative effectiveness of men and women who occupy leadership roles in groups or organizations. Eagly, Karau, and Makhijani quantitatively reviewed seventy-six studies that compared women and men managers, supervisors, officers, department heads, and coaches.[18] Within the leadership research reviewed, effectiveness was measured by subjective ratings anchored by poor leader and outstanding leader. When all studies in the literature were aggregated, female and male leaders did not differ in effectiveness $(d = -0.02,$ 95 percent confidence interval contained zero). However, although the overall finding indicated men and women were equivalent in effectiveness, that generalization was not appropriate in all organizational contexts. In particular, follow-up analyses indicated that findings from studies that investigated military organizations differed from the rest. When military organizations were excluded from analyses, the weighted mean effect size indicated that female leaders were rated as slightly more effective than male leaders $(d = -0.12)$. Thus, when a particularly masculine setting was removed (i.e., military), the results suggested that overall, women are perceived to be more effective as leaders in remaining contexts.

Interestingly, there also was evidence that effective leadership by women and men varied as a function of raters and measure. For example, judges as well as subordinates favored women in their ratings $(ds = -0.12$ and -0.19, respectively), whereas four other categories of raters (leaders, supervisors of leaders, peers of leaders, and mixed or unclear) favored men $(ds = 0.07$ to $0.31)$. In regard to type of measure, men were viewed more favorably than women when ability was assessed $(d = 0.28)$ relative to measures of effectiveness and motivation $(ds = -0.01$ and 0.01, respectively). Women also were rated more favorably than men when satisfaction measures were compared $(d = -0.16)$. There were no gender differences on performance measures $(d = 0.05)$. However, the magnitude of these effect sizes did not hold when the authors removed outlier studies, suggesting that reliable conclusions cannot be drawn from these findings.

The magnitude of the overall effect size also was moderated by the traditional masculinity of the role and the sex of the subordinates. Comparisons of leader effectiveness favored men more and women less to the extent that the leadership role was male-dominated and that the subordinates were male. Recall that if military studies are included, there was no overall gender difference. The remaining small and insignificant difference is important because it suggests that despite barriers and possible challenges in leadership, women who serve as leaders are in general succeeding as well as their male counterparts. Similarly, despite the reviewed meta-analytic findings reviewed earlier that suggest that female leaders appear to behave somewhat differently than male leaders, these findings suggest that they appear to be equally effective. Furthermore, even though the data suggest that men may excel in some areas and women may excel in others, there appears no empirical reason to believe that either gender possesses an overall advantage in effectiveness.

Emergence of Leaders

Given that men and women appear to vary on several leadership dimensions, it also seems important to know whether gender-related differences exist in the initial emergence of leaders. For example, if emerging as a leader within a group is less about performance and more about factors such as lifestyle advantages (e.g., fewer family obligations), it would be likely that men gain leadership roles in organizational settings more often than women. In a meta-analysis of seventy-five studies examining the emergence of leaders in initially leaderless groups, Eagly and Karua showed that in both laboratory and field studies, men emerged as leaders more frequently than women across different types of leadership ($d = 0.32$), but that a number of situational variables moderated this tendency.[19]

As expected, men emerged more frequently than women on task ($d = 0.41$) and unspecified ($d = 0.29$) measures of leadership, whereas women emerged more frequently than men on leadership when it was assessed with social measures ($d = -0.18$). For additional analyses, the authors combined the task and unspecified studies and examined variables that moderated the gender difference when the studies were combined ($d = 0.32$). Interestingly, male leadership was particularly likely in short-term groups and in groups carrying out tasks that did not require complex social interaction. Specifically, the tendency for men to emerge as leaders decreased to the extent that leadership was assessed after a longer period of social interaction ($d = 0.58$ if less than twenty-minute interaction, $d = 0.09$ if more than one meeting was held). Thus, male leadership was more prevalent in sessions of twenty minutes or less than in longer sessions that consisted of more than one meeting. As time and interaction progress, group members likely gain information about attributes other than gender and this additional knowledge may establish expectations about members' contribution, thereby diminishing the importance of expectations based on stereotypes of gender.[20]

In contrast, women emerged as social leaders slightly more than men. Specifically, the tendency for men to become leaders lessened when tasks required complex social interaction ($d = 0.55$ for high complexity, $d = 0.23$ for low complexity); tasks that did not require complex interaction yielded a strong tendency toward male leadership. Presumably, women's positive interpersonal contributions became relevant to leadership tasks requiring negotiation and extensive sharing of ideas. Overall, these findings underscore that societal gender roles influence leadership behavior. The reported gender differences in leadership emergence might be explained in part by gender-role tendencies for men to be oriented to the group task, whereas women tend to be more oriented toward facilitating social behaviors.

The major finding in this quantitative review was that gender differences in emergent leadership depended largely on the type of leadership measured—in the overall analysis the emergent difference was relatively small. One basis for interpreting the average effect sizes for leader emergence is to compare them with average effect sizes produced by other quantitative reviews, especially those already reported in the other areas of leadership reviewed. Recall that Eagly and Johnson's review of gender differences in leadership style found near zero mean effect sizes for interpersonal and task styles, but a mean of 0.22 for the tendency of women to adopt a more democratic and participative style than men do. This review suggests small to moderate tendencies for men to emerge as overall leaders and a small tendency for women to emerge as social leaders.

Evaluation of Leaders

Because gender stereotypes may cause behavior to be interpreted differently for female leaders, considering the issue of leadership evaluation also is important. Eagly, Makhijani, and Klonsky's synthesis of 147 experiments that examined evaluations of female and male leaders whose behavior had been made equivalent by the researchers found that evaluations were less favorable for female than for male leaders, as indicated by a small weighted effect size ($d = 0.05$) that significantly differed from 0.00 (which indicates no difference).[21] However, although people seem to evaluate female leaders slightly more negatively than equivalent male leaders, the bias for female leaders to be devalued was larger in specific contexts. Female leaders were devalued relative to their male counterparts when they adopted equivalent leadership styles that were stereotypically masculine (i.e., style was autocratic and directive) as well as when their evaluators were men. In contrast, female and male leaders were evaluated favorably when they adopted equivalent leadership styles that were traditionally feminine (i.e., democratic or interpersonally oriented). The finding that devaluation of women in leadership roles was stronger when leaders occupied male-dominated roles and when their evaluators were men suggests that women's occupancy of highly male-dominated leadership roles produces a violation of people's expectations about women. Male evaluators may experience female leaders as a more threatening intrusion because leadership is traditionally a male domain.

The authors also found that the tendency to favor men over women was larger when the dependent variable was the leader's competence or rater's satisfaction with the leader rather than the perception of leadership style. Thus, the measures that were more purely *evaluative* (i.e., competence or satisfaction) yielded stronger evidence of the devaluation of women's leadership. When specific leadership style was the moderator, two of three styles examined (interpersonal orientation and potency) did not produce gender differences. However, women were perceived as more task-oriented than men. This perception, contrary to what would be expected, may reflect a tendency to view women's behavior as more extreme when it conflicts with the female stereotype. The autocratic leadership style produced significantly more favorable evaluations of male than female leaders ($d = 0.30$), but only trivial differences were found for roles occupied mainly by men ($d = 0.09$) than for those occupied equally by men and women ($d = -0.06$). There was a greater tendency to favor male leaders in male-dominated leadership positions of business and manufacturing than in organizational contexts not involving business or manufacturing. These results highlight that men's styles may be less consequential in that their leadership is not questioned and they therefore enjoy greater latitude to carry out leadership in a variety of styles.

In summary, the extent to which people are biased to evaluate female leaders less favorably may reflect a form of prejudice, whereby leadership behavior enacted by women is often evaluated less favorably than the equivalent behavior enacted by men. Thus, the extent to which women may encounter negative reactions when they behave in a clearly agentic way may constrain their leadership style. Therefore, it may be partly out of a result of the pressure to *not* exert agentic behavior that females exhibit more communal, collaborative, and less hierarchical behaviors than men when they lead. More seriously, devaluation of female leaders may suggest that women encounter very serious barriers to leadership roles and advancing to higher levels within organizations.

Motivation to Perform Leadership Roles

The finding that women were slightly less likely to emerge as leaders has a probable variety of causes that potentially include the different leadership styles that we reviewed. However, it may also be argued that among these causes, women on average are less motivated to meet the requirements of the managerial role to the extent that it is traditionally defined in masculine terms. Research on gender stereotypes suggests that men, compared with women, are believed to have personalities that are described by Bakan's term *agentic* and that are characterized by aggressive, assertive, ambitious, dominant, forceful, and leader-like qualities.[22] This agentic emphasis is reflected in most of the subscales of the Miner Sentence Completion Scale (MSCS), which is the standard measurement test for assessing motivation to manage.[23] The subscales of the MSCS named Competitive Games, Competitive Situations, Assertive Role, Imposing Wishes, and Standing Out from the Group all reflect a traditional masculine profile. In contrast to the agentically oriented subscales, two additional subscales, Authority Figures and Routine Administration, have quite a different focus. Individuals who score high on the Authority Figures subscale are comfortable in a subordinate role in relation to their supervisors. Scoring high on Authority Figures would indicate that one may be especially good at maintaining relationships with supervisors, whereas scoring high on Routine Administration indicates a willingness to carry out everyday administrative activities—both traits that are more associated with the female stereotype. In sum, the majority of the subscales of the MSCS are defined in terms of stereotypically masculine qualities, whereas only two of the subscales emphasize aspects of the managerial role that might be considered more stereotypically feminine.

In a synthesis of fifty-one studies that examined gender differences in individuals' motivation to manage, Eagly, Karau, Miner, and Johnson found that men had higher motivation to manage than women on the overall MSCS scale ($d = 0.22$).[24] As predicted, men also scored higher than women on the five agentically oriented subscales: Competitive Games ($d = 0.31$), Competitive Situations ($d = 0.15$), Assertive Role ($d = 0.27$), Imposing Wishes ($d = 0.19$), and Standing Out from the Group ($d = 0.12$). In contrast but in line with expectations, women scored higher than men on the Authority Figures ($d = -0.17$) and Routine Administration Functions ($d = -0.09$) subscales. Thus these findings suggest that it would be unwise to infer from the overall effect size that men are generally more motivated to lead than women. Rather, it appears that men may be more motivated to lead in contexts or organizations in which they are well matched by agentic requirements of the managerial role, whereas women are more motivated when the leadership role involves characteristics that have been traditionally viewed as more consistent with a female gender stereotype. However, when interpreting the effect sizes in this particular review, it should also be noted that the findings were gathered from research conducted on relatively homogenous samples of respondents (i.e., business school students) in relatively controlled settings (i.e., classrooms). Therefore, these findings may not generalize. Furthermore, given that the selection of respondents in this area of research is from populations of business managers and business students, studies conducted in the general population may yield even smaller effect sizes.

Eagly and Johnson's findings (reviewed earlier) that male managers were somewhat more autocratic and directive in their leadership styles than females seems compatible with some results of the current meta-analysis. In particular, men's higher motivation on the Assertive Role and Imposing Wishes subscales and women's higher motivation on the Authority Figures and Routine

Administrative Functions subscales supports the 1990 results that suggest men take a more command-and-control leadership style. It also is important to consider women's lesser motivation on some dimensions in light of Eagly et al.'s later findings that suggested that women were devalued, relative to men, for leadership behavior that was stylistically masculine, especially if it was auto-cratic or directive. Experience with devaluation or discrimination may deter women from being motivated to adopt the more directive and assertive mana-gerial features that are reflected in the MSCS assessment. However, the overall mean effect size was small; women's lesser motivation does not necessarily mean that they are less effective. Despite the generally masculine definition of the traditional business manager role, women showed a stronger motivation in relation to some aspects of the role.

In summary, the results from the five meta-analyses reviewed here suggest that gender differences, when they exist, are quite small and often trivial (see Table 9.1 for a summary) and that situational and organizational variables often moderated the gender-related differences that were obtained. Nevertheless, the reported gender-related differences may reflect prejudice directed toward fe-male leaders who adopt more masculine styles when such styles are viewed as violations of the norms associated with the female role. In the next section we discuss in more detail how gender socialization and gender role theory may help one understand the differences and similarities in leadership among women and men.

SOCIAL ROLE THEORY

Social roles are generally defined as socially shared expectations that apply to persons who occupy certain social positions or are members of a particular category.[25] Gender role theory maintains that people develop expectations for their own and others' behavior based on their beliefs about the behaviors that are appropriate for men and women.[26] Similarly, people develop expectations about behavior that is appropriate for leaders within an organizational setting.[27] Within such settings, expectations regarding gender and leadership will interact and sometimes conflict. The potential contradiction in roles may help explain differing behavior in male and female leaders. The idea that leaders are per-ceived simultaneously in terms of their gender and their organizational role is consistent with the more general concept of gender-role spillover, which is "carryover into the workplace of gender-based expectations for behavior."[28] Gender-role spillover has different consequences for women than for men. In situations where expectations are informed by gender roles in organizational settings, the consequence may be that women are not regarded as generic managers but as female managers or women bosses. By fulfilling people's ex-pectations concerning leadership, women violate conventions concerning ap-propriate female behavior.

The existence of different expectations for men's and women's attributes and social behavior has been consistently documented in research on gender stereotypes.[29] Men are expected to express high degrees of agentic qualities, including being independent, masterful, assertive, and competent. Women are expected to possess high levels of communal attributes, including being friendly, unselfish, concerned with others, and emotionally expressive. These gender role expectations are assumed to arise from the distribution of women and men into different specific social roles in natural settings—especially family and occupational roles. The distinctive agentic content of the male gender role is assumed to derive especially from men's typical roles in the society and economy. The distinctive communal content of the female gender role is assumed to derive especially from the domestic role as well as from occupational roles occupied disproportionately by women (e.g., secretary, nurse, teacher). Role theory assumes that gender differences in social behavior are partly caused by people's tendency to behave consistently with their gender roles.

To the extent that gender roles exert some influence on leaders, female and male occupants of the same leadership role may behave differently (i.e., gender-role spillover). Thus, according to this argument, there is a likely influence of gender roles on leadership behavior, especially to the extent that one would be evaluated harshly for stepping outside of the prescribed gender role in an effort to be an effective leader. This social role analysis thus departs from the traditional reasoning that male and female leaders who occupy the same role display the same behaviors.[30]

As Eagly and colleagues maintained throughout their reviews, prejudices may result when there is perceived incongruity between the female gender role and typical leader roles. In particular, the reviews highlighted that women were less autocratic and directive, were rated as less effective when ability and performance were assessed, were slightly devalued as leaders in relation to men, and were less likely to emerge in contexts of task leadership. However, these differences were small in magnitude. Moreover, women also were more interpersonally oriented, democratic, and transformational—all characteristics that apparently bode well for leadership given the overall finding that women were evaluated as more effective than men despite exhibiting styles that may be traditionally less valued in organizational contexts. Ultimately, the results from the meta-analytic work of Eagly and colleagues draws attention to the fact that discussion of gender differences in leadership may be potentially overblown and that the differences, when they exist, are relatively small.

FEMINIST LEADERSHIP AS AN ALTERNATIVE MODEL

One criticism of traditional styles of leadership is that they have been examined within models of leadership that have been developed primarily by men and focus on individuals rather than groups.[31] Thus, the research reviewed here was based on models of leadership that are hierarchical. New approaches to leadership have been offered by several feminist authors with the suggestion that important principles of feminism can contribute positively to alternative models of leadership. However, a leadership style that conforms to the way women are expected to behave based on their gender role is not the same as leadership that is feminist.

Although a concise and agreed-on definition of feminist leadership does not exist, a new model of feminist leadership emerged from discussions that were held as part of the Feminist Leadership Initiative in the Society in the Psychology of Women (August 2002 through August 2003). This model conceptualizes leadership as a social process that moves away from describing the traits of leaders—one that can encompass the diversity of women's experiences while simultaneously reflecting the goals of feminism. This model would focus on creating an inclusive setting in which members work collaboratively, encourage broad participation, shared decision making, and an appreciation of diverse work styles. Leaders would promote open discussion and democratic participation, share resources, and help "subordinates" by empowering rather than exploiting them. Additional important principles to consider in proposing a feminist leadership model include reducing power hierarchies and addressing sources of oppression. In particular, this includes a need to explore how race, culture, class, and other individual, group, and social systemic differences interact with gender to affect the experience of group members. In this way, feminist leadership needs to be more than prioritizing the advancement of women and the dismantling of gender inequality; feminist leadership should consider different cultural experiences and be informed by gender, race, ethnicity, sexual orientation, and class. Differences must be not only tolerated but given equity in regard to how they inform values, behaviors, and decision making within an organizational context. Thus, to enact feminist leadership, leadership must be conceptualized as constantly negotiating the shared context, goals, and interactions among *all* members of an organization. In a hierarchical structure (which is not inherently cooperative or consensus-driven) it is highly unlikely that there will be much encouragement for decisions to be made collaboratively or for empowerment to be an objective. Thus, feminist leaders need to work within or challenge the hierarchies that characterize most organizations.

It is quite possible that this proposed form of leadership also would be good for organizations. For example, a Catalyst study indicated that companies with higher representation of women in senior management positions financially outperformed companies with proportionately fewer women at the top.[32] Although there is no evidence that women in this study led in a feminist manner, the traditional leadership styles that the meta-analyses suggested were more common of women (e.g., interpersonal orientation) lend hope to crediting a feminist model as a legitimate model of leadership that has benefits for individuals and organizations.

We recognize that all approaches to leadership are value based—even if the values are not explicitly stated (e.g., hierarchical). Feminist leadership challenges the hierarchies of status and power embedded in traditional leadership by enacting feminist values of deconstructing power hierarchies and establishing more egalitarian relationships. It recognizes that diverse individuals bring different skills, abilities, and values that allow them to contribute in different ways and is inherently collaborative and process-oriented. Furthermore, a feminist understanding of leadership aims to integrate understandings of multiple forms of oppression (e.g., sexism, racism) and resist the effects of these oppressions. When leadership is approached as collaborative, with multiple people involved not as followers but as cooperative leaders themselves, leadership can create social change.

NOTES

1. U.S. Bureau of Labor Statistics, *Women in the Labor Force: A Databook* (2005); retrieved July 21, 2005, from www.bls.gov/bls/databooknews2005.pdf.

2. Catalyst, *Women in the Fortune 500* (February 2, 2005); retrieved July 21, 2005, from www.catalystwomen.org/pressroom/press_releases/2-10-05%20Catalyst%20Female%20CEOs%20Fact%20Sheet.pdf.

3. J. C. Rost, *Leadership for the Twenty-First Century* (Westport, CT: Praeger, 1993).

4. H. Gardner, *Leading Minds Anatomy of Leadership* (New York: Basic Books, 1995).

5. B. Bennis and B. Nanus, *Leaders: The Strategies for Taking Charge* (New York: Harper and Row, 1985).

6. K. B. Boal and R. Hooijberg, "Strategic Leadership and Research: Moving On," *Leadership Quarterly* 11 (2000): 515–49.

7. R. F. Bales, *Interaction Process Analysis: A Method for the Study of Small Groups* (Cambridge, MA: Addison-Wesley, 1950).

8. V. H. Vroom and P.W. Yetton, *Leadership and Decision-Making* (Pittsburgh: University of Pittsburgh Press, 1973).

9. B. M. Bass, *Leadership and Performance beyond Expectations* (New York: Free Press, 1985).

10. B. M. Bass, *Transformational Leadership: Industry, Military, and Educational Impact* (Mahwah, NJ: Lawrence Erlbaum Associates, 1998).

11. B. J. Avolio, *Full Leadership Development: Building the Vital Forces in Organizations* (Thousands Oaks, CA: Sage, 1999).

12. L. V. Hedges and I. Olkin, *Statistical Methods for Meta-Analysis* (Orlando, FL: Academic Press, 1985).

13. A. H. Eagly and B. T. Johnson, "Gender and Leadership Style: A Meta-Analysis," *Psychological Bulletin* 108 (1990): 233–56.

14. J. Cohen, *Statistical Power Analysis for the Behavioral Sciences*, 2nd ed. (Hillsdale, NJ: Lawrence Erlbaum Associates, 1988).

15. A. H. Eagly, M. C. Johannesen-Schmidt, and M. L. van Engen, "Transformational, Transactional, and Laissez-Faire Leadership Styles: A Meta-Analysis Comparing Women and Men," *Psychological Bulletin* 129 (2003): 569–91.

16. B. J. Avolio, B. M. Bass, and D. I. Jung, "Re-Examining the Components of Transformational and Transactional Leadership Using the Multifactor Leadership Questionnaire," *Journal of Occupational and Organizational Psychology* 72 (1999): 441–62.

17. J. D. Yoder, "Making Leadership Work More Effectively for Women," *Journal of Social Issues* 57 (2001): 815–28.

18. A. H. Eagly, S. J. Karau, and M. G. Makhijani, "Gender and Effectiveness of Leaders: A Meta-Analysis," *Psychological Bulletin* 117 (1995): 125–45.

19. A. H. Eagly and S. J. Karau, "Gender and the Emergence of Leaders: A Meta-Analysis," *Journal of Personality and Social Psychology* 60 (1991): 685–710.

20. R. J. Webber and J. Crocker, "Cognitive Processes in the Revision of Stereotypic Beliefs," *Journal of Personality and Social Psychology* 45 (1983): 961–77.

21. A. H. Eagly, M. G. Makhijani, and B. G. Klonsky, "Gender and Evaluation of Leaders: A Meta-Analysis," *Psychological Bulletin* 111 (1992): 3–22.

22. D. Bakan, *The Duality of Human Existence: An Essay on Psychology and Religion* (Chicago: Rand McNally, 1966).

23. J. B. Miner, "Sentence Completion Measures in Personnel Research: The Development and Validation of the Miner Sentence Completion Scale," in H. J. Bernardin and D. A. Bownas, eds., *Personality Assessment in Organizations* (New York: Praeger, 1985), pp. 145–76.

24. A. H. Eagly, S. J. Karau, J. B. Miner, and B. T. Johnson, "Gender and Motivation to Manage in Hierarchic Organizations: A Meta-Analysis." *Leadership Quarterly* 5 (1994): 135–59.

25. B. J. Biddle, *Role Theory: Expectancies, Identities, and Behaviors* (New York: Academic Press, 1979).

26. A. H. Eagly, *Sex Differences in Social Behavior: A Social-Role Interpretation* (Hillsdale, NJ: Lawrence Erlbaum Associates, 1987).

27. J. S. Phillips and R. G. Lord, "Schematic Information Processing and Perceptions of Leadership in Problem-Solving Groups." *Journal of Applied Psychology* 67 (1982): 486–92.

28. B. A. Gutek and B. Morasch, "Sex-Ratios, Sex-Role Spillover, and Sexual Harassment of Women at Work," *Journal of Social Issues* 38 (1982): 55–74.

29. A. H. Eagly and V. J. Steffen, "Gender Stereotypes Stem from the Distribution of Women and Men into Social Roles," *Journal of Personality and Social Psychology* 46 (1984): 735–54.

30. R. M. Kanter, *Men and Women of the Corporation* (New York: Basic Books, 1977).

31. B. Lott, "Introduction to Models of Diverse Feminist Leadership: Reconciling the Discourses on Leadership and Feminism," in J. Chin, ed., *Feminist Leadership: Visions and Diverse Voices* (Washington, DC: American Psychological Association, in press).

32. Catalyst, *New Catalyst Study Reveals Financial Performance for Companies with More Women at the Top* (January 26, 2004); retrieved July 21, 2005, from www.catalystwomen.org/pressroom/press_releases/2004Fin_Per.pdf.

10

Tokenism Theory: What Happens When Few Women Work with Many Men

Mary B. Hogue and Janice D. Yoder

The world of work is changing. More women than ever before have entered the workforce, and increasing numbers of working women are entering jobs that have traditionally been thought to be the rightful domain of men. Whereas in the past, working women primarily remained teachers, nurses, or secretaries, many now are choosing careers as physicians, construction workers, and CEOs. This change has made it so that women often find themselves outnumbered by men in the workplace, and women who choose to work in male-dominated fields or who find themselves outnumbered by men at work experience obstacles to successful performance. Such obstacles can include a lack of recognition of their achievements or difficulty being perceived as qualified to do the job. These barriers and others can significantly limit women's actual job performance, and various lines of reasoning have been developed to explain the barriers to success faced by women. Some explanations for performance limitations may focus on how well the requirements of the job fit women or how well women fit the demands of the job. Social psychological explanations would look to the context, positing that the gendered nature of work leads women and men to operate in very different contexts with some work environments being more congenial to male workers. The complexity of the problem is such that each explanation is partly right, but no explanation alone provides a complete understanding.

In the late 1970s in her groundbreaking book *Men and Women of the Corporation*, Rosabeth Moss Kanter proposed tokenism theory to bridge the gap between these two approaches.[1] Her theory allowed knowledge from the domains of psychology and sociology to be combined to provide a fuller picture of the multifaceted difficulties faced by women who work primarily with men. By taking a social psychological approach to the interpersonal relations within work groups, Kanter has provided a more comprehensive means for examining women's work experiences. Her approach incorporates the more micro-level individual psychological processes with the more macro-level group structure approach.

In developing tokenism theory, Kanter analyzed the on-the-job experiences of "token" women working with a "dominant" group of male sales managers in a Fortune 500 company. She discovered that these women experienced performance barriers that were not experienced by their male co-workers, and she attributed these women's negative experiences to their proportional representation as less than .15 percent of their workgroup. In her seminal conceptualization of tokenism theory, Kanter explained the processes through which reduced representation leads to certain perceptual distortions that bring about predictable negative outcomes.

Although the number of women in the workforce is increasing and the number of women in low- and even mid-level management positions also is rising, some fields (especially higher-paying fields) as well as higher levels of organizational positions remain filled primarily by men. This segregation leads women working throughout male-dominated fields and in top-level management to often find themselves tokens in their workgroups, so although the overall workforce is changing, many workplaces remain segregated. Consequently, tokenism theory is an especially useful tool to understand the negative experiences that continue to plague many working women.

Since its inception, Kanter's theory has received considerable empirical support and has undergone important refinements, all of which have clarified our understanding of how group composition can affect the experiences of group members. As a social psychological approach, tokenism theory incorporates both the micro-level perceptual processes of group members as well as the macro-level contextual factors that impact and are a product of individual perceptual processes. In this chapter, as we discuss tokenism theory, we will explain the perceptual and interactional processes that occur when women constitute a significant minority of group membership. Our explanation will include a discussion of both the literature that supports and clarifies token effects and the modifications that have been made to Kanter's theory. We begin with a discussion of her original line of reasoning.

TOKENISM THEORY

Over a period of five years in the early 1970s, sociologist Kanter interviewed and observed employees at a large industrial supply company. Her research and conclusions were presented in *Men and Women of the Corporation.*[2] Specifically, Kanter focused on the experiences of a very small group of women sales managers working in a male-dominated department. Her case study consisted of analyses of interview data from twenty women in a 300-person sales force at a multinational Fortune 500 corporation as well as analyses of interview data from their colleagues and supervisors. She discovered that the experiences of the twenty women were very similar to those of one another and very different from those of their male co-workers. For example, she found that women (but not men) reported that they had been told that their job performance could affect the organizational prospects of other women in the company, and she further discovered that as a group, women (but not men) reported being excluded from important career-building activities, such as invitations to out-of-town business meetings. Kanter's research led her to conclude that these women were performing their jobs under very different conditions than those faced by their male co-workers. To explain how the women's experiences came to be so similar to one another's and so different from those of the male sales managers, Kanter developed tokenism theory.

Essentially, Kanter's theory is a structural theory of group composition that explains how perceptions and interactions are affected by the numerical proportions of demographically distinct group members. According to Kanter, one significant determinant of achievement for individuals within groups is the ratio of minority to majority group membership. Using a continuum to describe group composition, Kanter explained that groups can be at one end virtually uniform, with all members demographically similar. At the other end, they can be balanced, containing members of all social types. When groups are skewed to the extent that the imbalanced ratio of majority to minority members is eighty-five to fifteen or greater, minority group members are called tokens. At this ratio, rather than being perceived and treated as individuals, tokens tend to be perceived and treated as symbols of the category that distinguishes them from the majority. Token status leads many women to work longer hours with increased effort (often resulting in job burnout) or conversely, to withdraw from performance attempts (often leading to reduced job performance and compromised career aspirations). Significant numerical underrepresentation affects perceptual processes, which in turn affect interaction processes and performance. To better understand how the negative consequences of tokenism occur, we examine the perceptions that arise in demographically skewed work groups.

PERCEPTUAL PROCESSES

As just stated, significant numerical underrepresentation affects perceptual processes, interaction processes, and ultimately performance. Tokenism theory holds that group structure, specifically the proportional representation of different demographic groups, impacts group-related perceptions. When a particular demographic category is present but rare in a given group, this rarity leads to three types of perceptual distortions. The first is *visibility*, in which group members' attention is drawn more easily to notice demographically rare individuals who readily appear to be different from most group members. Second, *assimilation* occurs when group members perceive tokens' attributes as fitting preexisting beliefs or stereotypes associated with their demographic category. Finally, *contrast* is the exaggeration of group differences that results in in and outgroup perceptions holding the dominant group as the ingroup and tokens as outsiders. Information from social cognition theory readily can be used to explain these perceptual distortions.

At work, as in our daily lives, we encounter so much information that we are unable to fully process all of it. Thus we selectively attend to incoming information that will receive further processing. This is the beginning of meaning making that is assigned to the information; it is the initial stage in one's attempt to make sense of a situation. Attention is drawn by many things. When demographically dissimilar individuals are together, that dissimilarity captures group members' attention. It becomes a basis for understanding what to expect in the situation. Attention is drawn to tokens because their numbers make them stand out, and once attention is captured, an inference is made as to the importance of the attention-grabbing feature.

Women and men represent two demographically dissimilar categories. This draws attention, but attention is only the beginning of perception. Ultimately, perception is the interpretation of the information to which we attend. When women and men work together, gender will become a salient cognitive category used to interpret information.[4] When the gender category is activated by attention drawn to the significantly reduced number of women in a situation, because they are different from the majority and because the majority is a number great enough to constitute at least 85 percent of the present group, the token women will not be perceived as belonging. In such a situation, a token woman will be thought of merely as a "woman." She will not be viewed to be a "sales manager," an "executive," or a "carpenter." These are attributes that do not fit her category but rather better fit the male category.

Once each individual is identified with the appropriate category, category membership becomes the basis of understanding in the situation. Once group members are identified as fitting a particular category, they are believed to possess all attributes and characteristics held in that category and not to possess the attributes and characteristics in the opposing category.[5] Categorization makes it likely that token women will be perceived as belonging to, fitting, and even being representatives of the female stereotype, a stereotype that holds that women are communal and supportive. This is a perception that is in contrast with the male stereotype that men are agentic and competent.[6] Such stereotypical beliefs lead men in solo situations to be viewed as macho father figures, an idea that stands in opposition to the view of women solos working with a group of men. These women are seen as playing the role of mother, secretary, or bitch.[7]

Stereotypes can have profound effects on perceptions, but these effects cannot occur unless the stereotype is activated. Some environments seem to be better at categorization and stereotype activation, a process that leads to the belief that members of a particular category have more in common with one another and less in common with members of other categories.[8] These perceptual phenomena occur for men who notice, stereotype, and contrast themselves against token women. They also occur for women tokens, who are more aware of themselves as women in the situation and of the negative stereotypes associated with their group and feel a heightened responsibility for representing their sex.[9]

When this is applied to Kanter's three perceptual processes, we see that especially in a gendered environment such as work, attention is drawn to token women, and the visibility of these women makes it more likely that gender schemas will be activated. Once activated, all characteristics, attributes, and behaviors of token women will be interpreted consistently with the activated stereotype. Moreover, this will lead group members' perceptions to be drawn to similarities among the women, and an exaggeration of the believed differences between the women and the men in the group will occur.[10] Once these between-group distinctions provide a means for comparing aptitudes and capabilities, members of both groups infer that those in the majority are better suited, are more deserving, and belong more than tokens do. Because members of the dominant group determine the culture of the group, both groups will perceive tokens as not fitting the culture. These perceptual distortions lead to negative work outcomes.

INTERACTION AND PERFORMANCE PROCESSES

In her original conception of tokenism theory, Kanter suggested that token group membership will create performance pressures on tokens, which will affect their work negatively. To better explain token effects on interactions and performance, we return to the three perceptual processes that Kanter specified: visibility, assimilation, and contrast. Within a work group, these processes affect both dominants and tokens.

Dominant Group Members

Visibility

The attention of dominants is drawn more keenly to tokens, but it is drawn to the fact that the tokens are women, not to their achievements. When dominant group members' attention is not focused on tokens' achievements and when dominant group members are in a position to evaluate the performance of tokens, they tend to give tokens lower performance evaluations and not as keenly recognize token women's talents as compared with the evaluations given to women when women constitute a larger proportion of a work group.

This effect was demonstrated in a field study examining the relationship between sex proportion and the performance evaluation of 3,014 high-ranking officers in the Israeli Defense Forces. The performance of female officers was rated lower than that of male officers when the female officers were tokens, but female officers' performance was rated higher than male officers' performance when women constituted a larger proportion of the work group.[11] Another field study, this time examining data from 453 Canadian federal female and male managers, found that compared with the performance evaluations men gave to token women, men gave significantly higher performance evaluations to women who worked in groups that were not skewed to the extent that the women were tokens.[12] Because the attention of men who are charged with evaluating the performance of token women is drawn to the category membership of the token women, they can miss instances of successful performance, and when this occurs, the effect disadvantages token women as compared either with dominant men or with nontoken women.

Assimilation

Negative token effects clearly arise from visibility, but they accompany the perceptual and interactional processes of assimilation as well. When tokens' attributes are distorted to fit preexisting stereotypical beliefs, role encapsulation occurs, during which others view tokens as only suitable to stereotype-consistent jobs.[13] Token women are not seen as individuals with differing characteristics and abilities, but are viewed and treated as homogenous symbols of the female category. Viewing tokens as women rather than workers allows members of the dominant group to believe that they understand what behaviors to expect from the token women who have grabbed their attention, and they treat them accordingly. The activated female stereotype leads dominant men to believe not only that women *are* communal rather than agentic but also that they *should be* communal rather than agentic. This belief affects dominant group members' behavior in predictable ways.

Because being a representative of the female category does not fit with being a member of the leader stereotype, for example, token women are less likely to be selected as group leaders and will have a difficult time acting as leaders when appointed.[14] Furthermore, because token women are perceived as representing women in general, group satisfaction often is low when lone women are present.[15] This may occur because the female stereotype does not include the expectation of task competence, especially in a traditionally male-typed job. Moreover, assimilation of token women into the female stereotype can lead men to counteract women's success at work through what has been referred to as benevolent sexism.[16] For example, when a male co-worker expresses concern for a woman's safety or suggests that perhaps he should help her with a difficult task, his seemingly helpful behavior in actuality limits her ability to successfully perform all aspects of her job. So even when stereotyping leads to apparently chivalrous behavior by men, women's performance can be negatively affected.

Contrast

Stereotype activation and use also is implicated in the third perceptual distortion discussed by Kanter. Contrast occurs when group members' perceptions are drawn to believed differences between demographic groups, and it, too, has a significant impact on group interactions. The contrast of tokens with dominant group members frequently leads the majority to form seemingly impenetrable boundaries that marginalize tokens from informal supports that otherwise might assist their performance and promotion.[17] During such informal interactions as spending break time together, meeting on the golf course, or even chatting at the water cooler, career-assisting information frequently is shared. Not only are tokens left out of career-enhancing social activities, but by ignoring tokens and boosting one another, dominants also strengthen their own in-group cohesiveness. Kanter documented that the presence of token women works to increase solidarity among dominant men. For example, when a man prefaces a statement with "I probably shouldn't say this in mixed company," this simultaneously emphasizes the culture of the dominant group and highlights that the woman is an outsider. Being treated as a marginalized "other" leaves tokens feeling isolated.[18] Actual isolation limits the career-enhancing opportunities of token women, but felt isolation limits tokens in other ways.

Token Group Members

It is not only the behaviors of dominant group members that impact token women's job performance. The perceptual distortions of dominant group members have direct and negative effects on token women's job performance, but research also shows that token women are subject to the same perceptual distortions that dominant men have. Furthermore, token women's work behaviors also are affected by their own perceptions.

Visibility

Token women seem to understand the effects of visibility on the perceptions and behaviors of dominant group members. In fact, the women in Kanter's original study reported feeling the need to work harder to have their achievements noticed, told of situations in which their abilities were overshadowed by their physical appearance, and also discussed the added pressure of trying not to perform so well that they might threaten their male co-workers.[19] Feeling this pressure to do just well enough but not too well may be one reason that token women are more likely to report feeling increased stress and role overload, to perceive exploitation, and to report sexual harassment.[20] Because token women must devote energy toward balancing their level of success and managing elevated stress arising from their distinctiveness, they often find their energies for achievement depleted.

Assimilation

Tokens, sometimes explicitly and other times implicitly, are aware both that they are viewed as representatives of women in general and that their success or failure will be viewed as indicative of expectations for the future success or failure of all women who follow. This can create enormous pressure for a token, and it could explain why tokens often find it easier to conform to expectations rather than challenge others' stereotypical beliefs.[21] If token women believe that they are not expected to do well at their jobs or even that they are not expected to attempt certain jobs, such conformity limits job choice, career aspirations, and career progression. This conformity often keeps women out of higher-paying fields or keeps them from attempting to achieve higher positions within their companies.

The feeling that one does not fit or is not suited to a work situation can lead token women to experience stress.[22] It also can have profound effects on the job satisfaction, job choice, and organizational commitment of token women, and it even affects their expectations of performance in and acceptance by their work groups. Effects on tokens' expectations were demonstrated in a laboratory experiment in which female and male participants were asked to take part in two problem-solving tasks, the first independently and the second with a group whose composition was manipulated by the experimenters so that some participants anticipated being tokens and others did not. After being provided with written information about their future partners (information about personality traits and demographic characteristics), participants were asked a series of questions about their expectations for the future group experience. Women who anticipated being gender tokens (especially those with low confidence in their own task ability) were more likely than nontoken women and more likely than token men to want to change to a different group, to want to change the gender composition of their own group, and to expect to be stereotyped by others. These results suggest that women need not actually be tokens to be affected by tokenism. Mere anticipation of tokenism (along with low self-confidence) can be sufficient to induce negative tokenism effects.[23]

A related argument concludes that being in the minority can generate stereotype threat among stigmatized groups.[24] Stereotype threat arises when one fears being viewed through the lens of a negative stereotype, especially in a valued domain.[25] The fear inherent in stereotype threat can be one's concern for the impression others will have of her or him or concern one has for maintaining her or his own positive self-image.[26] Stereotype activation makes it so that being outnumbered is threatening for members of the token group, especially when performance is important (as it is at work). Feelings of threat negatively affect the tokens' expectations for their future performance, often leading to decrements in actual future performance as well. Concern that one is not expected to perform well can make an individual not attempt a particular task, or such fear can actually reduce performance when the individual attempts to function in the environment that induces stereotype threat. Research has shown that women's expectations of token status can lead them to attempt to either change to a group in which they will not be tokens or change their own group structure so that they will not be tokens. Further research shows that if such structural changes are not possible, token women's actual performance will be negatively affected by stereotype threat arising from their token status.

Contrast

Thus far, we have discussed how the perceptual distortions of visibility and assimilation affect the perceptions and behaviors of token women, but the third distortion, contrast, affects token women as well. Recall that when individuals are categorized, their category membership is contrasted against those in an opposing category. This results in decreased opportunities for token women. If a situation is such that men dominate, a culture will be created that will reward male but not female attributes.

This pattern was demonstrated in a study of the first female students allowed into West Point Academy.[27] These women described the fact that fraternization policies had been put in place ostensibly to discourage dating, but those policies served to isolate the women from any informal interactions with men, even those that might aid their performance. Not only were the women formally isolated, but they stood out as different from the men, and men had always been successful at West Point. Men were expected to be aggressive and competitive, but women were different. Because they were not the same, there was no expectation of aggression, competitiveness, or even success for the women.

Another study showed how contrast effects occurred for employees at a summer attraction assigned to one of three groups. In one group, two men worked in a gift shop with sixteen women. In another, one woman worked with six men in an isolated food stand. The third group was at a gender-balanced main food location. Unlike a traditionally male-typed military academy, these workers found themselves in the more gender-neutral job of concession worker. When employees were asked to describe their experiences at the end of the summer, the lone token woman reported experiences different from the reports of her co-workers. The token woman reported that she never felt that she fit with her work group, and she was observed spending as much of her break time as possible away from her work site. Her daily experience was such that she always was viewed in comparison with the men with whom she worked. In her work unit, three other workers were men; therefore the culture that developed was better suited to the dominant group. This woman quit at the end of the summer.[28]

It is clear from field studies and laboratory experiments alike that the perceptual distortions of visibility, assimilation, and contrast have negative consequences for token women. By connecting individual perceptual processes with social interaction processes, Kanter provided a more comprehensive means to understanding the performance-damaging experiences of many women attempting to take advantage of the doors that have been opened to them during and since the beginning of the women's movement of the 1970s. Through Kanter's theory, women no longer are blamed for the trouble they experience. However, Kanter's original conceptualization of tokenism theory was insufficient to provide a full explanation of token experiences.

REFINING THE THEORY

Gender and Tokenism

In her original conceptualization of token theory, Kanter suggested that the tokenism processes previously discussed would affect any demographic group representing less than 15 percent of total group composition. Although considerable research has been compiled to support her arguments for women tokens, there is solid evidence that the same is not necessarily true for underrepresented men.

Tokenism processes for women have been demonstrated across a wide array of occupations and manipulative experiments. For example, research with military cadets found that women were readily visible, even in uniform; that in basic training, women scored higher than men on tests measuring psychological stress; that women felt socially isolated and disapproved of by peers; and that women reported role conflicts between masculinized expectations for cadets (e.g., "command" voices) and stereotypes for themselves as women (e.g., fragile).[29] Similar tokenism effects have been confirmed in women in the fields of police officer, construction worker, firefighter, corrections officers in male prisons, physicians, academics, and executives.[30]

The women in each of these studies reported some form or even multiple forms of the negative outcomes associated with visibility, assimilation, and contrast, but the same was not necessarily true for men. For example, in an interview study, researchers found that women but not men in elite positions (e.g., company president or CEO) reported barriers to career progression such as being excluded from informal networks with male peers, an exclusion that hindered women's job performance.[31] Another study of executives compared women executives' perceptions and expectations with those of more subordinate women, then did the same for men.[32] These researchers found that compared with subordinate women, female executives reported lower satisfaction with future career opportunities and expected to encounter more promotion obstacles, such as not fitting into the organization's culture. These differences were not found when data between subordinate and executive men were compared. The reason could be that women (but not men) executives and executive (but not subordinate) women expected more future obstacles because their experiences as they climbed the executive ladder already had been fraught with obstacles. This reasoning is supported by a survey of human resource managers in 304 organizations.[33] This survey showed that 72 percent of non-traditional managers reported that what they perceived to be the top barrier to their advancement was that traditional (white male) managers were already in place, and they believed that this limited the promotion of women and people of color because those in power are more comfortable interacting with their own kind.

There is more direct evidence that negative effects do not necessarily transpire for token men. Recall from the previously mentioned studies of executives that the perceptions and expectations of male executives differed from those of female executives. A follow-up study found that the actual career progressions of men differed from those of women as well.[34] In contrast to token women executives who were more likely to report not fitting into the organizational culture and difficulty getting developmental assignments, male executives were more likely to report that developmental opportunities were handed to them and that mentoring significantly facilitated their career success.

Clearly, the expectations and experiences of token men do not necessarily mirror those of token women. A closer examination of male token effects shows that for white men in the female-dominated fields of nurse, social worker, librarian, and teacher, their own perceived masculinity and work attitudes may be threatened, but these men often are advantaged with pay and promotion.[35] Contrasting attitude data have been collected to show that token male flight attendants expressed the favorable work attitudes of job satisfaction and organizational attachment.[36] In general, though, no data have been found to oppose the conclusion that men's pay and promotion are positively affected by token status because men's pay typically is advantaged when they work in female-dominated fields.[37] Research seems to clearly indicate that although men may experience some of the negative psychological outcomes of token status, their actual achievements are not affected negatively in the ways that women's are.

Given this mixed bag of outcomes for men, what has been called men's glass escalator (as opposed to women's glass ceiling) seems to reflect universal male advantage rather than benefits attributed to simple numeric proportion.[38] In our society, white men are typically advantaged over members of other groups. The fact that these men do not fall victim to the same negative effects that women face when in a token position suggests that it is more than simple numerical underrepresentation that brings about harmful token effects. The outcomes Kanter thought were due to proportions alone really result from the combination of token proportions with stigmatized status, most commonly operationalized as being female in a male-dominated and masculinized context.[39]

Status and Tokenism

The addition of the status explanation to tokenism theory allows us to better understand why negative tokenism effects occur for women but do not fully occur for men. Status is the relative social position that accompanies certain characteristics and guides behavior, even when we are not explicitly aware of it.[40] In our society, women's status tends to be lower than that of men.[41] Because social status reflects the hierarchical position of individuals within a group, it influences the perceived value of each group member relative to the others. As a status characteristic, gender conveys information about the value, worth, and capabilities of women relative to men as well as the behaviors (subordinate or dominant) that are appropriate for each group.[42]

Determinations of status lead to expectations for ability. Within a task situation, such as those at work, higher-status individuals are believed to be more able to successfully perform the group's task. Such status construction becomes circular. Higher status group members are believed to be better able to perform, and then they are provided more opportunities to behave in ways that will lead to success, thereby fulfilling the original prophecy that these individuals are more valuable in the group.[43] For example, high-status group members are allowed to (and in fact are expected to) behave instrumentally, whereas low-status individuals are expected to be more communal. When group members observe dominant group members making task contributions and actively engaged in the task then see those dominants successful in their behavior, group members' status beliefs are confirmed. Because they are perceived in the group (by dominant members and by themselves) as less valuable, women are given and attempt fewer task contributions. Instead, they are expected to provide support for those who are actively engaged in the task. When they and other group members observe token women performing low-status behaviors, again, status beliefs are confirmed. So, in the same way that the female stereotype specifies not only that women are but also that they should be communal, low-status beliefs do the same. Not only *are* low-status group members expected to be less successful at the task, but because they are less valuable, they *should be* less successful and therefore given fewer opportunities for success.

If a woman who holds a normatively lower position is also a token with the spotlight on her, then not only is the female stereotype activated but its accompanying low-status expectations are simultaneously activated so that multiple low-status expectations are applied to her. The expectation will be that she is less competent than the high-status members of the dominant group. It will not be appropriate for her to perform well, so her performance will be more harshly judged. Her achievement and advancement will be both inappropriate for her status and perceived as a challenge to the status of the men in the dominant group. Role encapsulation, keeping her in a subordinate position, along with boundary heightening, which strengthens the distinction between high- and low-status group members, will allow men to feel more secure in their high-status positions.

If not for the expectations that arise when one's low-status position becomes salient, the negative effects of tokenism would not occur. Mere reduced representation can make a group member more visible, but being in the spotlight will not be threatening to a person who is expected to perform well. Increased stress arises when a person is in the spotlight only if the spotlight is shining on decreased performance expectations. Similarly, the negative consequences of assimilation are not solely due to stereotype activation and the resulting perceptual processes. The negative outcomes of assimilation occur when the activated stereotype contains low-status expectations, such as the unsuitability of the token for high-status power, privilege, or reward. When men are tokens and the male stereotype is activated, it contains high-status expectations, such as increased competence and value, two attributes associated with power, privilege, and reward. This stereotype activation does not handicap a man in the same way that activation of the female stereotype can handicap a woman. And finally, contrast processes would be unnecessary if not for status beliefs. Dominant men would have no need to contrast themselves so severely against token women if not for status-related outcomes. To not lose their power or to keep the reward that accompanies a high-status position, men must be distinct from low-status tokens. Thus, it is not underrepresentation alone that brings negative token effects but the combination of being a low-status person and rare in a group that leads to negative outcomes.

Race/Ethnicity and Tokenism

Gender is not the only demographically related status characteristic. Race/ethnicity also conveys status information.[44] Research extending demonstrated tokenism patterns beyond gender to race/ethnicity is minimal, though, and may be culturally specific. Available data, however, seem to support the status argument. For instance, a study of African American elite leaders found evidence of depression and anxiety as well as loss of black identity, multiple demands, felt isolation, and pressure to confirm one's competence.[45] The subjective experience of distinctiveness is especially strong among African Americans who commonly find themselves in positions as solos, an extreme form of tokenism. Studies of women firefighters demonstrated that differing stereotypes for African American and white women can each lead to role entrapment, but in qualitatively different ways for each group. Black women reported being overburdened in response to their stereotype as self-sufficient in contrast to white women, who described being underburdened as a result of their stereotype as fragile.[46] Again, this is a status-related effect. Women firefighters are often gender tokens privileged by their race/ethnicity in their firehouses in contrast to African American women firefighters, who typically are relegated to token status based on both their subordinated race/ethnicity and gender. Given that the fundamental basis for tokenism effects is status difference between tokens and dominants, further research exploring how race/ethnicity-status combines with numeric underrepresentation is warranted.

REDUCING TOKEN EFFECTS

When women represent less than 15 percent of a work group, their numeric underrepresentation combined with their lower status leads to perceptual distortions that bring about predicable negative outcomes. To better understand how to counter this process, some researchers have moved away from the simple documentation of negative effects and toward explorations of methods to facilitate tokens' success. Given Kanter's emphasis on proportions, the most obvious solution became increasing numbers themselves. The benefit of increased numbers remains unclear. Research in this area is mixed with some reporting more favorable outcomes when proportions exceed 15 percent and contrasting research highlighting intensified boundary heightening in the face of intrusive numerical increases.[47] The inconclusiveness in this literature may well rest in the clearly established understanding that tokenism effects themselves are more complex than simple proportional representation.

If negative token effects arise through numeric underrepresentation of low-status group members, then raising the status of women tokens should alleviate those effects. To test the hypothesis that raised status could counteract negative token effects, in a laboratory experiment researchers assigned gender token women to lead one of three groups.[48] Women leaders of all-male groups performing a masculine-typed task were (1) simply appointed to be leader; (2) appointed and trained beforehand (i.e., provided with task-relevant knowledge); and (3) appointed, trained, and legitimated by credible organizational personnel (a male experimenter). Legitimating is one means of allowing normatively lower-status women to be perceived as fitting a high-status position. Only the leaders of groups who were appointed, trained, and legitimated were able to facilitate group performance, suggesting that higher-status dominant men perceived it to be appropriate to be led by token women who were trained and legitimated. This finding suggests that it may be possible to override negative token effects within a context of skewed proportions.

Another line of research attempting to ameliorate token effects has followed successful tokens, comparing them to both less successful tokens and similarly successful dominants. Successful tokens reported relying on good track records, nurturing relationships, proactive management of their own career, mentoring, and developmental job assignments.[49] At times these women were perceived by themselves and others as belonging to the higher-status group. Rather than being seen merely as women, they were viewed as workers, in which case they no longer supported or identified with their still disadvantaged out-group of origin. Such findings are disturbing but not surprising, especially given our understanding of the felt need of high-status group members to be identified as such so that they are able to receive the power and privilege that accompanies such a position. Anecdotal individual boundary crossing fails to challenge societal structures that place women in a subordinate position relative to men, so the core of tokenism theory as a structural theory grounded in both numeric group structure as well as societal status structure remains.

To more fully understand the complexity of harmful token effects, further research is necessary. Specific incidents of status change can be found, cited, and even studied; however, the structure of society is not altered. That means that the inferior position of women and the perceptions created by that status structure are not altered in any way that would generalize from those specific instances. Instead, tokens who overcome are anomalies, and special cases do not undermine the stereotypes that are developed and strengthened with each confirmation of the existing status structure.

THE PROMISE OF TOKENISM THEORY

At its inception during the revival of the women's activism in the 1970s, tokenism theory was a monumental concept. Until then, many believed that women, by virtue of their sex, were not suited to certain positions. They were not thought capable of performing certain jobs. The prevailing belief was one of individual accountability. Through her research and the theory she developed, Kanter explained that job performance is not fixed by one's demographic characteristics. She argued that job performance is largely determined by work environment, going on to suggest that all workers, even those in the same work group, do not perform their jobs under identical circumstances. This took the focus away from victim blaming toward an understanding that could provide different solutions. The focus shifted from "What is it about women that limits their success at work?" to "What is it about the work environment that prevents women from succeeding and how does this prevention occur?" Reframing the problem in this way allows more creative solutions to be developed. The solution is not to prevent the unsuccessful individual from attempting different types of work. Rather, the solution is to structure work environments in such a way that all workers are able to succeed.

Those who find themselves few of a kind among a majority of others, especially when the few are lower status than the majority, are working in a context very different from that of most workers. For high-status dominants and low-status tokens, the context activates perceptual processes like visibility, assimilation, and contrast that make token achievement more difficult. Consequently, workplace discrimination (e.g., difficulty being hired, receiving biased evaluations, wage disparities, and reduced respect) becomes a product of the combination of the system and those within it. This remains a monumental concept because it implies that the achievement of subordinated social categories such as women, racial and ethnic minorities, and people with disabilities is not decided simply by their own fixed demographic characteristics. Instead, tokenism theory suggests that achievement can be dynamically altered as social structures change because changes in social structure affect changes in perception, which in turn lead to different behavioral outcomes.

The persisting promise of tokenism theory lies in its intersection of individualistic psychological processes (e.g., perceptual effects) with broader sociological approaches (e.g., the effects of group structure) into the more social psychological approach we have discussed. Such an integrated approach allows for better awareness of the processes that lead to the discrimination faced by women who work in male-dominated fields or work groups. Only through this better understanding can such discrimination be effectively thwarted.

NOTES

1. Rosabeth Moss Kanter, *Men and Women of the Corporation* (New York: Basic Press, 1977).

2. Ibid.

3. Janice D. Yoder, "Rethinking Tokenism: Looking beyond Numbers," *Gender and Society* 5 (1991): 178–92.

4. Susan T. Fiske and Shelley E. Taylor, *Social Cognition*, 2nd ed. (New York: McGraw-Hill, 1991); Cecilia L Ridgeway, "Interaction and the Conservation of Gender Inequality: Considering Employment," *American Sociological Review* 5 (1997): 218–35.

5. Fiske and Taylor, *Social Cognition*; Ridgeway, "Interaction and Conservation."

6. Amanda B. Diekman and Alice H. Eagly, "Stereotypes as Dynamic Constructs: Women and Men of the Past, Present, and Future," *Personality and Social Psychology Bulletin* 26 (2000): 1171–88.

7. Kay Deaux and Brenda Major, "Putting Gender into Context: An Interactive Model of Gender-Related Behavior," *Psychological Review* 94 (1987): 369–86.

8. Fiske and Taylor, *Social Cognition*; Delia S. Saenz, "Token Status and Problem-Solving Deficits: Detrimental Effects of Distinctiveness and Performance Monitoring," *Social Cognition* 12 (1994): 61–74.

9. Asya Pazy and Israela Oron, "Sex Proportion and Performance Evaluation among High-Ranking Military Officers," *Journal of Organizational Behavior* 22 (2001): 689–702; Patricia G. Devine, "Stereotypes and Prejudice: Their Automatic and Controlled Components," *Journal of Personality and Social Psychology* 56 (1989): 5–18.

10. Saenz, "Token Status and Problem-Solving Deficits."

11. Pazy and Oron, "Sex Proportion and Performance Evaluation."

12. Monique Lortie-Lussier and Natalie Rinfret, "The Proportion of Women Managers: Where Is the Critical Mass?" *Journal of Applied Social Psychology* 32 (2002): 1974–99.

13. Kanter, *Men and Women of the Corporation*.

14. Jennifer Crocker and Kathleen M. McGraw, "What's Good for the Goose Is Not Good for the Gander: Solo Status as an Obstacle to Occupational Achievement for Males and Females," *American Behavioral Scientist* 27 (1984): 357–69; Janice D. Yoder,

Thomas L. Schleicher, and Theodore W. McDonald, "Empowering Token Women Leaders: The Importance of Organizationally Legitimated Credibility," *Psychology of Women Quarterly* 22 (1998): 209–22.

15. Crocker and MacGraw, "What's Good for the Goose Is Not Good for the Gander."

16. Peter Glick and Susan T. Fiske, "The Ambivalent Sexism Inventory: Differentiating Hostile and Benevolent Sexism," *Journal of Personality and Social Psychology* 70 (1996): 491–512.

17. Kanter, *Men and Women of the Corporation*.

18. Joanna L. Young and Erika Hayes-James, "Token Majority: The Work Attitudes of Male Flight Attendants," *Sex Roles* 45 (2001): 299–319.

19. Kanter, *Men and Women of the Corporation*.

20. Pamela B. Jackson, Peggy A. Thoits, and Howard F. Taylor, "Composition of the Workplace and Psychological Well-Being: The Effects of Tokenism on America's Black Elite," *Social Forces* 74 (1995): 543–57; Janet Rosenberg, Harry Perlstadt, and William R. Phillips, "Now that We Are Here: Discrimination, Disparagement, and Harassment at Work and the Experience of Women Lawyers," *Gender and Society* 7 (1993): 415–33.

21. Jackson et al., "Composition of the Workplace and Psychological Well-Being."

22. David J. Maume and Paula Houston, "Job Segregation and Gender Differences in Work-Family Spillover among White-Collar Workers," *Journal of Family and Economic Issues* 22 (2001): 171–89.

23. Laurie L. Cohen and Janet K. Swim, "The Differential Impact of Gender Ratios on Women and Men: Tokenism, Self-Confidence, and Expectations," *Personality and Social Psychology Bulletin* 21 (1995): 876–84.

24. Michael Inzlicht and Talia Ben-Zeev, "Do High-Achieving Female Students Underperform in Private: The Implications of Threatening Environments on Intellectual Processing," *Journal of Educational Psychology* 95 (2003): 796–805.

25. Claude M. Steele, "A Threat in the Air: How Stereotypes Shape Intellectual Identity and Performance," *American Psychologist* 52 (1997): 613–29.

26. Inzlicht and Ben Zeev, "Do High-Achieving Female Students Underperform in Private."

27. Janice D. Yoder and Jerome Adams, "Women Entering Nontraditional Roles: When Work Demands and Sex-Roles Conflict: The Case of West Point," *International Journal of Women's Studies* 7 (1984): 260–72.

28. Janice D. Yoder and Laura M. Sinnett, "Is It All in the Numbers? A Case Study of Tokenism," *Psychology of Women Quarterly* 9 (1985): 413–18.

29. Yoder et al., "Empowering Token Women Leaders."

30. E. Marlies Ott, "Effects of the Male-Female Ratio at Work: Policewomen and Male Nurses," *Psychology of Women Quarterly* 13 (1989): 41–57; Clara Greed, "Women in the Construction Professions: Achieving Critical Mass," *Gender, Work, and Society* 7 (2001): 181–96; Janice D. Yoder and Patricia Aniakudo, "Outsider within the Firehouse: Subordination and Difference in the Social Interactions of African American Women Firefighters," *Gender and Society* 11 (1997): 324–431; Janice D. Yoder, and Lynne L. Berendsen, "Outsider within the Firehouse: African American and White Women Firefighters," *Psychology of Women Quarterly* 25 (2001): 27–36; Lynn Zimmer, *Women Guarding Men* (Chicago: University of Chicago Press, 1986); Liliane Floge and Deborah

M. Merrill, "Tokenism Reconsidered: Male Nurses and Female Physicians in a Hospital Setting," *Social Forces* 64 (1986): 925–47; Carlotta J. Young, Doris MacKenzie, and Carolyn W. Sherif, "In Search of Token Women in Academia," *Psychology of Women Quarterly* 4 (1980): 508–25.

31. Sally Ann Davies-Netzley, "Women above the Glass Ceiling: Perceptions on Corporate Mobility and Strategies for Success," *Gender and Society* 12 (1988): 339–55.

32. Karen S. Lyness, and Donna E. Thompson, "Climbing the Corporate Ladder: Do Female and Male Executives Follow the Same Route?" *Journal of Applied Psychology* 85 (2000): 86–101.

33. Catalyst, *Women in Corporate Leadership: Progress and Prospects* (New York: Catalyst, 1996).

34. Lyness and Thompson, "Climbing the Corporate Ladder."

35. Christine L. Williams, "The Glass Escalator: Hidden Advantages for Men in the Female Professions," *Social Problems* 39 (1992): 253–67.

36. Young and Hayes-James, "Token Majority."

37. Michelle J. Budig, "Male Advantage and the Gender Composition of Jobs: Who Rides the Glass Elevator?" *Social Problems* 49 (2002): 258–77.

38. Williams, "The Glass Escalator."

39. Yoder, "Rethinking Tokenism."

40. Theodore W. McDonald, Loren L. Toussaint, and Jennifer A. Schweiger, "The Influence of Social Status on Token Women Leaders' Expectations about Leading Male-Dominated Groups," *Sex Roles* 50 (2004): 401–9.

41. Edwin P. Hollander, "Leadership, Followership, Self, and Others," *Leadership Quarterly* 3 (1992): 43–54.

42. Murray Webster and James E. Driskell, "Status Generalization: A Review and Some New Data," *American Sociological Review* 43 (1978): 220–36.

43. Ridgeway, "Interaction and Conservation."

44. Ibid.

45. Jackson et al., "Composition of the Workplace and Psychological Well-Being."

46. Yoder and Berendsen, "Outsider within the Firehouse."

47. E. Marlies Ott and Hubert M. Blalock, "Status Inconsistency, Social Mobility, Status Integration, and Structural Effects," *American Sociological Review* 32 (1967): 790–801.

48. Yoder et al., "Empowering Token Women Leaders."

49. Lyness and Thompson, "Climbing the Corporate Ladder."

11

Power, Control, and Gender: Training as Catalyst for Dysfunctional Behavior at the U.S. Air Force Academy

Jamie L. Callahan

It is easier and more common to treat symptoms than to find and address underlying causes of problems. This axiom holds true not only for medicine but also for organizational interventions. The recent attempts by the U.S. Air Force (USAF) to respond to allegations of sexual assaults at the USAF Academy (USAFA) is an example of treating symptoms at the expense of ignoring underlying causes. In this chapter, I analyze the symptoms of dysfunction at the USAFA to uncover the potential causes of the problems.

Early in 2003, national media outlets began reporting about sexual assaults at the USAFA. Throughout 2003 and even extended through summer 2005, allegations of assaults, cover-ups, investigations, and USAF corrective actions filled the news. Many expressed disbelief that such a scandal would ignite at the USAFA, the elite proving ground for the USAF. As a female USAFA graduate, however, I was surprised that it had taken so long to become public.

A scandal that has not yet been as widely publicized is the rate of eating disorders among USAFA cadets. Recent media reports have highlighted that the U.S. military is having problems with overweight soldiers (CNN, 2005), at least half of whom had engaged in unhealthy weight loss strategies, such as bulimic behaviors, in an attempt to meet weight requirements. Eating disorders have been a hidden problem at the USAFA since the 1980s when a study revealed that the rate of bulimia among female cadets was three times the national average among college students.

I contend that the existence at the USAFA of these two problems—sexual assaults and eating disorders—is related. Although the current sexual assault scandal has been widely interpreted as an organizational culture that perpetuates violence against women, the reality is that the likely underlying catalyst for the scandal affects both women *and* men. I suggest that the sexual assault and eating disorder problems experienced at the USAFA find their roots in cadet training practices that deprive individuals of personal control. Thus, in this chapter, I describe how these training practices contribute to creating an atmosphere that leads to dysfunctional behaviors by both male and female cadets.

Current actions to address the presenting problem of sexual assault have included replacement of senior leadership and a flurry of awareness training programs. Although they are visible and appeasing, these types of responses are reactionary and fail to address the underlying catalyst that fosters the dysfunctional behavior. This underlying catalyst is the practice of rendering new cadets powerless in a process of stripping individuals' old identities to remold them in the image of an elite USAF officer. This deprivation of power or control causes some cadets to seek avenues in which they *can* exert control. Though there are many potential outlets, both positive and negative, to exert control, two visible and devastating negative outlets may arise directly from the deprivation of power that occurs in early cadet socialization training. Male cadets may attempt to exert control over female cadets, and female cadets may attempt to exert control over their own bodies.

In the sections that follow, I provide an overview of my qualifications to offer an interpretive perspective of the context and some background on the USAFA context. I offer an interpretation of dysfunctional behaviors as gendered responses to power deprivation in cadet training, and I conclude with implications for research and practice.

BACKGROUND

My current interest was triggered by the sexual assault scandal and aftermath at the USAFA in recent years. Because of my personal experience as a USAFA cadet, I instinctively felt that the corrective actions reported in the media—such as replacing leaders, offering awareness training, and segregating men and women —would not resolve the complaints regarding sexual assaults. I believed the problem was much deeper but had not thoughtfully reflected on the possible underlying cause of the assaults. I began to more systematically reflect on my experiences and more closely monitor media reports regarding the academy to gain a better understanding of the current context.

I have a unique perspective regarding the situation at the USAFA. As a female graduate of the academy, I have personal experiences with the culture and practices of the context. As a professor of human resource development, I also have been trained as a social scientist. Because this chapter is a result of my exploration of self in the USAFA, I first must offer some context for my analysis of the academy. To that end, it is important for the reader to be able to visualize who I am.

As I write this article, I stand just under five feet, two inches, weigh approximately 118 pounds, and wear a U.S. size 4 petite that is slightly big for me; I weighed exactly the same when I was a senior cadet at USAFA. However, because I was considered too close to my maximum weight allowance at that time, my squadron monitored my weight on a regular basis. To this day, I remember the comment made by one of my male squadron mates as I waited to be weighed in one day, "You know, Jamie, you'd be really cute if you would just lose five or ten pounds." Today, almost twenty years later, I finally realize that I am not and was not fat; nevertheless, the psychological scars are still there.

I can also speak to issues of sexual harassment. Although I was fortunate to have never been assaulted, I knew quite a few female cadets who said that they had been assaulted. Some reported it, some did not; some left, some stayed. On the other hand, I realize now that sexual harassment was such a fundamental part of the training routine that at the time, I didn't even realize it was occurring. Following examples cited by Dunivin in "There's Men, There's Women, and There's Me: The Role and Status of Military Women," I was just trying to be one of the guys and fell into a routine of unquestioning acceptance. Part of getting rid of an individual's identity to mold a new one includes stripping the identity of sexuality. In the process of stripping one's sexual identity, practices are used that can easily be associated with sexual harassment. For example, pushing the men by referring to them as "girls" or "pussies" or using explicitly sexual terms to label uniform parts or to measure cadence for marching in formation. Oddly, until I separated from the USAF and completed my doctoral work, I never considered these common behaviors sexual harassment.

THE USAFA

Integrity first, Service before self, Excellence in all we do.
—Core values of the USAFA

Military service academies in the United States (Army, Air Force, Navy, Coast Guard) are undergraduate institutions that typically have approximately 4,000 cadets. The caliber of applicants and the rigor of academics at these institutions have earned them the reputation of being public Ivy League universities. Cadets are required to take a *minimum* of eighteen credit hours per semester, to hold nonpaying squadron jobs, and to participate in mandatory extracurricular or intercollegiate activities. Unlike most college students, they have only approximately six weeks of vacation time per year (two weeks at Christmas, one week for Spring Break, and three weeks of summer vacation). The core mission of the institution is to educate, train, and inspire young men and women to become leaders of the USAF, dedicated to becoming career officers who give a lifetime of selfless service to the nation.

To initiate this process, cadets are socialized into the USAFA through Basic Cadet Training (BCT). When freshmen (otherwise known as doolies, derived from the Latin *dulia* which means "slave") arrive at the USAFA to begin BCT (or Beast), they enter a system in which personal characteristics are minimized.

Their civilian clothing is replaced with a uniform; men's hair is shaved and, until very recently, women's hair was cut short. Civilian glasses and contact lenses are replaced with black, horn-rimmed, "birth control glasses." Doolies in BCT may not go anywhere outside the squadron area alone, march at attention at all times, and participate in a series of activities designed to instill in them a warrior spirit and to teach them how to behave within the USAFA experience. In June 2003, the USAFA commandant indicated that "We're trying to get everyone to talk and think like warriors."

Interestingly, the Fowler Panel noted that BCT's real purpose was to create cohesiveness among team members of different socioeconomic statuses, classes, races, and genders but that many cadets felt that the system was meant to break the will of new cadets to remold them into a military image. This denotes a difference between espoused theory and theory in use regarding the purpose of BCT; it is quite likely that the tacit theory is what influences the development of the organizational culture.

GENDERED RESPONSES TO TRAINING PRACTICES

In Western society, women are socialized to feel successful if they are attractive and feminine like runway models; in other words, women are judged by their appearance and thinness. Men, on the other hand, are socialized to be masculine warriors, ready to engage in combat. Thus, prior to arriving at the USAFA, cadets have already been socialized by broad cultural influences associated with gender roles. Once arriving at the academy, cadets enter a basic training program designed in part to fundamentally alter their individual sense of identity. This practice is meant to initiate the cadet into desired cultural norms that reinforce what can be called a combat, masculine warrior image. Thus, influence transitions from the socius to the psyche and then back to the socius (see Table 11.1). This section discusses how this chain of influence impacts both male and female cadets.

Culture is transmitted in multiple ways, one of which is training associated with socialization. An organization's existing culture influences the nature and contents, both implicit and explicit, of socialization training. In turn, new

TABLE 11.1. Chain of Socius-Psyche Influence

	Pre-BCT (Socius)	BCT (Psyche)	Post-BCT (Socius)
Male cadets	Combat masculine warrior (CMW)	Loss of control = sexual assault	CMW reinforced
Female cadets	Attractive feminine model (AFM)	Loss of control = eating disorder	CMW and AFM in conflict

members are introduced to the culture through socialization training and help maintain that culture. Individuals pay attention to others' actions and their consequences and make decisions about their own actions based on the consequences of others.' In this way, implicit understandings of accepted cultural practices are generated—what is rewarded and what is punished. In the case of the USAFA, BCT plays a vital role in the transmission of cultural expectations, many of which are tacit.

Culture is maintained because social practices tend to be inserted into routines, often unconsciously, through our responses and reactions to events occurring around us. The repetition of practices over time and space creates routines that help individuals navigate their daily lives. Disruption of those routines can be traumatic; concentration camps, battle under fire, and religious conversions are given by sociologists as examples of situations in which existing routines are shattered and replaced with new ones. Those who are able to find some means of control in their lives are the ones who survive this "re-socialization" process. This concept of the consequences of breaking routines and resocializing is particularly enlightening for the USAFA because the initial training experience for new cadets involves shattering old routines to break down old identities and instill new USAF identities.

By removing power from the new cadets, that power is strengthened in external figures. An external locus of control is indicated in cases of eating disorders; in other words, individuals feel that others have greater power over their actions or decisions, and as a result, they seek alternative outlets to experience a sense of control. Although the problem is indeed associated with the organizational culture, as suggested by the Hall memorandum and the Fowler panel, the patterns of action have been directed at addressing only the explicit problem at hand instead of exploring the tacit reasons for the existence of the problem.

The Female Experience

This cultural norm for women to be attractive, feminine models influences girls before they even come to the USAFA. This is a difficult norm to uphold while in BCT and during the academy experience in general. A common phrase directed at female cadets while I was in training was that they suffered from CHD—Colorado hip disease—even when they were well within weight limits. Unlike their civilian counterparts, female cadets wear uniforms that are not particularly stylish, contend with stringent weight standards with limited access to healthy low-calorie foods, and face regular hostility from male cadets who don't believe women should be allowed to attend the USAFA.

Due to the nature of BCT, young women may feel that they have lost control over their personal lives. Research suggests that eating disorders, such as bulimia, are responses to powerlessness that frequently occur in women who have an external locus of control. Another key factor in the occurrence of eating disorders is dissatisfaction with appearance, such that those who believe they are not thin enough are likely to manifest abnormal eating behaviors.

One of the goals of BCT is to create combat warriors; the USAFA Public Affairs newsletter, titled *Warrior Focus*, highlights the combat, masculine warrior culture of the USAFA. To adopt this image of a combat, masculine warrior, and therefore fit within the USAFA culture, women must unlearn almost two decades of socialization and adopt a persona that is counter to what they have been taught equates to success. In addition, they must combat forces that continue to encourage them to meet the attractive, feminine model cultural norms. As a result, women battle both a sense of loss of control during BCT and, especially after BCT, a heightened pressure to meet both masculine *and* feminine cultural norms.

Military women in general have a significantly higher rate of eating disorders, especially bulimia, than their civilian counterparts. Freshmen female cadets at USAFA experience bulimia three times more often than female freshmen at other colleges. Furthermore, evidence suggests that these conditions are not preexisting but that contextual military factors cause the eating disorder. These contextual factors may include the deprivation of control in BCT, stringent weight standards, and negative perceptions of the dominant (male) group.

The Male Experience

Unlike women, who are socialized to be attractive, feminine models, men are socialized to be more like combat, masculine warriors; this is especially true for men in the military. In general, men are seen as successful based on their achievements instead of their personal appearance. Furthermore, Western (particularly American) culture tends to objectify women and "frequently views sexual intercourse as an act of masculine conquest." A fear that one does not meet these standards of masculinity may result in acts of sexual aggression toward women. Studies of fraternities also have suggested that group dynamics of fraternity culture encourage sexual coercion; although there are no fraternities per se at the USAFA, cadets commonly believe that they are part of one big fraternity, and at the very least, individual squadrons easily take on characteristics of fraternities. Thus, male cadets are socialized to believe that achieving sexual intercourse is a sign that they meet the standards of the combat, masculine warrior culture upheld by the USAFA. Experiences that begin in BCT reinforce the cultural perception that men are supposed to be dominant, achievement-oriented, powerful, and masculine. As with female cadets, male cadets also experience a climate created in part by the USAFA training system in which cultural perceptions may lead to dysfunctional behaviors—for women, the dysfunction is bulimia, and for men, it is sexual aggression.

But also like the women, male cadets experience another factor that may cause their dysfunctional behavior. Since the 1940s, repeated research has indicated that rape is often the result of a need for control, particularly over women. If BCT removes a sense of personal control from cadets, this research suggests that they will seek an outlet in which to express control as a response. If negative sanctions do not result from sexual aggression, theory and research indicate that such behavior is likely to continue.

Thus, initial socialization training may influence dysfunctional behaviors in two ways—through the psyche and the socius. First, through the psyche, by removing a sense of personal control, cadets seek avenues to reestablish control; men may demonstrate dominance over women, and women may demonstrate dominance over their own bodies. Second, through the socius, by reinforcing cultural expectations regarding a combat, masculine warrior, cadet training increases a climate that accepts male (sexual) aggression and creates cultural conflict for women who attempt to meet standards for both men and women.

IMPLICATIONS

Although adjustments to the larger organizational and societal culture would certainly stem the problem with dysfunctional behaviors by both male and female cadets, a key overlooked starting point to facilitate such a culture shift is the initial socialization training (BCT) new cadets experience. There is a need to reassess the purpose of the current USAF and USAFA and adapt training strategies accordingly. Although many positive changes have been made over the years, they do not seem to be made in a strategic way, and the underlying premise of the training continues to be based in military training culture hundreds of years old. Training designers at the USAFA need to strategically reassess BCT (and perhaps the entire four-year training sequence) and ask questions such as:

- What kinds of missions is the USAF most likely to face?
- Do our current practices create physically and psychologically healthy USAF officers capable of operating in missions faced by the USAF today?
- How can we best prepare USAF officers (both male and female) to accomplish those missions?

The missions that U.S. armed forces often face in the twenty-first century are of a peacekeeping nature. It is very likely that the training needed to be successful in this type of mission is very different from the training needed in more traditional combat missions. Analyses of peacekeeping missions in Somalia and the Balkans suggest that the skills necessary to keep peace differ from those needed to win wars and that military forces tend to get in trouble because when under stress, they resort to combat skills. Thus, training to enhance a combat, masculine warrior image may disadvantage soldiers in a major scope of military operations.

Additionally, I submit that the combat, masculine warrior mission is a small percentage of the entire operations of the USAF. Even in wartime, the USAF tends to be much more removed from the need for such a cultural image than the services that are more likely to engage in hand-to-hand combat. Perhaps this very removal from a traditional military frontline combat role instigates a stronger push toward creating a warrior spirit among USAFA cadets and officials. Whereas other service academies have modified many more of their practices to be more inclusive and less overtly combat, masculine warrior in their cultures, the USAFA has lagged. Yet the USAF seems to have more problems with issues that stem from the attempt to create such a combat image. Is it possible that the USAF is trying harder to project such an image to account for the perception that it is the most antiseptic branch of combat arms?

Regardless of the cultural push for a warrior culture, the USAFA has an opportunity to stem some of the dysfunctional behaviors that manifest due to control issues. Instead of holding sexual harassment and sexual assault training, training designed to increase cadets' sense of personal control is more likely to influence the broader problems occurring at USAFA and improve cadet performance. In fact, the types of training provided to cadets currently may actually be more damaging to women in several ways.

First, increasing awareness of the problem without providing strategies and opportunities to make effective change may be very frustrating. Women bear the brunt of both the sexual assault dysfunctional behavior by male cadets and their own problems with eating disorders. There is little that the women can do to change the culture. They are typically given strategies to avoid getting assaulted; this merely removes them from being part of and accepted by the larger community to which they want to belong.

Second, female cadets in the class of 1993 were taught how to more appropriately wear make-up and to avoid drinking alcohol when socializing with male cadets because "boys will be boys." Recommendations from the 2003 Fowler panel also include admonitions for women to avoid situations that may be threatening by limiting exposure to alcohol consumption (by self or others). This suggests that guidance provided to female cadets in 1993 is consistent with guidance given to current cadets. On the surface, this type of training may seem benign or even beneficial, but it may foster cultural stigma for female cadets. Dunivin notes that women "fit in" with the USAF by becoming one of the guys. By not socializing with male cadets, female cadets risk even more alienation from the culture than they already experience. Alienation may actually increase the risk of assault!

APPLICATIONS

Human resource development (HRD) professionals in particular can play a key role in the remediation of the USAFA situation. Trained in organization development and training, HRD professionals can help an organization conduct strategic assessments for broad-scale organizational development and to subsequently create strategically aligned training to facilitate organizational goals. Furthermore, the USAFA may prove to be a learning case for the HRD profession for addressing issues of social justice within and across organizations. HRD professionals can influence the practice of social justice within the USAFA, and as a result of their actions, they can influence other organizations with similar cultural dysfunctions.

Specifically, the following actions provide a useful starting ground to begin to resolve the dysfunctions at the USAFA:

- Assemble a team of both male and female professionals from both military and nonmilitary backgrounds who have organizational evaluation and diagnosis experience.
- Conduct an organizational diagnosis that uses a systemic-based model to assess underlying strengths and weaknesses of the USAFA without making assumptions about what needs to be fixed. An example of such a model is the Schwandt dynamic organizational learning systems model. Although I have suggested that training is a key underlying catalyst for dysfunction at the USAFA, jumping immediately to address that issue without further in-depth analysis will likely result in the same surface symptom treatments currently taking place.
- Once data-based presenting problems are identified, resolutions should be developed strategically by incorporating voices from military and cadet personnel at the USAFA.

CONCLUSION

The Fowler panel noted that BCT was an important indoctrination point that influenced the climate for potential sexual assaults. Some of the fundamental cultural changes that the panel recommended would address issues of unhealthy behaviors by both male and female cadets. These recommended changes, however, are embedded within the text of the report and are not highlighted in the recommendations section; they would be complex, expensive, and time-consuming and have not been the observable focus of action by USAF leadership.

Changes to BCT are likely to meet with stiff resistance. Already alumni are complaining that changes to date at the USAFA and the first-year training have eroded the heritage and tradition of the institution. Although my own exploration of this issue has theorized about a potential overlooked cause for both sexual aggression and eating disorders, it has not been tested. It should be. Studies in the future should explore the relationship between issues of control and, at the very least, risk factors for sexual aggression and eating disorders.

More in-depth analyses could be accomplished by identifying those who have experienced such dysfunctional behaviors and then determining their locus of control. If control does seem to be a factor influencing dysfunctional behavior, training could be initiated to address issues of power and control and outcomes could later be assessed.

The issues of sexual assault and eating disorders at USAFA are indeed connected to culture and climate. However, the creation and maintenance of that culture and climate occurs in part through BCT; thus, training may be a common source of these unhealthy and dangerous behaviors. By changing the nature of power deprivation in BCT and by providing training to mitigate negative effects of loss of control, I contend that the USAFA will achieve much greater success in reducing both sexual assaults and eating disorders.

REFERENCES

Adams-Curtis, L. E., & Forbes, G. B. (2004). College women's experiences of sexual coercion: A review of cultural, perpetrator, victim, and situational variables. *Trauma, Violence, and Abuse, 5*(2), 91–122.

Anonymous. (1988). Bulimia rampant among Air Force Academy women. *Minerva: Quarterly Report on Women and the Military, 1*(2), 9.

Argyris, C., & Schon, D. A. (1974). *Theory in practice: Increasing professional effectiveness.* San Francisco: Jossey-Bass.

Billson, J. M. (1994). Society and self: A symbolic interactionist framework for sociological practice. *Clinical Sociology Review, 12.*

Bowden, M. (2000). *Black hawk down: A story of modern war.* New York: Penguin Books.

Dalgleish, T., Tchanturia, K., Serpell, L., Hems, S., de Silva, P., & Treasure, J. (2001). Perceived control over events in the world in patients with eating disorders: A preliminary study. *Personality and Individual Differences, 31*(3), 453–460.

Dunivin, K. O. (1994). Military culture: Change and continuity. *Armed Forces and Society, 20*(4), 531–547.

Dunivin, K. O. (1988). There's men, there's women, and there's me: The role and status of military women. *Minerva: Quarterly Report on Women and the Military, 6*(2), 43–68.

Fowler, T. K. (2003). Report of the panel to review sexual misconduct allegations at the U.S. Air Force Academy. U.S. Air Force Academy (Ed.), U.S. Air Force Academy.

Fraser, L. (2000). Don't eat, don't tell. Available online at www.alternet.org/story/10005 (accessed August 28, 2004).

Giddens, A. (1979). *Central problems in social theory: Action, structure and contradiction in social analysis.* Los Angeles: University of California Press.

Kamoche, K. (2000). Developing managers: The functional, the symbolic, the sacred and the profane. *Organization Studies, 21*(4), 747.

Kerzhnerman, I. (2003). *The significance of general locus of control beliefs, weight-specific locus of control beliefs and restraint in predicting binge eating behaviors in an eating disordered population.* Unpublished manuscript, Drexel University.

Martin, P. Y., & Hummer, R. A. (1989). Fraternities and rape on campus. *Gender and Society, 3*(4), 457–473.

McNulty, P. A. (2001). Prevalence and contributing factors of eating disorder behaviors in active duty service women in the Army, Navy, Air Force, and Marines. *Military Medicine, 166*(1), 53–58.

Peterson, A. L., Talcott, G. W., Kelleher, W. J., & Smith, S. D. (1995). Bulimic weight-loss behaviors in military versus civilian weight-management programs. *Military Medicine, 160*(12), 616–620.

Rada, R. T. (1978). *Clinical aspects of the rapist.* New York: Grune and Stratton.

Schewe, P. A., & O'Donohue, W. (1996). Rape prevention with high-risk males: Short-term outcome of two interventions. *Archives of Sexual Behavior, 25*(5), 455–471.

Schwandt, D. R., & Marquardt, M. J. (2000). *Organizational learning: From world-class theories to global best practices.* New York: St. Lucie Press.

Slade, P. (1982). Towards a functional analysis of anorexia nervosa and bulimia nervosa. *The British Journal of Clinical Psychology/The British Psychological Society, 21*(3), 167–179.

Sprengelmeyer, M. E. (2004). AFA tradition focus of panel: Lively debate marks session of oversight committee. *Rocky Mountain News.*

Turner, J. H. (1991). *The structure of sociological theory* (5th ed.). Belmont, CA: Wadsworth.

Tylka, T. L. (2004). The relation between body dissatisfaction and eating disorder symptomatology: An analysis of moderating variables. *Journal of Counseling Psychology, 51*(2), 178–191.

Waller, G. (1998). Perceived control in eating disorders: Relationship with reported sexual abuse. *International Journal of Eating Disorders, 23,* 213–216.

Weida, J. A. (2003). Commander's guidance 06–5: Agenda for change progress. *Warrior Focus.*

Welch, M. R., & Page, B. M. (1979). Sex differences in socialization anxiety. *Journal of Social Psychology, 47,* 17–23.

12

Gendered Ethics and Law in Cases of Corporate Executive Crimes and Punishments

Mary Lenzi

Do female and male CEOs execute their leadership roles similarly? Do they pay themselves and receive recompense from the law and society in a gender-neutral way? Before the current "tribunal" of business, ethics, and law, CEOs appear judged more according to stereotypes of men and women in power than according to any genderless ideal. One still wonders why a female CEO, Martha Stewart, cannot lie like a male CEO, Kenneth Lay, and "get away with it": The rise and fall of male and female CEOs show critical gender differences in development of their personalities and corporations. Specifically, I examine whether their gender played a similar role in their wrong actions, cover-ups, indictments, convictions, and legal sentencing.[1] Generally, the analysis employs philosophical ethics and moral psychology to examine and evaluate the role gender plays in the personal professional development of corporate executives and in their respective types of corporations, the homemaking life versus the energy industries.

Martha Stewart, founder and former CEO of Martha Stewart Living Omnimedia, was indicted for obtaining and acting on a private tip from her stockbroker about future price changes in her personal stock in ImClone and then lying to federal investigators when directly questioned about these actions.[2] Kenneth Lay, founder and former CEO of Enron, three years after the collapse of that company,[3] was federally indicted on eleven charges of fraud, conspiracy, and insider trading offenses (July 8, 2004). His trial and sentencing have been drawn out. On May 25, 2006, Lay's five-month-long trial ended. He was convicted on ten charges and his sentencing will be decided on September 11, 2006. With these test cases, I provide alternative analyses of the role gender plays in culture, ethics, and law that may result in better choices and fairer consequences for corporate executive males and females in the future. These analyses will further show the implications for countless people (employees, shareholders, and society) as stakeholders dependent on corporate executive effectiveness and ethics.

For simplicity, relevant factors in this debate appear from A through G as follows:

A: American corporate activities (ethics, laws, and outcomes)
B: Bosses' behavior
C: CEOs' cover-ups
D: Deception and detection
E: Executives exposed
F: Failings of CEOs; fallout in both corporate and public worlds
G: Gender and groupthink

In its five-part analysis, this chapter explores the mélange of these factors, according to theories and interpretations of the ego and individual gender, group dynamics and psychology, social forces and morality, and culture and law. Overall, the formative factor of one's gender, psychologically, historically, and culturally, is evident in leaders of corporations as in society. As in society, gender is not the only cause of the differences, however. My analysis of gender will be subsumed under the more general analysis of "groupism" versus "egoism," or what could be viewed as "cultism" versus individual "exceptionalism."[4] The strategy here is to engage readers in the ongoing dialectic of dialogue—analyzing and debating opposing and complementary arguments and viewpoints. Such dialectic is more than merely theoretical: It uncovers inconsistencies, conflicts, and controversy in individual cases of male or female CEOs, arguably because these strains prevail in the U.S. corporate subculture. This ongoing dialectic of gender continues to shape and determine our beliefs, judgments, and actions in our daily lives and work.

DIALECTICAL ETHICS AND CORPORATE CULTURE

When corporate entities and their executives do business, standards of right and wrong, helpful and harmful legal parameters, business codes, and standard practices are in place. The following excerpts from a televised interview in which Kenneth Lay (K.L.) and the commissioner of the Federal Energy Regulatory Commission (FERC) participated illustrate the point:

> K.L. claimed, "I have faith in the market when we get the rules right."
>   Interviewer: But the rules aren't right.
> *Commissioner Pat Wood* [FERC] remarked, "Every market needs a cop in order
>   to insure competitiveness."
> K.L.: "That's what our antitrust laws are all about. If people are abusing the
>   marketplace, if they're colluding, if there's conspiracy, then in fact there
>   are ways to handle that."[5]

Nevertheless, these so-called rules were insufficient: They remain indeterminate and open to individual interpretation and changing contexts.[6] The corporate entity and its subsidiary structures emerge and transform in response to rapidly changing ways of doing business in the national and multinational corporate world. As will be shown, equally important are the public business personae of the CEOs as gendered persons and corporate figureheads. Public systems of law and social morality must continually be revised to modify, check, and balance the historical and cultural effects of gender typing in the CEOs' corporate successes and failings.

From the personal perspective, Confucius would say that people prosper when they "enjoy their enjoyments and profit from their profits." Alternatively, when corporate greed and power become ends in themselves, enjoyment of work, profit, and money turns to misery. The CEO mastery of the corporate self and others (the corporation) may turn into self-enslavement; profiteering may turn into losses, social isolation, and even imprisonment. We need to examine how the mere fact of one's gender determines individual roles and expectations, whether affecting or causing the disparities in achievement and outcomes, enjoyment and anguish from the goods and harms borne from executive leadership and performance.

From the social perspective of the CEO, "above all, do no harm," is an ancient, commonly held Hippocratic (medical) ethic that should apply to corporations and CEOs. To be attentively engaged with and responsive to others are critical attributes of the good person and the good CEO. For by so being, one can better foresee and avoid harming others. Again, CEOs' gender may play a significant formative role in decision making to prevent harm and loss for those dependent on their effective, ethical leadership.

The ethics of personal and corporate character development seem preferable, or at least complementary, to the customary social contract theory of business ethics.[7] This implied or explicit contract entails the social and legal coordination of (genderless) rational, self-interested individuals obligated under contractual arrangements in business as in other areas of society and government. Next, in the evaluation of top executives' ethics, I show that CEOs use multiple ethical systems and business factors to make decisions and assess consequences. Furthermore, hidden gains and losses resulting from CEO decisions and transactions are all subject to conflicting categories of appraisal. For instance, how does a corporate executive weigh short- versus long-term profits and penalties and public and legal oversight? How do CEOs reason about eventual exposure of their personal morality, as well as business deeds and misdeeds, especially given the increased likelihood of having criminal charges brought against them as individuals?

First, general ethical and legal systems are appropriate in evaluating the character and illegal actions of CEOs as corporate leaders. Specifically, however, my analysis also maintains that the prevailing psychology and social morality of gender typing are crucial in shaping corporate executive morality, wrongdoing, and punishment. To exemplify the ambiguities and potential conflicts in any ethical analysis of the cases in question, I merely note some of the ordinary maxims: know thyself, might makes right, only the strong survive, the golden rule, nothing in excess, the golden mean, quid pro quo, and help one's friends, harm one's enemies. In the end, one might contend that CEOs remain beholden to the bottom line of profit making, regardless of their gender or the means employed.

Second, genderless systems of government and the law apply equally to all citizens, but they also must adapt to regulate the changing business world. On one hand, though they may be corporate CEOs, all individuals, regardless of gender, race, or creed, are deemed equal under the law. Governmental and legal systems rely heavily on the ethics of justice, which social contract theory presumes to be genderless. Contract theories and frameworks, which are disparate in form and application, range from theories of fair redistribution of economic benefits and burdens in society to the extremes of libertarianism and free-market capitalism. Except to prevent fraud and coerced contracts, no intervention in the marketplace is justifiable, according to the latter.[8]

In my analysis, these theories and structures are insufficient to inform, shape, and control CEOs' moral development. Constitutional government, laws, and business codes of ethics can only provide necessary frameworks for corporate executive decisions. As such, they cannot mandate virtuous business leadership. Because character is an inward condition of the self, and action an outward expression, noble character in a CEO or business leader cannot be imposed from the outside. Significantly, gender identity also is both an inward and outward state of being oneself. External systems, such as codes, laws, and gender typing merely impose standards and expectations for CEOs and corporations. In *The Protestant Work Ethic and the Spirit of Capitalism* (1904), social theorist Max Weber suggested that rigorous attempts at rationalization, in the present cases, through rules and gender typing, might result in the decline rather than the progress of reasonable ethical values and social freedom.

Third, any virtues and vices must rest on mutual trust and reciprocity. By one definition, "the corporation is a voluntary association maintained through contractual arrangements."[9] Contractual trust then becomes the social glue that ensures the ethics and reliability of business contracts. Without it, parties to such contracts would instead have to resort to the use of force to compensate for deficient character and morality. Truthfulness is the foundation of trust in the corporate contractual world. Lying and deception become key factors in the charges and cases against Stewart and Lay. The differing legal charges, the intent and content of their lies and the consequences of lying seem to reflect gender stereotypes.[10]

Finally, as I will show, though all aforementioned systems of ethics, business, and law espouse genderless policies, gender still plays a leading role in the personal and professional development of men and women in power, as in the cases of Stewart and Lay.

CASE COMPARISONS AND CONTRASTS

Before their criminal indictments, Martha Stewart (b. 1941) was founder and CEO of Martha Stewart Living Omnimedia (1993–2003), and Ken Lay (b. 1943) was Enron's first chair and CEO (1986–2001). Despite noticeable parallels in their corporate positions, their different actions, indictments, and convictions continue to cause controversy along gender lines. The controversy stems not only from Stewart's and Lay's individual gender but also from the gender of those judging and observing their cases as they unfold. First, we must determine whether Stewart and Lay experienced differential treatment in the federal judicial system, including the sentencing for their wrongdoing.

According to the legal fact sheets, federal charges for Stewart included obstruction of justice, conspiracy, and false statements.[11] Stewart's appellate lawyers denied the last charge. Moreover, the major issue in the Court of Appeals was "whether the prosecution must prove that one knew that a false statement was criminal."[12] The Court of Appeals dismissed her case in January 2006; as of May 26, 2006, Stewart has filed another appeal to overturn her conviction on civil insider trading charges. In the Stewart case, the finer distinctions of legal interpretation and other ambiguities of business law are at stake regarding truth telling (see later discussion in this chapter). Unlike Lay, Stewart was not indicted for insider trading. According to the letter of the law, insider trading occurs when someone profits from selling stock after obtaining "material, nonpublic information from a company 'insider,' namely an official, or someone who has access to data that could move the stock."[13] Stewart's indictable dealings, resulting from dining conversations with her stockbroker about the sale of her ImClone stock (notably *not* her own corporation's stock, as in the case of Enron executives), managed to prevent a personal loss of a mere $45,673. On that same day, "December 27, 2001, more than 7.7 million shares were traded and the price fell from $63.49 at the opening of trading to $58.30 at the close."[14] Whereas Stewart's individual transactions had relatively little negative effect on others, Lay and other Enron executives were accused of bankrupting investors, raiding retirement funds, and culling corporate coffers. Despite the greater seriousness of the charges and guilty convictions against Lay, he has not been sentenced at the time of this writing.

Meanwhile, Stewart, contrary to the wishes of the judge and her lawyer, chose to serve jail time in advance of the Appellate Court decision. While Stewart was serving time at the female federal prison, given the sexist label of Camp Cupcake, her daughter, Alexis, explained that her mother wanted to get back to her work and put this mess behind her: For Stewart, "her life is her company."[15] Even Sigmund Freud would concur: For someone "to be well" means "to live and work well" (*lieben und arbeiten*). Work, and Stewart's love of it, gave focus and purpose to her life. As her case plays out, the sixty-three-year-old Stewart conveyed to the public that she just wanted to get back to the "good life,"[16] not merely one of finely designed homes and ornamental gardens but one characterized by a good job with money to perpetuate her self-sufficiency and fulfillment long into retirement. Unlike Lay, Stewart voluntarily served jail time, so she could return (more) cleanly to her former status as a leader in the home industry. Such a strong interconnection between Stewart's private and public life supports my analysis of gender's role in the intertwined personal and public schema of business.[17]

When Lay was CEO, Enron defrauded the public out of billions of dollars, perhaps because he exerted control over the country's energy policies and supplies. Lay, sitting in high political places on state and federal boards, directly influenced the power and gas industry, advising both Bush presidents. In his long corporate and political career, Lay enjoyed the status of a "brave new world's" economic ideologue and cult leader. Armed with a doctorate in economics and extensive academic and corporate experience, beginning as an economist with Exxon and culminating in a leading role on the FERC, Lay preached and practiced the economic liberalization model of nonregulation of gas and electricity monopolies, on which Enron also was modeled. Think tanks and academia, notably Harvard Business School, praised the "Enron model" of doing economics in business and politics.[18]

To begin in the middle, I tentatively pose these basic questions regarding the role and effect of gender in the two cases. Given disparities before the law and in the courts—the quick sentencing and the continuing intense public scrutiny of Stewart, versus the secretive, drawn-out course of Lay's trial and sentencing—did gender influence the differing courses of their cases and outcomes? Alternatively, were any differences due to the finer distinctions of past and new corporate laws? Did differences result from the varying crimes for which Stewart and Lay were originally charged? Because Lay's case has not completely played out in the legal system at this point, no apt closure or definitive conclusions are possible. This history is still being made and hence ripe for ongoing analysis and interpretation.

GENDERED BIOGRAPHIES OF CEOS

Specifically to illustrate my claim of corporate gender bias, I must briefly examine the biographies of Stewart and Lay. Both have high-profile business personae. The public perceives both as aloof, logical, calculating business people: They seemed not to attend enough to their workers, their company's shareholders, and society's stakeholders; they attend, instead, to themselves, their profits, and businesses. Both wrongly capitalized on their personae: Stewart on her celebrity cult image and Lay on his insider political status. Given these similarities, one rightly questions why their legal proceedings and outcomes have unfolded quite differently over many years (2001–2006).

The ethics and institutions of democratic justice, construed as embodying gender neutrality and equality before the law, appear inadequate. Neither Stewart nor Lay learned and acquired leadership virtues by respecting generic (genderless) abstract duties, laws, and codes, or by means of social shame or approval, or by lawful monetary rewards and punishment. Due to the weight of gender difference, I contend that these same systems of moral development can compromise or diminish one's humaneness.

First, as background, I find that in capitalistic society, capital attains independence and has its own individuality, whereas living persons can become dependent on capital to the point of sacrificing their individuality.[19] One could also see individuals sacrificing others by maximizing their own capital. In either case, one's humaneness is compromised, if not sacrificed.

The law itself illustrates this rationale. Legally corporations are deemed persons under federal law. In the 1970s, the Civil Rights Code added corporations to the list of persons having civil rights and protection. Although corporations are genderless in theory and before law, their in-the-flesh CEOs are male and female, and, as a result, incur different consequences and appraisal of their actions. Their personal professional development differs and also mirrors gender differences in their corporate personalities and organizations. I must still demonstrate the claim that the development of personal–capital connections is the extension of oneself, as CEO, outward into the corporation.

Stewart, as a college student and then as an educated, intellectual woman and young wife worked as a model to earn money. Nevertheless, she developed her brand of the brainy beauty. Stewart, like another female, Gloria Steinem (founder and former chief editor of *Ms. Magazine*), had humble origins. Both, however, attended an exclusive "Seven Sister" school, Barnard and Smith, respectively. Both modeled professionally, capitalizing on their good looks. After becoming a mother, Stewart stopped modeling and followed in her father-in-law's profession by becoming a stockbroker, which she quickly abandoned after some financial setbacks. As a result, Stewart found her profession in home-making, starting a catering business in her basement, and the rest is history.[20]

Now, we can consider whether Stewart had equal opportunities as a female of her generation to be a self-determining woman and professional business-person. Rather, was not the norm that such a woman would be supported by her interpersonal family relationships and emotional domestic attachments? Stewart's self-development and the growth of the Martha Stewart brand name and business are noticeably different from the career paths of males in her life. For instance, Stewart was a wife, mother, and entrepreneur in home economics, a field more primed for female leadership than oil and gas industries or stock brokerage firms. As apparent from the men in Stewart's life, her stockbroker father-in-law and lawyer husband, the normal course of professional male development seems more determined by culture and history. Male education, training, social conditioning, and career opportunities encourage them to assume leadership in law and business.

In contrast to Stewart, Lay followed the more traditional, typically male track to success. His steady, direct path to the top of his industry in energy appeared unimpeded by any domestic relationships. The story of Lay, as the former Enron CEO, diverges from that of his female CEO counterpart. Along gender stereotypic lines, Lay merged his business and political power, unlike Stewart, who merged home economics with a megacorporate business. Stewart was a domestic guru, a home network icon, with a cult following of female devotees—housewives and mothers. Lay was a public force who had powerful friends like the Bush family and business connections to the U.S. Energy Commission and public oil and gas industries. The globally connected Lay was on the 1990 Houston Economic Summit of Industrialized Nations, which hosted former British Prime Minister Margaret Thatcher. Unlike Stewart as CEO of her corporation, Lay certainly attained a wider sphere of interlocking national and international political influence and economic power.

Some philosophical background may serve well in evaluating these gendered biographies. Reviewing the eighteenth-century Age of Reason provides a pertinent historical foil for this CEO gender analysis. French philosopher Jean-Jacques Rousseau put forth different male-female theories of virtues and moral education, in the education of the brother and sister in *Emile* (1762). Females are to learn patience, charm, subservience, moderation, flexibility, and resilience. Males are taught courage, wisdom, self-respect, strength of will, and independent, self-sufficient thinking and behavior.

Turning to the desirable traits for the moral business personality, however, one can see the need to appropriate a combination of both male and female virtues, or perhaps a common set of virtues for both genders, for example, to integrate flexibility with strength of will, resilience with wisdom, and moderation with courage and integrity. Ideally, such integration of virtues, paired with ingenuity, inventiveness, and the pursuit of excellence in one's work would shape the successful, virtuous personality in corporate business.[21]

My analysis reveals other significant gender differences in CEO personalities and their corporate configurations. These may account for new twists in the nature and cover-up of their respective corporate wrongdoing.

THE NATURE OF GENDERED CEO CRIMES: TRUTH, CONCEALMENT, DISCLOSURE

First, I resume the saga of Stewart with particular regard to the rationale underlying the criminal legal charges of her deception and lying to federal investigators. Lawyers for Stewart have claimed that the government has employed diversionary tactics in the past and evidently in its timing and logistics of the case against her.

1. Stewart's lawyers argued that the charges against her were made "because the Department of Justice is attempting to divert the public's attention from its failure to charge the politically connected managers of Enron and WorldCom."[22] Given her lawyers' rationale, one may infer further that the government employed this diversionary tactic in the Stewart case for reasons similar to those used in bolstering the case for the U.S. invasion and occupation of Iraq.[23]

2. Stewart's lawyers also asked whether the federal government doggedly pursued the case against her "because [Stewart] is a woman who has successfully competed in a man's business world by virtue of her talent, hard work and demanding standards."[24] The presupposition is that being demanding and ambitious in her line of work is more of a deficit for a powerful executive female than for a male. Rather than being admired for her commanding personality, Stewart has become infamous (at times despised) for her perfectionist personality. Yet she would prefer to ascribe this trait to her strong drive for business excellence and success, and perhaps it accounts for this same success. In her letter to U.S. Judge Miriam Goldman Cedarbaum (July 15, 2004), Stewart revealed, "I was often chided for being a 'perfectionist' by my competitors, peers, and the press, but the way we looked at our business was that we were 'teachers' and what we taught had to be based in *fact, truth and 'highest standards of perfection.'*"[25]

On this particular point, four editorial asides are in order.

1. Note these underlying distinctions regarding the various standards of "truth": truth under the law and in legal investigations, in contrast to the "truth" of the "teacher," as adopted in the educational line of her work. Stewart deemed that being demanding about the standards of truth was necessary for operating Martha Stewart Living Omnimedia, founded on teaching successful living. Perhaps we are to assume further that these standards of truth would differ from those used in other industries, such as Enron's corporation and other professions.
2. One can evaluate the morality and consequences of Stewart's perfectionist personality in the social, corporate world. Though someone like Stewart may be earnest in teaching, by controlling and directing oneself from within, one may still be unable to control external forces to which any human personality is subject. Hence, to identify and tolerate one's own limitations in confronting those of others and of the external world would constitute necessary and beneficial self-knowledge for any professional corporate executive as well.
3. The basic rationale of her appellate lawyers strongly implies that sexism is a constraining factor in the case for Stewart.[26] Moreover, gender typing if not outright sexism most likely lies beneath the surface, because historically stereotypic gender roles underlie our social and cultural underpinnings, whether or not we are conscious of their influence or effects.

   Viewing this editorial commentary in light of the appellate proceedings and facts in the Stewart trial, her lawyers further proclaimed:

   > It is truly extraordinary when you have perjury committed at a trial—both by an outspoken juror and by a key government witness. First, we have a

man who lied his way onto the jury by falsely denying his prior arrest for a
gender-based crime. Then a key government witness—himself a high-
ranking employee of a law enforcement agency who functioned as part of
the prosecution team—commits flagrant perjury on the stand.[27]

There seems to be enough lying going around for everyone on both
sides to participate. However, the more long-lasting destructive lie
overlaying these charges is that of gender-equity between corporate males
and females.

Interestingly, the news report just referenced included the following
passage, which sets up another rationale.

4. Allegedly, the Securities and Exchange Commission seems to be using
"the Stewart case to significantly expand its ability to charge people with
insider-trading abuses."[28] The commission then is using a female CEO as
its sacrificial lamb in its crackdown on future executive misdeeds. "In an
informal Website poll, a majority of over 64,000 readers said the government was not being too hard on Stewart."[29] Herein are two equivocal
forces: Residing alongside gender typing is an abiding core belief that
given the ideals and system of U.S. constitutional democracy, most citizens expect that males and females will be treated fairly. In particular,
Americans hold that the law must judge all individuals as equals, despite
the diverse outcomes for those charged with similar crimes in the system.

Lay's wrongdoings, to which I now turn, typify at the executive level male
behavior regarding truth telling and cover-ups in the guise of Enron's complex business arrangements. Because "many of the accounting and legal
issues...were vetted by outside experts, that could make it more difficult for
prosecutors to convince a jury that the executives acted with intent to de-
fraud."[30] Consequently, any legal or ethical analysis entails variable, con-
tentious interpretations. One must read behind the lines of the virtual ledger
sheets at Enron and its affiliates. Lay maintained he was out of the loop of the
goings on at Enron, even though the facts suggested otherwise:

> Oct. 23, 2001 stands out as a particularly bad day for Ken Lay. As word
> circulated that [Enron]...was under investigation for balance-sheet shenani-
> gans, the CEO tried to pull Enron's stock out of a tailspin by arranging a special
> conference call with analysts: "We're not trying to conceal anything," he told
> them. "I'm disclosing everything we've found." After laying down the phone,
> Lay gathered Enron's employees via a live web cast and teleconference, and
> tried to reassure them too. "Our liquidity is fine," he said of the company that
> was about to flame.[31]

The two faces of Lay's business personae are clearly seen and voiced through
both sides of Enron—insiders (Enron "analysts"), and outsiders (thousands of
investors and employees).

In a similar fashion, defense lawyers for Stewart claimed, "Martha Stewart has done nothing wrong. The government is making her the subject of a criminal case designed to further expand the already unrecognizable boundaries of the federal securities laws."[32] However, a critical difference between their cases is obvious in the elaborate political and economic intricacies of "accounting" that Lay and Enron affiliates employed. Stewart was a novice in these regards. This distinction also seems gender-related. Because the corporation remains primarily a male subculture, a female CEO has fewer material and business connections with other female executives and government officials to pull off the intricate scheme of outsourcing and virtual business and accounting arrangements invented and implemented by Enron.

In a related strain of this argument, New Age cover-ups can appear worse than the actual crimes of the CEOs involved. Truth has become virtualized, electronically fantasized, submerged, or lost in convoluted business arrangements and partnerships. Hypocrisy, the lack of any authentic connection between one's image and words can be more heinous than one's deeds, and the appearance of wrong actions more culpable than their actuality. One may define the difference by assessing, comparing, and contrasting the consequences of their corporate executives' misdeeds with the public fallout from Enron versus that from Stewart's corporation.

Regardless of these alternative accounts, the ethical and legal rationale of lawyers in the Stewart or Lay cases could both be argued apart from any stereotypic gender analysis or by resorting to gender stereotypes. To illustrate this paradoxical point, his lawyers could similarly contend that Lay (like Stewart) is being targeted or scapegoated due to the government's diversionary tactics—to distract the public from fraudulent corporate activities increasingly practiced since the 1990s as a way of doing big business at home and abroad.

MORAL PSYCHOLOGY AND SOCIAL MORALITY OF GENDER

Moral Psychology

The public's responses of love and hate, fear and admiration, seem meted out differently for rich, powerful men than for women. Therefore, I must examine the requisite background research and findings in gender psychology. Harvard moral psychologist Carol Gilligan opens her groundbreaking book, *In a Different Voice: Psychological Theory and Women's Development*, with a scene from Chekhov's *The Cherry Orchard*. We find the success story of the businessman Lopchin, a "self-made man," whose father and grandfather had both worked on this cherry orchard, which he purchased from its female owner, due to her money problems. After buying the woman's estate, he cuts down the cherry orchard to replace it with vacation homes, reasoning that others like him "will see a new life. [The businessman prays: 'Lord, thou gavest us immense forests, unbounded fields and the widest horizons, and living in the midst of them we should indeed be giants'] . . . at which point the woman interrupts him saying, 'You feel the need for giants—They are good only in fairy tales, anywhere else they only frighten us.'"[33]

Similarly, we too might view CEOs as giants whom we admire and fear: We little people are beholden to them, and, like other dependent people, we are deeply ambivalent in loving and despising them for what they are and have become, what they have and own in excess, and what they have done with their success. For instance, when asked "why people hated her," Stewart replied that she would like to think that she was no different than anyone else with respect to people hating or loving her, yet realized that perhaps she was hated because she was perceived as "a perfectionist," "arrogant," and "extremely rich."[34] In light of this psychology of gender, I may hypothesize that the bigger these giants grow, the more the public lusts for them to stumble, to fall, often cutting them down to normal-sized people, sometimes destroying themselves and their own good in the long run. I tentatively identify this repetitive history as an indication of a leveling syndrome.

Gilligan found that "what emerges in these voices is a sense of vulnerability that impedes . . . women from taking a stand, what George Eliot [the male pen name chosen by this female novelist] regards as the girl's 'susceptibility' to adverse judgments by others which stems from her lack of power and consequent inability 'to do something in the world'" (p. 66). As overcompensation, these females assume and act as if they must do every task to perfection. This ideal of perfectionism causes a backlash against contemporary women, such as Stewart and Senator Hillary Clinton (whom some detest due to her political power). For performing well in their respective professions, these women are harshly leveled and even debased.

Could Stewart ever have known or anticipated that perfecting her own voice and trade late in middle age would ultimately cause her to be cut down, deemed criminal in the eyes of the court and in public opinion? That is, Stewart did not merely achieve the pinnacle of corporate executive success; instead, she also reached the point of serving jail time, home and work confinement, and parole until March 2007. However, ironically also because of gender, she continues to have many followers who are loyal to her brand and cause. The last part of this chapter examines why she and her corporation gained new advocates after her ordeal with the courts and choice to serve jail time to clear her name.

While Lay continued to live the lie, free, trying to sweep Enron's damages under the rug and passing guilt onto other corporate associates, Stewart decided to go to prison for lying to the wrong people—overly demanding federal prosecuting investigators. Why? Because a female CEO cannot lie like a male and get away with it? To illustrate this point, when directly asked, "It isn't true that you're the closet Secretary of Energy?" Lay replied, "I'm not the closet anything."[35] In other words, Lay claimed he felt no need to hide his wide range of national and international economic influence over the energy industry. In fact, his actions and style of public interactions speak otherwise: With his employees, shareholders, and the public as stakeholders in the energy industry, Lay was not forthcoming with explanations of his leading role in the fall of Enron.

Tentatively, we may reason that Stewart, unlike her CEO male counterpart (Lay), had failed to learn how *not* to speak about lies or alleged crimes to official legal authorities. Though this distinction may constitute some degree of legal difference in courts of law, how much does or will it figure into their moral guilt and innocence? Perhaps Stewart simply has better morals than some of her CEO peers, and her initiative in choosing jail time demonstrates her moral fiber, or at least moral scruples. This claim, however, requires scrutiny.

First, one could argue that a woman CEO who wants to be treated equally in corporations and under the law should learn to act more like a male CEO. Such assimilation is required for women to attain the social goal of genderless justice. Gender blindness seems fundamental, not only for realizing fair opportunities and freedom but for the good of individuals and society. Thus, once women liberate themselves from their stereotypical feminine virtues of charm, selflessness, and nurturance, they can be freer to become equal members of society, industry, and history. Those homey virtues of care—docility, patience, and passivity—are most successful in the private space of love and family, but apparently not in the public and business domains.

Women then may effectively assimilate to the male spaces of the common culture and public domain by means of equality in education and in the workplace. Thereby they become "normed" in "maleness," which is viewed as the standard of success outside the home, in business and in politics. Yet when such accommodation and assimilation to male standards lead to women's noticeable success, such equality can backfire. Consequently, the old sexism and fear of the other reemerge at a higher or different level of awareness. Existentialist feminist philosopher Simone de Beauvoir (*The Second Sex*, 1949) described female reality and image as "the Other": One group places itself as the One against the Other. According to this scheme of the sexes, others (females) need not be viewed as or treated the same as those in one's group (males).

This dynamic of otherness can explain groupism and determinations of insiders and outsiders with regard to the gender of corporate executives, their crimes, and punishments. Morality of the group or people in question must be examined in conjunction with these moral psychological claims. Lay may be more admired and feared than Stewart and, consequently, more hated or severely punished in the end due to his gender. As a male CEO he was more capable and better connected; thus, he was better able to merge his corporation and political prowess. Having close connections to U.S. presidents and the Department of Energy, Lay attained greater political and economic power and control. Because of Lay's prominent stature and range of influence, his activities adversely affected many more people and sectors over a longer time (the stock market, employee funds, and pensions), than did Stewart's wrong actions.

Social Morality

Businesses and their executives are, like the rest of society, embedded in a much larger world with its own ethics, norms, and practices. Perhaps due to the growing appropriation of humans and corporations by mass communication technology and globalization, leaders in business as in politics have become iconic figureheads.[36] In his psychoanalytic theories, Freud identified the dynamics of the group, as a certain esprit de corps, generated and sustained by the group ego. Different virtues and vices are deemed necessary for leaders versus followers, as different members of the group. Countervailing passive and aggressive forces work toward decentering self and group, as in business, government, and the military. Increasing privatization and subcontracting, which split up the groups, removing them from the control of centralized power and group leadership, provide current evidence supporting Freud's ideas. Even a cursory look at the fractured fact sheets that detail Enron's conglomerate build-up reveals a breakdown into subgroupings of all sorts. Especially notable is the infamous Arthur Andersen LLP and other off-balance-sheet corporate partnerships.

Social psychology further supports the thesis that gender affects the moral and legal evaluation of CEO crimes and punishment. French sociologist Émile Durkheim claimed: "Society [is] a psychic being that has its own particular way of thought, feeling, and action, differing from that peculiar to the individuals who compose it."[37] Furthermore, he proposed that morality is itself a "social reality," a "social product": "It is the authoritative judgment of one's group."[38] Human morality is a rationalistic, individualistic, legalistic set of rules and rule following. As such, morality sets up patterns of prescribed and proscribed behavior, overall producing habit, regularity, and constancy: "Throughout the diversity, human particular duties are everywhere the same" (pp. 32–33). As Durkheim further argued, "A spirit of discipline socially coordinates individuals and groups alike," and such a learned "discipline" is one of the most basic elements of morality (p. 33). Yet as individuals, they may object that all discipline is restraint on behavior, a denial of self-determination, and even of doing business.

Moreover, such individually variable attachments to social groupings entail a hierarchy normed among the diverse groupings and membership in which the self is invested. For Durkheim, the three main groupings are family, state, and humanity (p. 74). These three are above other subgroupings, such as gender, class, race, profession, job, and religion. If one adopts this rationale, it remains difficult to pick one morality for the group, another for the person, and a third for gender. One might object there should be another (supervening) morality, which works for the good of all and applies universally and objectively.

Returning to ongoing corporate cases, group followers and leaders alike can become either self-sacrificial lambs or predatory wolves. So, too, the "fall guy" may be a powerful leader, as when in January 2002 a former Enron executive committed suicide, either to save face and avoid further disgrace or to escape inner guilt. However, individual truth sayers often suffer an equally terrible fate. A notable exception is whistle-blower Sherron Watkins, an former Enron vice president who was named *Time*'s Person of the Year for 2002.

From the other side of public perception, that of infamy, note the rapid fall of Lay's corporate social personality from "Wall Street hero into public enemy number one." "In the Enron hearings' biggest week so far, the man who wasn't there [was] ... *Time*'s Person of the Week."[39] The title of the BBC News Business Report, "Kenneth Lay: A Fallen Hero," mirrored the precipitous fall of the Enron conglomerate in the guise of its leader.[40]

REPERCUSSIONS FOR CORPORATE MANAGEMENT ETHICS, LAW, AND SOCIETY

To assess the repercussions of these CEO crimes and punishment, we must remember their roots. From 1995 through 2001, *Forbes* named Enron the "most innovative company." Lay announced that his corporate "we" would "like to think of ourselves as the Microsoft of the energy world.... Enron multiplied its market capitalization more than nine-fold in a decade, became the U.S.'s seventh biggest company and the world's largest energy trading firm."[41] The eventual unfolding of the Enron conglomerate overturned the old saying, "what's good for General Motors is good for America." Instead, in retrospect, what was good for Enron was *not* good for America and especially bad for Enron, its chief executives, employees, investors, and the public's stakeholders in the oil and gas supply industries.

Enron's belief and persuasive power about the need to sustain open markets and trade energy *futures* just like other commodities caused *The Economist* to describe the firm as an "evangelical cult" with Lay as the "messiah." After Enron's 2001 collapse and "crucifixion" by the public and former followers of its leaders, the fate of the messianic Lay became uncertain. Despite the legal odds stacked against him, Lay still maintains publicly, "I want to see Enron survive."[42] Despite the long legal battles, in his July 2005 attempt at plea-bargaining, Lay displayed good faith in vowing to pay $4 million from his own profits to Enron's depleted employee pension funds.

Likewise, Stewart also may claim rebirth for herself and her corporation. Alternatively, is it more likely that the group may survive the demise of its leaders? Realistically, after being imprisoned and caught up in legal proceedings and appeals, how can these former giants (as CEOs) use their leadership expertise and former power to help their corporations survive? On one side of this dialectic, one wonders whether it is a question of her corporation surviving Martha Stewart or of Martha Stewart surviving her image, now tarnished by a federal conviction of criminal guilt and imprisonment. On the other side, it would seem odd that Martha Stewart Living Omnimedia (or the *Oprah Winfrey Show*) would survive without either one of these females at the helm.

Despite CEOs' beliefs that they are worth more than the sum of their employees' value, if the corporation can effectively separate itself from its tarnished leaders, it may reinvent itself in a new business. For example, Arthur Andersen Accounting has been reborn as Accenture. The myth of the phoenix resonates in the revival of such businesses that continue to rise out of their ashes. Stewart can reemerge due to expertise in her business and her many followers, as Lay too may someday accomplish due to his corporate expertise, political connections, and seasoned finesse.

Returning to our psychoanalytic line of reasoning, Freud claimed that God did not create humans in His own image, but that humans created God(s) in theirs. Analogously, we may presume that Enron or Martha Stewart Living Omnimedia did not remake the public in its image. Instead the public—stakeholders of society, labor, and the marketplace—fashioned corporations and leaders in their own image. Martha Stewart, the brand and being, has undergone a makeover and redemption. The new CEO, Susan Lyne, is strikingly similar in appearance to Stewart herself. As CEO surrogate for the paroled Stewart, Lyne is working with television moguls and Donald Trump in reversing Stewart's role from victim of the legal system to born-again queen of the good home life. (Stewart appeared in the fall 2005 line-up with two television series and a radio channel, *The Apprentice: Martha Stewart* was canned by Donald Trump in 2006 and subsequently canceled by the television network, but her daily talk show *Martha* and Martha Stewart Living Channel on Sirius Satellite Radio continue to be successful.)

Another noteworthy development in the Stewart story is the merger between K-Mart and Sears. With K-Mart's $11.5 billion buyout of Sears on November 24, 2004, inmate Stewart "made $32.7 million without lifting a finger. So does crime really pay? How can a woman behind bars be experiencing such a reversal of fortune?"[43] Apparently, Americans rally around the downtrodden in interesting ways, for example, when they embrace Stewart as the comeback kid. She is no ordinary American or common criminal, but an ex-con of the highest stock.

In comparison to the Stewart case thus far, male stereotyping may prove to affect Lay's case and its aftermath more adversely in his corporate revivalism. First, one could argue that the public and the courts treated Stewart quite leniently and summarily. They did not judge her wrongdoing harshly because she is a female queen in the home industry with a devoted grassroots following. On the contrary, due to a grassroots swelling of malaise and thirst for revenge against politically powerful male CEOs, citizens may perceive someone like Lay as swindling the public wholesale where it hurts most—in oil and gas supplies and workers' pensions, vital goods in daily life and work. The gender card may continue to influence their developing legacies, particularly in their personal fates and future business ventures.

Second, I may appropriate my analyses drawn from moral psychology and social morality of gender, groupism, and exceptionalism. For in the dialectic and dynamic opposition of insiders and outsiders, male CEOs like Lay apply different standards to insiders (corporate and political leaders on their side, in the elite group) than outsiders (employees, stockholders, average citizens in society). In contrast, in the life and corporation of Stewart, typical outsiders to the big business subculture of capital generation and mass production, namely, homemakers and mothers, identified vicariously with and enjoyed the rise and success of Martha Stewart Living Omnimedia. Stewart's corporation entered personally into their homes daily. In contrast, Lay's political dealings and business transactions often took place behind closed doors with his inner circle of presidential friends and corporate associates.

I now turn to a different but important long-term implication of profiting from one's corporate crimes and poor management practices. In this regard, first note these salient facts:

> In the past, 1940–1960s CEOs have made 40 to 50 times more than their laborers. By the 1990s, they earned 400–500 times more than their employees did. Broadly speaking, the effect of this widening gap between executive and employee compensation, with no caps set at either the top or bottom (apart from the government requirement of minimum hourly wage), has been decreasing income for the bulk of workers at the same time executive income has soared.[44]

Ethically speaking, compensation for top executives of both sexes should remain proportionate to the corporation's real assets and holdings, as is typically the case in European and Japanese corporations.

In reality, money in hand is worth more than the virtual potential stuff of the CEOs' dreams of future payoffs. They must balance their heightened sensibility with their actual power. Instead of acting on their power perceived through their own filters and those of insiders, CEOs should consider the others outside the corporate subculture who depend on them. If they did this, the ratio of CEO pay to that of their employees would better reflect CEOs' input and the productivity stemming from sound fiscal practices and socially responsible leadership.

In a broader social context, both consumerism and corporate greed may stem from common social expectations. Insiders and outsiders alike, the consumer and the corporate elite may share a belief in ever-increasing capital and renewable goods from an imagined fount of limitless market expansion and unchecked consumerism.[45] In these regards, the CEO's gender seems less relevant than what I have found elsewhere in this inquiry. For instance, female CEOs and business executives Stewart, Gloria Steinem, and Oprah Winfrey may incorporate themselves, and amass and spend their wealth in gender-typical ways; yet male and female corporate executives are similarly subject to these genderless beliefs in endless capital and goods.

The foregoing evaluation has demonstrated different influences on gender formation and typing in the nature of male or female CEO crimes and consequences. I may reasonably conclude that (1) human nature—moral and gender psychology; (2) nurture—moral education, acculturation, and social morality; and (3) political society—law, economic policies, and regulations must all work together to persuade CEOs to submit to rules of just behavior, fair exchange, and cooperative business interactions.

If, as discussed in the beginning, Freudian psychoanalysis was correct in claiming happiness is "to live and to work well," then the role and functionality of the state and its institutions—family, education, business, and the courts, can be judged as more or less fulfilling their functions when we may live and work well together in society. However, institutions, such as businesses, will ensure that universal desires for happiness are met only if they are set up justly. The best methods by which justice, fairness, and liberty are able to achieve the broad ends of happiness remain indefinite, to be determined by the culture and its subcultures, such as corporations and legal systems.

To address gender typing, which is embedded in business subcultures and in society, contemporary feminism has generated its own branches of ethics, psychology, economics, history, and philosophy.[46] In particular, the field of gender ethics centers on empathy and responsibility for oneself and others. Instead, however, the fields of business and law have historically preferred the social contract theory of ethics as the main framework for just contracts. As argued, Stewart, Lay, and their respective corporations developed and were also shaped and judged by larger cultural and ethical systems of gender typing of males and females in business and in power. Consequently, both the law and the public have perceived and treated these CEOs differently. In retrospect, which ethical framework would have better suited the CEOs in question? Which will be more appropriate for top executives in the future?

CONCLUSION

Before 2001,

> Americans treated their fraudsters with even more leniency than the Europeans. However, changes to the federal sentencing guidelines in 2001 and 2003 [Sarbanes-Oxley Act 2002] have raised the stakes.... Since George Bush set up a corporate fraud task force in July 2002, the workload of the Department of Justice (DOJ) has soared. Federal prosecutors have charged some 700 defendants in around 300 cases of alleged fraud, including over 30 chief executives [who represent 10 percent of CEOs].

One could object that they have not accomplished much in terms of legal settlement and sentencing in these cases.[47] Furthermore, long, costly government litigation against individual executives is not the best way to correct abuse of power in U.S. corporations.

Unlike Stewart, Lay has not yet been sentenced. Not until May 25, 2006, was his Houston trial complete, perhaps because the burden of proof required the prosecution to show evil intent in his case. Regardless of whether these CEOs were criminally negligent or innocent, ignorant, self-deceived, or simply amoral in their executive decisions, their gender differences as CEOs, evident also in their respective corporations (the good, home life versus public energy industries), are unavoidable but not considered blameworthy. Though similar in their record money-making abilities and elitism, Stewart and Lay differ in their gendered corporate crimes and consequences. Moreover, I have argued that they are loved and hated, admired and feared according to gender typing and expectations of men and women wielding power in politics and business.

Despite the facts stacked against them and the ensuing legal judgments for or against them, as former CEOs, both Stewart and Lay still appear firmly committed to their own innocence for what they did or did not do while heading their businesses.[48] As they proclaim, they had their reasons for their actions, derived from what they deemed were acceptable goals. At any rate, they believe themselves and their decisions generally trustworthy. Perhaps they trusted that their decisions were good and necessary at the time, given their CEO leadership role. The ethics of analysis and the law have judged them differently. Apparently, the CEOs lacked the relevant psychological and moral self-awareness connections about their own genders, corporate characters, and self-images, in contrast with those originating or imposed from the outside.

Fortunately, U.S. constitutional government is one of checks and balances, as are other key institutions of society and business. Harmful transactions of rogue CEOs and freewheeling, out-of-control marketplaces are checked, corrected, and balanced, as are government laws and policies. The years and sentences to come may continue to manifest this dynamic.[49] The pendulum may swing back to the center, fairer and more balanced than the past for both male and female corporate executives.[50] On May 25, 2006, as this volume went to press, Kenneth Lay was found guilty on all charges in Houston, Texas, Enron's former home quarters—six counts of guilty by the jury for security fraud, conspiracy, and insider trading, and four more convictions by the judge for personal banking fraud. (Jeffrey Skilling too was convicted on 19 out of 28 charges.) The judge will determine Lay's sentence on September 11, 2006, 5 years after fateful 9/11, and the collapse of Enron.

NOTES

I thank Martha Drummond and our editor, Margaret Karsten, for their editing suggestions.

1. Controversy ensued over the differing defense pleas and legal sentences for the Fastows (former husband-and-wife corporate executive team for Enron). Their court cases were argued according to gender differences and roles: Mrs. Fastow claimed undue hardship for their children if she was sentenced to jail.

2. See "Securities and Exchange Commission Bars Peter Baconovic from the Stockbroker Business," UPI, August 30, 2004.

3. C. Thomas, "The Rise and Fall of Enron," *Journal of Accountancy Online* (April 2002); Arlette Wilson and Walter Campbell, "Enron Exposed: Why It Took so Long," *Business and Economic Review* 49(2) (2003): 6–10.

4. See Mary Lenzi, "Freud: The Mind/Body of the Eroticist," *British Journal of Psychoanalytic Studies* 1(3) (1999): 315–26; Sigmund Freud, *Group Psychology and Analysis of the Ego* (New York: Liveright, 1921); Peter Gay, *The Freud Reader* (London: Norton, 1988).

5. "Blackout," *PBS Frontline*, March 27, 2001; available online at pbs.org/frontline (accessed on September 1, 2004).

6. See J. D. Rest, M. Narvaez, and S. Thoma, *Post-Conventional Moral Thinking: A Neo-Kohlbergian Approach* (Mahwah, NJ: Lawrence Erlbaum Associates, 1999); Patricia H. Werhane, *Moral Imagination and Management Decision Making* (New York: Oxford University Press, 1999); Terri L. Herron and David L. Gilbertson, "Ethical Principles vs. Ethical Rules: The Moderating Effect of Moral Development on Audit Independence Judgments," *Business Ethics Quarterly* 14(3) (2004): 499–502.

7. See Patricia H. Werhane, *Persons, Rights, and Corporations* (Englewood Cliffs, NJ: Prentice Hall, 1985); Lynn Sharp Paine, "Managing for Organizational Integrity," *Harvard Business Review* (March/April 1994): 106–17; Robert C. Solomon, *A Better Way to Think about Business: How Personal Integrity Leads to Corporate Success* (New York: Oxford University Press, 1999).

8. John Rawls, *A Theory of Justice*, rev. ed. (Cambridge, MA: Harvard University Press, 1999); John Rawls and Erin Kelly, eds., *Justice as Fairness: A Restatement* (Cambridge, MA: Harvard University Press, 2001); Susan Moller Okin, *Justice, Gender, and the Family* (New York: Basic Books, 1989); Robert Nozick, *Anarchy, State, and Utopia* (New York: Basic Books, 1977); Will Kymlicka, ed., *Local Justice: How Institutions Allocate Scare Goods and Necessary Burdens* (Newbury Park, CA: Sage, 1992); Michael J. Sandel, *Liberalism and the Limits of Justice*, 2nd ed. (Cambridge: Cambridge University Press, 1996).

9. See James Gaa, "Introduction to the Special Edition on Accounting Ethics," *Business Ethics Quarterly* 14(3) (2004): 349–54.

10. For feminist philosophies of trust and truth telling, see Annette Baier, "Trust and Antitrust," *Ethics* 96 (1985–86): 231–60; Nel Noddings, *Caring: A Feminine Approach to Ethics and Moral Education* (Berkeley: University of California Press, 1984); Onora O'Neill, *Bounds of Justice* (Cambridge: Cambridge University Press, 2000).

11. See "Securities and Exchange Commission Bars Peter Baconovic."

12. Robert G. Morvillo and John J. Tigue, lawyers for Martha Stewart: "Trial Update," June 4, 2003.

13. Keith Naughton, "Martha Breaks Out," *Newsweek* (March 7, 2005): 44.

14. Morvillo and Tigue, "Trial Update," June 10, 2003.

15. *Larry King Live*, interview, November 14, 2004.

16. Martha Stewart, press conference, September 15, 2004.

17. Though Stewart's confinement to home and office were to end in mid-August 2005, because she violated certain home restrictions, her home confinement was extended three weeks. Her parole ends in March 2007.

18. Briony Hale, "Kenneth Lay: A Fallen Hero," *BBC News*, January 24, 2002, available online at news.bbc.co.uk/1/hi/business/1779445 (accessed on September 1, 2004).

19. Heidi Hartmann, "The Unhappy Marriage of Marxism and Feminism," in James Sterba, ed., *Social and Political Philosophy* (Belmont, CA: International Thomson, 1995), pp. 364–76.

20. See "Martha Stewart, Multi-Media Lifestyle Entrepreneur," Martha Stewart Biography, *Academy of Achievement, A Museum of Living History,* available online at www.achievement.org (accessed on September 1, 2004).

21. Stephen Barr, "Women in Senior Executive Service Consider Themselves Influential, Study Finds," *Washington Post* (June 2, 2004): B2. Note that the modest rise of women in business management does not parallel rising female incomes and purchasing power. According to the *Society for Women in Business Management* (2004 Report), women comprise 14 percent of America's upper management, holding positions as chief financial officers. However, women make 95 percent of their household purchases. Female dominance in purchasing is not reflected in the very small percentage of female managers and corporate executives.

22. "Stewart Convicted on All Charges," *CNN Money Report* (March 5, 2004).

23. After the September 11, 2001, terrorist attacks on the United States, the United States attacked Afghanistan in an attempt to dismantle Al Qaeda and find Osama bin Laden. Failing in this effort, the United States constructed its case based on faulty evidence and interpretations of Iraq's nuclear capabilities and attacked that nation without establishing actual connections between it and Al Qaeda.

24. Jake Ulick, "Martha Indicted, Resigns," *CNN Money Report* (June 4, 2003).

25. Stewart's letter to The Honorable Miriam Goldman Cedarbaum, U.S. District Judge, Southern District of New York, July 15, 2004; emphasis added.

26. Walter Dellinger, appellate lawyer for Stewart: "Trial Update," July 16, 2004.

27. Morvillo, Abramowitz, Grand and Silberberg, P.C., "Reply Memorandum of Law in further support of Martha Stewart's Motion for New Trial pursuant to Federal Rule of Criminal Procedure 33," April 14, 2004: 1–10; Robert Morvillo and John Tigue, "Trial Update: Press Statement," June 4, 2003; Dellinger, "Trial Update Statement."

28. Keith Naughton, "Martha Breaks Out," *Newsweek* (March 7, 2005): 44.

29. Ulick, "Martha Indicted, Resigns."

30. Carrie Johnson, "Former Enron CEO to Face Criminal Charges," *Washington Post* (July 7, 2004).

31. Julie Rawe, "The Case against Ken Lay," *Time Magazine* (July 19, 2004).

32. Morvillo and Tigue, "Trial Update: Press Statement."

33. Carol Gilligan, *In a Different Voice: Psychological Theory and Women's Development* (Cambridge, MA: Harvard University Press, 1982), p. 5. Also see Eva Feder Kittay and Diana Meyer, *Women and Moral Theory* (Savage, MD: Rowman and Littlefield, 1987); Eva B. Cole and Susan Coultrap-McQuin, eds., *Explorations in Feminist Ethics* (Bloomington: Indiana University Press, 1992); Virginia Held, *Feminist Morality* (Chicago: University of Chicago Press, 1993); Alison Jaggar, "Caring as a Feminist Practice of Moral Reason," in Virginia Held, ed., *Justice and Care: Essential Readings in Feminist Ethics* (Boulder, CO: Westview Press, 1995).

34. Stewart's letter to Cedarbaum, pp. 1–2.

35. Follow-up interview, May 22, 2001, for *PBS Frontline*: "Blackout," March 27, 2001, available online at www.pbs.org/frontline (accessed on September 1, 2004).

36. See Jim Collins, "The Misguided Mix-Up of Celebrity and Leadership," 2001 Annual Essay, *Corporate Social Responsibility,* available online at www.csrwire.com (accessed on September 20, 2005); Michael Macoby, *The New Corporate Leaders: The Gamesman* (New York: Simon and Schuster, 1976).

37. Emile Durkheim, *Moral Education: A Study in the Application of the Sociology of Education* (New York: Free Press of Glencoe, 1961), p. 65.

38. Ibid., pp. 90–91; 86–87.

39. Frank Pellegrini, "Person of the Week: Kenneth Lay," *Time Online Edition* (February 8, 2002), www.timeonlineedition.com (accessed on September 1, 2004).

40. Hale, "Kenneth Lay: A Fallen Hero."

41. Ibid.

42. Ibid.

43. *Newsweek* (November 29, 2004): 40.

44. Naughton, "Martha Breaks Out."

45. This, at least, is the argument of other analysts, including Paul Lawrence and Nitin Nohria in *Driven: How Human Nature Shapes Our Choices* (New York: Wiley, 2001); Paul Lawrence, "The Biological Base of Morality?" in *The Ruffin Series* No. 4 (2004), pp. 59–79; John De Graaf, *Affluenza: The All-Consuming Epidemic* (San Francisco: Berrett-Koehler, 2001); Mary Lenzi, "Plato and Echo-Feminism," chapter 6 in Judith Presler and Sally Scholz, eds., *Peacemaking: Lessons from the Past, Visions for the Future* (Amsterdam and Atlanta, GA: Rodopi Press, 2000), pp. 90–104; Friedrich Nietzsche, "To the Teachers of Selfishness," in Walter Kaufman, ed. and trans., *The Portable Nietzsche* (New York: Viking Penguin Press, 1982).

46. Marianne A. Ferber and Julie A. Nelson, eds., *Beyond Economic Man: Feminist Theory and Economics* (Chicago: University of Chicago Press, 1993).

47. "Bosses behind Bars," *The Economist* (June 12, 2004): 59–60. See also "Cracks in the Crackdown: A Spitzer Loss May Signal a Shift for White-Collar Crime," *Newsweek* (June 20, 2005): 46; and "Does the Punishment Fit?" *Newsweek* (July 25, 2005): 18; see Robert Solomon, "Victims of Circumstances? A Defense of Virtue Ethics in Business," *Business Ethics Quarterly* 13 (2003): 43–62.

48. Morvillo and Tigue, "Trial Update Press Statement." See Paul Krugman, "Enron and the System," *New York Times*, Op-Ed (March 4, 2004); Allan Sloan, "Lay's a Victim? Not a Chance," *Newsweek* (July 19, 2004): 50.

49. *Washington Post* (July 25, 2005): Given New York Attorney General Eliot Spitzer's continuing crackdown, "a noticeable randomness, or, at any rate imprecision has developed since Stewart's quick-paced legal sentencing." Subsequent convictions and reversals of the courts (June–July 2005) indicate contrary results: Either the punishment more than fits the corporate crime, or not at all. The already complex concepts of executive wrongdoing and befitting punishment have become more muddled. For instance, Bernie Ebbers, former CEO of WorldCom, though initially harshly convicted, has launched a serious legal appeal, especially in light of the U.S. Supreme Court's overturning a conviction (June 2005) for Arthur Andersen's unusual accounting practices in the Enron debacle. See Alison Jaggar, ed., *Living with Contradictions: Controversies in Feminist Social Ethics* (Boulder, CO: Westview Press, 1994).

50. Lynn Sharp Paine, *Value Shift: Why Companies Must Merge Social and Financial Imperatives to Achieve Superior Performance* (New York: McGraw-Hill, 2003); Marvin T. Brown, *Corporate Integrity: Rethinking Organizational Ethics and Leadership* (Cambridge: Cambridge University Press, 2005); Carolyn Kay Brancato and Christian A. Plath, *Corporate Governance Handbook 2005: Developments in Best Practices, Compliance, and Legal Standards* (Conference Board, 2005).

Index

Page numbers followed by f or t indicate figures or tables.

About the Editor and Contributors

Margaret Foegen Karsten is Professor in the Department of Business and Accounting and Coordinator of the Print Business Administration Distance Program at the University of Wisconsin-Platteville, where she teaches management and human resource management courses. She developed a *Management, Gender, and Race* course and has taught it for many years. Her books include *Management, Gender, and Race in the 21st Century* (2005) and *Management and Gender: Issues and Attitudes* (1994), in addition to over twenty other professional publications. She has presented at many national and regional conferences, has received several grants, and has held various administrative positions. Her current research interests include career paths of executive women and the impact of intellectual distance between students and professors on learning.

Tamara A. Bruce is a doctoral student in the Industrial/Organizational Program at Michigan State University. She received her bachelor's degree in psychology from Smith College. A former member of the Women's Health Sciences Division of the National Center for Posttraumatic Stress Disorder in Boston, she continues to be interested in the impact of harassment on mental and physical well-being. Her current research focuses on the intersection of multiple forms of discrimination, including racial, sexual, and sexual orientation harassment.

D. Anthony Butterfield is Professor of Organizational Behavior in the Department of Management at the Isenberg School of Management, University of Massachusetts-Amherst. He received his doctorate in organizational psychology from the University of Michigan. His research interests center on issues of leadership and gender, and his work with colleague Gary Powell has appeared in many journals, books, and conferences in both management and psychology.

Jamie L. Callahan is Assistant Professor in the Educational Human Resource Development Program at Texas A&M University. Her primary research interests focus on emotion management and its relationship to organizational learning, leadership, and culture in a variety of public, nonprofit, and for-profit settings.

Donna Castañeda is Associate Professor in the Psychology Department of San Diego State University–Imperial Valley Campus. Her research focuses on issues of gender, culture, and sexuality in close relationships; sexual risk behavior among Latinas; and structural aspects of service delivery systems in provision of health services to Latino communities. She is presently engaged in cross-national research examining the HIV/AIDS prevention needs of Mexican women working in the maquiladora industry at the U.S.–Mexican border.

Eros R. DeSouza is Professor in the Psychology Department at the University of Illinois. During the summer of 1992, he was a fellow at the Center for Advanced Study in the Behavioral Sciences, Stanford University, and in 1999 became a State Farm Insurance fellow for incorporating technology into instruction. DeSouza has many publications on gender issues in prestigious journals. Presently, his main research focus is on the study of bullying and sexual harassment from a psychological, legal, and cross-cultural perspective.

Joan E. Gale is an equity partner in the Labor and Employment practice group of Seyfarth Shaw LLP and works in the Chicago office. Co-chair of the firm's Family and Medical Leave Act (FMLA) Task Force, Gale is a frequent speaker on the FMLA and has handled several FMLA cases. Her practice is exclusively dedicated to representing management in employment matters and is split nearly equally between litigation and advice and counseling.

Shelly Grabe currently holds a postdoctoral fellowship position at the University of Wisconsin–Madison. She received her training from Michigan State University and the Universities of Missouri and Washington. Her research interests are in the area of the psychology of women and include an examination of how the treatment of women's bodies as objects contributes to the process of marginalization of women via threats to their psychological well-being. Shelly is a member of the Society for the Psychology of Women and the Society for the Psychological Study of Social Issues. She has taught a course on the Psychology of Women and is currently teaching Basic Statistics at the University of Wisconsin. She is a recent recipient of the Ruth L. Kirschstein National Research Service Award for her research on women's body objectification.

Michelle C. Haynes is currently a sixth-year doctoral student in social psychology at New York University. Her research interests focus on social, cognitive, and motivational biases as they affect organizational settings. Currently she is pursuing various lines of research, including the extent to which attributional rationalization contributes to sex bias in the workplace and the formulation and consequences of beliefs about affirmative action programs.

Madeline E. Heilman is Professor of Psychology at New York University. For over twenty years she was Coordinator of the Industrial/Organizational Psychology program, which is now part of the University's Social Psychology program. After earning her doctorate from Columbia University in 1972, for eight years she was a member of the faculty at Yale's School of Organization and Management. She also spent the 1998–99 academic year as Visiting Professor at Columbia University's Graduate School of Business. An author and coauthor of over sixty published articles, she has been on the editorial boards of the *Journal of Conflict Resolution*, *Organization Dynamics*, and *Organizational Behavior and Human Decision Processes*. Heilman currently serves on the boards of the *Journal of Applied Behavioral Science*, the *Journal of Applied Psychology*, and the *Academy of Management Review*. Her research has focused on sex bias in work settings, the dynamics of stereotyping, and the unintended consequences of preferential selection processes.

Mary B. Hogue is Assistant Professor of Human Resource Management at Kent State University. She earned her doctorate in industrial/organizational psychology from the University of Akron. Her research examines the impact of gender and status on work experiences.

Janet Shibley Hyde, the Helen Thompson Woolley Professor of Psychology and Women's Studies at the University of Wisconsin–Madison, received her education at Oberlin College and the University of California, Berkeley. She has taught a course in the psychology of women since 1973, first at Bowling Green State University, then at Denison University, and now at the University of Wisconsin. Her research interests are in the psychology of women, human sexuality, and gender role development. Author of the textbook *Understanding Human Sexuality*, she is a past president of the Society for the Psychology of Women and is a Fellow of the American Psychological Association. She has received many other honors, including the Heritage Award from the Society for the Psychology of Women for career contributions to research on the psychology of women.

Mary Lenzi is Assistant Professor of Philosophy at the University of Wisconsin–Platteville. She received her bachelor's degree from Bryn Mawr College and her doctorate from the University of Pennsylvania in 1989. She teaches courses in the history of philosophy, theoretical and applied ethics, political philosophy, and feminist philosophy and has published articles on these topics. Currently she is coediting a book, *Problems for Democracy*, in the *Philosophy of Peace* series.

Julie Manning Magid is Assistant Professor of Business Law at the Kelley School of Business, Indiana University. Her courses focus on law, ethics, and business. Currently, her primary areas of research include underdeveloped areas of Title VII and emerging areas of business law. She has a particular interest in inter-disciplinary approaches to these issues.

Rudy Nydegger, a Professor at Union College and at the School of Management in the Graduate College of Union University, is Chair of the Faculty and of the Graduate College Executive Committee. His previous faculty positions were at Rice University and Baylor College of Medicine. Rudy has written many articles in peer-reviewed journals, has served on editorial boards of the *Journal of Personality and Social Psychology* and the *Management Development Forum,* and was an ad hoc reviewer for several other journals. In 2002, his paper "Managing Computer Programming Teams" won the Best Paper Award at the European Applied Business Research Conference in Rothenberg on der Tauber, Germany. Nydegger has been actively involved in the Psychological Association of Northeastern New York and the New York State Psychological Association, serving in many leadership positions, including president, of both. The former organization named him the recipient of its Distinguished Psychologist Award, and the latter presented him with its Distinguished Service Award.

Carmen A. Paludi Jr. is Senior Scientific Advisor for a major defense company. He has held positions in government, industry, academia, and private consulting, including those at Air Force Research Laboratory, Sanders Associates, the MITRE Corporation, Maden Tech Consulting, Integrated Devices Sciences, New Hampshire Technical College, and the Advanced Electronics Technology Center–University of Massachusetts. Besides technical expertise, he brings nearly thirty years of technical and program management experience to Human Resources Management Solutions, where he is Principal Staff Consultant. He is the author of over twenty technical journal articles and numerous presentations to national and international conferences, panels, and technical meetings. He has served on many working groups throughout his career, including several at the Joint Chiefs of Staff and the Office of the Secretary of Defense.

Michele Paludi is the author/editor of 23 college textbooks and over 130 scholarly articles and conference presentations on sexual harassment, psychology of women, and career development. Her book *Ivory Power: Sexual Harassment on Campus* (1990), received the 1992 Myers Center Award for Outstanding Book on Human Rights in the United States. Paludi was one of six U.S. scholars selected to serve on the U.S. Department of Education's Sub-panel on the Prevention of Violence, Sexual Harassment, and Alcohol and Other Drug Problems in Higher Education, which she chaired. She was a consultant to and a member of former New York Governor Mario Cuomo's Task Force on Sexual

Harassment. An expert witness for court proceedings and administrative hearings on sexual harassment, Michele is President of Human Resources Management Solutions. She is currently a School of Management faculty member at the Graduate College of Union University.

Jane D. Parent has over thirteen years of management experience in the fields of cost analysis, marketing, and finance working for such companies as Grumman Aerospace (currently Northrop-Grumman), United Technologies, National Semiconductor, and Siemens, AG. Drawing on her business experience, Jane is currently doing research in the area of individual adaptation to organization changes, individual and team empowerment, and management trends in organizations.

Gary N. Powell is Professor of Management and Ackerman Scholar at the University of Connecticut. He received his doctorate in organizational behavior from the University of Massachusetts–Amherst, and his research interests focus on gender and diversity issues in the workplace. Powell is the editor of *Handbook of Gender and Work*, coauthor of *Women and Men in Management* (3rd ed.), and author of *Managing a Diverse Workforce: Learning Activities* (2nd ed.).

Joan E. Riedle is Professor of Psychology at the University of Wisconsin–Platteville. Her academic interests are in the areas of gender stereotypes, sex-role socialization, and ethical issues in social dilemmas. She has been honored by the University of Wisconsin–Platteville and by the National Academic Advising Association for excellence in academic advising.

Janice D. Yoder is Professor of Psychology of the University of Akron. She earned her degree in social psychology at the State University of New York, where her work with Ed Hollander on leadership and Bob Rice with cadets at West Point focused her interests on women in nontraditional occupations and tokenism theory. She won the university's and college's teaching awards at the University of Wisconsin–Milwaukee, is a Fellow in the American Psychological Association, and served in various positions for the Society for the Psychology of Women (APA Division 35), including president in 2000–2001. Her textbook *Women and Gender: Transforming Psychology*, is expected to be released in its third edition in summer 2006.